EXPERT SYSTEMS

for Reference and Information Retrieval

Supplements to
COMPUTERS IN LIBRARIES

1. Essential Guide to dBase III+ in Libraries
Karl Beiser
ISBN 0-88736-064-5 1987 CIP

2. Essential Guide to Bulletin Board Systems
Patrick R. Dewey
ISBN 0-88736-066-1 1987 CIP

3. Microcomputers for the Online Searcher
Ralph Alberico
ISBN 0-88736-093-9 1987 CIP

4. Printers for Use with OCLC Workstations
James Speed Hensinger
ISBN 0-88736-180-3 1987 CIP

5. Developing Microcomputer Work Areas in Academic Libraries
Jeannine Uppgard
ISBN 0-88736-233-8 1988 CIP
ISBN 0-88736-354-7 (softcover)

6. Microcomputers and the Reference Librarian
Patrick R. Dewey
ISBN 0-88736-234-6 1988 CIP
ISBN 0-88736-353-9 (softcover)

7. Retrospective Conversion: A Practical Guide for Libraries
Jane Beaumont and Joseph P. Cox
ISBN 0-88736-352-0 1988 CIP

8. Connecting with Technology 1988: Microcomputers in Libraries
Nancy Melin Nelson, ed.
ISBN 0-88736-330-X 1989 CIP

9. The Macintosh ® Press: Desktop Publishing for Libraries
Richard D. Johnson and Harriett H. Johnson
ISBN 0-88736-287-7 1989 CIP

10. Expert Systems for Reference and Information Retrieval
Ralph Alberico and Mary Micco
ISBN 0-88736-232-X 1990 CIP

11. EMail for Libraries
Patrick R. Dewey
ISBN 0-88736-327-X 1989 CIP

12. 101 Uses of dBase in Libraries
Lynne Hayman, ed.
ISBN 0-88736-427-6 1990 CIP

13. FAX for Libraries
Patrick R. Dewey
ISBN 0-88736-480-2 1990 CIP

14. The Librarian's Guide to WordPerfect 5.0
Cynthia LaPier
ISBN 0-88736-493-4 1990 CIP

15. Technology for the 90's
Nancy Melin Nelson, ed.
ISBN 0-88736-487-X 1990 CIP

16. Microcomputer Management and Maintenance for Libraries
Elizabeth S. Lane
ISBN 0-88736-522-1 1990 CIP

17. Public Access CD-ROMS in Libraries: Case Studies
Linda Stewart, Kathy Chiang, Bill Coons, eds.
ISBN 0-88736-516-7 1990 CIP

18. The Systems Librarian's Guide to Computers
Michael Schuyler, ed.
ISBN 0-88736-580-9 1990 CIP

19. Essential Guide to dBase IV in Libraries
Karl Beiser
ISBN 0-88736-530-2 1990 CIP

20. Essential Guide to UNIX in Libraries
D. Scott Brandt
ISBN 0-88736-541-8 1990 CIP

21. Integrated Online Library Catalogs
Jennifer Cargill, ed.
ISBN 0-88736-675-9 1990 CIP

EXPERT SYSTEMS

for Reference and Information Retrieval

Ralph Alberico
and
Mary Micco

Meckler
Westport • London

Library of Congress Cataloging-in-Publication Data

Alberico, Ralph.
Expert systems for reference and information retrieval / Ralph Alberico and Mary Micco.
p. cm. -- (Supplements to computers in libraries ; 10)
Includes bibliographical references.
ISBN 0-88736-232-X (alk. paper) : $
1. Expert systems (Computer science)--Library applications.
2. Reference services (Libraries)--Automation. 3. Information retrieval. I. Micco, Mary. II. Title. III. Series.
Z678 . 93 . E93A4 1990
025 . 5 ' 24 -- dc20 89-49456
CIP

British Library Cataloguing in Publication Data

Alberico, Ralph
Expert systems for reference and information retrieval. -
(Supplements to Computers in libraries ; 10)
1. Information retrieval. Applications of expert systems
I. Title II. Micco, Mary III. Series
025. 524

ISBN 0-88736-232-X

Meckler Corporation, 11 Ferry Lane West, Westport, CT 06880.
Meckler Ltd., Grosvenor Gardens House, Grosvenor Gardens, London SW1W 0BS, U.K.

Printed on acid free paper.
Printed and bound in the United States of America.

Contents

Acknowledgments vii

Introduction ix

1. What Is an Expert System? 1

2. Anatomy of an Expert System 31

3. Modeling the Reference Process 65

4. Review of Expert System Projects 85

5. Knowledge Engineering for Reference and Information Retrieval 107

6. Knowledge Representation and Information Retrieval 145

7. Building a Solid Foundation: A Vocabulary Control System 185

8. Designing the User Interface 223

9. Developing a Microcomputer-Based System 255

10. Methodologies for Designing Large Expert Systems 291

11. The Future of Expert Systems and Artificial Intelligence in Libraries 317

Bibliography 343

Index 385

Acknowledgments

This book is dedicated to our families for persevering with us. We would also like to acknowledge the support and encouragement of the folks at JMU and IUP, and the unflagging enthusiasm of Dr. Irma Smith, "expert" reference librarian. Special thanks to Tammy Crawford, Debbie Ryman, Jerry Gill, Jeff Clark, and Jody Hess and to the able staff of the IUP Media Center, including the Media Services Department, which produced the high-quality graphs for this book.

Figures used with permission are acknowledged in the text. Sections of Chapter 9 first appeared in the 1989 *Proceedings of the Fifth National ACRL Conference* (Ralph Alberico,"Expert Systems as Interactive User Aids" pp. 316–318).

Introduction

This book is about expert systems, one of the most rapidly changing, confusing, fascinating topics in computer science, psychology, linguistics, information science. . .and a number of other disciplines too numerous to mention. Expert systems were barely mentioned just a few short years ago. Now there are hundreds of books and articles on the topic. As the name implies, the subject has its share of hyperbole but there is real promise as well. What is an expert system anyway? The field is so new, and so rapidly evolving, that defining the term **expert system** is not an easy task. For now let's say an expert system is a group of computer programs, along with knowledge, information and databases, which act together to simulate the problem-solving and decision-making processes of a human expert within a relatively narrow domain. Attempting to simulate intelligent behavior is an intellectual challenge of the highest order. One must first be able to identify intelligent behavior. There is the problem of language. How is the system to communicate with its users? How much should it be trusted? How can expert knowledge be represented? It should be evident that building an expert system is no small undertaking.

A Puzzle with Many Pieces

Expert system development is a puzzle whose pieces are scattered among the disciplines. Computer scientists are exploring new paradigms in their discipline. Cognitive psychology is a growth area. Human cognition, memory, and problem solving are the focus of unprecedented attention. Linguists are attempting to understand the nature of language. Engineers, medical doctors, physicists, geologists — specialists from every field of endeavor — are tackling the challenge of building intelligent artifacts. Programs billed as expert systems come in all sizes and shapes.

Expert systems have also attracted attention in the library and information field. There is potential in numerous areas. Reference and information retrieval have been the two areas of greatest activity. For us, they are also the areas of greatest promise. They are also the areas with the most unanswered questions and some of the most daunting challenges. Problems which were once thought intractable are now being solved. But new problems are arising. Field tested, operational systems are rare. Philosophical issues range from E to E (epistemological to ethical).

This book will attempt to address the development of expert systems for reference and information retrieval. It is no surprise that expert systems for electronic information retrieval are so many in number. The computer, of necessity, is already there in an electronic information retrieval system. Why not build some intelligence into the way the system searches for information? We know that most online searching is still done by intermediaries. Augmenting the expertise of the intermediary has been the goal of expert systems for information retrieval. Some of the retrieval systems have been around almost from the beginning. So the domain we have selected is not as narrow as it may first seem. We can't possibly address either all of the technical issues, or all of the philosophical ones.

The field is also in an early evolutionary stage — far from settling down. We haven't even gotten to something like the Model T yet. Reference and information retrieval are areas of unbounded territory when it comes to expert systems. Our goals are modest. We would like to give the reader a basic understanding of a field which is advancing by fits and starts across a broad front. Some of the more advanced projects will be described, but a case will also be made for the small-scale use of this technology by educated lay people. Although this book will discuss research processes and strategies within the context of expert systems, it is not really a book about reference service or online searching. However to develop an expert system, it is crucial to understand the cognitive processes of human experts within the system's domain, so a good deal of attention will be paid to the heuristics employed by skilled reference librarians and online searchers. We will assume a certain amount of familiarity with the basic principles of reference service and automated information retrieval. On the other hand we will assume relatively little knowledge of expert systems.

Why Expert Systems?

This book is directed to librarians and other information professionals and to students of reference and information retrieval. Most of our examples relate to the work done by information intermediaries. We have drawn heavily from the literature of information science. We have tried to cite the most important studies and to supplement our references with recommended readings. Writing this book, we encountered the same problem many of the systems we describe are attempting to alleviate. The literature of expert systems is amorphous. There are many possible routes to different pieces of the expert system puzzle. One can find information related to expert systems in many subject literatures, in many formats. As is often the case on an active research front, communication tends to be informal. And in this computer-intensive field, communication is often electronic as well. We got to many of the conference proceedings but we missed the electronic mail. Interestingly enough one of the expert retrieval systems (Fox, 1987) addresses the dispersal of knowledge within a domain among so many different print and electronic formats. The vocabulary of the field changes constantly. It's hard to tell where the latest breakthrough is going to come from. An intelligent retrieval system would have helped.

There are definitional problems which arise when discussing expert systems. The term "expert system" has been applied to simple microcomputer systems which occupy a few kilobytes of memory and to tremendously complex systems which took years to develop and include thousands of lines of code. The terminology can be confusing and the terms and the hyperbole associated with them (**expert systems**, **artificial intelligence**) still offend the sensibilities of many who feel quite comfortable using other varieties of computer software. One of the purposes of this book is to demystify expert systems and artificial intelligence.

It is doubtful whether expert systems will ever replace true human expertise and that is not our position. Rather, we view these programs as consultation systems. Maybe it's unfortunate that so many systems are billed so presumptuously as artificial intelligence or expert systems. But the vocabulary has stuck, and we also will refer to the programs we discuss as expert systems. In this book, however, the term "expert system" is meant to imply simply another medium to be consulted, like a reference work or an online database. Real expertise is scarce and much of it is never recorded in written form. No matter what it is called, capturing and attempting to transfer expert knowledge is an activity that has proven worthwhile enough to have attracted the attention of just about every profession.

Eventually expert systems may evolve into a new medium of knowledge transfer (Stefik, 1986). It's hard to predict whether they'll have anything near the impact of the printed book as a medium of knowledge transfer. Right now, what we see are mostly prototype systems. And there are big differences between small-scale projects and major systems. The systems we'll be discussing are more properly called advisory or consultation systems. In the short-term future, both large-scale projects and small systems are more likely to be developed for experts by experts than for consumers of expertise within different domains.

Small systems have value because they are more accessible and can teach us much about basic principles and some of the problems that have yet to be resolved. It is possible to experiment with expert system technology on a relatively small scale. Large systems will be beyond the capabilities of most searchers and reference librarians, but so is producing a new reference book or online database. Nevertheless, it is important to understand the basic design principles underlying large systems in order to evaluate them and assess their usefulness for reference and retrieval tasks.

There is nothing magical about expert systems. They should be evaluated with the same criteria applied to reference sources or online databases. To evaluate them and their potential, one must first understand general design principles for expert systems. One must also have some sort of conceptual model of the search process, and be familiar with the barriers to effective information retrieval. One of these days, it will probably be possible to buy expert systems. These are among the things people will be looking for:

- the **quality of the knowledge** a system contains. We can develop impressive methods of encoding, storing, and connecting to knowledge, but if that knowledge doesn't somehow reflect the expertise of human beings, it will be useless. As we'll see the idea of a "refereed" expert system isn't so far afield.
- the **source of the knowledge** in the system and how it got there. Expert systems are group efforts requiring the cooperation of domain experts and developers. The manner in which a system's knowledge is acquired will have a great impact on its value.
- the **ease of use** of a system, and the efficiency with which knowledge is represented and organized. An expert system is unlikely to provide the responsiveness of a human expert but the knowledge it contains should be organized and presented logically. On the surface, the system should act in a similar way to the way a human expert would act.
- a system's **utility within a given environment**. As fascinating as a system may sound, it won't remain fascinating if it doesn't work. Systems must be accepted by those for whom they were intended.

Outline of Chapters

This book will attempt to provide the background needed to address the concerns described above. Here is a brief chapter-by-chapter outline.

Chapter 1 provides a brief history and basic overview of the broad field of artificial intelligence. Expert systems are often referred to as applied artificial intelligence. A basic introduction to artificial intelligence will help show where expert systems fit in the big picture. This chapter discusses some of the more famous expert systems and outlines some of the types of applications for expert systems.

Chapter 2 covers the anatomy of a simple expert system, describing the basic components and the ways in which they interact with one another. Examples written in the artificial intelligence (AI) language **PROLOG** are provided.

Chapter 3 reviews some of the models of the reference and information retrieval process. One of the prerequisites to developing an expert system is an understanding of the cognitive processes of human experts in the system's domain.

Chapter 4 looks at some of the more interesting attempts to develop systems which emulate some or all of the functions performed by online searchers and reference librarians. The field is evolving too rapidly to do an exhaustive survey. It would be easy to get bogged down in technical details. Our goal for this chapter is to describe systems which illustrate concepts which will be further discussed in subsequent chapters.

Chapter 5 is concerned with the process known as knowledge engineering. Emphasis is on describing some of the techniques for identifying expertise, and acquiring expert knowledge from human experts.

Chapter 6 discusses some of the formalisms for representing expert knowledge with a computer and describes some of the techniques being used to represent knowledge.

Chapter 7 examines some of the methodologies for organizing and representing the subject knowledge which will serve as the underpinning for reference/retrieval expert systems. Prototype systems for enhancing subject access and using hypertext to improve subject access are described.

Chapter 8 focuses on the user interface, looking at the functions a user interface for an expert system should perform.

Chapter 9 presents a case study of developing a small-scale, microcomputer-based expert system for business reference.

Chapter 10 analyzes some of the design issues associated with the development of large- scale expert systems for reference and retrieval.

Chapter 11 looks at developments on the technological horizon and presents a scenario of future systems for reference and information retrieval.

1
What Is an Expert System?

Characteristics of Artificial Intelligence Research

Before delineating the features of expert systems or discussing their development, we need to look at research loosely categorized as **artificial intelligence**. Expert systems have evolved from a long tradition of artificial intelligence research. The field is named artificial intelligence because all of its subfields have the common goal of simulating with a computer the processes of human intelligence.

This interest in modeling human intelligence is not new. It has been around since long before computers were invented. But since the dawn of the computer era, the research focus has expanded. As cognitive scientists learn about the processes that produce intelligent behavior, they attempt to identify components and procedures, then codify them into series of systematic steps. The steps can then be programmed into a computer and simulated. The feedback provided by humans using those computer systems then enables researchers to further refine their models of intelligence.

Artificial intelligence focuses on symbolic, nonalgorithmic problem-solving methods. Our intelligence relies on our ability to manipulate symbols, including but not limited to numbers. The languages of artificial intelligence (**LISP** and **PROLOG** are the most famous) enable us to process symbols very efficiently, using predicate calculus. These logic-based systems, reliant on deduction, are very different from traditional programming. We no longer work out step-by-step procedures for resolving a given problem. Instead we collect the facts plus the relevant rules of thumb, or **heuristics**, then derive conclusions. When either the knowledge or the rules of thumb to encode are derived from humans, recognized for their expertise in a given domain, then these systems are expert systems.

Artificial intelligence research focuses on pattern matching. We make sense of our world by recognizing patterns and/or relationships which give meaning to objects and events we encounter. Once we identify a familiar pattern, we recall similar patterns from long-term memory. These remembered patterns will be used to fill in details that are left out and also to recognize incongruous details, or unfamiliar variations in the pattern, as, for example in systems for scanning brain X-rays to identify possible tumors or abnormalities.

There are a number of areas of artificial intelligence research which hold promise for libraries. Among the more promising areas are:

- **Natural language processing** is the branch of artificial intelligence which is concerned with understanding and generating natural languages like English, Russian, and Japanese. Much of the earliest research in AI focused on natural language and natural language processing systems have been among the early successes in the field. Among the areas of natural language processing which have the most potential for libraries are **textual analysis** and **machine translation**. Textual analysis systems attempt to summarize or interpret text, and machine translation systems attempt to automatically translate text from one language to another.
- **Speech recognition and synthesis**, while related to natural language understanding, is often treated separately. The goal of this research front is to develop machines which can respond to, interpret and generate spoken words. Speech recognition systems have been some of the earliest and most dramatic successes in the field.
- **Robotics/Computer Vision**, are the areas of artificial intelligence which attempt to simulate human perception and motor abilities in machines. Robotics aims to create machines which act as intelligent agents within the physical world and which are capable of manipulating their environment to a greater or lesser degree. Robots equipped with vision systems may one day shelve and retrieve books from stacks and perform routine inventory functions.

  Computer vision, a closely related area of research, aims to provide machines with the ability to analyze sensor data and recognize objects in the physical world. Computer vision like human vision involves both **sight** and **perception**. There is also computer vision research on machine recognition and understanding of printed texts. **Optical character recognition (OCR)** is an offshoot of computer vision which allows computers to recognize and convert to machine-readable form both typeset and hand-written texts. OCR may one day make possible the transition from a printed to an electronic information environment by allowing libraries to convert to machine-readable form the vast amount of information already in the printed store.

- **Intelligent tutoring systems** attempt to model learner characteristics, diagnose gaps in knowledge, and develop strategies to address the needs of specific learners. Intelligent tutoring systems are already being designed to assist and educate library clients by providing help with the more elementary navigation tasks in the library.
- **Neural networks** simulate the biological processes of the human brain and nervous system. Neural networks are often considered separately from artificial intelligence but they are closely related. Neural networks have been used for digitizing hand-written text, proofreading, and other pattern-recognition tasks.
- **Expert systems** are designed to codify and automate the knowledge and heuristics of human experts in a variety of narrow domains. In libraries there are a number of possible applications, such as the provision of reference assistance to users as well as a variety of other information management tasks, including acquisitions, cataloging, indexing, database searching, interlibrary loan, and automated information retrieval.

Of all the branches of artificial intelligence, expert systems hold the greatest potential. Expert systems will therefore be the major emphasis of this book. But the other areas of AI also have potential and there is a great deal of overlap between expert systems and the other branches of AI. Therefore, before discussing expert systems in depth, we will provide an overview of other artificial intelligence technologies.

Natural Language Processing

Understanding and generation of natural language is a major AI research front. Until now computers have seemed formidable and difficult to communicate with, mainly because they accept only a very limited number of commands which must be precisely specified. Although menu-driven and icon-based systems have simplified the end-user's communication with the machine, researchers are actively working to develop computers that can understand and respond appropriately to the spoken work.

Such systems need to accommodate at least three levels of linguistic analysis.

1. **Acoustic/Phonetic**
2. **Morphological/Syntactic**
3. **Semantic/Pragmatic**

Acoustic/Phonetic Analysis (Speech Understanding Systems)

Sounds are represented as a plot showing the energy level at various frequencies. Input is translated into words. One difficulty is determining where a word begins or ends. Even the human ear is not infallible at this task. A young woman who visited New York for the first time returned home to tell her relatives that everything cost "a nominal egg;" puzzled they asked her to clarify this. The expression she heard was "an arm and a leg." Researchers are working on both inputting sounds and creating them.

The complexity of this task is directly related to the number of distinct syllables the computer system must recognize. A syllable, as a recognizable unit of speech, consists of a vowel and its surrounding consonants, pronounced together. Since there are over 10,000 syllables in English, it is very difficult to isolate any particular one. In sharp contrast, Japanese has only about 500 syllables from which all Japanese words are constructed. Speech recognition techniques based on syllable identification thus play an important role in current research.

Ambiguities in natural language communication are usually resolved through our expectations about familiar situations and contexts. Thus, a computer language understanding system must not be confined to signal processing; it must also accommodate meaning. Spoken stress and intonation patterns provide additional clues. Pitch drops at the end of a factual statement but rises at the end of a question, doesn't it? One common technique for speech understanding is to identify possible interpretations, and then use AI techiques to select the most plausible.

Two of the better known speech understanding projects were **SUR** (Speech Understanding Research Project), funded by DARPA (Defense Advanced Research Projects Agency) during the 1970s, and **HEARSAY**, which was developed at Carnegie Mellon University (CMU).

HEARSAY consisted of two separate programs. HEARSAY-I used syllabic analysis plus a knowledge of syntax and semantics to enable a voice-only command to play chess against the computer. HEARSAY-II analyzed a spoken sentence on several different levels at once, and communicated through a common area called a **blackboard** in order to arrive at a final interpretation. Syntax and semantics provide severe constraints on acceptable word combinations. Consequently, they serve very effectively to prune impossible interpretations of input signals. These speaker dependent programs claim to have achieved a recognition accuracy rate of over 90 percent (Firebaugh, 1988).

HEARSAY-II is considered one of the most influential AI programs ever written. It pioneeered the idea of using multiple independent knowledge sources, each working on a different aspect of a problem. It was also among the first AI programs to employ a series of **demons** — subprograms that wait until a condition is true before activating. Since

HEARSAY, these design principles have been used in many other applications. Clearly, this is the most effective design for taking advantage of parallel processing, a new way of handling information which many contend will revolutionize computing (Reddy & Zue, 1983, Fennel & Lesser, 1981).

HARPY, also developed at CMU, used a network of speech-pattern templates to understand speech in limited domains. It applied heuristics to prune unlikely interpretations from the options considered. It could also generate patterns for all sentences it could understand. HARPY's accuracy rate was over 95 percent. It succeeded, however, only because it stored every possible pronunciation of every possible sentence that could be spoken using its artificially restricted syntax. Similar systems support paraplegics and other handicapped people. Applications are restricted to very narrow domains. Simply stated, this is not a feasible technique with which to approach the wide diversity of unfettered human communication.

During the period 1971–1976, with funding from the ARPA project, a great deal of progress was made, then interest waned until federal funding was resumed in 1983. One of the more productive projects in recent years has been the "intelligent typewriter" project under the direction of Frederick Jelinek of IBM. The goal of the project is to develop a speech-driven typewriter system.

The system has performed at a 95 percent recognition rate for IBM's 5,000-word office task vocabulary. Although its performance is impressive, a number of obstacles will need to be overcome before such systems will be put into widespread use:

- It is still difficult to achieve this level of performance in "real time." In other words the user must pause between words to allow the software to catch up.
- Most systems in current use have to be taught to recognize the user's unique voice patterns.
- Systems will need to greatly increase their vocabularies and level of comprehension of human input.

A modern system being marketed commercially is the **Kurzweil Voice System 3000**, a sophisticated automatic speech recognition system which can handle an initial vocabulary of 1,000 words/phrases. Its performance improves through use. It can be trained in any language and the vocabulary can be increased.

Voice Synthesizers/Speech Production Systems

Acoustic/phonetic analysis is also used in speech production as distinguished from speech recognition systems. On one level are systems that read aloud a provided text. There are currently a number of such voice synthesizers on the market. One of the better known suppliers of such systems is the Kurtzweil Applied Intelligence, Inc. of Waltham, Massachusetts.

Much more challenging are speech production systems that answer questions and respond appropriately to human input. Again, there are such systems already on the market, but they work in limited domains with restricted vocabularies. One such system is on display at Epcot Center in Orlando, Florida.

Morphological/Syntactic Analysis

Computerized analysis focuses on discerning the syntactic features of an utterance, then selecting from several possible interpretations. For example, given the following:

"Can companies litter the environment"

One needs to know which of the two possible meanings is intended. **Disambiguation** is one of the more difficult challenges for natural language understanding programs.

An ambitious reference project that focuses on syntactic analysis is **LUNAR** (Fischler, 1987). LUNAR answers questions about the chemical characteristics and soil composition of lunar matter retrieved by the Apollo moon missions. The system is designed to only handle reference questions related to its collection of data on lunar rocks. Its first step is to parse the request. Let's use the following request as an example.

"What is the average concentration of aluminum in 'high alkali rocks'?"

The phrase "high alkali rocks" corresponds to a set of entries in the database, and "aluminum" is identifiable as one of the attributes. The phrase "average concentration" is recognized as a particular set of computations that the system knows about, so the computation is made and the answer given to the inquirer. LUNAR has an extensive grammar that covers a subset of English and can handle some pronouns and definite determiners. Thus, it can establish a limited dialogue capability.

LUNAR (Woods, 1977) exemplifies a question-answering system in which the parser provides a structural description of the question. Interpretation rules identify the logical connections among the linguistic elements that correspond to database entries. Retrieval operations are performed using the query expressions produced by the interpretation rules.

LUNAR worked reasonably well, but was restricted to a particular limited domain. Thus, it was much too specialized to function for tasks like general reference service. Nevertheless, LUNAR demonstrates that we do not have to achieve full communication in order to be able to retrieve information by automated means.

The **LIFER** system is another approach to creating English-language interfaces. LIFER is designed to allow a nonlinguist to tailor a natural language "front-end" to a given application. It works with database management systems and other types of computer software. LIFER allows a system designer to specify the processes to be carried out on natural language inputs by writing pattern and response expressions. These are similar to the patterns used by the famous program **ELIZA,** which will be described later. One of LIFER's better features is its ability to handle **ellipses**. For example, in the series of questions "How tall is John? How old? And Mary? the last two questions would be correctly interpreted as "How old is John?" and "How tall is Mary?" (Hendrix,1978)

An intriguing by-product of the research in this area has been the introduction of commercial, microcomputer-based, natural language front-ends for databases. They accept typed requests in standard English, then convert them to the syntax of a particular database. **Clout** from Microrim is an example of such a product. Typical of the requests it handles are queries such as: "Find all the salesmen with sales over $500 a week." It will convert this English sentence into the syntax of the database "list salesman, sales where sales > 500." Symantec, Inc. of Sunnyvale, California, is also marketing a natural language processing package. The program, called Q & A, can be customized to serve as a front-end for any database management system.

Parsing

As the first step in understanding human language, the computer parses a sentence to determine parts of speech. It locates the the primary verb and noun subject by matching the words it encounters to its store of knowledge about words and how they are used. This involves use of a **lexicon** (dictionary) with definitions of likely words. The lexicon also contains a morphological analysis of words. The analysis is used to determine the form and structure of each word, as well as the relationships between words and their roots and derived forms. Parsing takes advantage of conventional regularities in the forms of sentences. Sentences are diagrammed and the function of each element is determined. Among the commonly used parsing techniques are:

- **Augmented transition networks (ATNs)**: a method of breaking a sentence down into finer and finer parts
- **Top-down parsing**: analyzing a sentence according to its anticipated structure
- **Bottom-up parsing**: analyzing a sentence by evaluating words from left to right, while checking out all possible syntactic structures as the analysis progresses
- **Semantic grammar parsing**: rewriting a sentence according to units of meaning, rather than adhering to traditional syntactic conventions.

Semantic/Pragmatic Analysis

Analyzing sentences is just a first step in getting a computer to understand natural language. At a deeper level, we must understand what is being said and fit it into the larger context of our world knowledge and the general sense of the message being communicated. The purpose of this analysis is to grasp the meaning of a sentence.

Roger Schank (1984) describes some of the difficulties of understanding language in his very readable book, *The Cognitive Computer*. He discusses in depth four major problems in understanding natural language.

1. Ambiguity
2. Imprecision
3. Incompleteness
4. Inaccuracy

Ambiguity

Multiple Word Meanings

A single word can frequently have two or more different meanings. For example, examine the following two statements.

The pitcher is erratic.
The pitcher is full.

There is no syntactic clue to assist in deciding whether the speaker is referring to the person who pitches in ball games or a container designed for liquids. How can a computer be programmed to "distinguish" the many subtle shades of meaning in more complex examples, such as the verb "to give."

1. John gave Mary a book.
2. John gave Mary a hard time.
3. John gave Mary a night on the town.
4. John gave up.
5. John gave no reason for his action.
6. John gave a party.
7. John gave his life for freedom.
8. John gave Mary away. (Schank, p.93)

Syntactic Ambiguity

A sentence can be interpreted in more than one way. Let's take the following sentence as an example.

Tim hit the man with the bat.

It is not immediately clear whether Tim used the bat as a weapon or whether the man who was hit was holding the bat when Tim hit him. This kind of ambiguity can only be resolved by relying upon contextual cues.

Unclear antecedents (anaphora)

Another problem is the use of pronouns to replace previously used nouns. The antecedent is not always clear. Consider the following sentence:

John punched Bill because he wanted to marry Edna.

Does the "he" refer to John or Bill?

Imprecision

We often use vague or imprecise terms. For instance, consider the meaning of the phrase "a long time" in the following statements.

I've been waiting in the dentist's office a long time.
The corn is dying because it hasn't rained for a long time.
Dinosaurs ruled the earth a long time ago.

In each case the interpretation of "a long time" differs, and depends to a large extent on the context. We have all waited in a dentist's office for what seems an eternity, yet we all know that the office closes at five o'clock and everyone goes home. This is a very different time frame from the span of time since dinosaurs roamed the earth. The question still facing researchers is how to store sufficient knowledge in a computer to enable it to make distinctions which are based on general knowledge unaffected by the syntax or semantics of the sentences themselves.

Incompleteness

We do not always say all that we mean. Schank gives the following example. "John went in. He ordered a bacon double cheeseburger and a milkshake. He paid for it and found a nice spot to sit and eat in the park across the street." (Schank, p.117)

In order to comprehend this situation we must supply considerable knowledge from our general world view. We have no difficulty determining that he must have gone into a fast food restaurant and there is nothing incongruous in this behavior. If however, he had ordered escargots then we would have had to pause and reconsider our interpretation, since it does not fit with our expectations. Escargots suggest an expensive French restaurant where you sit down for a meal and there are no takeouts. None of this is evident from the sentences themselves.

Inaccuracy

Humans do not always write gramatically correct sentences. Even in published material, it is not unusual to find spelling errors, incomplete sentences, incorrect punctuation, and unintentional ambiguities. The human reader can make allowances for such errors and quickly determine the intended meaning. Getting a computer to do this is much more challenging.

This happens quite frequently in libraries and is more of a problem with computerized systems, which tend to be less forgiving than printed reference works. It is not at all unusual to see a reader using a term like KLU KLUX KLAN, instead of KU KLUX KLAN.

Over the years a great deal of time and effort has gone into developing natural language understanding programs. All of the commercially successful ones have limited the domain in which they are expected to function.

These projects are feasible and function reasonably well because the domains involved are fairly small and more or less clearly defined. These systems are not expected to form abstract generalizations, or to modify themselves on the basis of experience. They are simply expected to answer basic questions in their field.

By way of contrast, a challenge of the future is to build a system that can read all the bills that might ever be voted on in Congress, and then detail the ways to handle them. The knowledge base involved is massive. Congressmen themselves have difficulty coping with this problem, and must depend on their ability to read and listen, to acquire and integrate new knowledge. Our computers still cannot do this. They cannot even add to their store of knowledge from their experience within a limited domain. They must be painstakingly programmed by a knowledge engineer. "[I]t is clear that until we can develop programs that learn from their experiences we will not have achieved true intelligence." (Schank, 1984) Efforts to do this are actively underway.

The task of a reference librarian is somewhat less ambitious than achieving complete understanding. Rather, it is to make a good match between the user's information need and the relevant material held in the collection. Some techniques used in natural language interfaces to database management systems might adapt well to reference services functions.

Achieving True Understanding: Schank's Conceptual Dependency Model

Schank's conceptual dependency model is one of the more nearly successful natural language understanding techniques in use. The goal is to convert sentences describing an event into a representation of the event itself. A set of **semantic primitives** conveys the sense of what is said. Primitives can be classified in terms of primitive acts, primitive states, and rules relating them. (Feigenbaum,1981)

The following are typical primitive **acts** the system recognizes:

- **ATRANS**: transfer of an abstract relationship, such as possesion-changing actions. To give, to sell, to exchange, to swap, etc.
- **MBUILD**: construction of a new conceptual (mental) structure from an old one, involving deciding, inferring, and imagining
- **MTRANS**: transfer of mental information between people or within a person
- **PTRANS**: transfer of the physical location of an object
- **PROPEL**: applying physical force to an object

Primitives are used to represent whole classes of words which have a similar sense. For example, the words **push**, **shove**, **kick**, and **bat** can all be reduced to the primitive PROPEL.

Every event is segmented into:

- an **actor**
- an **action** performed by that actor
- an **object** on which the action is performed
- a **direction** in which that action is oriented

For example:

INPUT: John sold Mary a book

INTERNAL REPRESENTATION

ACTION:	ATRANS			
ACTOR:	John			
OBJECT:	book		ACTION:	ATRANS
TO:	Mary	—>	ACTOR:	Mary
FROM:	John		OBJECT:	money
			TO:	John
			FROM:	Mary

OUTPUT:
Mary gave John some money and John gave her a book.

PARAPHRASES:
Mary bought John's book. Mary paid John for a book.
Mary has a book. John has money. Mary wanted John's book.

INFERENCES:
John didn't want the book anymore.
John had already read the book.
Mary will read the book.
John needed the money.

A number of intellectual activities are involved in understanding a text. First we must, of course, parse the text. The next step is to paraphrase it, to help discover its meaning. Finally, an **inferencer** extrapolates relevant information. Soon it becomes obvious that each sentence must be understood in a context larger than itself. This serves, among other things, to limit the inference explosion. The techniques used by

Schank involve conceptual chaining of ideas. Scripts determine the links between chains. A major problem is that, in many instances, no predefined script exists for a situation. Without a script the computer is unable to provide utterances with the context needed to derive meaning from them. In addition to scripts, general principles and rules for planning are needed.

Summarizing Text

Schank's work consisted of a number of smaller projects. In 1979, all of the elements of Schank's research were combined and a new intelligent program was generated. The program, called **FRUMP** (1979), was hooked up to the United Press International news wire. FRUMP was able to summarize the stories that it understood in several different languages. However, FRUMP could not learn from its experience nor add to its knowledge base.

The research continued using small experimental programs such as **CYRUS** in 1979 and **IPP** in 1980. CYRUS, a professional and personal history of Cyrus Vance, could answer questions about which it had no direct knowledge. When asked if Mrs. Vance had ever met Mrs. Begin, it searched for a situation when both women were likely to be present, then it assumed they had met. It did, in fact, find a state dinner in Israel that occurred during a trip where Mrs. Vance did accompany her husband. It assumed the rest.

The major focus of IPP, the Integrated Partial Parser, was its ability to add to its knowledge structures by forming new structures as a result of what it read. For example, after analyzing a number of news bulletins about Basque terrorist attacks where policemen were shot, IPP was able to conclude that "terrorist attacks in Spain are often shootings of policemen in bars by Basques" and added this knowledge to its knowledge base.

Many other programs that purport to produce summaries of stories within limited domains are now available .

Most of today's computer programs and database management systems unfortunately do not have any understanding or deep knowledge of the data stores they contain. They have a great deal of data but no information. They are not capable of knowledge, that is to say they have not been programmed either to analyze or to summarize that data or to draw meaningful conclusions from it. In the library world we have over sixteen million MARC records in our database and can do brute force searching for a keyword or combinations of keywords. But so far we have not incorporated much intelligence in our systems for managing this vast resource.

One may well question whether a deep understanding of every library user's information need is either possible or even desirable. Maybe we don't need that kind of deep understanding to develop systems which are useful. It should be possible to come up with basic search primitives and categories of information-seeking needs in order to provide the best possible match between what is available in the collection and what the client is seeking. A natural language front-end should be able to translate the user's query into an optimized search strategy for submission to databases deemed relevant.

Computational Linguistics

Computational linguistics attempts to extract meaning from language in order to develop within the computer a deeper understanding of human expression. Joseph Weizenbaum's ELIZA program represents an early attempt to build a system that could understand natural language. It uses pattern matching and some clever syntactic tricks, such as a parser that converts pronouns — "you" to "me" etc. — to make the conversation seem more natural.

ELIZA was designed to simulate a Rogerian therapist. Users of ELIZA carry on a dialogue just as if they were on a psychiatrist's couch. The program uses several slick programming techniques to ask predetermined questions, and contains canned responses to specifically identified keywords. For example, if a person uses the word "no," it will respond "don't be so negative." ELIZA plays the role of a psychiatrist interviewing a patient and is very cleverly done. It appears almost to be responding to things being said to it. A word pattern evokes an appropriate response from ELIZA. For example,

I am ________
Why are you ________?
I am very sad.
Why are you very sad?

If the words "father," "mother," "brother" or "sister" appear in the input, ELIZA responds by saying, "Tell me more about your family."

When ELIZA cannot find a word pattern that matches, there are some phrases that can be randomly selected as generic responses, such as: "Tell me more," "In what way?" "Can you think of specific examples?"

All men are alike.
In what way?
They are always bugging us about something or other.
Can you think of specific examples?
Well, my boyfriend made me come here.
Your boyfriend made you come here?

Although it has delighted many generations of novice users, and is very popular in introductory programming courses, the approach typified by ELIZA is no longer considered a viable technique for natural language understanding.

Another famous program that delved into natural language understanding was Terry Winograd's **SHRDLU**, written as a doctoral thesis at Massachusetts Institute of Technology (MIT) in 1972. It was written in **LISP** and dealt only with a very limited world: a tabletop with simple geometric objects such as blocks, cylinders, and boxes. A robot arm follows instructions from a human operator given in natural language and carries on a reasonable conversation about it. A dialog with SHRDLU goes something like this:

> Find the block which is taller than the one you are holding and put it in the box.
> *By "it," I assume that you mean the block which is taller than the one I am holding.*
> What does the box contain?
> *The blue pyramid and the blue block.*
> How many blocks are not in the box?
> *Four of them.*
> When did you pick it up?
> *While I was stacking up the red cube, a large red block and a large green cube.*
> Why?
> *To get rid of it.*

SHRDLU proved that by combining syntax with semantics and some useful heuristics, it is possible to build a program which responds intelligently to natural language commands. It did have some limitations, however. It could not remember what went wrong when failure occurred, nor could it improve its performance.

Machine Translation

In the 1950s, fueled by the need to provide translations for the increasing volume of scientific literature appearing in Russian and Japanese, work began on computer translation from one language to another. It did not appear too complex of a task, but to this day we do not have completely satisfactory translation systems (Pierce, 1966).

Early efforts include keyword dependent programs like ELIZA, described above. Such programs quickly showed up the limitations of the "dictionary approach" because the programs lacked any deep understanding of the text being analyzed. The classic and often quoted example is: "The spirit is willing but the flesh is weak." This was translated into Russian as: "The vodka is good but the meat is poor."

To overcome this sort of limitation, it was at one stage proposed that the machine translators provide a list of all the options for each term. Then an expert system would make the needed judgments based on context.

The spirit is willing but the flesh is weak

This yields the following set of options:

The	character is	consenting but the	flesh is	lacking strength
	courage	inclined	meat	impoverished
	alcohol	disposed	pulp	feeble-minded
	mood	ready	body	weak
		has goodwill		poor

Such printouts were supposed to benefit human translators and increase their productivity. Translators found the lists more confusing than helpful. In their own information processing, human translators quickly eliminated many of the options presented; the list approach was considered a waste of time.

Efforts to use semantic and syntactic analysis to narrow the choices continue, but clearly an in-depth understanding of the context (pragmatics), and a knowledge of linguistic conventions in the two languages is required for succesful translation to occur.

Robotics/Vision

Robotics focuses on the development of computer-based systems which act as intelligent agents within the physical world. A related area of research is computer vision. Is it possible for a computer to make sense out of digitized two-dimensional images stored as a matrix of individual dots, called pixels? This is still considered one of the most challenging problems in artificial intelligence. Artificial intelligence techniques make it possible to analyze and interpret pictures. Various clues are used to make this task easier, including color, depth, texture, and motion. The most difficult task is to identify the components of the picture. Two techniques in use are **edge detection** and **model-based recognition**.

Research into vision systems for robots seems very remote from the library world. Yet it is not difficult to imagine a seeing robot that can scan call numbers, and shelve or retrieve books, take care of the odious chore of inventory, scan shelves for misfiled books, and a host of other menial tasks. Another possibility for the future is to charge robots with performing tasks that are too dangerous for human operators. It is not hard to imagine extensive use of robotics technology in mass deacidification projects, where dangerous chemicals are often used.

Vision systems are affecting libraries in other ways as well. Already there are systems that can correctly identify texts written in many different fonts, and even some hand-written messages, by using pattern recognition. They can be trained to learn new fonts, and also to make informed guesses. Guesses can be displayed on a screen and the user is asked to confirm or correct the selection.

Proofreading requires rather more skill, but is also within the bounds of possibility. We are all familiar with the spelling checkers included with most word processors, and usage and grammar tools such as **Writers Workbench** from Bell Labs. The focus is on the detection and correction of writing errors. Such systems can be programmed to assist an experienced proofreader rather than taking over the function.

Intelligent Tutoring Systems

Another focus of artificial intelligence research is intelligent tutoring systems which adapt to the learning style of the student, providing guidance, instruction, and support in performing complex tasks. Initially much of this work was funded by the Defense Department, which had the goal of training unskilled recruits to use and maintain high-tech equipment. Applications to information retrieval and decision support systems are obvious. Every search for information is a learning process. People need help in locating and interpreting data that will subsequently satisfy information needs. Any intelligent tutoring system designed to serve as a reference assistant would need to address a number of different stages of the search process.

Stage 1: Exploration

Each researcher needs to get a "feel" for the topic, to find out what information is available, and what the scope of the subject is. Clients often need instruction about tools available and correct terminology. For example, not "left" but "starboard."

Stage 2: Negotiation

The researcher begins to refine and delimit the scope of the information need based on feedback provided by the system. The topic is modified into a manageable project. If not enough material is uncovered, the topic can be broadened. Conversely, if too much is retrieved, the search can be narrowed to a relevant subtopic. For example, a request for "media and minorities" was reduced to a study of "employment opportunities for black women in television." An intelligent system could very appropriately guide and instruct the user in the various options, and provide a browsing capability as well.

Stage 3: Data Collection

Some researchers want all the information in the system on their negotiated topic. Here the issue becomes what databases to search and how to access them. Clients must determine the primary relevant subject area, and what type of materials interest them. Should the search be restricted to periodical literature and/or to reference books, or monographs, or all three? Clearly, intelligent instruction tailored to each specific need is required.

In addition, the system demands all the capabilities currently in place to dial access a whole raft of databases as well as the Online Public Access Catalog (OPAC), the circulation records, and interlibrary loan. Obviously, a fully automated system would not only identify desired items, but also enable the client to check their current whereabouts and have them delivered if necessary.

Stage 4: Detailed Analysis and Evaluation

Small, experimental expert systems already assist researchers by ranking for relevance the output of database searches using a variety of algorithms. In addition, hypertext programs make possible sophisticated note-taking systems whereby researchers extract the material they want and arrange it efficiently with a variety of different access and display mechanisms. (See Chapter 7 for more details.) One of the difficulties with today's search systems is that too much is being retrieved and users experience cognitive overload.

Stage 5. Final Checks and Adjustments

As any project nears completion, researchers frequently return to their sources to verify a point or to check some factual data. Consequently, the search strategies used and types of material consulted will be very different even for similar research projects. A tutoring system would need to keep track of the user profile, and maintain a constantly changing image of research progress for each project. Without those capabilities an intelligent tutoring system wouldn't be able to be fully helpful and supportive for real world research projects.

Intelligent computer-assisted instruction that adapts to the level of the user and provides specific instruction as needed is still a decade away in most information retrieval systems. But all the necessary technologies exist; it remains for the researchers to focus their efforts and deliver marketable, cost-effective products.

Error Detection and Correction

Intelligent tutoring systems can identify errors as they occur, and suggest corrective action. **DEBUGGY** from Xerox is a good example of such a system. It teaches students how to subtract and is based on a detailed cognitive analysis of the errors students do or can make. Heuristics discover the kinds of errors a student is making. Once this is established, the system proceeds to ask the student to practice a carefully selected subset of problems to reinforce the concept that is causing difficulties.

The **LISP TUTOR** used in freshman programming classes at Carnegie Mellon University teaches students how to write LISP programs. It detects errors and alerts students to problems as well as suggesting corrective action.

In the dialog that follows a student has been asked to write a factorial function in LISP. The function should take a number argument, n, and compute the factorial of n. The factorial of n is calculated by multiplying n * n-1.... For instance,

(factorial 3) = 3 * 2 * 1 = 6.

By definition the factorial of 0 is 1.
The system then presents this skeleton code and asks the student to fill in where appropriate.

```
(DEFUN fact (n)
    (COND ((FUNCTION) <ACTION>
    <RECURSIVE CASE>))
```

When the student types in the word "equal" to replace "FUNCTION" the system responds:

"I assume that you are trying to test if the number argument is equal to the number zero. There is a special function for testing equivalence to zero. Try to use that function instead of EQUAL. What code can you write to test if the condition for terminating case is true? Try writing a predicate."

The student changes "equal" to "zero."

The system responds: "Did you mean zero (y or n)?

A student who is not having difficulty will not see any of these prompts.

For an information retrieval system, the common types of errors have been categorized below. Expert systems technology will provide a means to diagnose these errors interactively during an information retrieval session, and proffer corrective action via suggestions to the user.

Type I error: The concept selected may be too narrow or specialized resulting in an unrealistically low number of hits.
For example: "sodomy cases in Pennsylvania."

Type II error: The concept may be too broad resulting in so many hits that the user is overwhelmed. For example: "education for the handicapped."

Type III error: The user's terms may not represent the term of choice in the discipline. Much relevant material will remain buried. For example: inputtimg "playwrights" when the taxonomy dictates "dramatists."

Type IV error: A user may search in the wrong database or an ineffective information package. For example: Searching for material on the Dead Sea Scrolls in the current *Magazine Index*.

On a slightly less ambitious scale are numerous adaptive systems which provide practice or training. Some will adapt themselves to different cognitive styles; others will attempt to explain errors.

GUIDON from Stanford University (Clancey, 1987) is an intelligent tutoring system in the medical domain. It trains students in diagnosis, and is built on **MYCIN**, a medical diagnostic system which is among the most famous of all expert systems. Instead of asking for symptoms and then offering a diagnosis, GUIDON will present test cases as patient histories. Students make the diagnoses. If a diagnosis is the same as MYCIN's, the student is congratulated; otherwise the system displays rules where there were discrepancies between the student's diagnosis and MYCIN's rulebase, and the student is asked to try again.

In libraries we are starting to see examples of simple tutoring systems. Typical examples are:

- **POINTER**, developed by Karen Smith of SUNY-Buffalo, is a menu-driven system, which interactively guides the user through the library collection. It even includes a screen on **Useful Sources of Ideas for Term Papers** (K.F. Smith, 1986).
- **INFORMATION MACHINE**, developed by Jeff Fadell, Judy Myers and others at the University of Houston. It uses an IBM PC presentation manager, keeps statistics, and covers general information, directions, basic library research strategies, etc. There is even a tutorial on using the "red books." This system, which has been available to the public for over a year, displays about 360 screens.. The same team is also working on an expert system to assist users in selecting the appropriate periodical indices for a given subject search.
- **ANSWERMAN**, developed at the National Agricultural Library, uses the First Class expert system shell to guide the user in areas of ready reference and database searching (Waters, 1986).

Before long, we can expect to see many more such efforts.

Neural Networks

Discussions of neural networks are common in artificial intelligence literature. Although neural networks do address some of the same issues as artificial intelligence, they are fundamentally different in their approach to solutions. Neural networks attempt to mimic biological processes and structures of neurons in the brain, whereas artificial intelligence programs attempt to identify and execute higher-level processes and relationships that are often based on logic or linguistics. Because of these distinctions, expert systems have focused on problems that require the application of a fixed set of logical rules and related facts within a specific domain — for example, the very specific rules from *Anglo-American Cataloging Rules* (*AACR*).

Expert systems perform very well with such tasks, but this technology has not been nearly as succesful in processing raw sensory data, such as sonar signals under water. Neural networks, on the other hand, seem especially promising for organizing and identifying patterns in this kind of variable data. They can quickly learn new patterns. They have also been fortuitously applied to recognition of hand-written text. **Nestor-Writer**, which runs on an IBM PC/AT, will read handwritten text that is entered with a digitizer. More significantly, it can teach itself entirely new symbols on the spot.

Still another very active research area at the moment is the modelling and analysis of primitive brain functioning. MIT labs have been working on simulating primitive impulses of the insect brain to develop intelligent behavior in small robots (Hapgood,1988). The designers identified certain low-level behaviors and then programmed circuit boards to respond to sensor signals as follows.

The first behavior is "explore." So long as no obstacle is detected the robot insect sets off in widening circles to explore its environment. Should it encounter an obstacle as detected by its sensors, it goes into "escape" behavior and attempts to negotiate around the obstacle by moving left. This did not do much for its chances of meeting another cockroach and forming a relationship, so a "follow" behavior was added. If the roach encountered a moving object, it would follow it. If the object remained stationary for longer than a given threshold, the roach would switch to "escape" behavior to go on its way. When two roaches met head on, they would glare at each other for a while and then one would switch to escape and the other would follow. While interesting, the relevance of this technology to information retrieval seems at present rather remote.

Expert Systems

The most promising AI technology for libraries is expert systems. The key feature of expert systems today is that they involve modelling the thought processes of human experts who are very familiar with the given problem domain. If you are going to build an expert system that will serve as a reference assistant, it must be done by sitting down with expert reference librarians and asking them to codify the heuristics or rules of thumb that guide them in their decision making. By definition, one cannot build an expert system without at least one resident expert. The rest of this book will be devoted to an examination of some systems that have already been developed and to a discussion of the technical issues involved.

History of Expert Systems

Humankind's interest in analyzing thought processes, in understanding the working of the human brain, dates back eons. Various disciplines approach this from different points of view. In medicine, efforts have been directed toward helping those whose brains are not functioning correctly. For centuries it was believed that such people were possessed. Priests were regularly called upon to exorcise demons.

Physicians have tried remedies, ranging from opium to electric shock, as they have attempted to better understand the inner workings of the brain. Even transplants have been considered seriously—and not so seriously. Popular literature is full of stories of inculcating human intelligence into other life forms. Dr. Frankenstein built an artificial person, and thereby created one of the great horror stories of all time. Psychologists concern themselves with measuring intelligence, and study factors that influence its development. Linguists investigate how language develops and how humans communicate.

Interestingly enough, some of the most directly relevant work to libraries is being sponsored by intelligence agencies. Espionage agencies are working on automated translation of scientific journals and automatic interpretation of machine-readable data. Intelligence agencies are also involved with broader projects whose goal is the intelligent storage and retrieval of the masses of information which come in from all manner of sources.

Practical interest in artificial intelligence has coexisted with a number of theories. **Cybernetics** provided the first theoretical base for the evolving interest in modelling by machine the activities of the human brain. Norbert Wiener, from MIT, in 1948 defined cybernetics as the science of communication and control in both the animal and the machine. Cybernetics attempts to construct, analyze, manipulate, and apply formal models representing the organization of either physical entities such as brains and machines, or symbolic entities, such as information systems, languages, and cognitive processes. In the United States, however, a narrower definition prevailed. Cybernetics, as used in the United States, designates principally the narrow field of information feedback systems in engineering.

In mathematics, George Boole (1815–1864) is notable for combining the logic of the philosophers with the rigor of mathematics to yield Boolean algebra. In the preface to his book, *An Investigation of the Laws of Thought on Which Are Founded the Mathematical Theories of Logic and Probability* (1854), he makes the following bold claim: "The mathematics we have to construct are the mathematics of the human intellect."

Not until computers were readily accessible was serious interest shown in building machines that could think! In 1937, Claude Shannon, a graduate student at MIT, used Boolean algebra to describe the operation of electrical switching circuits. His ideas led directly to the still prevailing binary system of information storage.

First Generation, Pre-1956

Warren McCulloch, one of the founding fathers of artificial intelligence, was a philosophy major who went on to medical school. He began his research on epilepsy, head injuries, and the central nervous system. As director of the Laboratory for Basic Research in the Department of Psychiatry at the University of Illinois, he made a major contribution in formulating a neural net model of the brain. This model, which proved later to be fundamentally flawed in its assumption that neurons behaved strictly digitally, was nevertheless very influential. His model consisted of a network of synapses and neurons which he postulated behaved in a binary fashion, that is firing or nonfiring.

Alan Turing (1912–1954) is credited as the first to see clearly the possibilities of thinking machines. In 1950 he astounded the computer community with his now famous article, "Computing Machinery and Intelligence." He suggested that computers can be programmed to exhibit intelligent behavior. He also proposed the "Turing Test." A person and a computer were hidden behind a screen. Another human subject was then challenged to question both and attempt to determine which answers issued from the computer. If the subjects failed to distinguish, then one could assume that the computer was, in fact, exhibiting intelligent behavior by carrying on a conversation.

Games and Game Playing

The same year, Claude Shannon, considered as the third founding father of artificial intelligence, suggested computer chess. This challenge was accepted quickly by many others and, to this day, continues to intrigue. Shannon shared Alan Turing's conviction about the possibility of machines thinking. He and Turing were friends who spent many hours in animated discussions. It is reported (Firebaugh, 1988, p.17) that Turing once exclaimed: "Shannon wants to feed not just data to a Brain, but cultural things! He wants to play music to it!"

In 1953, Shannon published a paper entitled "Computers and Automata," in which he raised a number of provocative questions that AI researchers have been addressing ever since. These include:

- Can a machine ever be programmed to learn?
- Can a computer be programmed to program itself?
- Can a self-repairing machine be built that will locate and repair faults in its own components?

Second Generation: 1956–1970

In a very active intellectual climate John McCarthy, an assistant professor of mathematics at Dartmouth College, and his friend Marvin Minsky at MIT organized a two-month, ten-man study of artificial intelligence carried out during the summer of 1956 at Dartmouth. This marks the first time that the term "artificial intelligence" appeared in print. The conference was a milestone. It brought together, for the first time, men who would dominate the field of artificial intelligence for the next twenty years. Alan Newell and Herbert Simon from Carnegie Institute of Technology (later Carnegie Mellon University) were the most advanced of the group. At that time they were working on the **Logic Theorist**, which evolved into the **General Problem Solver**.

The early AI effort was directed toward building an artifical inteligence program that could solve any problem. General Problem Solver was designed to prove thirty-eight of the fifty-two theorems of Chapter 2 in Whitehead and Russell's *Principia Mathematica.* The Logic Theorist caused quite a stir when it was unveiled. Newell and Simon went on to the very ambitious project of creating a General Problem Solver that would tackle any problem presented to it. Attempts to complete this program went on for many years before it was finally abandoned in favor of discipline-specific systems. Even though unsuccesful, this research helped clarify the formidable challenges involved in simulating intelligent behavior in whatever domain (Charniak & McDermott, 1986).

Although this period started with high hopes and expectations, few were realized by 1970. Instead, through the research and experimentation, it was discovered that artificial intelligence was a great deal more complex, and more challenging, than anyone had anticipated. Solving general problems would require far more powerful computers than anything available at the time.

Much of the work then was done in a small cluster of University and research labs. The problems were classified as "toy problems," small enough to be manageable, focused enough to explore defined problems. Many early projects have become classics. For example, **BAGGER** was a rule-based system designed to pack groceries in bags, ensuring that the fragile items, such as eggs and bananas, were on top and heavier items underneath.

Similarly, the "Monkey and Bananas" problem is a classic planning problem. The monkey is forced to overcome a variety of obstacles while he attempts to reach the bananas. He has to know what he is holding in his hands, and put things down in order to grasp other things. He has to negotiate around a heavy sofa, which he cannot move, and move a ladder to reach his target, a bunch of bananas on the ceiling.

ANALOGY, another toy problem solver, was designed as a system that could perform at an acceptable level on the MENSA I.Q. test (Evans, 1963). The problem is to select an answer; figure X, such that A is to B, as C is to X. The key here is a clear set of well-defined rules. Once these are in place, problems become trivial (Winston, 1984).

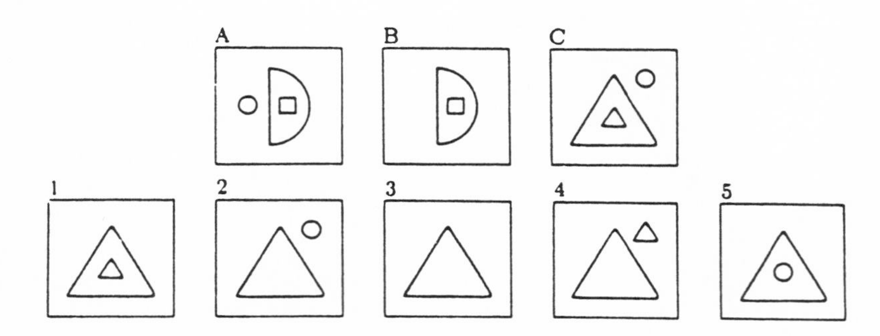

Figure 1.1. Analogy intelligence tests

One of the larger systems built during this period is **MACSYMA**, designed in 1968 by Carl Engleman, William Martin, and Joel Moses at MIT (Boden, 1975). MACSYMA is a powerful problem-solving program with the capability of performing over 600 distinct mathematical operations, including but not limited to, differentiation, integration, vector and matrix algebra, and solving systems of equations. It has gone through much growth and change, and it is still in active use on a daily basis in research laboratories all over the United States.

Edward Feigenbaum, a student of Newell's, became a very articulate spokesman for artificial intelligence. His **DENDRAL** program, 1968, one of the first expert systems, is still one of the most successful. It uses three steps to identify the structure of a parent compound from an input formula, mass spectrometer, and magnetic resonance data.

DENDRAL is a landmark program, because it was the first time someone sat down with a human expert to determine the heuristics, as well as the constraints involved in solving a complex problem. Because it was the first program to focus on highly specific expert knowledge rather than general approaches to problem solving, **DENDRAL** represents a major paradigm shift in AI research.

In this particular case the goal was to compose a hypothesis about what organic compound was being analyzed. The raw data was being provided by the mass spectograph. There is no scientific algorithm for mapping the mass spectrum of a compound into its molecular structure. This is where the skill, experience, and expertise of human experts come into play.

DENDRAL used a three-phase approach which has since been applied to many other problems (Charniak & McDermott, 1986):

1. **PLAN**. All configurations are reduced to those consistent with constraints derived from the mass spectrum.

2. **GENERATE**. The system generates all structures that meet the given constraints.
3. **TEST**. The system then ranks the output according to the quality of the fit. If it cannot find one unique identification of the chemical, it lists the most likely structures with an indication of relative probability

1970–1982: The Lean Years

Although large systems were developed, tested, and marketed during this period, funding was difficult. There wasn't much hope for practical applications of problem-solving theory and research. Many thought the applications of AI research were limited to the category of knowledge-based systems, often referred to as expert systems.

The effort to discover general approaches to problem solving was largely abandoned and more systems were modelled on the knowledge of human experts. Heuristics, or rules of thumb, were used to guide the activity of the new generation of more practical systems. The systems developed during this period were typically larger and more ambitious than the toy systems of the earlier period. Among the systems developed during this period are some which are still used today.

PROSPECTOR is an expert system designed to make decisions in mineral exploration. Richard O. Duda of SRI International wrote it in 1970. It uses a forward-chaining algorithm, depends on human expertise, and has to deal with uncertainty. It added an explanation facility to explain its reasoning and justify its conclusions. It performs at the level of an expert hard rock geologist, and quickly proved itself successful at prospecting. It predicted a molybdenum deposit near Mt. Tolman in Washington State, which was subsequently confirmed by core drilling at a value of $100 million.

MYCIN, started in 1972 and completed in 1976, was a production rule-based expert system for infectious blood disease diagnosis and therapy recommendation. Although it performed consistently at an expert level, it never won acceptance in the medical community; probably because it was restricted to a narrow domain of infectious blood diseases, and most patients exhibit other symptoms as well. Physicians did not deem it essential. Ethically, the doctor is ultimately responsible. This raises an intriguing possibility. If the doctor does make a human error which could have been prevented had he consulted a standard medical expert system, could he be sued?

XCON (also known as **R1**) is a rule-based, forward-chaining system still used today to configure the VAX and PDP-11 computers sold by Digital Equipment. It was first developed in 1978 by John McDermott of

Carnegie Mellon University. Its domain concerns computer-system components. When a customer buys a big computer, there are many components which must be organized along input/output busses. Moreover, all the appropriate electronic modules must be placed in the proper kind of cabinet in a suitable slot of a suitable backplane.

Getting all the components arranged and placed in the most efficient manner is a task known as **configuration**. It is very tedious and error-prone because a large computer typically has hundreds of possible options with a very large number of possible combinations. Currently XCON is a 2500 rule system and is still growing. It routinely handles orders involving one to two hundred components, with a knowledge base of over three hundred parts. It has amply demonstrated that a rule-based system can embody all the configuration knowledge needed to do configuration well. Perhaps we will live to see a system that handles reference books as efficiently!

1982–Present: The Golden Years

After twenty-five years of sputtering along quietly but persistently in research labs and back rooms, the exciting possibilities of the artificial intelligence research were recognized; thus dawned a second computer age. The transition from computers that calculate and store data to computers that can reason and inform has been made. We no longer process data, but knowledge. The period we are now in is often referred to as AI's golden age. There is no doubt that computers now do much more than simply calculate. Whether or not the promises of this golden age will be realized remains to be seen.

In 1982, *Time* magazine's Man of the Year was a computer. But the single event that propelled artificial intelligence to the forefront actually occured in Tokyo, Japan. In October, 1981 at the International Conference on Fifth Generation Computer Systems, the Japanese unveiled a ten-year plan to dominate the computer industry, which they view as vital to their economic future. They aimed not only at traditional forms of the industry but also at the establishment of a "knowledge industry in which knowledge itself would be a saleable commodity like food and oil." (Feigenbaum & McCorduck, 1983)

The American AI community was both incredulous and alarmed. In the 1960s no one had taken seriously the Japanese initiative in small cars. Then, in the 1970s, the Japanese announced plans to dominate consumer electronics. Later, the microelectronic chip market was a target. History will show whether the Americans were right to have reacted with alarm to this new, larger challenge to the American computer industry.

As a result of this supposed threat to a major American industry, government and industry both invested heavily in AI research. Understandably, there was a great deal of hype, and many unfulfilled promises. Of the more notable was the **Star Wars** program, which was intended to shield America from nuclear attack. This led to the 1983 announcement of the five-year Strategic Computing Program. One of its stated goals was to encourage research in AI technologies, such as expert systems, natural language processing, computer vision , speech recognition, and planning systems. Emphasis shifted from basic research into intriguing questions, to developing practical applications of the models proposed.

A number of large computer vendors jumped into the arena. Artificial intelligence research was now the fashionable thing to do, and real progress was made in large-scale, commercially practical expert systems. Most notable were the efforts of Texas Instruments, which hosted a series of free, nationally broadcast seminars. The other factor that contributed considerably to the rapid spread of the new expert systems technology was the ubiquitous personal computer. Although not suitable for large expert systems development, it is is very appropriate for a layman armed with an expert system shell. A layman can quickly bring up a

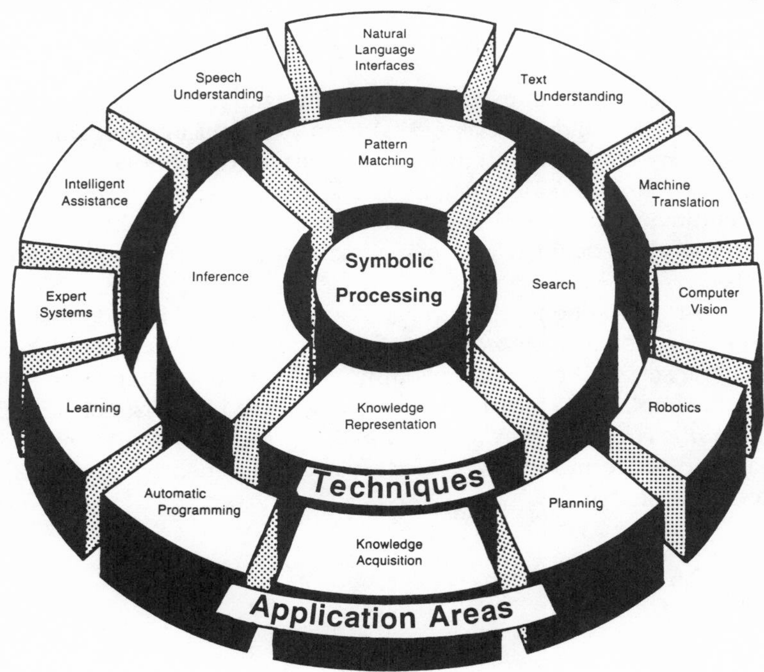

Figure 1.2. Elements of artificial intelligence

small application and explore its possibilities. We already see a plethora of such experiments in reference rooms across the country.

A wide variety of programs have been developed in many different fields performing a range of different tasks. Figure 1.2 represents an effort to classify them according to the function they perform and the type of problem they address.

As we have attempted to show in this chapter, artificial intelligence techniques and particularly expert systems offer some exciting potential for improving library services. It remains to be seen if this technology can be effectively harnessed. In the next chapter we will consider some of the technical problems of developing an expert system and introduce some of the general principles of expert system design.

Recommended Readings

A number of books provide a general overview of the field of artificial intelligence. Patrick Winston's book on *Artificial Intelligence*, now in its second edition (1984), provides insight into the theory behind it. Firebaugh (1988), a more recent text, approaches it from a layman's view with numerous examples.

For those interested in exploring issues in natural language processing, the Schank & Childers book (1984) is an excellent introduction, besides being very readable with many humorous accounts of failures. *The Eye, the Brain, and the Computer*, by Fischler and Firschein (1987), adds a different dimension because it explores the concept of intelligence and the nature of the cognitive and perceptual capabilities of people and machines.

The most comprehensive reference book in the field is undoubtedly Barr and Feigenbaum's *Handbook of Artificial Intelligence* (1981), a three-volume set, with contributions from many of the leading figures in the field. A simple introductory handbook is offered by Mishkoff called *Understanding Artificial Intelligence* (1988). For the more serious reader, Charniak and McDermott (1986) offer a very comprehensive and rather more technical study.

2
Anatomy of an Expert System

Artificial intelligence aims to duplicate human information processing with a machine. Among the significant challenges propelling current research are: vision, natural language processing, machines that can learn from their mistakes, intelligent tutoring systems that can adapt to the user's learning style and identify the types of errors being made, and neural networks which imitate the processing patterns of the human brain. Less exotic and far more commercially successful have been expert systems. Expert systems aim to codify the knowledge of human experts in specific problem domains, thus making that knowledge available for others to use.

Expert system technology has clearly come of age, and numerous library applications are now under consideration. We are still in the early stages of assimilation and accommodation. The first step is appreciation of the values and benefits artificial intelligence can bestow on libraries. Then comes assimilation of procedures involved and a grasp of the mechanics. A few library professionals are at this stage, building experimental prototypes or "toy" systems. An even smaller group of more advanced researchers is pushing out the frontiers. Members of the more advanced group are taking on larger and/or more ambitious projects. As they progress, their mastery of this new technology increases along with their ability to accommodate it to the specialized needs of existing library services. Eventually there will be new services centered around expert systems technology.

Two separate but interrelated issues are immediately apparent:

1. Before really significant expert systems components can be modularized and integrated into existing library automation, more **robust** methodologies must exist. Components must run on the same machines, supported by the same operating systems as the majority of existing library applications.
2. Ways to deal with a vast array of large knowledge bases must be developed. Most of the commercially successful expert systems deal with tightly restricted areas of knowledge. The literature cautions developers to select clearly constrained problems in narrow domains. Systems targetted to special-

> ized user populations are recommended. Developing expert systems to serve very large and heterogeneous end-user populations (like the clients of libraries) radically alters the dimensions and complexity of the knowledge bases which must be developed.

Libraries, which tend to serve large diverse client groups, and deal with broad spectrum knowledge, are a major challenge for expert system development. Before examining some of the emerging solutions to library-related problems and assessing their value, we will examine the anatomy of simple rule-based expert systems. Subsequent chapters will treat more complex systems.

Formalisms for Expressing Knowledge

The first crucial task in designing an expert system is to establish a formal, structured mechanism for communicating with the machine. This requires encoding information about library clients and collections. Also needed are instructions, or rules if you will, to enable the computer to understand what is required of it. Most of us are familiar with at least one of the standard programming languages, like **BASIC** or **Pascal**. They are procedural, that is, every step must be spelled out in detail. They consist of sets of instructions and have few, if any, mechanisms to describe a closed world of known facts.

Logic-based languages such as **PROLOG**, on the other hand, are a convenient way to manage descriptions. The description of a given world or universe consists of both facts and rules. Once we have set up the world description, we can ask questions about that world if we express the query as a goal. Fundamental to the whole process is the formalized description. Every expert system is initiated by specifying the known facts and articulating the rules to be imposed on the relationships that may develop (Rogers, 1987).

Specifying Facts in a Knowledge Base

Natural language has proven to be an unsatisfactory vehicle for specifying facts to a computer. The richness, variety, and tremendous ambiguity of natural language all mitigate against it being used as a medium for computer description.

Many expressions convey the same idea:

Joe smashed his toe with a chair.
Joe's injury was a result of dropping a chair on his toe.

Joe's toe was injured by being smashed by a chair.
The chair smashed Joe's toe.

These four sentences vary considerably in syntax. Their meaning, however, is very similar. In expert systems, it is necessary to reduce this variety to simple patterns of expression that can be used repeatedly. These patterns also help perform grouping functions to reduce the number of rules to write and process. The above cluster of statements can be simplified into such a pattern:

injured (<person> <body part> <instrument>)

The term **injured** can be thought of as a **predicate** which describes the **relationship** between three **objects**: a person, a body part, and an instrument. The predicate can be applied to the specific instance cited earlier as:

injured (Joe, toe, chair)

To generalize it to cover contingencies such as :

Jim cut his finger with the glass.
Helen skinned her knee on the sidewalk.
Henry shot himself in the foot with a pistol.

we change the pattern to:

reported (<person>,<injury>,<body part>,<instrument>)

which results in the following instances for our fact base:

reported (Joe, smashed, toe, chair)
reported (Jim, cut, finger, glass)
reported (Helen, skinned, knee, pavement)
reported (Henry, shot, foot, gun)

From this set of facts we can obtain information. Queries are formulated as goals, then the system seeks to obtain answers by pattern matching. It seeks a match in the database and unifies the items that are given.

Let us set up a query to find out if anyone has been reported hurt by a gun. We must know the form of the predicate and the position of the known item. Reported (Who, Hurt, Where, gun) ? The system will search for that pattern, and finding a match on gun will inform us that Henry was reported shot in the foot with a gun. This pattern-matching process is described as unification.

Obviously, what we can do with simple predicates or fact statements is quite limited. Fortunately, we can add rules to the system.

Let us explore a small system in which we set up rules to determine citizenship. First, we provide facts relating to place of birth, and family relationships. Here again, we standardize the predicates. We need at least two, namely, born-in (<person> <place>), and parent-of (<adult> <child>). The predicate stands first, followed by the subject and object, e.g., (parent-of Helen, Mary). This can be translated to mean Helen is the parent of Mary, or Mary's mother is Helen or Mary is the child of Helen.

Adding Rules

After expressing a number of facts, the system designer also puts in rules or heuristics that enable the derivation of new facts based on what is already known. Let us formulate two simple rules for citizenship:

1. Mary is a citizen of Australia if Mary was born in Australia.

In predicate logic this becomes:

```
(citizen-of Mary Australia):-
      if (born-in Mary Australia).
```

A second corollary rule is obviously needed:

2. Mary is also a citizen of Australia if Helen is Mary's mother and Helen is born-in Australia.

```
(citizen-of Mary Australia) :-
      if (parent-of Helen, Mary) and
        (born-in Helen, Australia)
```

Now we may set up a small expert system to demonstrate how a knowledge base of facts about family relationships and origins can, with a few simple rules, derive new facts through the process of unification.

```
Born-in (Susan, US)
Born-in (George, US)
Born-in (Pat, England)
Born-in (Richard, England)
Born-in (Mary, England)
Born-in (Fred, France)
```

```
Parent-of (Mary, Susan)
Parent-of (Fred, George)
Parent-of (George, Pat)
Parent-of (Susan, Richard)

  (Citizen-of <Person> <Country>):-
      if (Born-in <Person> <Country>).

  (Citizen-of <Person> <Country>):-
     if (Parent-of <X>,<Person>) and
            (Born-in <X> <Country>)
```

Person, Country, and X are considered variables or unknowns.

Setting Up Goals/Queries

Having set up the knowledge base of facts and rules, we are ready to interrogate our system by setting up a query or goal to satisfy. For example: (Citizen-of Mary Australia)?. Having verfied that this pattern exists in the database, the system will simply respond T / True or F / False.

We can ask further questions such as:

In what countries is Pat eligible for citizenship?

Answer: England (born there), and US because his father was born there.

List citizenship for everyone in the database.

Answer:

Susan born-in	US	&	England	because mother born there
George "	US	&	France	because father born there
Pat "	England	&	US	because father born there
Richard "	England	&	US	because mother born there
Mary "	England,			
Fred "	France,			

Who are citizens of England?

Pat, Richard, Mary, all born there, also Susan because mother born there.

Since there are two rules for citizenship, both are checked. This method is recursive because every relevant instance in the knowledge base is checked to establish whether or not it is true. This procedure can be very inefficient, so methods have been derived to control or prevent unnecessary backtracking. If we accept the first instance as true, we can then stop the search. If Mary is born in Australia, we can immediately determine that she is a citizen of that country. There is no need to check whether any of her ancestors were born there (Clark & McCabe, 1984).

Directing the Flow of Logic

Goal Seeking/Backward Chaining Systems

When designing an expert system, there are numerous choices to make about the searching mechanisms that will determine the firing order of the rules. Many different techniques are available.

It is also necessary to ascertain the most efficient way to organize rules. An often-used technique involves grouping rules by goals. Then we must develop a set of guidelines to determine which of the relevant rules to fire and in what order. This is the purpose of the inference engine, now a standard component of most expert system shells.

Most simple systems use **goal seeking** and **backward chaining**. We set up a goal and then chain backwards through the knowledge base, checking relevant predicates until all solutions are found. Others, particularly diagnostic systems, are forward chaining. We are given some facts, perhaps symptoms, then we search forward through the database of production rules looking for matches.

The following example (BORLAND, 1986) illustrates a goal seeking/backwards chaining system written in Turbo PROLOG, an inexpensive version of the AI language PROLOG. It is also possible to use a special development tool called a **shell** to develop a small expert system. PROLOG was chosen for this example because, unlike shells which often supply components of the finished system, PROLOG requires the developer to build each component. PROLOG will therefore provide a more complete picture of the separate problems which need to be addressed when developing a system, and the components of a functioning expert system.

We will use it to determine who are the suspects in a murder mystery. The system is set up as a series of facts and rules. In order to satisfy our original goal of identifying the suspects, we must first satisfy a number of subgoals. In each case we match the predicate pattern and then replace/unify unknown variables with known facts.

```
Who killed Susan?

Can you find the suspects?
/* Who dun it */

person( allan, 25, m, football_player).
person( allan, 25, m, butcher).
person(barbara, 22, f, hairdresser).
person(bert, 55, m, carpenter).
person( john, 25, m, pickpocker).
had_affair( barbara, john).
had_affair( barbara, bert).
had_affair( susan, john).
killed_with( susan, club).
motive( money ).
motive( jealousy ).
smeared_in( catherine, blood ).
smeared_in( allan, mud ).
owns( bert, wooden_leg ).
owns( john, pistol ).

/* Background-knowledge */
operates_identically( wooden_leg,  club).
operates_identically( bar,  club).
operates_identically( pair_of_scissors, knife).
operates_identically( football_boot, club).
owns_probably( X, football_boot )   if  person( X,_,_,football_player).
owns_probably( X, pair_of_scissors)    if person(X,_,_,_,_).
owns_probably(X, Object)    if owns(X, Object).

/* suspect all those who own a weapon with which susan
     could possibly have been killed*/
suspect(X)  if  killed_with(susan, Weapon)  and
                operated_identically(Object, Weapon)  and
                owns_probably(X, Object).

/* suspect men that have had an affair with susan */
suspect(X)  if  motive(jealousy)  and  person(X,_,m,_)
                and   had_affair(susan,X).

/* suspect females who have had an affair with a man
     with whom susan had an affair */
suspect(X)  if  motive(jealousy)  and  person(X,_,f,_)
                and  had_affair(X, Man)
                and  had_affair(susan, Man).

/* suspect pickpockets whose motive could be money */
suspect(X)  if  motive(money)   and  person(X,_,_,pickpocket).
```

Figure 2.1. Who killed Susan?

For example : We set up a goal of **suspect (X)**.

The system searches for the predicate "suspect." It locates four rules for suspects.

1. Suspect: all who own a weapon which could possibly have killed Susan.
2. Suspect: men who have had an affair with Susan.
3. Suspect: women who have had an affair with a man who has also had an affair with Susan.
4. Suspect: pickpockets whose motive could be money.

From just the first of these rules we see that:

> Suspect (<X>) if killed-with (<Victim>, <Weapon>) and
> operates-identically (<Object>, <Weapon>) and
> likely-to own (<Person>,<Object>).

The system now selects the first subgoal to determine "if killed-with (<Susan, <weapon>)" and will quickly find "killed- with (susan, club)." Having satisfied this subgoal in the rule, the system moves to the second condition "..operates_identically (<Object>, Weapon)." Because we know that the weapon was a club, this is substituted in < Weapon>.

Next we set out to search for objects that operate-identically to a club. We find several that qualify: a bat, a wooden-leg, and a football boot. Note that unless the system designer decides that the pistol can also be used as a club and puts this fact in the database, this connection will not be made and we will fail to extract the very significant fact that John owned a pistol that could very well have served as the murder weapon.

The next step is to find out who is likely to own any of these objects. From that the system can determine the first group of suspects. Allan is a football player and probably owns a football boot. Bert has a wooden-leg, which operates-identically to a club. Therefore, Allan and Bert become our first suspects.

The second rule searches for men who may have had an affair with Susan. We turn up John. Moving to the third rule, we search for any woman who may have had an affair with a man having an affair with Susan, i.e., with John. The only one to qualify is Barbara.

Lastly, we check for people who might have had a money motive. John is our man, because he is a pickpocket by trade. Our final list of suspects then is Allan, Bert, John, and Barbara.

Weighting or Ranking of Outcomes

Obviously, this elementary system would be much more useful if it ranked the suspects. Clearly Allan or Bert, who own items that could be weapons but otherwise had little motive, are less likely to be the murderer than is someone who had an affair with the victim or the victim's lover. More likely is someone with more than one possible motive. John may have been jealous, but also he was motivated by greed for money. Barbara was only jealous. If we present this in the form of a Venn diagram (Figure 2.2), John becomes our primary suspect. We see the need for weighting, whether accomplished through supplementary rules or by ranking each possible motive. A ranking system can be developed with a probability value then assigned to each suspect as shown in Figure 2.3.

In larger and more sophisticated systems, Bayesian analysis is used to calculate the weightings but Turbo PROLOG, used for these examples, does not offer this capability.

Explanation and Verification

When the system presents a list of suspects, even a ranked list, almost all people will demand to know how it was determined. Very few of us are so lacking in curiosity as to accept computer output unquestioningly. Thus, a feature of the better expert system shells today is built-in mechanisms for explanations. At the very minimum, you should be able to trace the rules that fired and understand how each suspect was chosen. John was selected as our prime suspect because he is a pickpocket and might

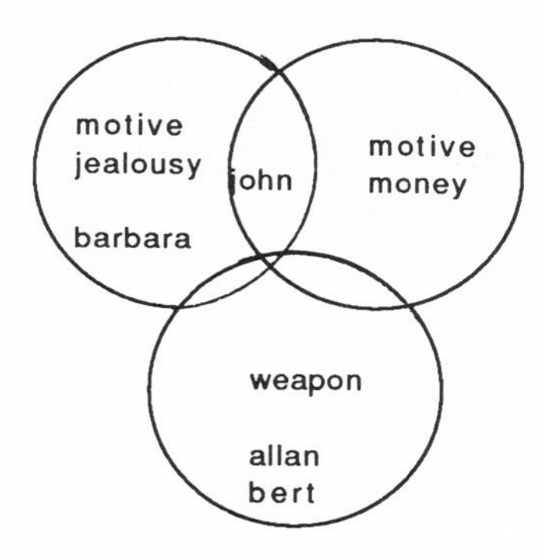

Figure 2.2. Venn diagram

0.80	jealous greedy weapon
0.72	greedy weapon
0.70	jealous weapon
0.60	jealous
0.50	greedy
0.30	weapon
0.00	

Figure 2.3. Probability rating scale

have had a money motive. He also had had an affair with Susan and may have been jealous. Explanation facilities will be discussed in greater detail in Chapter Eight.

Forward-Chaining Systems

The inference procedure used in cases where the desired outcome is not certain is known as **forward chaining**. The procedure begins with known facts and conditions then works forward to possible solutions. The difficulty with this method is that it can very quickly lead to a **combinatorial explosion** with overwhelming numbers of options to consider.

A good analogy is a quest through a maze. In forward chaining you enter at the top with no clear idea of where to find the exit. By a process of trial and error and the elimination of blind paths you gradually work closer to the exit and eventually find a solution that satisfies all constraints.

Figure 2.4. A maze

A library example of a forward chaining or data driven search might look something like this:

If a disease is mentioned and the disease term includes subcategories,

Determine which are of interest and use the tree structure to search for them.

If a disease is mentioned, and a chemical is mentioned, and the chemical is a drug, maybe drug therapy is of interest.

Obtain data to verify and, if necessary, attach the drug therapy subheading to the name of the disease.

If there is a registry number for the chemical in the knowledge base, incorporate it in the search strategy.

In brief, the search is driven by the data rather than by the goal. The values provided in the search request determine the direction taken in the search.

Changing Closed Worlds/the User Interface

The above examples dealt with closed worlds. The only information accessed and processed was already contained in the system, except for the initial goal. Similarly, a brute force keyword search technique simply accepts a list of keywords, grouped to indicate desired relationships, and then performs a search without further interaction between the system and its user.

An information specialist's approach is markedly different. Probing questions narrow and refine the initial user query while the search strategy is being worked out. For any expert system to be viable it, too, must be able to interact with end-users. New data, acquired through this interaction, has to be added dynamically to the database where it will influence the choices being made, remaining active for the duration of that search. A user interface can be written in such a way that when the system gets to a certain rule it will prompt the user for the information it needs to select one of several options.

Let us examine, for example, a simple tree identification system (Figure 2.5). Rules have been grouped in clusters. The first group deals with the **family** to which a tree might belong.

When the system begins with the first rule in this group, setting family as the goal, the very first condition it encounters says "if class is gymnosperm...." Since the class is not known, the system sets **class** as a subgoal and the first goal, family, is put on hold until the subgoal class is satisfied. Now the system goes chasing off to find the rules that deal with the class of the tree (Rules 5 and 6). The system begins with the first rule in this cluster, and here the first condition asks if the type is tree. Since the type is not known, the system sets a second marker at this second goal and goes off to find out the type. Rules 7–10 deal with type, and the first rule in this group asks if the stem is green.

The system has no information on the stem, but does locate a prompt, which is presented to the user as a question to be answered at this point in the process. The user responds to prompts for the rules that are being fired, specifying that the stem is woody, the position upright and there is one main trunk. From these facts the system concludes that the type is tree, thereby satisfying the goal of determining the type.

Having accomplished this subgoal, the system backtracks to the previous goal of determining the class, inserts the newly acquired information that the type is tree, and prompts the user about the shape of the leaves. Since they are not broad and flat, we can determine that we are

SAMPLE TREE IDENTIFICATION SYSTEM

RULES

```
Family is cypress :-        if   class is gymnosperm
                              and  leaf shape is scalelike.

Family is pine :-           if   class is gymnosperm
                              and  leaf shape is needlelike
                              and  pattern is random.

Family is pine :-           if   class is gymnosperm
                              and  leaf shape is needlelike
                              and  pattern is 2 even lines
                              and  silvery band is yes.

Family is bald cypress:- if   class is gymnosperm
                              and  leaf shape is needlelike
                              and  pattern is 2 even lines
                              and  silvery band is no.

Class is angiosperm :-      if   type is tree
                              and  broad_flat_leaves is yes.

Class is gymnosperm :-      if   type is tree
                              and  broad_flat_leaves is no.

Type is herb:-  if  stem is green.
Type is vine:-  if  stem is woody and position is creeping.
Type is tree:-  if  stem is woody and position is upright
                       and one_main_trunk is yes.
Type is shrub:- if  stem is woody and position is upright
                       and one_main_trunk is no.
```

ATTRIBUTE	TRANSLATION	PROMPT
stem	The stem of the plant	Is the stem woody or greens?
position	The position of the stem	Is the position of the stem upright or creeping?
one main trunk	The plant does/not/have one main trunk	Does the plant have one main trunk?
Leaf shape	The leaf shape	Is the leaf shape needlelike or scalelike?
broad_and_flat_leaves	The shape of the leaves is/not/broad and flat	Is the shape of the leaves broad and flat?

*written in pseudocode.

Figure 2.5. Tree identification system

dealing with a class of gymnosperm. Once the class is known, the system backtracks to the original goal of type and plugs in that the class is gymnosperm. The user responds to prompts that the leaf shape is needlelike and the pattern random, and our system has satisfied rule number 2 and correctly informs us that we are looking at a pine tree.

In this small system prompts were provided for a number of items that can readily be observed by the user as she attempts to identify the plant. Among the attributes of plants for which prompts exist are stem color, position (either creeping or upright), type of trunk, and type of leaf. The actual prompts used are shown in the bottom right column of Figure 2.5.

In most expert system shells, prompts to elicit required information from the user can be specified for any attribute. It is also usually possible to create helpful explanations in the form of English-like sentences (referred to as **translations**). For example, in Figure 2.5, stem is defined as "the stem of the plant." The value-seeking prompt asks the user whether "the stem is woody or green." This information will be added to the dynamic database. If the stem is green, it is an herb. If the stem is woody, the next question is whether the plant is creeping or upright. If it is upright, it is a tree. If it is not, it is a vine.

Additions to Working Memory

While most expert system shells include prompts and translations, in PROLOG the ability to add to working memory is not built in. The mechanism for obtaining needed information and providing explanations must be added by the developer in the form of a consultation module, an example of which is shown in Figure 2.6. This module, which forms a part of the inference engine, will permit the system to ask its user for additional information, to manage this user input, to match it with production rules, and to keep track of (or "remember") the responses. The rules, "positive" and "negative," are used to match the user's yes or no responses with production rules. The rule "remember" makes assertions with yes and no responses used for pattern matching. "Asserta" adds new facts to a dynamic database, where facts about the problem currently being considered are stored. Finally, after a session is concluded, the "clear_facts" rules remove the search-specific facts that were added during the consultation so that the next user will have a fresh start.

When the production rules are in place, the simple dialog shown below will prompt the user for information, asking the appropriate questions as determined from the flow of logic.

```
ANIMAL IDENTIFICATION SYSTEM

Please answer the following questions to identify your animal.
Has it hair? Yes
Does it give milk? Yes
```

SAMPLE CONSULTATION MODULE
written in Turbo Prolog

```
goal
    run.
/* this goal initiales the system */
clauses
    run:-
        animal_is(X),!,
        write("\nYour animal may be a(n) ",X),
        nl,nl,clear_facts.

/* If an animal is located with the required attributes it is printed out */
    run:-
        write("\nUnable to determine what"),
        write(" Your animal is. \n\n"), clear_facts.

    positive(X,Y) if xpositive(X,Y),!,
    positive(X,Y) if not(negative(X,Y)),! and ask(X,Y).
    negative(X,Y) if xnegative(X,Y),!.

/* the system determines if x y is positive or negative by the user */
    ask(X,Y):-
        write(X," it ",Y,"\n"),
        readln(Reply),
        remember(X,Y,Reply).

/* the users response is stored in the database */
    remember(X,Y,yes):-
        asserta(xpositive(X,Y)).
    remember(X,Y,no):-
        asserta(xnegative(X,Y)), fail.

/* after a consultation the system resets the values to blanks */
    clear_facts:-
        retract(xpositive(_,_)), fail.
    clear_facts:-
        retract(xnegative(_,_)), fail.
    clear_facts:-
        write("\n\n Please press the space bar to Exit"),
        readchar(_).

/* example of an animal rule */
    animal_is(cheetah) if it_is(mammal), it_is(carnivore),
                          positive(has,tawny_color),
                          positive(has,black_spots),!.
```

Figure 2.6. Sample consultation module

Does it eat meat? Yes
Has it pointed teeth and claws? Yes
Is it tawny-colored? Yes
Has it black spots? No

Has it black stripes? Yes
Your animal is probably a tiger.

Answers are added to the dynamic knowledge base for the duration of the search. Facts in the dynamic knowledge base are used to guide the system toward a solution. As soon as the animal is identified, the system will "clear_facts," that is, eliminate all inputs for the current query, and reset those values to unknowns.

The mechanics of end-user interfaces vary widely from package to package. There are no standards at present, despite the fact that it is one of the most critical factors in user acceptance of expert systems. It should be given careful consideration when selecting any expert system shell.

Using Decision Trees

One of the first steps in designing any expert system is to develop a set of typical test cases with which the system must be able to deal. We use these test cases to extract the significant attributes involved and organize these by means of a **decision tree**. Then we are ready to begin writing the necessary production rules (Yin, 1987). Let us look at a simple animal identification system (Figure 2.7).

The attributes we select are designed to identify each animal uniquely within the group we have selected. In this case, the attributes are:

ATTRIBUTE LIST

1. Mammal (has hair, gives milk)
2. Carnivore (eats meat, has pointed teeth and claws)
3. tawny color
4. Black spots
5. Black stripes
6. Mane
7. Ungulates (has hooves, chews cud)
8. Long neck
9. Black stripes
10. Antlers
11. Bird (has feathers, lays eggs)
12. Flies
13. Bird of prey
14. Webbed feet
15. Wing span over 5ft.
16. Can't fly
17. Swims

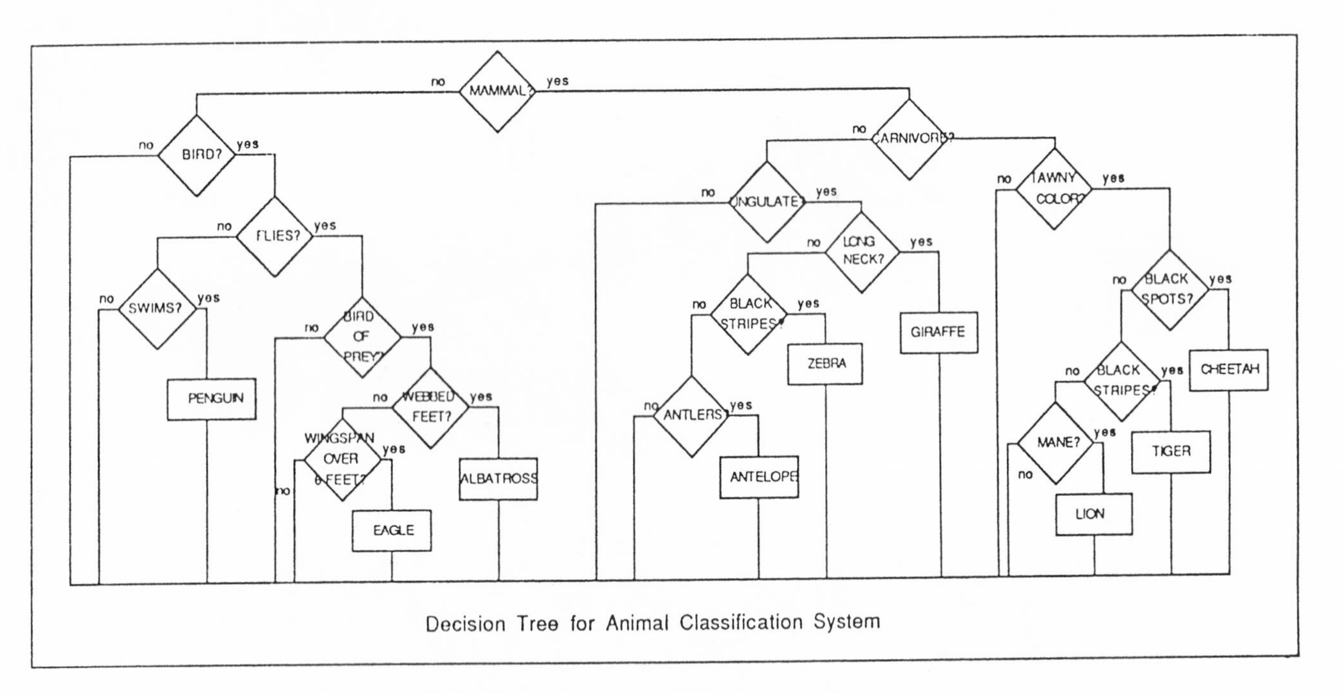

Figure 2.7. Animal classification decision tree

The major distinction is whether these animals are mammals or birds. From there we move one level of specificity in the hierarchy to determine whether the mammals are carnivores or ungulates. Birds are grouped according to whether they fly or not.

Objects and Their Attributes

Since the objective of the system is to classify the objects by their distinguishing attributes, part of the development process of any expert system involves making lists of the objects and their attributes, whether we are dealing with diseases, troubleshooting equipment, identifying a sonar signal, or simply naming an animal.

Each attribute is applied as a YES/NO (binary) decision. The animal either has or does not have the characteristic singled out.

OBJECT/ATTRIBUTES LIST

Breed	**Attributes ***	
Carnivores		
Cheetah	1, 2, 3, 4	
Tiger	1, 2, 3, -, 5,	
Lion	1, 2, 3, -, -, 6	
Ungulates		
Giraffe	1, -, -, -, -, -, 7, 8,	
Zebra	1, -, -, -, -, -, 7, -, 9,	
Antelope	1, -, -, -, -, -, 7, -, -, 10	
Birds		
Albatross		11, 12, 13, 14
Eagle		11, 12, 13, -, 15
Penguin		11, 16, 17

*The numbers used refer to the Attributes List above.

Once the attributes are determined, then we write distinct production rules for each animal, including for each one any reference to a major category.

```
animal_is (cheetah):-     if it_is (mammal) and
                          it_is (carnivore) and
                          *positive (has tawny_color) and
                          *positive (has black_spots).
```

```
animal_is (lion):-        if it_is (mammal) and
                          it_is (carnivore) and
                          *positive (has tawny_color) and
                          *positive (has mane)
```

* positive indicates that the user has reponded yes to a prompt.

A number of expert systems in libraries are using this sort of decision tree structure to build interactive pathfinders in the reference room. One example, reported at the ASIS Midyear 1988, dealt with an expert system that could recommend the most suitable biographical reference tool depending on the user's answers to a series of questions.

Pruning/Narrowing the Search Space

Perhaps the most valuable asset expert systems can bring to large database searches is the capacity to narrow the search space by **intelligent pruning**. Even in this very small system, as soon as we determine that the user is interested in a mammal, all the rules that deal with birds are ignored. The response of the user to each question is used to narrow the system's path through the database, thereby eliminating no longer necessary rules from consideration.

Depth First/Breadth First/Hill Climbing

Directing the search flow efficiently is the primary function of the inference engine, and one of the major driving forces behind metarules and modules. In the example, (Figure 2.8) the Lawn Boy mower trouble shooting diagnostic system, the user has a whole range of possibilities to consider in order to detect the malfuntion.

The owner of the lawn mower must first determine whether or not the motor starts and runs properly. A brute force approach works through all the possibilities systematically from first to last without any effort to eliminate unnecessary steps. A number of different strategies have been proposed to make the search more efficient.

Take the case of the lawn mower that won't start. The first strategy, **depth first**, entails selecting one possibility, the ignition for example, and then testing every rule involving the ignition: spark plug fouling, no spark, defective switch, broken switch lead circuit, hi-tension lead grounded or shorting out, incorrect air gap, etc. Only after exhausting the procedures for all these rules would the search process then shift to the fuel supply as the potential source of the starting problem.

The second common strategy, **breadth first**, involves moving across every branch in the tree, systematically checking first the spark plug, next

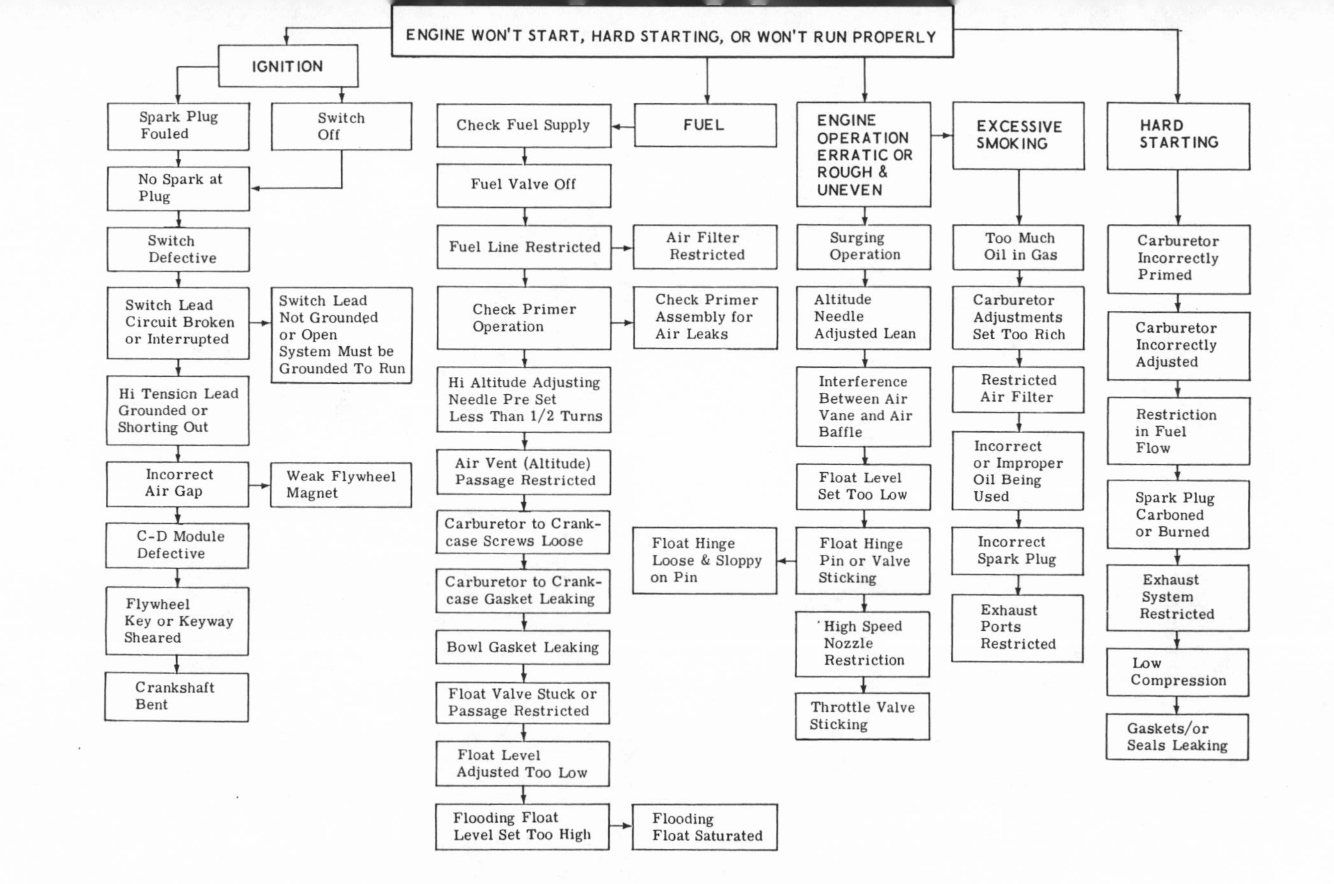

Figure 2.8. Lawn Boy lawn mower repair troubleshooting

the fuel supply, the altitude needle, the amount of oil in the gas, and then the priming of the carburetor. Both these strategies are blind or uninformed, since the firing order being used is not at all affected by information on the progress of the search, except for tracing the moves from the origin, and tests to prevent getting stuck in an endless loop.

Hill climbing strategy, on the other hand, uses local information to decide which is the best path. We seek to maximize movement toward the goal and minimize lost motion (Firebaugh, 1988). For example: A team of mountain climbers equipped with only an altimeter and compass (no topological maps) find themselves in heavy fog on the side of a mountain. What is the optimum strategy to reach the summit?

One solution would be to walk 100 feet north and note the change in the altimeter reading. Returning to home base, repeat the process to the east. With a little trigonometry, we can calculate the direction of the maximum gradient. After a few hundred feet, repeat the process. When, eventually, all directions lead to a reduced gradient, we are at the summit.

In our lawn mower repair system, after completing one test cycle we can assess our progress, and proceed from there. If, after cleaning the fouled spark plug, it starts but is running erratically, then we can move to checking the surging operation.

Metarules

The larger the expert system and the more rules involved, the greater the need for pruning the search space and organizing or controlling the flow of logic. In the lawn mower repair system, several distinct groups of rules can be identified. The first set deals with ignition problems, the second with fuel supply, the third with engine operation, another with excessive smoke, and the last with hard starts. Once the rules have been grouped by specific application in this way, they are separated into modules, to be accessed only when indicated by **metarules**. For example:

IF the engine operation is erratic or rough and uneven and
there is excessive smoke,
THEN invoke-module "SMOKING MODULE".

This will speed up the flow of logic by reducing the number of rules to be accessed in seeking a solution.

The Inference Engine

Once a system gets larger it quite often occurs that more than one rule is ready to fire at the same time. To overcome this sort of difficulty and enforce consistency, another essential component of all expert system is the inference engine, which manages the rules. The following small rule-based system demonstrates how an inference engine works and why it is needed (Gilmore & Howard, 1985).

We are given the current facts: Fact1,fact2,fact3,fact4,fact5.

We have a rule base as follows:
Rule 1: If fact1 & fact2 & fact6, then conclusion1.
Rule 2 If fact2 & fact3 & fact4, then conclusion2
Rule 3 If fact2 & fact3 & fact4 &fact5, then conclusion3
Rule 4 If fact1 & fact2, then conclusion4
Rule 5 If fact4, then conclusion5
Rule 6 If fact3 & fact4, then conclusion6
Rule 7 If fact2 and fact3 and fact5, then conclusion7
Rule 8 If fact2 and fact3 and fact6, then conclusion8

The system moves into the **conflict set** all rules with antecedents that satisfy the given facts. In the above case the following rules are selected for possible firing:

CONFLICT SET

Facts Given

Rules Selected	Fact1	Fact2	Fact3	Fact4	Fact5
Rule 2		x	x	x	
Rule 3		x	x	x	x
Rule 4	x		x		
Rule 5				x	
Rule 6			x	x	
Rule 7		x	x		x

Firing all these rules simultaneously or in random order will result in inconsistent if not erroneous results. Therefore, a method to select a single rule from this conflict set must be derived, then followed consistently to guarantee uniform performance.

Conflict Resolution Strategies

In some expert system shells **conflict resolution** is tied to the most recent rule fired. The system keeps track of the firing history. In this case we are told that the following rules have already fired: Rule8, Rule7, Rule3, Rule2, Rule5, Rule4, Rule6 and Rule1. Rule1 is the most recent rule fired. If we decide to use the recency strategy, Rule 6 will qualify as the next to be fired. If we decide to go with the rule that has been active the longest, then Rule 7 will qualify.

Another common strategy is to fire the most specific rule with the largest number of conditions attached. In this case Rule 3 has four conditions which must be met before it is invoked. It will be the next. However, if we adopt a strategy of firing either the most general rule or the least specific, rule 5 has only one conditon to be met. It will be fired as the least specific.

Obviously, these strategies have little or nothing to do with the specific rules in a given system. They are generic and necessary to guarantee the shell's uniform performance. Understanding how such resolution strategies work, is important, however, in determining how to make a system perform correctly.

Hooks to the Outside World

In libraries, any expert system that proposes to do substantial work must be able to interface with and access existing databases. It is simply not practical even to consider duplicating the entire library collection in a PROLOG-type data structure that can be acted upon by rules. Most Online Public Access Catalogs (OPACS) store and access MARC records using relational database technology with inverted indices for key word searches. These systems perform set processing which is much more efficient at retrieving data than logic-based systems. What is needed is an effective interface that permits us to integrate the two technologies.

The expert system should interact with the library researcher, refining the information need, determining the most suitable information packages, and selecting the appropriate databases — in effect, guiding the search process. However, retrieving records that match a given search strategy is much more efficiently handled by existing systems so the expert system should also be able to pass control over to the OPAC or online search programs which already exist.

Blackboard Systems

In some of the more elaborate expert systems, a "blackboard" is provided for recording intermediate results. Three types of decisions appear on the blackboard: a **plan**, an **agenda**, and **solution elements**. Plan elements describe the overall or general approach to problem solving, that is, current plans, goals, problem states, and contexts. The plan may, for example, recommend first checking the ignition thoroughly, then formulating a series of other tests to refine, then eliminate each problem until the car is once again purring along. Agenda elements record the potential actions awaiting execution. These correspond to knowledge base rules that seem relevant to some decision already placed on the blackboard. The solution elements represent the possible solutions being considered plus the decisions made thus far.

The **scheduler** maintains control of the agenda and decides what to do next. To accomplish this, each item is prioritized according to its relationship to the plan. The **interpreter** executes a chosen agenda item by firing the corresponding rule. The **consistency enforcer** is responsible for **truth maintenance** and tries to ensure a consistent representation of the emerging solution. If new information is added, such as the discovery of a broken lead to the battery, it may impact on earlier conclusions that were reached without the benefit of this new insight.

Hayes-Roth has given his view of an ideal expert system. It even includes a natural language front-end for communicating with the end-user (Hayes-Roth, 1984, p.18).

Some of the more robust expert systems shells allow for a number of possible solutions to be considered at the same time, each one occupying a different world. All worlds are checked as each rule is fired until a world fails to satisfy a given condition. When this occurs that "world" or hypothesis is "poisoned" or removed from active consideration.

Choosing the Right Expert Systems Tool

The person who has decided to build an expert system is faced with a number of choices in deciding on the right expert systems tool.

A number of logic-based programming languages are available if the developer decides to build the whole system from scratch. The best known of these languages are **LISP** and **PROLOG**. An attractive alternative is provided by the many expert systems shells now on the market which provide as a minimum a built-in editor, a user interface, an inference engine, and a help facility. Using a shell enables the system developer to concentrate on the facts and rules involved. The disadvantage of these shells is that they often lack the flexibility needed for the application. Chapter 6 will provide a more detailed discussion of knowledge representation techniques.

The key characteristic of expert systems is that they solve problems through reasoning. Systems must have access to organized facts and heuristics, known as a knowledge base, and must be able to infer new

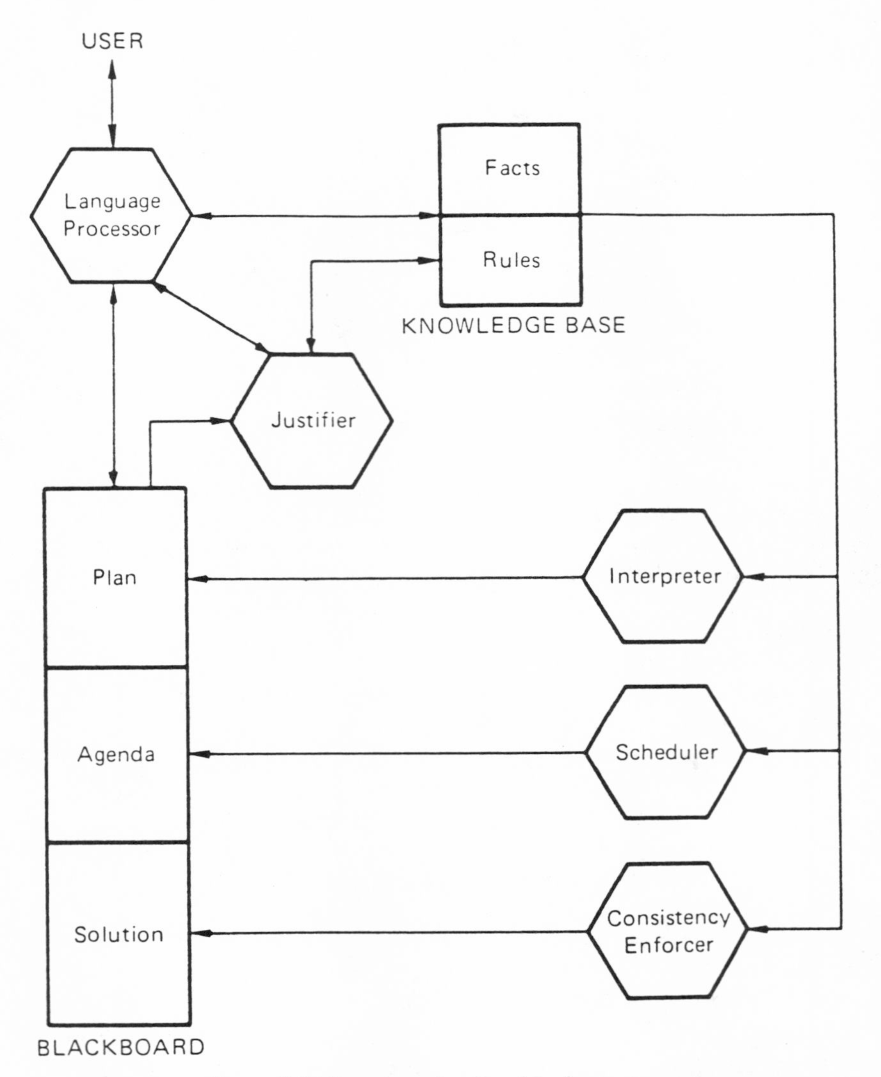

Figure 2.9. Components of an ideal expert system.

---

facts from the information given during a consultation session by using the heuristics or rules of thumb supplied by human experts.

An expert system consists of no less than three basic components.

1. **Knowledge base.** The central component of the system. It contains both factual and inferential knowledge. Facts, such as John is Mary's father, and rules or inferential knowledge,

such as if X is the father of Y and X is a citizen of America, then Y is also a citizen, comprise the knowledge base.

2. **Inference engine.** It consists of operating rules and principles. These are applied consistently to ensure that the system is stable and predictable. One of the more difficult tasks is deciding which rules to fire and in what order whenever a conflict appears.
3. **User interface.** The end-user interface enables communication with the user at several different levels. It must acquire needed input or data to add to working memory for the duration of the session. It can give definitions or translations upon request and can also explain any decision, showing the logic upon which it was based.

Symbolic Processing Languages

In the 1950s when the major high-level languages **Fortran** and **COBOL** were evolving, LISP, a language designed to permit symbolic processing, first appeared in research labs and universities. Over the years many other symbolic languages have been developed, including PROLOG, **OPS5**, **Flavors**, and **Smalltalk**. Each addresses a particular need of AI researchers.

Indeed, as research in artificial intelligence progressed, it expanded into many areas. Expert systems represent a small subset of this research by focusing on the application of logic and symbolic processing to tightly circumscribed problems in limited domains with clear sets of rules. However, because these systems have become commercially viable so quickly, they have attracted a lot of publicity and are now well within the grasp of the layman armed with an expert system shell.

How to communicate with the machine? Procedural languages, such as BASIC and Pascal, although limited in their expressiveness, enable us to convey explicit instructions about what we want done. Sort this, list it out, print it, etc. They do not, however, provide any organized method of pulling together what we know, the relevant background information, the surrounding context or, the common sense knowledge involved. Nor can we reason with or draw conclusions from what we already know.

Research in artificial intelligence has focused on how to represent and use knowledge that is useful and relevant to problem solving. Although a few expert systems have been written in conventional procedural programming languages, it is recognized that two declarative languages, PROLOG and LISP, are particularly well suited as artificial intelligence languages because they are both:

- **Symbol based.** They do pattern-matching with symbols, and are much less tightly structured than conventional languages.

There is no sharp distinction between program and data. Rather the user is able to enter facts and rules into a database. When a goal is set the system will search for a match in the database. There is no need for a detailed step-by-step algorithm.

- **Descriptive.** The emphasis is on stating relationships between symbols which can and do represent a wide variety of objects, rather than spelling out very precisely what every variable in the system represents. The whole system is generally more amorphous and dynamic.
- **Well supported.** They typically have a strong supportive system programming environment, including full-screen editors, powerful debuggers and tracing options, bit-mapped graphics, and well-developed online help facilities.

PROLOG (PROgramming in LOGic)

This language was developed at the University of Marseille in 1972 and is considered a backward-chaining, goal-seeking, logic-based language. Most of the examples in this chapter were developed using Turbo PROLOG from Borland, which unlike "purer" versions of PROLOG is a combination typed and declarative language. Although the syntax varies slightly from package to package and the quality of the editor and user interface varies much more, PROLOG has been widely adopted both here and overseas as the language of choice for expert systems. The programmer simply puts in the facts that are known and the rules governing the relationships between the facts. The task is to declare which effects should produce what outcomes. The programmer leaves to the language itself the burden of finding a solution to the problem. The system does this by searching through all the sentences for each condition, matching the condition with the conclusion of the sentence. When it finds a match, the conditions for that query represent a new query.

Execution of a PROLOG program, therefore, amounts to trying to satisfy a goal. It starts by trying to satisfy the list of subgoals, and if failure occurs, it backtracks and tries an alternative set of subgoals. If the system runs out of alternatives, then it has failed to achieve the goal. Since this whole process is recursive, efficiency is a serious problem. A discussion of techniques for improving efficiency is offered by Warren (1977). The power of PROLOG lies in the fact that the selection of goals and backtracking are built in, while in most other languages such operations would have to be explicitly programmed.

LISP (LISt Processor or Lots of Infuriating Superfluous Parentheses)

This language, developed in the 1950s by John McCarthy of MIT, is the second oldest programming language in use today and is the most widely used symbolic processing language in the world (Liebowitz, 1988). It was designed originally as a list-processing language, using functions to work primarily with symbols. It achieves its effect by the application of functions, rather than by changing the value of existing objects through assignment. A small number of primitive functions are used to build up very sophisticated programs. A key feature of the language is the heavy reliance on recursion as a control structure rather than iteration (looping), as is common in most procedural programming languages.

In America it has been widely used for advanced artificial intelligence projects, often forming the underpinning for several of the larger expert system shells. Of all the options available it is by far the most flexible and versatile. It is also used for natural language processing. But its strength is a problem for the inexperienced programmer because the whole expert system shell must be built from a small number of primitive functions. This process is very time consuming, difficult, and there is a long learning curve. Also, since it is not widely taught in computer science programs, it is difficult to find experienced programmers. With PROLOG a system developer can be writing rules within a hour or two of beginning to use the language.

There are several other disadvantages that are widely recognized. LISP programs are hard to read, particularly as the programs get longer. There are very many dialects of LISP. Although **Common LISP** was an attempt at a standard dialect, it is very large and seems to combine the features of all other LISP dialects rather than being selective. Finally LISP requires a lot of memory and can't be easily run on any but the most powerful machines.

Other Languages

Frame-Based Languages Such as Smalltalk and Loops

Marvin Minsky from MIT is credited as the first to postulate the hypothesis that knowledge can be represented in bundles called frames and then applied in intelligent systems (Minsky, 1975). These configurations provide additional expressive power because related facts can be placed as fillers into predefined slots and then linked together in a frame and accessed as a group. Any fact that binds to that frame makes all the other information accessible without the need to check numerous other predicates. By using pointers to link the frames together, it also becomes possible to inherit information from one frame to another.

Frames were developed because it is clear people draw upon a large collection of structures available in memory to represent previous experience with objects, locations, situations, and people. Frames are useful to group together in one data structure information about many aspects of the object or situation being described. They are also used to contain attributes that must be true of objects that will be used to fill individual slots and can describe typical instances of the concepts they represent (Rich, 1983).

Scripts, as proposed by Schank, are implemented as special purpose frames that describe a stereotyped sequence of events in a particular context (Schank & Abelson, 1977). The slots of a typical script include the following:

- **Entry conditions**: hungry, has money
- **Results**: conditions that will generally be true after the events described in the script have occurred: has less money, is not hungry, is pleased (optional)
- **Props**: slots representing objects typically occurring in the given script: tables, menu, food...etc.
- **Roles**: slots representing people: customer, waiter, cook, cashier
- **Track**: a specific variation on a more general pattern that is represented by a particular script: French restaurant
- **Scenes**: actual sequences of events that occur: enters restaurant, decides where to sit, moves to table, etc.

Two implementations of frame-based languages are offered as complete expert systems development environments and require considerable memory. The first is **KRL (Knowledge Representation Language)** developed by Bobrow and Winograd and **FRL (Frame Representation Language)** developed by Roberts and Goldstein.

Object-Oriented Languages

These, such as Flavors and Smalltalk-80, have taken frames a step further by providing not only related slots and fillers but also methods which are bound to the objects or classes of objects. The user can define methods that work only on objects of a specific class. Methods can be run automatically when an object is created if special procedures are required. They can be activated by message passing. For instance, when the number of hits is greater than 100, activate frame for Narrowing a Search. Methods can send messages to other methods and can pass parameters.

The techniques of object-oriented programming have been found to simplify many types of problems, since they free the programmer from the tedium of constructing complicated control schemes and scope rules.

Expert System Shells-Evaluation Criteria

Because of the time and considerable programming skill required to write a substantial expert system from scratch in any of these languages, many are turning to commercially available expert systems shells. On the market there are currently a large number of such tools of all sizes and types, offering a wide range of features. A number of evaluation criteria have been proposed.

Knowledge Representation Schemes

The first and most important criterion is the set of knowledge representation techniques supported by the shell. Over the years, many different knowledge representation schemes have been proposed, each specialized to meet a particular need (see Chapter 6). Gradually various expert systems shells have evolved that simplify the programmer's task with a built-in inference engine to manage the rule firing. They also offer an integrated set of compatible knowledge representation techniques. Usually, in large expert systems, there are multiple knowledge bases requiring a variety of techniques.

The more sophisticated shells today, e.g., **ART**, **KEE** and **Knowledge Craft** offer an integrated set of tools with the interfaces necessary to combine the rule-based systems built in PROLOG-like languages with frames to support inheritance as well as semantic nets, which allow us to deal with the expressiveness of natural language. They also have some provisions to connect with relational database management systems capable of handling MARC records, as well as supporting some features of object-oriented languages which allow messages and procedures to be associated with objects in the knowledge base. There are a number of different classes of expert system development tools (Gilmore & Howard, 1986).

Types of Shells

Simple rule-based tools. At the lower end of the price scale, these shells allow the developer to enter in a single knowledge base a series of if-then rules. They are very easy to implement and are suitable for small projects, but complex tasks quickly exceed their capabilities . The **Insight 2** package is an example of such a tool. So is **VP-Expert** from Paperback software. There are also a number of public domain expert systems that fall into this category. These tools differ widely in their sophistication.

Structured rule-based tools. Rules can be separated into modules or partitions arranged in a structured hierarchy and managed by a system of metarules. One of the key questions is to what extent knowledge is passed from one module to another. Is there inheritance? How is the flow of logic handled? Does it have the required flexibility? **Personal Consultant Plus** from Texas Instruments is an example of this class. While it has far more capability than simple rule-based tools, it also requires a great deal more memory — at least one megabyte of core memory to build a substantial system.

Induction tools. These work not by deduction, but rather induction. The knowledge engineer inputs numerous examples, indicating the correct conclusion for each. The system will then proceed to build a decision tree and the rules that will obtain the desired outcomes. **1st-Class** is an excellent example of such a package. It runs in 512K on a PC, is relatively inexpensive, and is easy to learn. It uses the familiar spreadsheet with rows and columns to be filled in as the system is developed. We have found it useful to check our logic because it seeks to optimize the decision tree and often points out weaknesses in our design. It is very easy to learn. It was used to develop **Answerman** at the National Library of Agriculture (Ruth, 1988).

Logic-based tools. These use the Horn clauses and goal resolution dictated by predicate calculus. Most of these tools are built on PROLOG. **ES/P Advisor** is an example of such a system. Since these packages do not significantly enhance the capabilities of PROLOG and, in fact, often are not as versatile, it would seem better to invest in a version of PROLOG that includes a user interface and editor. **Micro-PROLOG** with **Apes** and Turbo PROLOG both offer these features and are well supported and documented.

Frame-based tools. Often described as object-oriented, these generally offer a variety of knowledge representation techniques, including frames, in one package. The combination yields a great deal more flexibility to work with multiple and differing knowledge bases, to interact with the environment, to perform nonmonotonic reasoning (to deal with situations where the information is not static but is changing rapidly). They often include graphics capabilities and offer sophisticated end-user interfaces with windowing and the mouse. However, they are much more costly and generally require larger and more sophisticated hardware. ART, KEE and KRL are examples of such tools.

For those who wish to review specific development tools in greater depth, Jay Liebowitz's very readable *Introduction to Expert Systems* (Liebowitz, 1988) contains a comprehensive list.

Problem Characteristics

A careful analysis of problem characteristics should precede the selection of any shell, particularly in the library environment where there is a great deal of hardware and software already in place. Integration with existing hardware will be a very significant cost consideration.

Complexity and scope of the problem. If the goal is a small system of less than fifty rules requiring no modules — perhaps a pathfinder — then an inexpensive, PC-based shell will suffice. For more ambitious projects, and a modular design, then a more robust and costly system is required. Many systems have limits on the maximum number of rules which can be accommodated. Remember, complex tasks such as in-depth indexing of different sorts of documents require more rules.

Number of solutions presented. Some tools halt on finding one solution; others search exhaustively until all solutions are presented. Ranking the output according to a predetermined weighting scheme may be important. It wouldn't be wise to select a system for reference which stopped execution upon finding a single possible solution to a client's problem.

Certainty factors. In some systems, probabilistic knowledge is used as a means of assigning certainty to decisions and recommendations. Tools for developing reference systems should accommodate recommendations of varying levels of certainty, just as reference librarians do.

Arithmetic. Not all shells are capable of dealing with sophisticated numeric calculations. If this is important, then this should be a criterion in the selection process.

Inheritance and use of properties. In frame-based systems the developer is able to assign properties to objects which can then be inherited by other related objects. If all elephants are gray and have trunks, then Clyde, who is an elephant, inherits these properties. This greatly enhances the representational power of the system. Inheritance will be discussed in greater detail in subsequent chapters.

User Interface

Since ultimately the systems developed in a library will be used by non-programmers, it is critical that interfaces be well designed and as similar to standard English as possible. The following features of the user interface should be considered when selecting a shell.

Online help. Both quality and ease of access to online help needs to be evaluated. In many of the smaller shells, it is virtually nonexistent.

Translation and prompts. Some systems have a capability to enhance rules with translations for variables. It is also possible to generate sentence-length prompts to assist people as they interact with the expert system under development.

Multiple answers. If multiple answers are found and presented, some explanation of the rankings and probability factors should be provided.

Screen management facilities. At the very least, the system should be menu-driven. Screen management facilities should be flexible and capable of being customized to fit in with existing systems.

Development Facilities

The following capabilities in a shell will make the system developer's job considerably easier.

Tools for knowledge base creation/modification. A full-screen editing capability is desirable both for the initial creation of the knowledge base and for subsequent editing. The ability to make changes readily to the knowledge base is critical, since generally much more time is spent making changes to the rules than in the initial development.

Graphics. Some of the more expensive systems now feature bit-mapped graphic displays of the database. It is debatable whether they are worth the high overhead they place on resources, even though they undoubtedly have considerable appeal to those using expert systems.

Debugging and tracing. At the very minimum, the system should display a full trace of the execution, showing which rules fired and in what order. More sophisticated systems allow the end-user to ask **why** (or **why not**) or **how** a particular result was obtained. It is also helpful to have a **"what if"** capability to modify the inputs and perform sensitivity analysis.

Cross-reference or apropos facility. A useful feature is the ability to determine what knowledge structures are affected by a particular object or one of its attributes. Such a feature makes it much easier to track down and alter a rule that is malfunctioning. If you wish to change a predicate, such as "mammal," you can list out all the rules in the database that make a reference to "mammal."

System Interface

As mentioned previously any system that is going to function in a library environment must have hooks to existing databases, and also to existing procedural languages.

Software and Hardware Requirements

It goes without saying that any expert system destined for use in an information center should run on the same hardware as is used for other applications.

Language. Most expert systems obscure the underlying language and offer only a restricted form of it. Check that there is access to the underlying language and that manuals are provided. Some tools require that a particular language already be installed on the host, others come as a complete package. This should be checked before the system is acquired.

Compiler. Some programming languages (e.g., BASIC) are **interpreted**, that is each line of code is converted into machine-readable form as it is encountered. Other languages are **compiled**. The entire program (or expert system) is converted to machine-readable form in advance. If a shell can generate compiled systems, they will run faster and can be reproduced and ported to multiple machines. There is a trade-off, however, since with a compiled system it becomes much more difficult to look at and change rules.

Training and Support

At the very minimum a purchaser should insist on an adequate tutorial, a hot line for questions, and a sufficient supply of well-written manuals. The more costly packages offer training sessions, consulting support, and working examples.

Trends in Software Development

The move to supermicros. It is no longer necessary to buy an expensive LISP machine or a large mini- or mainframe. The new breed of super PCs with the 80386 or the 68030 processors, found in the Sun and Apollo workstations, can deliver sufficient power for all but the largest applications. This downsizing has considerably reduced the cost of expert systems and has brought the technology within the grasp of most institutions.

Declining software prices. The trend has been rapidly downwards. We have noted in the past year distribution of a number of reasonably priced, well-documented, PC-based shells, designed for the educational market. VP-Expert which lists for $249 from Paperback Software has a surprising range of features. **Exsys** by Exsys Inc. is a classical production rule system, with both forward and backward chaining and confidence factors. It is written in C and has a rule capacity of about 5,000 rules on a 640K machine.

Rules alone are not enough. Nearly everyone acknowledges that rules alone are often inadequate for complex tasks. In most cases a variety of knowledge representation techniques are required. In response to this need, many of the shells have added frame-like structures and object-oriented programming (Firebaugh, 1988).

The move from LISP to C. Some shells have shifted from LISP to **C** as the best language for a tool because of performance improvement.

Also C code can be ported more readily and there are more skilled programmers with a mastery of C available.

The need for embedded systems. A great deal of the research money that has fueled the development of expert system shells has come from the Defense Department, which has stressed the need to embed knowledge-based components in larger systems. Expert systems are being considered as just another function or subroutine called when needed by the user's main program. This means effectively that information specialists can begin to think of expert system components being added to existing software applications including but not limited to their online public access catalogs (OPAC).

Now that we've investigated the environments for expert system development, let's look at some of the models of the environments in which expert systems for reference and information retrieval will operate.

Recommended Readings

For the user interested in mastering one or more of the languages, there are a number of books on PROLOG, including several specifically directed at Turbo PROLOG. Yin's *Using Turbo PROLOG* will take the beginner through a number of applications of increasing complexity. It is well written and has numerous working examples of code. Another useful introduction to logic programming is offered by Jean Rogers in a *Turbo PROLOG Primer* (1987).

For the person interested in exploring LISP, Wylensky's *Lispcraft* (1984) has many examples and he offers a good explanation of inheritance.

A number of introductory books discuss designing expert systems and some of the issues involved (Harmon & King, 1985). Jackson (1986) and Liebowitz (1988) both offer reasonable handbooks. Although dated, Waterman's *A Guide to Expert Systems* is a very good place to start (1985). A more serious text that discusses the difficulties in building larger systems is entitled *Building Expert Systems* by Hayes-Roth, et al. (1983).

3
Modeling the Reference Process

Models as Knowledge Representation

Modeling human expertise is one of the most crucial stages of the expert system development process. A model is an abstract representation of human thought processes and behavior. An expert system may be thought of as a model — a highly formal, symbolic model for representing human expertise.

The things most frequently modeled in expert systems are problems within a domain and the ways in which experts deal with them. Problems related to reference and information retrieval are boundlessly complex. Despite the complexity of the domain, many models have been proposed, most of them before expert systems were ever even heard of. There is a large body of literature on problem solving in reference work and online retrieval. Though they share many basic concepts, reference work and online searching have some fundamental differences. In our examination, we will treat them separately. But before we look at the differences between the two task domains, and the different models which have been proposed, let's look at some of the elements which are common to both domains and to virtually all of the models.

Models are not perfect. Any attempt to develop an an abstract and systematic frame of reference for a something which includes the corpus of recorded knowledge **and** a high level of human interaction is bound to oversimplify. The interpersonal encounters and the information sources which are part of both reference and online searching are unpredictable and dynamic — difficult things to model.

The purpose of a model is not to develop the definitive way of representing the components of a complex activity. It is not important that a model be completely accurate. Like other models, models of the reference process have defects. No model can adequately represent what goes on in even the simplest reference transaction. Models have value because they provide us with a framework for understanding. A model can provide organizing principles. And organizing principles are certainly needed for structuring the symbols being manipulated in a computer program like an expert system.

Different paradigms have been applied to the study of the reference interview and the search process. Communications theory has been the dominant paradigm for at least twenty years and it still has many proponents. Recently, we've begun to see models based on theories of human information processing, theories which have also been important in AI research. No matter which paradigm is used, most models tend to focus on the same basic elements. The objective of the model is to describe those elements and how they interact with one another. Models of information seeking, at the broadest possible level, focus on four components: actors, objects, actions, and relationships.

Actors, Objects, Actions, and Relationships

Actors are entities that act. Actors are most often people, but in the world of the model, a machine could also be an actor. An information seeker, an intermediary, and more recently, a computer are all categories of actors. A college student asking a question is an actor. An online searcher, pressing keys and sending messages, is an actor. A computer program determining where information is displayed on a screen is an actor.

Objects are the things which are acted upon. Information-seeking models incorporate a variety of different types of objects. Information sources are the most common types of objects. But there are other types of objects. A reference book is an object. An index in a reference book is also an object. A term in an index in a reference book is an object, too. So is a database of reference books, or a query, or a record in a database, or a field in a record.

Models of the reference and search processes often describe **actions**. Query, recommend, reformulate, look up, explain, and evaluate are all action words that appear frequently in search models. The reference process is often described in terms of the actions that are performed by the reference librarian and the client. The actions performed by online searchers have also been described in great detail. Every online searcher has a repertoire of actions which she performs during a search.

Finally, information-seeking models are concerned with **relationships**. The relationship between actors — the reference/search interview — has been a favorite topic. The relationships between information objects have also been modeled. What is the relationship between a catalog and a collection? What is the relationship between a term and a document, between one term and other terms, between a query and a set of documents? Some of the objects we use are models themselves. A thesaurus is a model of the relationships among concepts within a subject domain. Another relationship which has been examined is the relationship between actors and objects. How is the literature used?

What do searchers do when they search a database? Isn't the goal of most user studies the development of a model of the relationship between people and information objects?

Some models are stronger in one category than another. A model of the concepts in a discipline that help us design a useful thesaurus doesn't have to be concerned with the relationship between professional intermediaries and their clients. At the deepest level, a model does not have to account for all of the vagaries of a complex encounter like a reference interview. On the other hand, an expert system which didn't attempt to model at least to some degree the human interaction in a mediated search probably wouldn't be very useful. Some models scrutinize a tiny microworld; others go for the whole ball of wax.

The value of a model is not in its complexity or in its simplicity. The value of a model lies in its ability to help us make sense of events in the real world. It's unlikely that anyone will ever develop a grand, unified theory which does justice to information-seeking behavior. But different investigators have studied just about every part of the process. We are beginning to understand a number of facets of the information-seeking process. And that understanding is leading us to take the first few tentative steps toward simulating the expertise of information intermediaries.

Now let's look at some models of the reference process, introducing basic concepts here and later focusing on the problems and opportunities unique to electronic access. First of all, it is important to differentiate between models which focus on sources of information and models which focus on users of information. The reference interview has been the most frequently modeled aspect of reference work. Users of information are the focal point for analyses of the reference interview. The most popular starting point for modeling the reference process has been the human communications model. This model has been adopted by both the online community and traditional reference librarians.

Communication Models

Communication models are built around the reference interview as a communication process. The communication process involves a query which must be negotiated to resolve an information need. The initial query is an attempt to describe an unknown in terms of what is known. This is the central paradox of the process. The job of an intermediary is to help a client reformulate the query in terms which can be matched to the collection and its syndetic structures. A query often needs to be reformulated several times as different objects within the collection are consulted. The job of the intermediary is to prioritize objects in the collection which may resolve the need expressed in the query.

The intermediary also helps the client reformulate the query to match each specific source consulted. Intermediaries also explain the use of information resources, usually within the context of the query. The actions taken by an intermediary can range from simply presenting the information seeker with a list of possible sources to extracting, organizing, and evaluating information. Almost all of the intermediary's actions with regard to the client involve communicative acts.

Messages are passed back and forth between the intermediary, the client, and resources in the collection. Messages travel through a **channel**, which must be opened for communication to occur. **Feedback** from the client affects the actions taken by the intermediary and feedback from the collection affects the actions taken by the client. In communication models, the client and intermediary exchange roles as sender or receiver as they interact.

The reference interaction is characterized as a multistep process during which decisions are being made. The classic work on the subject is by Robert Taylor (1967, 1968), who identified four levels of need:

- **Visceral need** is the information need of which the inquirer is only vaguely aware and which is unexpressed.
- **Conscious need** exists once the inquirer becomes aware of his need and begins to formulate his query in his own mind.
- **Formalized need** exists at the phase when the inquirer has expressed his need in a formal statement.
- **Compromised need** exists after the inquirer has had a chance to evaluate the chances that the information system will satisfy his need. Compromised need is what is expressed in the formal query to the information system.

The intermediary engages the client in a dialog which is intended to resolve the client's need at different levels. The goal of the negotiation between client and intermediary is a query statement which can be expressed in such a way as to achieve results from the collection. Before moving on to a new level, the need at the current level must be resolved.

An important aspect of the process is the continuous monitoring which takes place. Feedback controls the nature of the interaction. As each suggestion is made, the client's response is monitored and evaluated. It is often necessary to establish subgoals and consult sources to satisfy subgoals before the primary goal can be achieved. For example, before an "acceptable" query can be generated, subject heading lists and dictionaries need to be consulted to identify useful terms.

Taylor also describes "filters" for defining a search. Filters determine which possibilities the librarian will present to the user in response to a query. Among the filters through which a query must be passed are:

- the subject of the query
- the client's motivation and objective
- the client's personal characteristics
- the relationship of the query to the organization of resources
- the expected answer to the query

All of these categories are important to the successful resolution of the query. Some must be explicitly negotiated. It would be difficult to develop a query statement without the client articulating the topics in which he is interested. Others, such as the client's personal characteristics, may be implicit. Each of these categories has the potential to be the center of a far-reaching research agenda. As we will see in subsequent chapters, this model, which was developed over twenty years ago, incorporates elements which are important in today's expert system prototypes.

The Plumbing Metaphor

Models of the reference process often employ something which we'll refer to as a plumbing metaphor. Information is said to flow. Knowledge is referred to as if it were a liquid which flows through a channel from a reservoir to a receptacle. The collection of graphic records in a library is a pool of knowledge. The inquirer is a receptacle, waiting to be filled with knowledge and the librarian is a plumber who adjusts, regulates, and directs the flow. The librarian is responsible for inserting filters in the information pipeline, preventing unwanted material from reaching his client. The librarian taps the most useful reservoir of information and stops the flow when the "receptacle" is full.

This plumbing metaphor is certainly easy to visualize. Catalogs and indexes become valves, books are containers of information, information is absorbed by scholars. However, it is possible to become carried away with this metaphor. Information doesn't flow along one channel at a time in a single direction. It flows through many channels simultaneously. And the receptacle that is the human mind is never empty and impossible to fill.

Problems with Communications Models

There are a number of aspects of the reference process which aren't easily represented by a communication model. A reference interview cannot be described solely in terms of the communicative acts of the parties involved. A good reference librarian must be an effective communicator, but other qualities are also required. For general reference work, domain knowledge from a wide number of areas appears to be crucial. Most communication models (Taylor is an exception) make no attempt to address the internal store of world knowledge available to both the reference librarian and her client. The world view held by each of them and the extent to which shared knowledge may be assumed, has a great deal to do with the success of the encounter.

Another problem relates to the channel of communication which is emphasized by most communication models. Attention is paid only to substantive, verbally articulated messages. Much of the communication in a reference encounter is phatic. Its primary purpose is to open a communication channel so that a more substantive exchange of messages can occur. In real world situations, it also appears that reference librarians spend a lot of time reassuring clients that things are under control (even when they aren't). The reference process is self-referential. Nonverbal communication is also important, as evidenced by the large body of literature on the subject.

Many of the heuristics employed by the reference librarian are based on visual and other nonverbal cues provided by the client. Each encounter takes place in a milieu which includes a variety of elements, some of which are affective, many of which are nonverbal. Even if the nonverbal element were removed, language may be the irreducible problem, when it comes to modeling and simulating the reference process. It may never prove possible to achieve machine understanding of language, which is a slippery beast indeed. Language and intelligence appear to be related to one another. Language is also a social phenomenon (Winograd & Flores, 1986). We don't yet understand how language is used to communicate and it is discourse which lies at the heart of the reference process. We know how important context is to understanding. Furthermore, it is very likely that the meaning of the messages conveyed in a reference interview is socially determined. The world knowledge, cultural baggage, goals and expectations of each of the participants may have more to do with the success of the encounter than the content of the explicit messages being exchanged.

The options chosen and level of service provided are often determined by the intermediary's perception of the information seeker, the amount of time available and psychological state of one or the other. It is not uncommon to see an intermediary attempting to convince an information seeker to modify her query so that it is more reasonably resolved by using the local collection. How do we model that kind of a behavior pattern? Is that what Taylor was talking about when he referred to a "compromised" information need?

Models of the reference process as a communication process can help us identify the relationships between actors which need to be addressed by an expert system for reference. But it probably will never be possible to simulate a reference interview in all its complexity. The reference interview is one of the most intractable problems, because the focus is on the interaction between two or more very human beings. The reference interview is an incredibly rich and meaningful interaction. Because we are unlikely to be able to simulate it doesn't mean that it isn't worth studying. It won't matter if an expert system can't simulate a reference interview if the outcome of the client's interaction with the system is similar to the outcome of the client's interaction with a reference librarian.

Human Information Processing

Reference work is goal oriented, so it seems to lend itself to expert system applications. The paradox is that goals usually aren't recognized until after they've been achieved. The process also often involves multiple, parallel goals. Early interest in cognitive and behavioral aspects of information seeking were replaced by an interest in machine-mediated information retrieval. Now we've come full circle and need to understand how the human behaves in order to replicate that behavior in a machine.

Communication models provide one way of looking at the reference process. The focus of communication models is the interaction between the reference librarian and her client. More recently, other models have been applied, models which focus on the internal mental processes of the reference librarian and her clients. For example, Neill (1975) based his model on the problem-solving theories of the psychologist J.P. Guilford.

Some of the information-processing models have direct application to expert systems and artificial intelligence. Marilyn White (1983) has proposed a model based on the human information processing theories of AI researchers Marvin Minsky (1975) and Roger Schank (1984). One of the basic premises of those theories is that people relate to the world in terms of their previous experience. People maintain mental schema for organizing their knowledge of the world, and as new situations are encountered, they are related to existing knowledge structures. Knowledge structures are built through experience. The stereotypical knowledge structures which people rely upon to impose order on unfamiliar situations are referred to by Minsky as **frames**, and by Schank as **scripts**. White describes the reference interview in terms of the cognitive processes of the particpants, using as her starting point the frame theory first proposed by Minsky.

Frame-Based Models

According to Minsky, a frame is a stereotyped representation which is recalled from memory and filled in with particulars when a new situation is encountered. The blanks which need to be filled in are referred to as slots or terminals, and can refer to other frames or to complex procedures if necessary.

For example, Minsky describes a frame for a child's birthday party. There are slots for the kind of clothes the guests should wear, the type of gift to get and how to present it, the games to be played, the decorations to be used, and what kind of food, cake, and ice cream will be served. The specific details which go into those slots will vary from one birthday party to the next. But almost all birthday parties have these things in common and the person who has experienced a birthday party has probably developed a mental structure which he or she can refer to when invited to another birthday party. When invited to a birthday party, the gift slot in one's birthday party frame must be filled and choosing, buying, and wrapping a gift are all procedures associated with placing a value in that slot. Most people also probably have a **"making a purchase"** frame, which can be connected to the gift terminal in the **birthday party frame**.

White suggests that frames play an important role in the behavior of both participants in a reference encounter. At the beginning of the reference interview, each participant selects from memory a "master frame" which guides the direction of subsequent interaction. A client who hasn't participated in many reference interviews may call upon a frame for a similar interview situation, such as a **job interview frame**, and modify that frame based upon the reference interview experience. Most likely the reference librarian has a **reference interview master frame** developed from her experience with reference encounters.

It is the reference interview frame which monitors the reference process and causes other frames to be moved into the reference librarian's memory. As additional frames are moved into the foreground, the reference librarian attempts to place needed values in empty slots. White refers to other frames such as the user frame, the search strategy master frame, the problem frame, and a variety of frames related to specific categories of reference sources and specific subject areas (e.g., the **sources of biographical information frame**). The search strategy frame may be differentiated according to the category of information being sought. The reference librarian may have a **financial information about companies frame** and a **sources of poetry explication frame**. Each would be linked to a different type of search strategy frame.

Slots in many frames have default values. For example, in an academic library, the user frame might default to **"student"** for its **user type** slot and **"writing a term paper"** for its user motivation slot. The reference librarian can place needed values in empty slots by asking the client questions, referring to external sources like reference books or direct observation. The experienced reference librarian can call upon a complex network of interconnected frames. The user's frame for a reference encounter is less well developed.

As in the model proposed by Taylor (1968), participants exchange information to develop a common information base. Both Taylor's model and White's model break down the problem-solving process into a series of phases. The interview begins with each participant selecting a master frame. In the user's case the master frame is the problem frame. Additional frames are activated on each side as the process continues. Once the slots within a frame are filled, the process moves to the next level.

Filling a slot may involve invoking another frame with its own associated slots and procedures. This corresponds to Taylor's levels of need and filters. The initial query must eventually be posed in terms which match the access routes to information in the collection. As soon as decision is made to begin the actual search, control shifts to a search strategy frame which guides the selection and use of resources in the collection.

White concludes by pointing out that models based on transcripts of reference interviews (the method employed by Taylor, and most other theorists of the reference process) will need to be supplemented by models based on the internal knowledge structures of the participants. As we will see in chapter 5, a knowledge acquisition technique called protocol analysis has been developed to gain access to the internal mental processes of experts.

Scripts and the Reference Process

Schank (1984) has identified a knowledge structure called a script which is very similar to the frame schema described by Minsky. A script, like a frame, consists of stereotypical knowledge which can be applied to unfamiliar situations. People maintain scripts which are based on past experiences and which help them relate new situations to situations which have already been experienced. Scripts, because they contain knowledge, expectations, and assumptions related to categories of experience, help people to predict what will occur in a given milieu. Scripts also guide behavior. A script, like a frame, has categories which are filled with particular values as a situation is encountered.

Scripts also have **tracks**. Schank (1984) describes a restaurant script, with a track which would vary depending upon the type of restaurant. Different expectations are associated with a coffee shop track than would be associated with a French restaurant track. In a reference interview script, a public library track might differ from a university library track. Scripts also have **props**, **roles**, **entry conditions**, and **results**. It is easy to imagine a reference interview script which could be applied by either a librarian, a client, or both. The diagram of such a script might look something like this:

Reference Interview Script

Script: Reference Interview
Track: University Library
Props: Reference desk
Reference books
Computer terminals
Printed handouts
Student's notebook and pen

Roles: College student
Reference librarian

Entry conditions: Student has an assignment to write a paper.

Results: Librarian recommends useful information sources to student and teaches student how to use some of them.
Student locates information, reads and understands it and demonstrates that understanding in a written paper.

Scene 1: Student appraoches librarian with query.
Scene 2: Student and librarian discuss query.*
Scene 3: Student and librarian select and discuss information sources.*
Scene 4: Student looks at information sources.*
Scene 5: Student and librarian part company.

*These steps are often repeated a number of times.

This script represents expectations about what is going to happen in the encounter. The players can use it to help them understand their roles, but once the action starts, the dialog which occurs will be improvisational. In real life, each actor and scene would be multidimensional. There are all types of college students and as many different levels of motivation. The scenes could easily overlap one another. The discussion of the query and the selection and examination of sources can all happen simultaneously. Even the props, if we are talking about things like reference books, can influence the action. As they say, don't introduce a dictionary in Scene Three unless someone is going to use it in Scene Four.

So far we have concentrated on models of the relationship between actors in the reference process. Although it is often described, that relationship has never been convincingly simulated. Simulating a reference interview would mean teaching a machine to understand language and to communicate on human terms. A machine which could convincingly simulate a reference interview could pass the famous Turing test. No one has come close yet.

Language is one of the core problems of artificial intelligence. A few of the best known AI researchers have suggested that it may be an intractable problem (Winograd & Flores, 1986; Weizenbaum, 1976). It may be more productive, then, for expert systems to focus on models which are more easily simulated.

Models of Reference Sources

While the dialog between client and intermediary is a vital part of the reference process which must be addressed in any model, some models have placed their primary emphasis on the relationship between expert intermediaries and information objects. Part of the intermediary's expertise lies in his ability to interact with his clients. Another part of the intermediary's expertise lies in his ability to interact with the collection and its contents. Simulating expert knowledge of information sources is a much more tractable problem than simulating the knowledge required for human communication.

One dimension of all of the models is the store of knowledge which is drawn upon to "answer" reference questions. Jahoda has described the scenes in the reference script with a strong focus on the role of information resources. The goal described by Taylor is a "compromised need," a query which has been defined in terms of results which the collection can be expected to provide. According to Jahoda (1977) achieving that goal first requires translating a specific request into a request for categories of information.

Next it is necessary to match those categories of information to types of library tools. Once useful tool types have been identified the librarian must select from types of library tools, specific tools likely to provide the specific information required. Meta-level tools like indexes, abstracts, and catalogs (which Jahoda called lead-in tools) are often required to help identify possible sources for the information being sought.

Occasionally it is necessary to rely upon meta-level tools which focus on physical location (e.g., union lists) to identify sources of information which are not locally available and to direct the information seeker to locations where those sources are available. Finally, the vocabulary of the client's query must be translated to the vocabulary of the specific information tools selected. These processes lend themselves quite naturally to expert system development. If we are interested in results, they are the areas with the most promise of paying off.

Another important aspect of the intermediary's interaction with the collection is the extraction of "answers" from information stores. Extracting the "answer" encompasses explaining the use of recommended tools, as well as simply presenting the client with a list of possible sources. Presenting the client with a list, even if no explanation is proffered, almost always involves some sort of a ranking process. Given several possible sources for the required information, the librarian is likely to recommend trying one first and then another — moving from the items with the highest likelihood of a payoff to long shots. Remember the certainty factors which determine which expert system rules fire first. The ranking process is also a good example of reasoning under uncertainty. Extracting information involves solving problems of intellectual access and problems of physical access.

It is often necessary to physically move from one place to another before the intellectual presence of some specific piece of information can be verified. There are different levels of difficulty in extracting information. Isolating a specific data element from a table or chart is much easier than extracting information from text. It is much easier to identify a financial ratio or a demographic statistic than it is to find "the causes of the Russian revolution" in a historical text. Locating answers in text (where narrowly defined "answers" are presumed to exist) is often a multistep process involving a fair amount of negotiation.

Classification and Categorization Schemes

The use of subject classification schemes also plays a role in the intermediary's interaction with information sources. One common strategy is to go to the call number area of the reference collection where books on the desired topic will be found and then to browse for the type of tool likely to answer the question. For example, for a definition of a term from genetics, one might go to the biology section of the shelf and look for genetics dictionaries. As the size of the collection increases, this strategy becomes less effective and more formal access methods must be used. Subject access is a thorny problem. The subject relationships between information objects and the ways of describing and structuring them will be described extensively in Chapter Seven.

Categorization is important in almost all models and categorization is one of the cornerstones of artificial intelligence. Clients, information needs, and reference sources have all beeen categorized. The categorization of information objects is the most pervasive activity in librarianship, explicitly in cataloging and indexing, and implicitly, when answering reference queries. Expert systems for reference and retrieval, if they are to

Tool-Descriptor Matrix

KNOWNS \ WANTEDS	1. Dates	2. Events	3. Illustrations	4a. Properties	4b. Statistics	5. Organizations	6. Persons	7. Addresses, locations	8a. Citations	8b. Document locations	8d. Verification of publications	9a. Abbreviations	9b. Words, phrases, definitions	9c. Abstracts, annotations, recommendations of publications	9d. General information	10. Unspecified or other	
12. Abbreviations						D							D				12.
13. Dates		HM Y				Y	Y		I		I		Y	I	HM Y		13.
14. Events	EH M		AE MY		EHM Y	EM	EH MY	EH MY	CI				EH MY	I	EM P		14.
15. Illustrations				H	H								H		H		15.
16. Organizations	EH M	EN Y	E MP		NE	N	EMN	EG HN	CI	C	CI	D N		GI	EH NP		16.
17. Persons	BDE H	BD EH	BE MY	BE HY	BE HY	BE	BEM	AB EM	BC I	C	CI		BD E	GI	BEM PY		17.
18. Places	EHM	EH MY	AE HM	AD EH	AD EH	N	AE	AD EH	CI	C		D	D	I	AE HM		18.
19. Terms or subjects	DE HM	EM	AD EHM	DE H	EH NY	N	BE Y	E	CG I	C	CI	DE	DE H	GI	EH M		19.
20. Titles					I N P				CG I	C	CI P	I		GI N P	EG IP		20.
21. Unspecified																	21.
	1.	2.	3.	4a.	4b.	5.	6.	7.	8a.	8b.	8d.	9a.	9b.	9c.	9d.	10.	

Figure 3.1. Jahoda's tool-descriptor matrix (from Jahoda Gerald et al., The Reference Process: Modules for Instruction. ERIC ED 136765, 1976.)

be successful, must take advantage of existing categorization schemes. Expert systems must also make explicit the implicit categories reference librarians use to identify potential sources of information.

A *	Atlases, Maps
B	Biographical sources
C	Card catalogs, union lists
D	Dictionaries
E	Encyclopedias
G	Guides to the literature
H	Handbooks, manuals, and almanacs
I	Indexes, bibliographies, and abstracts
M	Monographs, texts
N	Non-biographical directories
P	Primary publications. This includes dissertations, reports, primary journals and coference proceedings
Y	Yearbooks
*	Letter code used for characterizing type of answer-providing tool in Figure 3.1

Figure 3.2. Jahoda's types of answer-providing tools

Jahoda (1977) developed a matrix for matching types of reference works to types of required information. Along one axis are categories of wanted information. Along the other axis are categories of known information. In the cells formed by the intersection of the two axes are types of reference works likely to provide the type of wanted information, given the type of known information. Expressed as an **If...Then** rule, the information derived from a cell in Jahoda's matrix would look like this:

If KNOWN is NAME and WANTED is ADDRESS
then CATEGORY is DIRECTORY

Jahoda tried using encoded rules based on this schema to answer a sample of twenty-eight reference questions. The experiment had mixed results and Jahoda was led to conclude that successful automation of the reference process, if it was possible, was an elusive goal.

As fraught with problems as it may be, the categorization of information objects is a more easily achievable goal than the simulation of the reference interview. We know that certain classes of information carriers exhibit common properties. Numerous categorization schemes have been proposed. Most group tools functionally. Terms which often show up in the titles of reference works, terms like "**index**," "**dictionary**," "**di-**

rectory," and "**encyclopedia**" are indications that there is widespread agreement on the properties of different classes of information sources.

But it's hard to tell whether the mental categorizations used by intermediaries coincide with the schemes for functionally classifying reference works. Our understanding of the cognitive processes of reference librarians is still very primitive. Benson & Maloney (1975) suggest that each individual tool may be viewed as a microcosm of the larger system. Perhaps if we can understand in greater depth how the simplest tools are used, we will increase our understanding of more complex systems.

Models of Online Searching

Artificial intelligence research evolved from general theories of intelligence to practical attempts to solve problems. Ambitious attempts at modeling intelligence in a general sense have largely been failures. Representing commonsense knowledge seems to be an insurmountable problem. More modest attempts to explicitly represent and apply specialized knowledge from a very narrow domain have been more successful. In a similar manner models of online searching tend to be more explicit and less ambitious than models of the traditional reference interview. Models of the online process are also much more likely to have evolved into prototype expert systems. Perhaps this is because online searching is a more constrained and highly structured universe than reference is. The fact that the information store being consulted by online searchers is in machine-readable form also has a lot to do with the relatively larger number of expert systems for online information retrieval.

Some online models subject the query to linguistic and computational analysis. Others examine the behavior of the people using information systems. Behavioral studies tend to focus on the consumers of information referred to in the jargon as end-users, or on professional information intermediaries. King (1974) and Eisenberg (1975) provide good reviews of user behavior, and Belkin & Vickery (1985) provide a good review of searcher behavior. An exhaustive analysis of user behavior is beyond the scope of this book, though the subject will be treated in greater depth in Chapters Five and Eight. In this chapter, we will turn our attention to studies of online searchers and attempts to model searcher behavior.

Online models involve a different sort of information objects — online databases with characteristics which require different approaches. The sheer size of some online databases makes them qualitatively different from books. Online files also tend to be more structured than printed works. An additional actor is added to the scene — the search program to whose actions the searcher must respond. Although search programs don't show the many personalities of human actors, they are far from uniform. Different actions are also involved; you don't truncate or adjacency search, or perform Boolean operations (at least consciously) when using printed documents.

Relationships differ, too. The information source being consulted is more remote. With the addition of the search software as an actor, the possible number of relationships increases. There is still the relationship between the intermediary and the client. There is also the relationship between the intermediary and the machine. Clients may also interact with the computer. Sometimes there is a bewildering flow of messages between the client, the searcher and the machine. Each human participant responds to different messages being presented by the machine; the process of the search anbd the subject content of its results both require attention.

Online Search Strategy and Tactics

Bates (1978) was one of the first to develop behavioral models of information searching. Although her model is intended to accommodate all types of search behavior, it seems especially suited to an online environment. In a series of separate articles Bates addresses the overall strategies guiding searcher behavior, and the specific techniques or tactics employed by searchers. Bates relates search strategies to models of the reference process. A strategy is an overall approach to the search, the master plan which the searcher uses to guide her moves as the search progresses. Tactics are defined as moves a searcher makes to further the progress of a search. Bates's emphasis is not on overall strategies but on very specific tactics. She also focuses on the search itself and not on the presearch interview or the post-search evaluation of results. In contrast to the general strategic and theoretical approach taken in most models of the reference process, her approach is more explicit and narrower.

Bates (1979a) describes and categorizes twenty-nine specific tactics used by experienced searchers. Search tactics are placed in four categories:

> **Monitoring tactics** are used to evaluate the progress of the search; for example, using the **Display Sets** command in DIALOG to look at sets created and compare them to the initial query is a monitoring tactic.
>
> **File structure tactics** are techniques for taking advantage of the structure of records, files, and online services; for example the **bibble** technique involves looking for an existing bibliography to avoid duplication of effort.

> **Search formulation tactics** are used in the design of a complex query; for example, the **parallel** tactic broadens the search formulation by making use of synonyms for the concept terms in the initial query.
>
> **Term tactics** are used to help the searcher select and modify specific terms; for example, the **neighbor** tactic is used to identify terms by examining alphabetically and conceptually adjacent terms.

Bates (1979b) also examined the "idea tactics" which searchers use to generate new approaches to a search. Idea tactics are used by searchers as they develop approaches to solving specific types of information problems. Bates emphasizes the importance of changing one's mental structure, of switching perspectives as a way of generating new ideas. This is analogous to selecting a different frame in the model of the reference interview proposed by Marilyn White. In contrast to the twenty-nine search tactics (Bates 1979a), the seventeen idea tactics (Bates 1979b) are not concerned with formulating a query in explicit terms. Rather they are concerned with developing a mental approach to the concepts in the search.

Idea tactics are more related to the searcher's thought processes than to the searcher's behavior while online. Idea tactics are further categorized as "idea generation tactics" or "pattern breaking tactics." Among the purposes for which idea tactics are invoked are to "unblock a search," to develop a conceptual framework for a search, or to shift the focus of a search. Idea tactics have names like "**brainstorm**," "**jolt**," "**focus**," and "**reframe**" — mental processes more than physical actions.

According to Bates, it is likely that some librarians employ a rational approach to the search process while others use a more intuitive approach. Fidel (1984, 1985), who also studied the tactics used by searchers, has also described two distinct searching styles. The **operationalist search** is concerned with precision. The operationalist searcher uses a variety of system capabilities to generate a set which matches as closely as possible the original query presented by the client. The **conceptualist search** is concerned with recall. Focus can shift away from the initial query. Conceptualists begin with a primary facet representing the most important concept in the query. The conceptualist searcher generates a main set and a group of subsets; each subset represents a different facet of the initial query. Operationalists make most of their moves at the operational level, forming the initial query into a Boolean expression where each concept is given equal weight. Conceptualists make most of their moves at the conceptual level, identifying a primary concept and then creating subsets which represent its different aspects.

Techniques used by searchers in the presearch interview have also been analyzed. Concept formation and strategy development are important goals of the presearch interview. Meadow & Cochrane (1981) in their excellent textbook on online searching identify a number of basic strategic approaches to the search process. Approaches like the **building block approach** (building a search formulation one facet at a time) or the **citation pearl growing approach** (starting with a known item and using it to identify other related items) are familiar to most online searchers. Harter (1986) has also written a textbook which does a good job of covering the theory of online searching. As we will see in the next chapter, many of the strategies and tactics described in the literature have found their way into prototype expert systems.

Heuristics are the rules-of-thumb which experts employ in their work. Harter & Peters (1985) review the literature on search strategy and tactics and classify heuristics used by searchers. According to Harter and Peters, the heuristics used by searchers fall into six broad categories.

Heuristics Used by Online Searchers

1. overall philosophy and approach
2. heuristics related to language of problem description
3. heuristics based on file structure
4. heuristics for concept formulation and reformulation
5. heuristics for decreasing or increasing recall and precision
6. heuristics for cost effectiveness (Harter and Peters, 1985)

Most of Harter and Peters' categories could as easily be applied to the use of printed reference sources. The same is true of most of the other models of online search behavior. However, there are a few differences which should be noted. The online searcher who typically is offering a fee-based service and working with expensive online databases faces a different situation from the reference librarian working with a printed collection which is already bought and paid for. Online search expenses are unpredictable. The online interview, unlike the reference interview, almost always involves a discussion of search costs, which in turn have an impact on the approach selected. The online searcher's behavioral strategy is tightly bounded by time and money constraints.

Another difference between models of reference and models of online searching is the emphasis in online search models on tactics rather than strategies. The reference process is guided by the discourse between the participants. It is an open-ended process. Online searching is more restrictive. The online search process is largely guided by the messages provided by the host computer system. Each message requires a discrete, usually physical, response from the searcher. The searcher must rely upon a repertoire of actions to which the host system is able to respond. Hence the emphasis on tactics.

Online files have significant advantages over printed files. The ability to combine concepts with one another makes for more evocative queries. The cumulative nature and size of online databases are pluses. So is speed. But there are disadvantages as well. Online systems suffer from opacity. The user can't see as much as can be seen with printed sources. With online systems, the chances of stumbling upon important information by accident is nearly nonexistent when compared with printed files. Locational and visual cues can't be relied upon to the extent that they can with printed sources. The mental models developed by reference librarians often incorporate cues of this sort. Online searchers have to rely upon other types of cues. This issue will be addressed more thoroughly in Chapters Seven and Eight.

Saracevic (1988) and his colleagues have done an extensive analysis of searcher behavior. One of the areas in which human experts consistently outperform machines is knowing when to move from one phase of the process to another. A good human intermediary has to know when enough information is available to attempt a solution to the problem at hand. Saracevic's study suggests that too much preparation time and too much planning can have an adverse affect on search outcome. An expert system like an expert human needs to know what it knows. Online searching is a truly interactive process which takes place under very real time constraints. Effective expert systems will need to function in real time as human experts do.

During a reference interview or an interactive search, partial solutions are continuously posed. Each search goes through a few cycles as it progresses. Information obtained from users isn't obtained all at once in a single lump but in bits and pieces, interactively. Information obtained from an online database is also acquired incrementally. And events which occur in later cycles are affected by information moving both ways during earlier cycles.

As we'll see in the next chapter, the more sophisticated systems attempt to simulate the cognitive processes of skilled search intermediaries, including the ability to shift from one phase to another based on the current image of the search problem. Many of them are based on models of the process which were established decades before it became feasible to bring computing power to bear on problems of reference/retrieval. Many of them also attempt to incorporate the tactics and explicit knowledge found in recent models of online searching.

Recommended Readings

Taylor (1967, 1968) remains the classic theorist of the reference process. The text by Jahoda and Braunagel (1980) provides one of the better schematic analyses of reference work. The Summer 1975 issue of the journal *RQ* is devoted entirely to reference theories and includes among others a very readable paper by Benson and Maloney (1975). King and Palmour (1974) provide an interesting critique of user studies and Eisenberg (1983) reviews the literature on end-user searching. Belkin and Vickery (1985) provide a thorough review of information interaction with a decided focus on expert system issues. White (1983) provides the best AI-oriented model of the reference process.

Bates, Fidel, Harter, Saracevic, and Vigil have all written extensively on modeling the online searching process and all are represented in the bibliography. Belkin, Kalfass (1984), H.M. Brooks, and Wersig (1984) are all engaged in projects with the goal of modeling and simulating information-seeking expertise. The books edited by Dietschmann (1984) and by Ingwersen (1986) and his colleagues also include a number of papers related to topics covered in this chapter. Finally, the book edited by Warren (1985) includes papers applying economic and social models to information systems.

4
Review of Expert System Projects

This chapter will review some of the more interesting attempts to apply the theories discussed in the previous chapters. Not all of the systems discussed here are true expert systems but all of them attempt to incorporate to some extent the expertise of human intermediaries. We may be jumping ahead of ourselves by describing actual systems before we address the processes of identifying appropriate classes of problems, acquiring knowledge from experts, and designing systems. On the other hand, those subjects can be quite abstract. The reader who hasn't been exposed to a few actual systems may have a difficult time understanding the abstractions treated in later chapters. Therefore we have decided to first provide a brief overview of some of the many systems which have already been developed.

There have been quite a number of efforts to automate some or all of the reference/online search process. It is now one of the most fertile areas of information science research. Most of the systems developed so far attempt to provide access to existing online files, but the earliest systems were concerned with improving access to printed reference sources. Query formulation was the first problem to be addressed. Current systems have more ambitious goals.

Common Knowledge

As we have seen both reference and online information retrieval are complex problem-solving processes. The starting point for developing a computer program to solve problems is to identify the problem(s) to solve. Then it is necessary to determine what kinds of knowledge are needed to solve the problems which have been identified. All of the systems we will describe in this section incorporate (to varying degrees) these types of knowledge:

- things we know about **information systems**
- things we know about **information seekers**

- things we know about **databases/collections**
- things we know about **intermediaries' expertise**

Evolving Systems

All of them are based on some sort of a model. The more sophisticated ones model the flow of information from one type of problem-solving process ("expert") to another, simulating the phases of the mediated information seeking process. Other systems are based on models of information sources within some domain.

The amount of information stored in machine-readable form is still relatively small. Current estimates (Alpert, 1989) are that machine-readable information accounts for only approximately 2 percent of the existing corpus. Another 3 percent is estimated to be in microform. That leaves somewhere in the neighborhood of 95 percent of recorded information still in print format. It is on the vast storehouse of printed information that early systems had their focus. The focal point of the earliest systems was not on printed information sources themselves but on reference tools which provide access to sources.

Another generation of systems is based on restructuring source texts in an attempt to answer questions which are answerable by the knowledge stored in printed works. Lately, emphasis has shifted to improving access to information files which are already in machine-readable form. It is important to differentiate between systems which take existing knowledge, mostly from the printed store, and radically restructure it for machine accessibility and systems which are designed to provide more intelligent access to currently available electronic databases.

Let us first examine some of the early systems which were designed to improve access to traditional reference books. The emphasis of those systems was on categorizing and describing printed reference sources in terms of queries they satisfy.

Antecedents: A Biographical Reference Assistant

Weil (1968) was among the first to use a computer to provide something other than traditional bibliographic access to reference works. Weil chose a relatively narrow domain (biographical reference sources) that was still complex enough to be worth attempting to categorize. Weil described biographical reference works in terms of the types of people they profiled. In essence, she developed a language for describing the attributes of the people profiled. Biographical sources, the people they profile, and the characteristics of those people are the information objects she investigated. Her system centered around the relationships among those objects and between those objects and typical queries for biographical information.

Weil developed two premises about biographical reference sources that explained why those sources lend themselves to a system like the one she devised.

1. Specific sources are almost always confined to people who have some common attribute. There are biographical sources including only women (**attribute: sex**), others for chemists (**attribute: occupation**), others for Britons (**attribute: nationality**) and so forth.
2. Any given work is likely to include the same group of data elements for each person profiled. Typical data elements included are age, sex, spouse's name, address etc. A biographical source which includes information on degrees obtained by one of the people it profiles is likely to include similar information for other people it covers.

The descriptive database developed by Weil was designed to describe existing sources in her test collection, not as a totally abstract classification scheme. For example, there was no occupation code for **botanist** because none of her sources profiled botanists, but there was a code for **physicists** and another for **chemists** because there were sources which covered people in those occupations. There was also a code for scientists, but a tree structure was not employed and the system was therefore unable to take advantage of the hierarchical relationship between scientific occupations and identify a physicist as also belonging to the **scientist** category. Indexing was to the greatest level of specificity in the same way it is with many current online systems

Weil's system was coded in **COMIT**, an early AI language developed at MIT. The program matched the contents of a highly structured query to highly structured descriptions of biographical sources. Communication with the system was done in a batch mode. Requests were prepared in advance and submitted to the system at one time. The system attempted to find sources which matched the specifications of the query. Some data elements were referred to as "specifics" and *had* to be present in order for a source to be recommended. As the matching proceeded, sources which did not meet the specifications of the query were eliminated one by one. Once a list of possible "answers" was compiled, it was filtered through another procedure designed to rank the possibilities according to their likelihood of answering the query. The ranked list was then printed out for the inquirer.

The whole process seems rather primitive by today's standards, but it did incorporate a few features which are widely used in today's expert systems. A categorization scheme was used and the system followed a pattern-matching procedure. Reference sources were described in functional rather than bibliographic terms. Recommendations were ranked according to the degree of certainty that they could answer a query. A declarative knowledge representation scheme was employed. Since it dealt with a small number of specific attributes of a relatively small number of sources within a narrow domain, Weil's system might be characterized as a **fine grain** system. Around the same time that Weil's system was developed, another system with a much larger grain size was also developed.

Antecedents: REFSEARCH

The **REFSEARCH** system developed by Joseph Meredith (1971) and his colleagues took a broader view, taking as its domain the entire universe of reference works. The developers of REFSEARCH used a series of predicates to abstractly represent the qualities of reference works.

Meredith's system was intended to be instructional, to be used for teaching beginning librarians the basic principles of reference work. Meredith wanted to get away from the idea of teaching reference through intensive study of specific reference tools and move toward studying the "principles that would apply to the collection as a whole, to the sum of the data contained in the collection, and to the networks of paths leading to the data." (Meredith, 1971 p.177) In other words, Meredith wanted to move from a high level of specificity to a high level of abstraction.

A Categorical Scheme

Meredith's system was designed as a tutorial for students of the reference process, but in this era of expert systems, the ideas he described over fifteen years ago have acquired broader significance. The schemata he devised for representing knowledge about reference sources are quite similar to the methods being proposed by today's expert system designers. The REFSEARCH system described reference works in terms of the functions they performed, focusing not on the subjects treated but on the **types of tools** likely to resolve different **types of information problems**.

Handles

Meredith hypothesized that reference librarians solve problems by referring to internal representations of "**sure** sources of **types** of information which are **likely** sources of **specific** information." However, he was aware that experienced reference librarians are also able to go directly to sure sources of specific information. The system he developed attempted to duplicate the categorical rather than the specific approach. It would be impossible to descibe every specific reference work in terms of each specific piece of information it contained. Meredith envisioned a merged index to all of the reference works in a general reference collection, but he realized that such an index would become as large and as unwieldy as the collection itself.

As an alternative approach, he proposed a system of classified indexing which, instead of listing the specific things treated in each reference work, listed the types of things included in different reference works. His system is based on the premise "that every reference question has a 'handle,' that is a specific noun (or word or phrase used nominatively) that is not only central to the question but is also — in theory at least — indexable somewhere in the collection." (Meredith, 1971 p.177)

Meredith and his colleagues identified seventeen types of "handles," seventeen classes which cover the things that most reference questions are about. Meredith referred to these classes of handles as "channels." The channels represent the categories of information objects common in general reference questions. The channels are:

FIELDS
NONLIVING OBJECTS
PRODUCTS
HUMAN PROCEDURES
CONCEPTS
NATURAL PROCESSES
LIVING OBJECTS
ART WORKS
LANGUAGES
CORPORATE BODIES
WORDS
PLACES
PERSONS
EVENTS
DATES
ERAS
LAWS

Qualifiers

Once a list of nouns had been compiled, a list of adjectives for each of them had to be developed. The adjectives describing the channels (the subjects in his grammar) Meredith referred to as qualifiers. Each channel was associated with a specific group of modifiers. Qualifiers were "allocated" to specific categories of nouns. It wouldn't make sense, for example, to use a qualifier such as **LIVING** for a query whose handle was **EVENT**. So the LIVING qualifier was allocated to channels such as **PERSONS**.

Services

Developing a formal language for describing reference works requires predicates as well as subjects; those predicates are needed to describe the actions to be applied to subjects. Meredith called his predicates "services." Services function as verbs in his descriptive language. Nine services performed by general reference works were identified.

- DEFINES
- IDENTIFIES
- DISCUSSES
- LOCATES
- DATES
- QUANTIFIES
- CHRONICLES
- JUDGES
- PROVIDES FINANCIAL INFORMATION (represented by a $)

A Language for Describing Reference Works

In addition to channels, qualifiers, and services, special categories of qualifiers were developed for special services. Reference works could then be described as providing **bibliographies**, or having **pictures**, or including **maps**. Useful features commonly associated with reference books were thus accounted for. Special qualifiers, called **subcollections**, were also provided to describe the subject content of reference sources. A reference book which dealt with a specific topic area could be coded as part of a subcollection such as **MATHEMATICS** or **HISTORY**. Time periods and geographic delimiters were also included as "parts of speech" in the descriptive language.

Thus it could be said, using the parts of speech and acceptable combinations from this descriptive language for reference books, that:

> The *Dictionary of American Biography* IDENTIFIES, DISCUSSES, AND DATES, PROPER-NAMED, REAL, DEAD, AMERICAN PERSONS and it has the special feature of INCLUDES BIBLIOGRAPHIES.

The thing that distinguishes REFSEARCH is that it was one of the first systems to attempt to describe reference sources in terms of reference queries and to develop an abstract schema for relating reference works to the categories of information found in queries. People may disagree with the categories identified by Meredith and the values he selected to fill each of them. For example, he totally rejected the idea of coding books based on their level of understandability. Nevertheless, it was a system based on the syntax of the reference question, one of the few systems to pay as much attention to possible queries as to information sources which might answer them.

RESEDA

Meredith's system described printed reference works. Other systems attempt to derive information directly from printed sources. Those texts needn't be reference books, and in fact, usually aren't. A system based on restructuring the knowledge encoded in printed texts was developed by Zarri (1979, 1985). The **RESEDA** system is based on principles of linguistics. Zarri developed a meta-language for recording information found in standard printed works on medieval French biography and history. The knowledge contained in each work had to be laboriously restructured and translated into Zarri's meta-language before it could be manipulated with a computer. The goal of RESEDA is to use the knowledge base derived from the texts to answer natural language questions about the domain.

The Hepatitis Knowledge Base

The **Hepatitis Knowledge Base** (Bernstein, 1980) is another example of a system which is based on the restructuring and computerization of information from printed texts. The Hepatitis Knowledge Base is an example of a consensus system. The knowledge driving the system is derived from a consensus among experts. Consensus systems will be described in greater detail in Chapter Five, which deals with knowledge acquisition. Only the most influential works on viral hepatitis were used as the basis for the Hepatitis Knowledge Base. Information from the evaluated core literature was re-encoded and classified for easy retrieval of knowledge.

The project, sponsored by the National Library of Medicine (NLM), became in the words of its chief architects:

> a multi-disciplinary team effort to assemble a compact yet comprehensive body of information that could meet health practitioners' needs. The aim was to assemble knowledge on viral hepatitis which would contain substantive information relevant to a wide variety of questions (rather than bibliographic citations only); would provide information that is both current and the consensus of a group of experts; would be immediately respon-

> sive to inquiries (online access); and would provide access to variable levels of data supporting the substantive information, including citations to primary publications for more detailed study if desired. (Bernstein and Williamson, 1984, p.236, 237)

Knowledge from Text

Core knowledge from authoritative texts on viral hepatitis was restructured by taking individual paragraphs from separate sources and grouping them together under headings in hierarchical groups. Each group of "topic paragraphs" was accompanied by a "synthesis paragraph" which attempted to review, synthesize, and reconcile information derived from diverse sources. "Data paragraphs" were derived from experts' published works. Only data paragraphs which had been evaluated by a panel of experts were included. Data paragraphs were then linked to citations included in the original sources from which they were derived.

The Hepatitis Knowledge Base is interesting because it attempts to provide actual answers to questions rather than merely pointing to likely sources of information. Like many related projects it makes use of a hierarchical classification scheme but it is unique because the information in its knowledge base is taken directly from the published literature.

PLEXUS: A Knowledge-Based Reference System

PLEXUS, developed by Vickery (1986, 1987) Brooks (1985) and colleagues at the University of London, is another example of a system designed to augment the use of the printed literature. PLEXUS takes as its domain the acceptably narrow field of gardening, but its scope is nevertheless broad, since it seeks to represent real world knowledge about terms and concepts related to gardening and to refer its users to human experts and to gardening associations in addition to printed reference works. The knowledge base driving the system was developed with **PROLOG** but the user interface, inference procedures, and system housekeeping tasks were developed with **Pascal**.

PLEXUS is essentially a natural language system centered around the use of the facet classification scheme known as **BSO**, or **Broad Subject Ordering**. The system's knowledge base was developed by compiling a database of information resources related to gardening. Reference sources, associations, and individual experts are the primary resource categories included in the knowledge base. Creating the knowledge base involved creating original descriptions of information resources within the system's subject domain. Using the system involves matching terms in queries to terms in its dictionary. The context of query terms is determined by referring to categories and relationships included in the dictionary. For example, the system is able to distinguish the use of the term "blossom" as a noun and as a verb.

Front-Ends and Gateways

Now let us turn to systems whose goal is to provide more intelligent access to existing electronic databases. Early attempts were concerned with developing front-ends to databases. Query formulation and translation of the user's input to the syntax of the host system are the two areas which received the greatest attention.

The field has advanced to the point where there are a number of commercially available front-ends and gateways which are designed to provide search assistance to inexperienced end-users.

While many front-ends and gateways incorporate principles of natural language processing, it is difficult to categorize most of them as expert systems. Most are designed to make online systems easier to use by superimposing a query builder on the native language of the host system. Queries are often developed offline by prompting the user with menus and then submitted to the online service in what is, in effect, a batch mode. A few help with term selection and development of Boolean expressions and others translate natural language queries into the syntax of the host system.

Others provide assistance with database selection, and some help the user evaluate search results. But commercially available programs which address the search as an interactive process deal with searching at a conceptual level and provide real-time search assistance are rare. Features found in front-ends and gateways are also incorporated in the expert systems described here, but the expert systems are also knowledge based. Unlike traditional front-ends which focus on search syntax, expert systems tend to include explicit domain knowledge about the subjects covered by the databases they are designed to assist.

Commercial front-ends and gateways, therefore, are largely beyond the scope of this book. We might consider today's commercially available systems as first generation front-ends. The knowledge-based systems with which we're concerned here might be referred to as second generation front-ends. The reader who is interested in exploring first generation front-ends in greater detail is referred to Levy (1984), and Williams (1986), both of whom do a good job of reviewing the literature on front-ends and gateways.

First and Second Generation Front-Ends

First generation front-end concerns	Second generation front-end concerns
search syntax	explicit domain knowledge
query formulation	strategy and concept development
query translation	explanation and advice
Boolean searching	probabilistic searching
command driven	browser driven

Retrieval Through Dialogue

Oddy (1977) was among the first to develop a system which was capable of retrieving information by engaging the user in a dialogue. His system can't be characterized as an expert system either, but it was among the first to use **relevance feedback**, a technique which many of today's experimental systems include. Oddy's ideas will be discussed in greater detail in Chapter Eight. Another precursor of today's expert systems was a query formulation system called **CONIT** developed at MIT by Marcus (1983, 1986). It featured a common command language for access to several systems (**SDC**, **DIALOG**, **NLM**) and an instructional facility for assisting users of the common command language with strategy development. The approach was Boolean with a stemming algorithm used to generate search terms.

CONIT and IIDA

Meadow (1982) used Marcus's language and added to its translation capabilities a tutorial and analysis capability. His system (**IIDA**) could identify patterns in searchers' behavior and suggest more efficient approaches. Marcus's project continues to evolve and spawn new systems. Yip, an MIT graduate student, added a menu-driven dialogue and the ability to modify strategies based upon users' evaluation of initial results (Smith, Linda, 1987).

Marcus (1986) believes that Boolean retrieval will ultimately be shown to be more effective than statistical techniques but advocates Boolean systems which "bring human intelligence into play in a mixed initiative." Marcus also emphasizes the importance of separating the problem representation from any search strategies it implies. This separation makes it possible to derive multiple strategies from a single problem representation. Different strategies can be brought into play depending upon circumstances.

Knowledge-Based Systems

Only recently have we seen attempts to model the explanation, advisory and strategy development capabilities of human experts and to incorporate techniques other than Boolean searching. The current generation of search assistance software is more concerned with modeling the online search as a problem-solving process which goes beyond the formulation of a single, syntactically correct Boolean query. Terms are a concern but so are the concepts which terms represent. Knowledge forms the basis for the system's activities. The search is more likely to be treated as an interactive, iterative process which goes through a number of cycles before yielding results. Strategic issues assume importance along with tactical issues.

Blackboard Architectures

One thing most of the more ambitious attempts have in common is a way of managing problem-solving knowledge known as a blackboard architecture. The blackboard architecture was first discussed in Chapter One. Blackboard systems are based on a concept first implemented by Erman (1980) with the **HEARSAY II** natural language speech recognition system. A blackboard is an area of working memory where cooperating expert system modules can share information about the problem at hand. Feigenbaum (1985) describes a blackboard as:

> a scheme for the cooperation of multiple sources of knowledge in a common knowledge structure that represents the emerging solution and asks: What can I add to it? What do I know that can build onto this solution? It's an incremental, opportunistic process....

Cooperating Experts

Imagine a group of subject specialists, together in a room, working on a multifaceted problem. Imagine that the problem relates to pharmacology and that its solution will require searching a few different databases. One of the experts might be a medical specialist, another a chemist, and yet another an expert in searching databases. Journal articles, search aids, thesauri, and reference works might be available for consultation. Each participant is encouraged to contribute to the solution of the problem by calling upon his or her area of expertise. As the problem-solving process proceeds, each expert is able to go to the front of the room and write down his ideas on a blackboard.

One of the participants is selected as the monitor and attempts to integrate the knowledge contributed by the others. As new approaches are agreed upon, partial solutions can be erased from the blackboard and new ones can be written in. Some of the information on the blackboard will relate to the problem at a conceptual level. Other information on the blackboard might involve specific tactics to use with specific databases and other information might relate to the overall plan of attack, containing information like which databases to search first and which should be tried as last resorts. Separate areas of the blackboard are reserved for different facets of the problem. The blackboard becomes the vehicle through which the humans communicate with one another.

Problem Representation Schemes

Eventually the blackboard will contain a proposed solution to the problem derived from the combined expertise of the different individuals working on it and the reference sources which are available for them to consult. This is a cooperative problem-solving style which is not unusual at all. In a blackboard architecture expert system, the human experts are replaced by specialized knowledge bases and the physical blackboard is replaced by an area of computer memory. This metaphor seems to work especially well in expert retrieval systems.

In an expert system for information retrieval, part of the information held on the blackboard would be a representation of the current problem, and, if Marcus' advice is to be taken, it would be separated from strategies recommended by the system for its resolution. Remember the models of the search process. The search process is an open-ended, problem-solving process. It can move from one phase to another and back. It is also a multimodal process. Concept definition, term selection, browsing, query formulation, explanation, and evaluation are all possible modes for the different phases of the search process. Many different sorts of knowledge are required to perform an effective search. The blackboard architecture provides a useful mechanism for incorporating diverse knowledge sources in a single system.

CANSEARCH: A Menu-Based System

Pollitt (1986, 1987) was one of the first to use AI techniques for a database access system. Pollitt used PROLOG to implement a system for access to cancer therapy literature contained in the Medline database. Pollitt's system, **CANSEARCH**, presented a series of menus to the naive user whose responses triggered other menus in a hierarchy of menus. Users selected options from menus by touching a pressure-sensitive screen. No typing was required; all of the facets of a cancer therapy search were provided by the system. CANSEARCH sought to incorporate four types of knowledge: system knowledge, searching knowledge, subject knowledge, and user knowledge.

Frames for Medline Searches

Pollitt used a blackboard architecture to fill in slots of frames which correspond to the facets of typical Medline cancer therapy searches. Slots correspond to things like site of the cancer and type of therapy. Classes and hierarchies used in the MeSH trees of medical subject headings are preserved by the system. For example, the drug therapy frame activates a menu with different classes of drugs derived from the MeSH tree structure. Selecting a specific class of drugs in turn activates a menu displaying a list of individual drugs within that class. After the user was presented with a series of menus designed to fill in the values associated with a cancer therapy search on Medline, those values were used to generate queries which were submitted to Medline.

CANSEARCH is a hybrid system (written in PROLOG, using rules and frames) system which uses separate blackboards for different facets of a cancer therapy search. For example, there is a **site board**, where the firing of rules can read, write, copy or remove information related to the site of the cancer for which therapy information is being sought. Blackboards are also used to hold control information. It is information in the blackboards which determines the sequence of menus displayed to the user.

An important principle underlying Pollitt's system is "abstracting the search space." The search is constrained by expectations related to the characteristics of cancer therapy searches on Medline. Controlled vocabulary terms and the hierarchical relationships between concepts expressed in the Medical Subject Headings (MeSH) are used to guide the search process. Queries formulated by CANSEARCH are based on knowledge of typical searches, concepts within the domain, and the Medline query language.

An experiment was done to compare the performance of skilled human intermediaries to naive users assisted by CANSEARCH. Intermediaries outperformed naive users, but on a few occasions CANSEARCH did outperform the human expert. And many naive users were able to use CANSEARCH to develop effective searches.

Croft and Thompson (1987) and Brajnik, Guida and Tasso (1986) are all working on somewhat more ambitious projects. All aim to somehow decompose the search process, breaking it down into different phases as is done in most of the models.

IR-NLI: A Natural Language System

Whereas Pollitt used a menu-based approach with a relatively narrow domain, Brajnik, Guida, and Tasso (1986) developed a natural language interface for information retrieval. The **IR-NLI (Information Retrieval - Natural Language Interface)** system was designed to exemplify a number of trends in natural language processing.

Goals of IR-NLI (Brajnik et al, 1986)

ability to understand imperative sentences in natural language

ability to manage a simple dialogue with the user

ability to display a "graceful behavior," e.g., understanding incomplete or grammatically incorrect sentences, ability to handle anaphora and ellipsis, establishing the correct meaning where multiple interpretations are possible

ability to employ principles of pragmatics, the branch of linguistics that deals with language as it is actually used

ability to provide cooperation and support to naive users

Brajnik and his colleagues organized the types of knowledge required by an effective intermediary system into four broad categories:

1. knowledge about the user
2. knowledge about the target system
3. knowledge about the problem domain
4. knowledge about the intermediary's job

Does this sound familiar? This knowledge typology comes up again and again. Virtually all of the extant systems attempt to capture these types of knowledge, some emphasizing one type rather than the others.

Strategies and Tactics

Brajnik and his team divided the search process into four phases, each including a number of distinct tasks:

1. presearch interview
2. database selection and strategy design
3. execution
4. result evaluation

Using ideas first expressed in the models of Bates, Meadow, Cochrane [Atherton], Harter (cited in bibliography) and others, they identified five approaches employed by skilled intermediaries:

1. most specific facet first
2. lowest posting first

3. building block approach
4. citation pearl growing
5. successive fractions

In addition to the approaches, they identified a number of specific tactics, (following the models developed by Bates). Among the tactics which IR-NLI has in its repertoire are: **generalize**, **exhaust**, **reduce**, **parallel**, **pinpoint**, **super**, **sub**, and **relate**. The purpose of the tactics is expressed in their names.

The system was designed to have three areas of competence:

1. natural language understanding and dialogue management
2. modeling an intermediary's activity
3. generation of a workable search strategy

Modular Design

Different system modules accomplish different phases of the search process. An **understanding and dialogue module** translates the user's initial query into a formal problem statement known as the **problem internal representation**. The module controls the dialogue which is intended to elicit additional information from the user and build upon the initial problem internal representation. The knowledge needed for the process is drawn from two sources — a vocabulary and a knowledge base containing knowledge about linguistics. Remember the dictionary used in the PLEXUS system? This is a similar idea.

A **reasoning module** in IR-NLI attempts to model the intermediary's behavior by drawing upon a knowledge base of expert intermediary knowledge. The expert knowledge base contains rules relating to tactics, strategies, and approaches used by searchers, and a knowledge base of domain specific knowledge. Domain knowledge is "mostly terminologic" knowledge about the subject domain of of the target database. It is similar to the type of knowledge recorded in a thesaurus.

The job of the **formalizer module** is to generate formal, syntactically correct search strategies in the languages of specific systems. This is a task which is already within the scope of most commercially available front-ends.

Organization of Rules

The rules in the knowledge bases underlying IR-NLI are organized in a tree structure as "loosely connected knowledge islands." There are three types of rules:

- **domain rules** are used to carry out tasks assigned to the reasoning module

- **matching rules** attempt to identify clusters of rules which would be helpful in solving the problem at hand
- **conflict rules** add efficiency to the system by determining which of several possible rules would fire first in a given situation

Clusters of rules associated with particular approaches to information-seeking problems are activated by **matching rules** and sequenced by **conflict rules**. For example, if the information seeker indicates the existence of an important document which should be part of the search, a "pearl-growing," high-precision cluster of search rules might be activated. Clusters of interrelated rules are referred to as **tasks**.

IR-NLI employs a mechanism known as **task activation** to determine which chunk of knowledge is most appropriate for attempting to resolve the subproblem it is dealing with at any given time. This process is similar to the blackboard approach but rather than sharing a single blackboard, tasks are knowledgeable about one another and each task can call other tasks. In a blackboard system, the blackboard determines which of the system modules to consult for additional problem-solving information.

Each of the following phases of an IR-NLI session is associated with one or more of the following **task rule clusters**: presearch-interview; approach-selection; concept-analysis; and result-evaluation.

The tasks called upon to resolve the concept-analysis phase of the search are determined by the basic approach developed during the approach-selection phase.

Representing the Problem

A **problem internal representation (PIR)** serves as the global memory of the system and is divided into two parts, one of which contains problem information and the other which contains control information. The contents of this working memory are derived from the user, who indicates through a dialogue the topic she is interested in, and the domain knowledge base. The domain knowledge base, like a thesaurus, includes terms and term relationships.

The problem information part of the PIR is organized as a frame with subframes, each of which has its own associated slots. There is a separate subframe for each concept in the search problem. Each concept frame has slots for attributes of the concept. There is a slot for the name of each concept, another for the number of postings for concept terms, and another for the concept's level of generality. One slot contains a flag indicating whether or not the concept name is a controlled term. Other slots include related terms for the concept and related concepts derived from the domain specific knowledge base.

Remember frames can also be used to represent procedural knowledge. One subframe indicates the way in which separate concepts are to be logically combined and a subframe for the objective of the search as supplied by the user (e.g., high precision, high recall). Another subframe holds information on search limits requested by the user and another subframe is reserved for information on the desired output format. The user can specify the acceptable number of items, a sort sequence, and whether results should be delivered in print or online. The system also lets the user define which elements of records to print.

I³R: Probabilistic Knowledge-Based Retrieval

Another ambitious multimodal expert system for information retrieval is the one developed by Croft and Thompson (1987) at the University of Massachusetts. Croft and Thompson have described a prototype system for retrieving information from ACM computer science documents. The system, known as **I³R** combines probabilistic (statistical) search techniques with production rules in a blackboard architecture.

The system is able to employ domain-specific knowledge or statistical techniques. Domain specific knowledge is used to support inferences based on concepts from the subject domain being investigated. Probabilistic, relevance feedback techniques (Salton & McGill, 1983, Bartschii, 1985) are employed in situations where large amounts of domain-specific knowledge are not available.

Tasks Supported by I³R

query formulation
acquisition of domain knowledge
explanation
browsing
retrieval of results
evaluation of results

Phases of an I³R Consultation

query formulation and refinement
search
user evaluation

I^3R System Components

As in other systems discussed, the HEARSAY-II blackboard architecture is used to allow the system to move from one search problem-solving modality to another. I^3R, is a complex system which includes a number of major components.

The blackboard is the centerpiece of the system. In addition to working memory related to the problem at hand, it also contains a **plan** and an **agenda**.

Modules for different problem-solving activities are known as "**system experts**." Each is a collection of rules and knowledge pertinent to the resolution of a different specific problem-solving tasks. For example, there is a **request model builder**, a **user model builder**, and a **browser**. System experts are activated by the state of the blackboard. Compare this approach to Brajnik's "tasks," which can activate one another directly.

A **scheduler** controls activation of system experts based on the plan and agenda stored in the blackboard. The agenda supplies a list of possible actions which system experts can perform and the plan matches information on the current state of the problem with information on preferred actions associated with different problem states.

Another major component of I^3R is a **knowledge base**. The knowledge base contains structured information about documents, users, and concepts from the domain — sort of like a thesaurus in a higher stage of evolution.

Finally, there is an **interface manager** which manages the dialogue with the user and all input/output from the system.

The system experts posited by Croft and Thompson correspond roughly to the "tasks" identified by Brajnik, et al. Nor is it surprising that they also correspond to the parts of the search process present in most of the models discussed in the last section.

A Typical I^3R Session

A session with I^3R goes something like this. First a user model builder attempts to match user characteristics obtained via a dialogue to stored stereotypes which establish the overall goals and style of interaction for each specific session. Then a request model builder parses the initial query to obtain possible search terms and weights the terms. A **domain knowledge expert** uses knowledge obtained in previous modules to relate **user stereotypes** and query terms from the domain-specific knowledge base to infer possible search concepts and present them to the user. The user can consider concepts and possibly incorporate them in the strategy. As the process continues, the blackboard is being used for the shared development of a request model. Each cooperating system expert adds something different to the solution of the problem emerging on the blackboard.

A **search controller** develops strategies based on probabilistic retrieval and document clustering. A **browsing expert** assists the user in navigating the database. Browsing is important. Despite the systematic process implied by most models, information retrieval is still largely a trial-and-error process. Browsing is controlled by the user but the system can advise, explain, and navigate for the user. For example, term relationships can be graphically displayed with each term occupying a node and relationships occupying links between nodes. Another mechanism to aid the user is **the explainer**, which is designed to give the user insight into the system by referring to rules which fired in response to the condition of the blackboard.

As the session continues, the interface manager is also in contact with the blackboard. The blackboard provides guidelines on how to present information to the user and what to display. Prompts to the user and explanations for the user are placed in the blackboard and may be inspected by "system experts," which can possibly contribute to the solution of the problem by providing information to or eliciting information from the user.

Resolving Conflicts

In a complex system where many rules might apply at any given time, it is necessary to determine which group of rules is most likely to bring the problem closer to resolution. A scheduler selects activities and assigns priorities. Like the "task activation" process described in Brajnik, Guida and Tasso, the scheduler needs to know when to switch control from one system expert to another and when the limits of any given expert's ability to resolve the subproblem being considered have been reached. In other words, as Guida et al. have suggested, the system has to be able to "degrade gracefully." The type of knowledge required for the system to know its own limits is known as **meta-knowledge**.

Human reference librarians are usually very adept at "degrading gracefully." When a good reference librarian realizes a problem is beyond her capabilities she is likely to say, "I'm sorry I don't know much about sources in your topic area. Could I refer you to a [colleague, another library, an expert system] that does."

Just as knowledge in the knowledge base is structured and organized, information in the blackboard is structured and organized. The blackboard in Croft's system is divided into the following six areas:

- **a plan** — which is **instantiated**, or provided with givens, for each session
- **an agenda** — a list of possible actions determined by the plan

- **a user model** — which is based on stereotypes stored in the system
- **a request model** — this corresponds to the problem internal representation described by Brajnik, Guida, and Tasso
- **input/output requests** — for use by the interface manager
- **a system journal** — a log of the entire session which contains information about which rules fired and why and which is used by the explainer

The beauty of the blackboard as an organizing principle is that the blackboard is dynamic. It changes as different problems are presented to the system and as the solution for a specific problem develops.

In contrast to the blackboard, the knowledge base contains longer-term knowledge about information-seeking problems. The knowledge base is comprised of frames which describe the attributes of users, documents, terms, concepts, authors, and other data pertinent to the solution of information retrieval problems. The blackboard architecture provides structure and control for the system's short-term memory. Frames provide structure and control to the system's long-term memory. Sections of the knowledge base dealing with documents, terms, and concepts include statistical relationships as well as syndetic structures. Subject and probabilistic approaches can be combined. Much of the knowledge in the knowledge base is of the same type found in thesauri. Much of the knowledge found on the blackboard is of the same type found in the heads of human intermediaries.

Problem-Solving Systems

We've seen narrow domain systems and we've seen broad domain systems. We've seen systems which work with existing electronic records and systems which restructure (and convert to machine- readable form) knowledge for intelligent retrieval. We've looked at how a number of investigators have approached the problem-solving process by breaking big problems down into a series of smaller problems. We've looked at some of the things these systems have in common and the ways in which they differ. We've examined the ways in which each of the major subproblems have been approached. We know which lend themselves to machine solutions and which are problematic. We're aware that models tend to oversimplify and we know that many of the existing systems rely upon abstract models of the search process.

Now let's move away from the model world and into the real world. Now let's look at the ways in which real human experts work and some of the attempts to capture human expertise for machine problem solving.

Let's also consider some of the techniques for acquiring expert knowledge from skilled humans — techniques which we shall see are similar to the techniques employed by the skilled intermediaries whose behavior we are attempting to model.

Recommended Reading

The book edited by Davies (1986) includes descriptions of some of the better known projects. L.C. Smith (1987) and E. A. Fox (1987) provide the best reviews of the more sophisticated efforts to develop knowledge-based front-ends. Williams (1986) covers more traditional efforts. The *Proceedings of the American Society for Information Science* (ASIS) and the Association for Computing Machinery Special Interest Group on Information Retrieval (ACM SIGIR) often include papers of interest. The *Informatics* series (Informatics, 1985, Jones, 1983, MacCafferty, 1979) does a good job of covering the European scene. The journal *Information Processing and Management* and the *Journal of the American Society for Information Science* are the two best journals for finding out about knowledge-based retrieval systems.

Noteworthy projects not already discussed in this chapter include those of Edward Fox, Frei and Jauslin, and P.J. Smith, all of whom are cited in the bibliography. Medical informatics is the hot research area, and the book edited by Salamon (1986) contains papers describing several interesting medical projects. Other interesting papers are located in the books edited by Karna (1985) and by Jacobson and Witges (1986).

5
Knowledge Engineering for Reference and Information Retrieval

The task of acquiring expert knowledge and encoding it in such a way that it can be used by an expert system is known as **knowledge engineering**. Knowledge engineering is a tricky job — much more an art than a science. Real experts are difficult to identify and even when they can be identified are often at a loss when it comes to describing how they operate.

Tact and skill are required to accomplish the transfer of expertise from humans to machines. Interviewing and interpersonal skills are vital. Does this sound like a field in which reference librarians would be interested? Knowledge of artificial intelligence programming is also important. The ability to organize and classify knowledge is also crucial. Maybe catalogers have a role here as well. Knowledge engineering requires a variety of different skills. For large projects, it is not unusual for the knowledge engineering task to be handled by a team, with different individuals responsible for acquiring, encoding, and organizing human expertise.

Knowledge engineering for expert systems involves many subtasks, not the least of which is simply determining what constitutes knowledge within the domain. Identifying knowledgeable human beings who are willing to cooperate in an uncertain venture can be a real challenge. Obtaining knowledge from human experts can take months of hard work, and so can developing an appropriate structure for that knowledge. Expertise is a dynamic thing. The human expert must keep up with changing developments. So the knowledge engineer's job isn't finished once the first knowledge base has been compiled. Knowledge engineering is an ongoing process. Knowledge bases must be continuously updated, maintained, and evaluated.

We use the term "knowledge" a lot. After all, one of the definitions of "expert system" is a computer program which can draw inferences from a body of knowledge. But what do we mean when we use the word "knowledge?"

Gio Wiedenhold (1986) differentiates between **data** and **knowledge**. Expert systems, unlike most computer programs, operate on knowledge rather than data. According to Wiedenhold, data are objective facts which are subject to verification. Data can be collected with machines. A counter which records the number of people who enter and leave a building is collecting data.

Knowledge, on the other hand, is abstract and subjective and not easily verified. Knowledge comes from education and experience, not directly from the physical world. It is fuzzier and more general than data. Data is more precise than knowledge. The mental schema that reference librarians use to guide them in their work are knowledge.

Wiedenhold's test for differentiating data from knowledge follows:

> If you'd let a clerk update it: **Data.**
> If you'd trust an expert only: **Knowledge.**
> (Wiedenhold, 1986)

Knowledge engineering involves both obtaining knowledge from experts (**knowledge acquisition**) and developing formalisms for representing that knowledge (**knowledge representation**). In essence, knowledge engineering involves making abstractions of mental processes which are abstract to begin with. Before beginning a knowledge engineering project, one must determine whether the resulting system is likely to justify the challenging and time-consuming task of collecting and organizing knowledge. The developer will also need to determine whether the system is to be developed for experimental purposes or if the ultimate goal is something which will be used, and if so, by whom.

Kidd (1987) recommends a top down approach to knowledge engineering that incorporates many of the principles applied by systems analysts to conventional programming problems. The first step is to isolate and identify the problem to be solved. Then it is necessary to describe in detail the knowledge required to solve problems in the selected domain and to list the steps involved in applying knowledge to the solution of problems. Part of the process involves defining acceptable solutions to problems in the domain, developing a working model to guide the knowledge acquisition process, and establishing specifications of the finished system's capabilities. Finally, a plan for assessing the validity and completenesss of the knowledge base must be developed along with a strategy for updating and maintaining the knowledge base.

Problem Domains

Knowledge engineering lends itself best to problem domains where there is already a formal language for representing knowledge and problem solving. Kidd (1987) identifies classes of domains, ranging from those which already have a formal language for knowledge representation to those which can only be described in ambiguous terms.

For example, mathematics is characterized as a domain with a formal knowledge representation language. The success of early mathematical systems such as **MACSYMA** is evidence of the payoff of developing an expert system in a domain where there is already a formal language. Less formal domains such as medical diagnosis are also the subject of intense interest, but development often involves the additional challenge of creating a formal problem representation language. Many of the efforts in information retrieval have attempted to describe IR problems in formal terms.

Kidd also identifies deciding upon the system's modality as an important step in the development process. Breuker and Wielinga (1987) discuss the process of specifying what a proposed system will and won't do. The reference/retrieval process is multimodal but falls most clearly into the mode known as domain consultation. Consultation within a domain is the most common modality for expert systems. Kidd (1987) cites several studies which identify task categories common to domain consultation systems. Among the functions of consultation systems reviewed by Kidd (1987) are:

- negotiating with the user to develop a problem representation which is expressed in terms of the domain addressed by the system
- educating the user by answering questions about different aspects of the domain
- "Communicating advice to the user in a form that is focused, intelligible, and convincing. The single-solution output and trace-style explanations of current expert systems do not match this requirement."

These task categories parallel very closely the phases of the reference/search process posited by most theorists.

Once a domain and a modality have been identified it is necessary to acquire data from human experts. Typically, data are acquired verbally but there is growing support for machine acquisition. There is more to the process than data acquisition. The conversion of raw data to knowledge involves interpretation and the development of a model of expertise within the domain.

Prerau (1985) describes a project designed to identify fruitful domains for potential expert systems. Fifty experts from the corporate world were interviewed and over thirty application areas were considered. Those thirty areas were narrowed to eight possible areas, of which two were selected for detailed scrutiny.

Experts were presented with a list of desired attributes for an expert system problem domain. The list of prerequisites was used by the experts in the study to cull the list of possible applications and identify the areas of greatest potential. High-potential domains shared many of the same criteria.

Criteria for Expert System Development *

Domain is narrow and unambiguous enough to be manageable.

The domain is fuzzy enough to justify development time. The task can't be performed by a nonexpert.

Uncertainty and nonlinear problem-solving techniques apply within the domain.

Problem solving involves symbolic reasoning.

Procedural knowledge exists within the domain but there are enough exceptions to the rules to make an algorithmic approach impractical. Reference work, for example, isn't easily described in a procedures manual.

Sufficient development time is available. If systems were standardized, development time could be reduced because development work could be more easily shared.

Human expertise is available, but limited. Another criterion is that the tasks involved are boring for human experts, who would be more valuable solving higher level problems. Human experts must also be cooperative if the project is to succeed.

Any payoff is likely to exceed expense in terms of money, time, and user acceptance/satisfaction.

* Kidd (1987), Prerau (1985), Breuker & Wielinga (1987), Waterman (1986)

Reference as a Problem Domain

As a problem domain, how does reference/information retrieval work measure up to this list of criteria?

Reference/intermediary work takes place in a large complex, fuzzy search space. But as Philip Smith (1988) has pointed out, successful intermediaries must have some method of factoring and organizing the search space to make it manageable.

On one side of the problem space is the user, on the other side is the collection — the available store of recorded knowledge. Pieces of the puzzle needed to solve the problem are moved in and out of the problem space, which changes its shape as the search progresses. Facets of the problem are resolved by employing different resources in the collection. Neither the collection nor the user are uniform.

On the user's side of the problem space are:

- expectations
- abilities
- constraints (time, money, or intellectual ability)
- the user's conceptual image of the problem

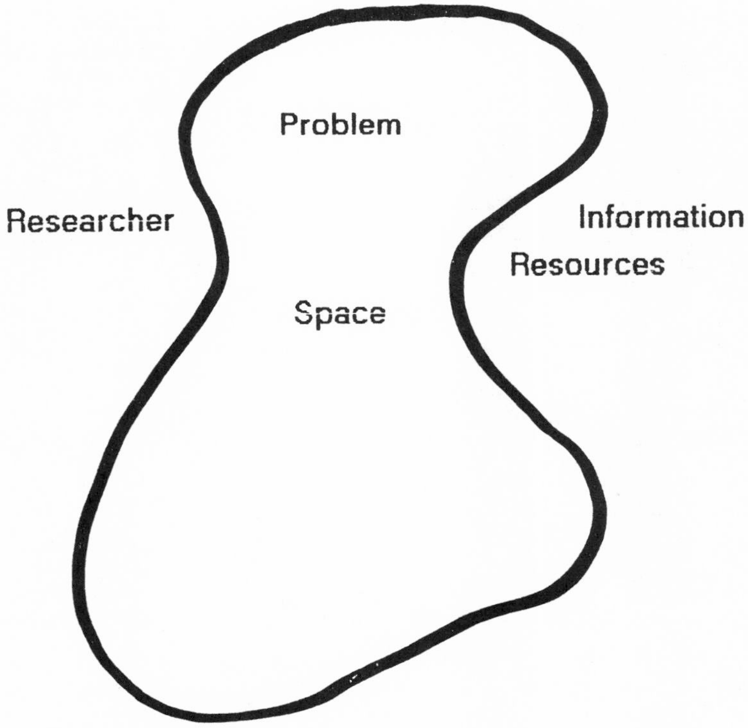

Figure 5.1. The problem space

On the collection side of the problem space are:

- documents
- search protocols
- formal descriptions
- query languages
- storage media
- syndetic structures and indexing techniques

As more information is obtained from and about both the user and the collection, the shape of the problem space changes. The question to ask when contemplating an expert system for retrieval tasks is whether the problem space is manageable. Stefik (1982) describes one class of expert system problems as involving "large factorable search spaces." Information retrieval almost certainly belongs to this class of problems.

With this type of problem it is essential to establish boundaries on the system's expertise. Like a human expert, the system must know when to stop, when there is sufficient information to attempt a solution, and when more information is required before a stab can be made. And if more information is required, the system must define what sort and how much and what steps need to be taken to acquire it. In addition to knowing when enough information is available to attempt a solution, a reference system must be able to determine when a query can't be satisfied by local resources and how to make the connection to external resources. In the case of an online search system, cost/benefit decisions must be made as well.

Types of Problems

Luconi (1986) lists four types of problems and the best method for machine solution of each type.

1. structured problems lend themselves to data processing
2. partially structured problems are appropriate for decision support systems
3. domains where relevant information can be encoded are suitable for classic expert systems
4. domains where knowledge cannot be feasibly encoded suggest **expert support systems**, which provide advice rather than answers

Reference work most likely falls between being a Type 3 and a Type 4 problem. It may lend itself to a support system which provides consultation but can't be expected to provide answers. A true expert system would be expected to provide answers like a human reference librarian does. Reference work is a little fuzzy as a problem domain. Goals aren't always obvious. The parameters of each encounter aren't easily predicted. Procedures can't be easily standardized. Stefik (1982) describes this type of problem as lending itself to a "hierarchical, generate and test" approach.

Sparck-Jones (1987) considers some of the specific problems associated with developing expert systems for information retrieval:

> Comparing the IR case with "classical" expert systems shows critical differences: documentary domains are very large and ill-bounded; the knowledge manipulated by the system is secondary, not primary — the user wants the knowledge in the documents, whereas the system deals with knowledge about the documents; and the way documentary knowledge is expressed, in its linguistic text, is part of that knowledge. Expert system design in this area comes up against very complex and ill-constructed knowledge. A straight expert system, moreover, will not be enough: user modeling will be required, implying the very challenging task of modeling the "anomalous state of knowledge," that is ill-defined lack of knowledge the user is seeking to remedy.

Another major problem in the application of AI techniques to information retrieval is the fact that the tasks to be performed in order to solve an information retrieval problem cannot be specified in advance. Nor are possible solutions to a problem easily verifiable as correct.

Big Systems/Little Systems

So the jury is still out on retrieval as a problem domain. It appears that consultation systems will predominate and that question-answering systems are less likely to be feasible. It is important to remember that developing a **MYCIN**-style system is a major undertaking which is beyond the scope of most libraries. But it is possible to use current microcomputer technology, working within smaller domains, to develop systems which have a primarily advisory/instructional role. (Small-scale systems will be treated in greater depth in Chapter Nine.) The first library systems will probably be developed by librarians for consultation by colleagues. Later, systems for clients will emerge — systems which will perform in a tutorial and advisory mode.

Bruce Buchannan one of the founding fathers of AI, recommended to a group of librarians at the 1987 ALA conference in San Francisco that the basic design principle for expert systems is "to keep the knowledge driving the system modular and explicit." Buchannan suggests that the best library applications for expert systems are those in which "a medium-sized body of knowledge is applied frequently by a variety of people." Such a medium-sized body of knowledge should be represented with a maximum of a few hundred rules. General reference doesn't seem to meet these criteria, but small ready-reference systems within narrow domains do seem to fall within the limits recommended by Buchannan, Prerau, and others.

There is evidence that small-scale systems, besides being easier to develop, are more likely to be accepted by the clients for whom they are intended. Kimura and his colleagues (1986) developed a medical expert system which (as is usually the case) was not accepted by the medical community. Kimura's system was designed to recommend antibiotics for therapy and to suggest appropriate dosages. The system was originally implemented on a large mainframe computer. People seeking to use the system had to go to a centralized workstation. Scaling the system down from a mainframe to a stand-alone, optical disk-based sytem and finally implementing it in the package of a hand-held calculator resulted in widespread acceptance. Users seem to want simple, inexpensive systems that supplement rather than replace experts. Experts such as the doctors for whom Kimura's system was designed seem less threatened by advisory systems which use familiar, off- the-shelf technology.

Focusing on Information Resources

Perhaps the easiest approach to knowledge engineering for library tasks is to focus first on information resources in a specific domain. A first step might be to choose a subject area and gather a collection of useful sources. Then the knowledge engineer could look at factors which separate the sources from one another, starting at the grossest level. The final goal would be to categorize the sources in order to develop schema for a knowledge base.

The resulting knowledge base wouldn't really represent the expertise of a human in the field but could still prove useful. One of the advantages an expert system can have over a human expert is the systematic, comprehensive way in which the domain knowledge base is constructed. In a reference system, a systematically built knowledge base would not overlook the rarely used information source or the long shot, which a human expert might neglect to consider.

Deriving a Knowledge Base from the Literature

Bernstein (1980) describes a National Library of Medicine project called the **Hepatitis Knowledge Base**. There are many interesting aspects to ths project, one of which is its underlying goal of dealing with both the quantitative (information explosion) and qualitative problems of information transfer. The Hepatitis Knowledge Base is also one of the first attempts to build a knowledge base through consensus. It represents an attempt to acquire knowledge for the knowledge base from multiple experts and to extract from the published literature high-quality chunks of knowledge. The final knowledge base is analogous to a publication that has been subjected to a rigorous peer review process.

The Hepatitis Knowledge Base bypasses some of the problems identified by Sparck-Jones by focusing on sources themselves and by restructuring knowledge from sources to provide users with information about the domain. The knowledge in the Hepatitis Knowledge Base is derived from documents, not human experts. But human experts are used to validate the knowledge extracted from documents.

Bernstein (1980) describes the Hepatitis Knowledge Base as a prototype system to facilitate information transfer rather than document access in biomedicine. Among the goals of the project are:

- to make available substantive information, instead of mere citations to documents
- to include current information which is also the consensus of a select group of recognized experts
- to provide online access to an information resource that contains textual passages which can be used to answer questions frequently posed by clinicians and medical researchers
- to link text in the knowledge base to primary publications from which it is derived

The problem domain of this prototype system was hepatitis diseases, an area for which there existed a large number of citations (16,000 titles in English for the ten years prior to the beginning of the project) and an area where the quality of published materials is mixed. A major goal was to reduce the quantity of information to be dealt with by information seekers and to increase the quality by filtering out inferior and redundant information, as well as by incorporating narrative text instead of bibliographic citations.

Review Articles as a Knowledge Source

The first stage in the knowledge acquisition process was to limit the number of knowledge sources to be incorporated in the knowledge base. This was done by using review articles as the initial qualitative filter. Review articles are useful for identifying the most important sources because:

- They tend to be written by human experts who were selected because of their expertise.
- They exclude low-quality material.
- They eliminate redundancy.
- They are based on experts contextual knowledge and are typically organized by applying a human expert's schema for representing the knowledge in a topic area to a large, diverse body of literature.

Forty review articles provided the source material for the first draft of the knowledge base. The articles chosen were those recommended by experts on hepatitis. The next step was to organize the information from the review articles and put it into a usable structure. Contents of review articles were cut into sections and pasted into a hierarchically organized body of knowledge. Paragraphs related to different aspects of a topic were grouped together under descriptive headings and preceded by a summary paragraph.

For example, the section of the Hepatitis Knowledge Base relating to transmission of the disease (Bernstein, 1980, p.186) is organized as follows:

Organization of the Knowledge Base

637H	**Modes of Transmission of hepatitis**
639H	Contact transmitted hepatitis
641H	Contact transmission of type A hepatitis
655H	Contact transmission of type B hepatitis
706H	Contact transmission of type non-A, non-B hepatitis
712H	Primate associated hepatitis
721H	Water borne hepatitis
728H	Food borne hepatitis
730H	Shellfish associated hepatitis
745H	Milk borne hepatitis
748H	Other food borne hepatitis

752H	Externally contaminated insects
761H	Biting insects
773H	Transfusion associated hepatitis
775H	"Average risk" transfusion materials
796H	High risk blood derivatives
800H	Safe blood derivatives
806H	Transplantation associated hepatitis
811H	Dialysis associated hepatitis
825H	Syringe associated hepatitis
836H	Hepatitis associated with exposure to health care providers
855H	Contaminated tattoo needles and vials of dye
857H	Hepatitis associated with illicit self-injection
965H	Hepatitis associated with other instruments
875H	Hepatitis associated with common use of wash water
879H	Hepatitis associated with penetration of bare skin
881H	Vertical transmission of hepatitis to neonates

One of the major challenges of developing the knowledge base was organizing separate pieces of information derived from a diverse body of literature. After the knowledge was organized, ten experts were asked to read the draft knowledge base and to note inaccuracies, gaps, and other problems.

The objective was to achieve a consensus among experts on the knowledge to be included under each of the headings in the hierarchically organized knowledge base. For occasions where there was disagreement among experts, decisions were arrived at by a vote. Cases where two or more experts disagreed with the contents of the knowledge base generally resulted in a modification of the section in contention.

Experts were asked not only to evaluate the contents of the knowledge base but to suggest possible changes in its organizational structure and to identify new material which should be incorporated. Experts were asked to limit evidence in support of suggested changes to information which had already appeared in the published literature. Participants in the development process (who were geographically dispersed over a wide area) communicated electronically with one another and with the knowledge base. Each also received a printed draft to critique.

Maintaining the Knowledge Base

A major problem was developing a mechanism for updating the knowledge base as new discoveries on hepatitis appeared in the literature. Since the original knowledge base was derived from review articles, its contents were initially three years or so out of date.

The updating problem was kept manageable by using citation analysis techniques to identify the most influential current literature on the topic. Citation lists from the forty review articles were analyzed and a core journal list was compiled. Eighteen journals thus formed the core source material for updating the knowledge base. Each expert read a selected group of articles on the topic which had appeared in the core journals. New knowledge was then synthesized and summarized by the expert panelists and added to the knowledge base. Panelists then communicated with one another until consensus was once again reached.

A final attempt to achieve consensus was the publication of a short form of the knowledge base in the *Annals of Internal Medicine* (Bernstein 1980). By this means, the medical community at large was invited to comment on the contents of the knowledge base and its organizational structure.

Human Experts as Sources of Knowledge

The formalized knowledge found in texts, however, is only one component of a human expert's knowledge base. Expertise often grows from experience and there is certainly a great deal of expert knowledge which has never been either articulated or recorded. Despite the wealth of literature in just about every domain, the vast majority of expert knowledge is almost certainly still found only in the minds of human beings.

Eventually we will have to focus on what is known about users and also on representing the cognitive processes of reference librarians and online searchers. A number of conjectural papers have been published in this area but there is surprisingly little empirical research.

Belkin (1986) and his colleagues have done extensive analysis of interactions involving information intermediaries, attempting to discover functions performed by intermediaries as they interact with clients. The purpose of this research is to identify those functions which can be simulated with a machine.

Belkin's theory of how interactions take place is centered around model-building. Instead of constructing a query statement, most of the interaction involves developing a representation of the user's problem. Focus is not on the development of formal queries but on the identification of concepts, goals, and constraints. According to Belkin, model building seems to almost always precede query formulation or source selection. Not surprisingly, in light of his emphasis on problem solving, Belkin proposes a blackboard architecture as the most efficient way of modelling search problems with a machine.

Memory and Cognition

An important, related area of research is the investigation of human thought, memory, and problem solving. Cognitive psychology, one of the precursors of artificial intelligence, provides many of the theories and is the source of most of the studies in this area. If we can understand the thought processes of humans in problem-solving situations, perhaps we can duplicate those processes in expert systems.

Slatter (1987) compares the architecture of a typical expert system to the organizational scheme proposed by the human information-processing model. Early models of human cognitive processing divided human information-handling processes into **short-term memory (STM)**, **long-term memory (LTM)**, and a **cognitive processor**. These correspond respectively to an expert system's global database (working memory), knowledge base, and inference engine. More recent models of human cognition posit considerable overlap, viewing short-term memory as working memory — the portion of long-term memory which is currently activated. There is also evidence that human information processing is massively parallel with many coexisting cognitive processes and representation schemes.

Cognitive psychologists have been influential in AI circles and George Miller is one of the most influential of the bunch. It was Miller (1956) who came up with the experiment which resulted in the famous theory that humans are only capable of dealing with about seven (plus or minus two) pieces of information at one time. If people can only handle seven simple ideas or symbols at a time, how are they capable of knowing so much?

Miller proposed that people organize their knowledge in categories he called **chunks**. The label for a chunk can be easily handled within constraints on human short-term memory. Each chunk can be dealt with as a primitive symbol. Pieces of knowledge are connected to one another in chunks. The chunk becomes a single unit, an abstraction of a larger body of knowledge — a collection of inter-related ideas which can be called forth from a single mental construct.

Najarian (1981) considers the implications of psychological studies of human memory and cognition for the design of library storage-and-retrieval systems. She was among the first to review the work of Miller (1956), Mandler (1967), Bruner (1973) and others within the context of library science. Among the possibilities suggested by this research to Najarian (1981, p.288): "It seems likely that organizational schemes that group subjects into categories that progress from the general to the specific would be more effective as search aids than those that do not."

Also among Najarian's suggestions: aids to orient the user, providing him with a diagram of the classification scheme and allowing him to relate the point at which he entered the system to other access points. Another recommended design strategy involves incorporating our understanding of the limits on the number of "chunks" of information a human can process simultaneously into information systems. Knowledge of the limits of short-term memory will help to determine the number of facets of a topic which can be handled at one time. Such research will also assist in display design by specifying the number of items to display at one time.

Modalities

Information-seeking problems of the sort requiring an expert intermediary are complex and include many classes of subproblems. Some subproblems require the intermediary to switch from one mode of interaction, or modality, to another. Different cognitive representations are required for different modalities. Breuker and Wielinga (1987) discuss the work of Clancey (1987), who found he had to totally restructure the knowledge base of the MYCIN system in order to have it function within a tutorial rather than a diagnostic modality. Breuker and Wielinga also point out that expertise is not limited to the ability to solve problems in a domain, but also includes the ability to communicate both the formulation and the solution to the problem. One of the capabilities almost always required of an expert system is the ability to explain its reasoning.

The reference process involves different modalities. Each is likely to involve different chunks of knowledge and to require a different way of interacting with the client. Among the major modalities of reference work are:

- identifying concepts and developing problem descriptions
- recommending sources and providing user instruction
- extracting specific data from an information store
- assembling a collection of sources and access tools, developing a reference collection for a subject domain

It is also almost certain that reference librarians use chunks of knowledge. Many reference problems can be solved by using compiled knowledge. For example, a recurring assignment in an academic library can often be handled by referring to a single chunk of compiled knowledge. The reference librarian is able to go directly to an answer without having to solve intermediate problems. She may not even be able to express the steps required to achieve the goal because they have been unconsciously compiled into a single step.

In the reference process, complex problems can be viewed in terms of moving inter-related pieces of information from long-term memory to short-term memory. Short-term memory has limited capacity so knowledge is chunked in broad hierarchical categories, each with its own label. The librarian's model of the user, the query itself, and other factors serve as "triggers" which cause specific chunks to be moved from long- to short-term memory. The reference librarian can refer to chunks of knowledge within an internal domain schema. Often chunks are hierarchically organized. For example, a business librarian could use the following schema to help him manage knowledge about one specific class of financial information sources.

A Chunk of a Business Librarian's Knowledge

sources-of-financial-information chunk
  financial-ratios chunk   sources with timeseries chunk
    Robert Morris Associates Annual Statement Studies chunk
      when-to-use-which-quartile chunk

As subproblems are resolved, the shape of the problem space changes and new chunks are brought into short-term memory. The problem-solving modality can also change as a reference interview proceeds. Designers of expert systems for reference and retrieval tasks will have to decide upon a modality for each phase of the system's interaction with its users. Different modalities will almost certainly require different sorts of knowledge structures. If the goal is a multimodal system, the knowledge underlying the system will have to be segmented. Reference work is nonmonotonic — that is, it can change as it proceeds. There is also evidence which suggests that humans are able to solve different parts of a problem in parallel. While explaining to a client how to use one source, a reference librarian may very well already be thinking about which other sources to consult if the one at hand dosn't work out. And with another part of her mind, the librarian may be formulating explanations for those sources which she hasn't even recommended yet.

We also have to be aware that the typical reference interview is taking place within a very constrained time context, in terms of both the amount of time available to resolve problems and the currency and volatility of source materials and data examined. The human expert has the ability to rapidly jump from one decision tree to another while passing along what is known about the problem. The human expert must also be able to easily shift from one problem-solving mode to another.

In addition to knowledge engineering projects which focus on the literature and projects which focus on skilled intermediaries, there are studies of the behavior of information seekers.

Information Seekers as Sources of Knowledge

Doyle (1986) investigated the cognitive processes of expert medical researchers as they scanned the contents of journals looking for items of interest to their research. The subjects of his study were asked to list the journals which were most important to their research. When new issues of selected journals arrived, experts were asked to come in and browse through them in the presence of the knowledge engineer. The subjects of the experiment were asked to think out loud as they used the journals. Verbalizations were recorded and moves from one section of a journal or article to another were noted by the knowledge engineer.

After the scanning session an interview was conducted. Subjects were asked to comment on the articles they reviewed and to discuss relevance, "citability," impact, etc. The subjects of the experiment were divided into three groups: novices, journeymen, and experts. The behavior and verbalizations of each group were studied and an attempt was made to find common behavioral patterns among the members of each group.

One set of results relates to the parts of the text ("textual inputs") which occupied subjects' attention. The highest priority parts of journals were **tables of contents**, **abstracts**, and the **results** sections of specific articles. Experts tended to pay less attention to the **discussion** sections of research articles than members of the other two groups. Since this was scientific literature, the articles themselves were divided into sections (**abstract**, **introduction**, **methods**, **discussion**, **results**, and **references**), making them amenable to this type of analysis. Inexperienced researchers read articles sequentially whereas experts moved from the abstract to the results section and then back to the methods section.

Doyle was also able to draw some tentative conclusions about the differences between experts, novices, and journeymen. Experts' relative lack of interest in discussion sections probably reflects their preference for developing their own interpretation of the data reported in the results section.

Verbal protocols obtained from subjects were analyzed for inferences related to searching and inferences related to evaluation. There were no differences in the searching and evaluation heuristics employed by experts and novices. Both tended to focus on relevance before making judgments on rigor or impact. Journeymen, on the other hand, achieved poorer recall than either experts or novices. Perhaps this is because novices were willing to explore more possibilities and experts have a richer internal representation with which to compare potentially relevant articles. Journeymen were unwilling to consider articles, which at first glance, didn't seem relevant, nor did journeymen have the extensive knowledge needed to recognize patterns which made articles relevant.

Studies like this one have some useful implications. For example, since results sections are of greater importance to experts, systems for expert users should derive keywords from that section. Another possible implication relates to the display of information in full-text databases. Maybe researchers should be able to indicate which sections are most important to them. Important sections could then be marked or displayed differently. Another possibility is incorporating the internal representations of experts into a system so it can recognize patterns and assist its users in identifying relevant items.

Documentary Knowledge Versus Behavioral Knowledge

A major part of developing a knowledge base is identifying expertise within the selected domain. At one level, expertise could be described as the experiential knowledge of practitioners. At another level, expertise can be derived from the literature. We already know that bibliometric measures can be used to determine "value" of published works.

Another source of expertise is the users for whom a system is intended. Different techniques have been used to acquire knowledge from experts, from the literature, and from users. We've already described attempts to extract knowledge from the literature and from users. In reference work the expert would tend to be a subject specialist with extensive experience. Before any substantive knowledge engineering project can begin, it is essential to locate a human expert who is willing and able to cooperate. Now let's consider some techniques for acquiring knowledge from human experts.

Knowledge Acquisition Techniques

Let's assume we've identified experts, selected a domain, and want to begin the task of acquiring knowledge for a system. Where to begin? The technique used by Doyle is known as **verbal protocol analysis** or **discourse analysis**. It is a popular knowledge acquisition technique but only one of a variety of different techniques that have been used.

Knowledge acquisition is widely acknowledged as the great bottleneck in expert system design. There are two possible roles reference librarians could play in the knowledge acquisition process. In a system for reference or retrieval tasks, a reference librarian would be the most obvious source for the human expertise that would need to be represented.

A reference librarian may also be a good choice as a knowledge interviewer. Similar skills are required of knowledge interviewers and reference librarians. Each must be able to elicit information from other people in a focused way in order to achieve a goal. There is debate in the AI community over the best qualifications for a knowledge engineer. Almost everyone views interpersonal and verbal skills as crucial for the knowledge acquisition phase of the process. So the skilled reference interviewer may one day become a knowledge interviewer.

Knowledge acquisition techniques may be divided into those which involve the articulation of expert knowledge or the observation of expert behavior and those which involve the use of machines to elicit knowledge. Let us first consider techniques which are based on observation and verbalization.

Interviewing Techniques

The most common class of methods for knowledge acquisition are those which involve direct human contact between expert and knowledge engineer. Typically, the contact takes the form of an interview that is similar in many respects to the reference or online search interview. In fact, the same advice and caveats provided for the reference interview apply also to the knowledge interview.

Anna Hart (1986) provides an excellent introduction to knowledge interviewing techniques. Directing the interview is one of the major responsibilities of the knowledge engineer, whose job it is to keep the interview focused and on track. The knowledge interviewer should have clearly defined goals for the type and amount of knowledge to be obtained from each session with the expert. The goals of the session should be shared with the interviewee.

Hart recommends treating a manageably small area in each session, and exhausting one area before moving on to the next. Before a line of questioning is abandoned, the knowledge obtained should be summarized to ensure nothing was missed and to allow the expert to correct any misconceptions of the interviewer. The interviewer should also inform the expert when the line of questioning is shifting to another area of the topic.

Good reference librarians observe many of these practices. Summarizing, explaining why a question is being asked, and keeping the interview focused on the client's problem are all common techniques.

Hart suggests that the most effective interviews are open-ended. It is best to let the expert use his or her own words. It is also a better idea to let an expert focus on typical or representative cases than to try to get the expert to discuss general principles. The interviewer shouldn't attempt to determine what is important until after the interview is finished.

Hart also describes some interviewing techniques which are widely used in knowledge acquisition. Among the techniques reviewed by Hart (1986, p.58) are:

Interviewing Strategies

Critical incident technique. This technique involves asking the expert to focus on interesting cases. The emphasis on difficult or unusual cases is likely to result in a more complete and detailed account from the expert. It is harder to remember less interesting or typical cases and they will eventually have to be considered, but it is easier to start with interesting cases.

Characteristics and decisions. This techniques requires the expert to provide a list of characteristics and discuss their implications. Given enough examples along with the decisions associated with them, it is possible to identify implicit rules.

Distinguishing goals involves differentiating evidence required to arrive at one goal from evidence which leads to alternative goals. This technique is useful for developing an idea of how the expert organizes her knowledge.

Reclassification. Working backwards from a goal, the expert specifies subgoals and conditions needed to satisfy the goal.

Dividing the domain. The expert begins by describing subgoals and conditions and then works forward to the goals with which they're associated.

Talk-through. This technique asks the expert to think out loud as he works, identifying decisions as they are made and explaining them. This is really a variant of the technique known as protocol analysis, which will be treated in greater detail in a later section.

Decision analysis involves asking the expert to compare the likely costs and benefits of all possible decisions for a given situation.

Hart (1986)

Waldron (1986) notes that interviewing techniques for knowledge acquisition are still at an early stage of development. He also recommends a structured, goal-oriented interview and identifies several different question types employed by knowledge interviewers. Compare the question types described by Waldron to the questioning techniques described in the extensive literature on the reference interview.

Question Types in Knowledge Interviews

Open questions are recommended for the preliminary stages of a knowledge interview; **what, where when, who,** and **why** questions encourge experts to discuss their expertise in general terms. Open questions are most useful for obtaining large amounts of information in a nondirective way.

Probes serve as follow-up questions to some aspect of the expert's answer to a prior question. Probes are designed to elicit additional information or expand upon some facet of a larger topic.

Reflective probes are used to clarify the interviewer's understanding of what the expert is saying by paraphrasing the expert's words.

Request probes are unambiguous requests for additional information or expressions of a lack of understanding.

Closed questions are considered by Waldron to be "restrictive and of limited value." Just like in the reference interview, most useful for verification.

Leading questions reflect the interviewer's preconceived notions, and, according to Waldron "should be avoided" just as they should be in the reference interview.

Waldron (1986) lists problems typical of knowledge acquisition interviewing, including:

- **goal ambiguity.** Tasks to be performed by the system being developed haven't been explicitly stated and/or expert and interviewer don't share common perception of system goals
- **vocabulary.** Within narrow domains meaning of terms can be ambiguous and experts tend to use specialized terms and jargon
- **limitations of verbalization.** Being able to do something and being able to verbalize what is being done are two different things
- **compiled knowledge.** Experts tend to develop automatic responses which are almost like reflexes; a complex series of primitive actions is collapsed into a single step; once knowledge has been compiled it becomes extremely difficult for the expert to decompile it into its component parts.

Finally, there is a tendency in interview situations to capture idealized rather than realistic representation of expert thought processes and problem-solving techniques. Because experts tend to present things the way they think they should be rather than the way they really are, it is probably not a good idea for a reference librarian to serve as her own knowledge interviewer. It sometimes takes a dispassionate observer to get an accurate observation of what really goes on in an encounter such as a reference interview. Serving as one's own knowledge engineer is analogous in many ways to acting as one's own lawyer, and probably about as advisable.

Protocol Analysis

Interviewing techniques can be quite useful for knowledge acquisition, but we have seen that there are also disadvantages. Protocol analysis is a method which retains many of the advantages of interviewing techniques while eliminating some of the disadvantages. Protocol analysis combines the introspection associated with interviewing with the objectivity of direct observation of behavior. Observational studies have been widely used in librarianship. The typical observational study besides being obtrusive does not provide the knowledge engineer with accesss to the expert's thought processes.

Protocol analysis, on the other hand, attempts to capture the thought processes of experts as they deal with problems. Protocol analysis is among the most common method of analyzing the reference process. In a reference interview, protocol analysis involves asking one or both of the actors to "think aloud" as the interview progresses. Some form of protocol analysis has been used by Taylor (1967), Brooks (1979, 1985, 1986) Belkin (1984, 1985, 1988), and Ingwersen (1982, 1986).

Ericcson and Simon (1984, p.263–64) list the basic assumptions underlying protocol analysis:

1. The subject's behavior can be viewed as a search through a problem space, accumulating knowledge (not always correct) about the problem situation as he goes. This gradual, step-by-step accumulation of knowledge can be represented by a problem behavior graph, the kth node of which represents the subject's knowledge after k steps of search.
2. Each step in the search involves the application of an operator, selected from a relatively small set of task-relevant operators, to knowledge held by the subject in STM [short-term memory]. Application of the operator brings new knowledge into STM, moving the subject to a new point in the problem space.
3. The verbalizations of the subject correspond to some part of the information he is currently holding in STM, and usually to information which has recently been acquired.
4. The information in STM, and reported by the subject, consists primarily of knowledge required as inputs to the operators, new knowledge produced by operators, and symbols representing active goals and subgoals that are driving the activity. A goal may take the form of an intent to apply an operator; in which case the protocol may contain explicit evidence for the application of operators.

The first step in a protocol analysis of a reference situation would involve asking a reference librarian to think out loud during or immediately after an interview. The subject would be asked to try to not miss anything and to verbalize his thoughts in the sequence they occurred. Ericsson and Simon (1984) contend that protocol analysis is most useful when done concurrently with the process being analyzed or immediately after, while subject can recall his thoughts, instead of later when the subject is more likely to infer what his thoughts were, providing an idealized rather than a real account of his reasoning process.

The analyses of reference protocols that have been done are more likely to involve retrospective protocols and direct transcriptions of interviews than they are to involve the reference librarian directly verbalizing his thoughts during the course of his work. Verbal protocols have also been developed for hypothetical situations. The knowledge engineer poses a situation and asks probing questions as the expert describes her thoughts.

The ultimate goal of a protocol analysis is to identify data in the protocol, to decompose the problem-solving process into its separate steps. A well-done analysis will result in a list of categories of information needed to develop an expert's image of a problem, a description of primitive operators and the operations they perform, and a sequence of operations.

Almost all operations can be reduced to more primitive operations. Verbal protocols tend to include higher level operators. For example, an expert might say, "I looked in *Statistical Abstract* and found the answer," instead of saying, "I remembered where *Statistical Abstract* was on the shelf and went to the general vicinity. When I spotted it I pulled it from the shelf and looked in the index which I know is in the back of the book. I tried looking under chickens and didn't find an entry so I tried looking under poultry, where I found an entry. I know that the numbers next to the index words refer to tables, not pages, so I turned to table number 1,114. I found the table and first ran down the labels for rows until I found the row labeled **number produced**. Then I looked at the columns until I spotted the one for 1986 Then I scanned that column until I found the entry I was looking for. There were 217 million chickens produced in 1986."

Contrast the expert's description of her activity with that of the knowledge engineer who is often required to describe higher level operations in terms of their more primitive components.

Protocol analysis is an attempt to capture the contents of the expert's short-term memory as she moves through a problem space. Today protocols are usually recorded on audio or videotape. The tape is used to create a transcript of all utterances. The transcript is analyzed and separate utterances are treated as data. The goal is to categorize the expert's actions in order to gain an understanding of the separate steps in the problem-solving process.

Part of the process involves coding the separate parts of the transcript in terms of the inputs, operators, and goals described in assumption 4 above. A task analysis may precede the protocol analysis. The information obtained from the task analysis helps the coder of the transcript determine how to label the expert's verbalizations by identifying goals and subgoals, the data needed to achieve them, and the tasks which need to be performed to acquire and process the data.

As a reliability check, it is not uncommon for more than one coder to analyze the same protocol. The task categories, encoding of utterances, and goals identified can then be compared with one another. If the agreement between the different coders is high then it is assumed that the data derived from the protocol are valid. Separate protocols in a problem-solving domain are then compared with one another to arrive at general models of problem solving within that domain.

Problems with Protocol Analysis

Protocol analysis is still somewhat controversial among psychologists, many of whom contend that it is a subjective technique which has never been validated. But for knowledge acquisition, protocol analysis seems to have more utility than traditional interviews or observation studies which provide only surface-level information.

Most knowledge acquisition techniques have difficulties with compiled knowledge, and protocol analysis is no exception. Increased expertise (gained through practice) leads to short cuts. This compiled knowledge is more difficult for the expert to verbalize because the expert is unconscious of the primitive operations which have been compiled. Protocol analysis is most effective when done concurrently or immediately following a problem-solving task, but in a reference interview a concurrent protocol could become very obtrusive (and could affect content of the interview).

There may be more hope for online searches where the searchers interactions can be recorded and where the searcher may be providing a verbal explanation to the client as she conducts a search. A videotape of a search along with a recorded search history could provide the raw material for a protocol analysis. However, it would still be necessary to capture the searcher's assessment of the client, which most likely would not have been said aloud during the course of the search.

Another problem relates to the nonsequential nature of human thought. Verbal statements are necessarily sequential while the thoughts being verbalized may very well have occurred simultaneously.

Ericcson and Simon warn against letting preconceptions of the coder influence the manner in which the transcript is coded, the "contamination of data by theory." The agreement rate among different coders tends to be low, one indication of the extent to which coders' preconceptions play a role in the encoding of verbal data. Finally, it is difficult to derive decision trees from a protocol. The coder is presented with a list of utterances. Coders have had difficulties agreeing on the utterances which represent a shift from one line of reasoning to another.

Now let's examine a hypothetical protocol. As is often the case, this protocol was developed by asking the human expert to focus on an unusual or atypical case.

I'm sitting at the reference desk, there's a lull in the action. A colleague is asking me about the schedule for next week.

The phone rings and I answer it. It's Professor X from the Math. Dept. She wants the married name of Marina Von Neumann, who she identifies as the daughter of John Von Neumann. I ask her if she means *the* John Von Neumann, and she says yes.

She also tells me that Marina is famous in her own right, a mathematician and a corporate executive, but she's a little fuzzy here, can't tell me when or where, "GE, or something like that I think."

I ask her why she wants Marina Von N's name and she tells me she wanted to suggest her as a speaker on campus. She and the chair of the Math Dept. would like to see more women from the sciences invited to speak on campus.

The first thing I thought about, before I even hung up the phone, because I talked to her about it was how easy it is to get a maiden name when married name is known, especially if the person is famous. The other thing I thought about was that getting a married name when a maiden name is the given would be much harder.

But I knew that John Von N. is pretty famous ... that should help. I thought there was a reasonable chance that I would find what she was looking for. A long shot but I'd try.

First I decided to check *Who Was Who in America.* I know they give information on the spouse but I wasn't sure if they give much information about children. I knew I wouldn't find Marina's address there which is what Professor X. really needed, but I needed some kind of backgraound on Marina before I continued.

At this point, my colleague who'd overheard the phone conversation interrupted my thoughts. She suggested, "Try *DAB*, he was an American citizen wasn't he?"

I think, OK, I'll try that but first check *Who Was Who...* and also *Who's Who* for Marina.

Marina's not in *Who's Who in America*, at least not under her maiden name, but her father is in *Who Was Who...* where I had to use the cumulative index to find out which volume he'd be in.

In *Who Was Who*, I find out

> John Von Neumann was married twice.
> His first marriage was in 1930.
> Marina, was a child of that first marriage.
> He died in 1957.

I still don't know how old Marina is, but think she was most likely no more than 27 in 1957 when her father died, since she is the progeny of a 1930 marriage.

Then I figure I might as well check the *DAB* since X is still standing there.

In the *DAB* I find the same stuff about marriage and death dates I already know. There's a lot more narrative. I scan through it quickly looking for words like "daughter," "child," "Marina." I find the following information which I think I might use.

Marina was named to the President's Council of Economic Advisers.

I think, "It doesn't say which president, doesn't say when, still don't know her birthdate. Could be Eisenhower, probably Kennedy though, maybe Johnson, but consider Kennedy first."

Then I start thinking about where to find a list of past presidents' economic advisors. Also think good thing her first name's Marina, not going to be too many Marina's on the President's Council. Maybe government documents, but we don't have them that far back, so I won't bother yet. Encyclopedia yearbooks, maybe, but old ones, probably in stacks on other side of the building. I guess I'll try *Facts on File*. Think it over a little more before I try something else. What do I know, where could I go for her married name?

I think more on Marina might be in biographies of her father, but I don't want to go that route yet, too much potential for a lot of work without a payoff. I'd have to look them up and chase all over the building.

Wait a minute, John Von Neumann was so famous, he died in '57, why not check his obituary in the *Times*, what a dummy, the obit's sure to list his survivors. Died in '57, maybe a 27-year-old woman — good chance she was already married. Pretty confident I'll find it now. Forget *Facts on File*.

First I check *Current Biography*, it'll have the cite to his obit. Maybe even eliminate the need for it by providing "the answer" but I'm not counting on it. Nothing I don't already know about Marina is there, but the citation to the obituary is.

Now I've got to go downstairs, get the *New York Times* on microfilm. It's a long article; I scan it. Sure enough, one of the survivors, Mrs. Robert Whitman. She was his only daughter by that marriage.

What to do now? First go upstairs and double check. Check biographical sources — science, industry, economics. First go back to *Who's Who* .... Marina Whitman, not there under '57 married name, might as well check her husband, several entries under name "Robert Whitman," just as I expected. Look at them, BINGO, here's one with the name "Marina" in it. Good, they're still married, living in Boston and the address and phone number are there, plus his affiliations. She should be easy enough to contact. Good thing her husband was listed. Her father I expected to be listed because he was so famous, but the husband, that was pure luck.

How do we analyze this protocol? And a simple protocol at that, one that doesn't even involve an interview of the usual sort. What are we to make of this? Where are the data in this protocol? Can the expert's individual thoughts be decomposed and scientifically analyzed? Are there any truisms to be derived? Are there any heuristics we can identify? Any rules to be derived?

Can we now say that IF the names of the members of a person's immediate family are needed, AND the person is dead, AND the person was famous, THEN an obituary is a good bet?

Is there any common-sense knowledge of the type which is beyond the scope of current technology at work here? How does the advice (even the unsought advice) from a colleague figure in? How much trust is there in advice provided by the client? Can advice provided by the client mislead the intermediary and reduce the chances of a successful encounter? Can we say that government documents were ruled out because they were a poor choice, or because they weren't in the building for the time period in question? Why did the subject add some details to the picture of the problem while neglecting others, such as whether or not Marina was the only daughter?

What kind of world knowledge is needed to know that John Von N. was a famous mathematician, and what "famous" means? And how do we represent the process which allows the skilled practitioner to go directly to the shelf for a possible sources, and to be thinking of a variety of possibilities, both strategic and tactical — all at the same time? We hope this simple protocol will give the reader an idea of the complexity of acquiring knowledge by analyzing verbal data.

The process of transcribing and analyzing protocols and extracting meaningful data from them is both tedious and intellectually challenging, and still controversial. We hope our simple protocol will also give you a feel for the potential of this technique as a knowledge acquisition tool.

Project MONSTRAT: Studies of Searcher/Client Interactions

Belkin and Windel (1984) report on research into user intermediary information interactions which was conducted as part of **Project MONSTRAT**, a multinational, multilibrary, interdisciplinary study of the search process. Discourse analysis techniques similar to those described in

Ericcson and Simon (1984) were used in three separate but related studies. Online interviews were observed and recorded, in some of which the investigator was one of the participants. The goal of one study was to gain some insight into the nature of the human interaction which takes place during the online search process.

Another study focused on the problem description activities and utterances initiated by expert intermediaries, information seekers, and retrieval systems. A third study attempted to understand the intermediary's use of subject knowledge by analyzing transcriptions of search interviews. The ultimate goal of all of the studies in the project was to obtain a sufficiently clear idea of the problem-solving and definition activities of intermediaries to simulate those activities with a computer.

Online search interactions were taped and the participants were also interviewed for their thoughts on what had transpired. Everything was transcribed and the entire protocol was then analyzed for utterances which served one of the ten search functions described in a model based on a task analysis of online searchers. Each function category includes activities designed to develop a clearer representation of the problem at hand. The MONSTRAT function categories cover the following aspects of the information interaction:

Information Search Functions

Belkin and Windel (1984)

Problem Mode (PM)
User Model (UM)
Dialog Mode (DM)
Problem State (PS)
Problem Description (PD)
Relevant World Builder (RWB)
Retrieval Strategies (RS)
Response Generator (RG)
Explanation (EX)
Secondary Communication (SC)

In the problem description study, utterances of both the intermediary and the information seeker were examined, and each utterance relating to one of the above categories was noted. Utterances relating to problem description were subjected to a more extended analysis. The results of the detailed study of problem description utterances led Belkin and his colleagues to the following conclusions:

1. Problem description activities are most consistently initiated by the intermediary, not the information seeker or the retrieval system.
2. Problem description is a multistep process involving identifying the problem type, specifying a topic, establishing constraints, and, possibly, identifying a problem context.
3. The mode of interaction for this function typically involves the intermediary questioning the information seeker.

The detailed analysis of all utterances associated with the search interview led the investigators to conclude that intermediaries and online systems are only capable of offering limited assistance to information seekers and that the range and depth of human interaction is highly constrained and does not even address many of the problem-solving processes posited as components of the search process. Another conclusion: the problem description function is largely based on the intermediary's schema for representing problem stereotypes and an effective problem description must arise from a dialog between humans or between a human and a machine. The searches with the greatest potential for success are those which are highly interactive.

Studies of Searcher Attributes and Behavior

Saracevic (1988) and his colleagues also did a systematic study of the cognitive aspects of the online search process. Like the studies of Belkin and his colleagues, the study focused on both users and searchers from a problem-solving perspective. Search problems were analyzed in terms of the level of problem definition, the client's intentions, the client's knowledge of the problem domain, and the client's expectations from the information system — i.e., the likelihood that the information system would be able to deliver the information being sought. Data were gathered by administering separate Likert scales to users. Users were asked to indicate the degree of problem definition, the specificity of their research, their level of background knowledge, and their level of expectation.

Another dimension of the search process which was investigated was the questions posed by users. Questions were analyzed in terms of their constraints (limits) and structure. Questions were also classified in terms of their domain, clarity, specificity, complexity, and inclusion of implied concepts. Data for this dimension were supplied by users and classifiers, who all worked with the same scales.

Perhaps the most interesting part of this study focused on searcher attributes and behavior. Searchers were tested for language ability, logical ability, and learning style using standardized psychological instruments. Online searching experience was another variable considered by the study and was measured by a questionnaire administered to searchers in the study.

The final dimension of the study was searches themselves and items retrieved. Searches were analyzed in terms of three subprocesses: **question analysis**, **strategy formulation**, and **search execution**. All iterations of each search were recorded and a transcript of the entire interaction between the searcher and the machine was made available. However this study did not focus on the presearch interview, clients were not present when searches were being done, and the interaction between client and searcher was not a dimension of the study. Items retrieved were studied in terms of relevance, recall, precision, and overlap.

This was a massive study with numerous conclusions. Those most closely related to knowledge acquisition include:

- Relevance of results was better for problems which users identified as being well defined.
- Relevance and precision were higher for problems where users expected to find existing public information.
- Users' level of internal knowledge of the problem domain had no impact on relevance or precision.
- Certain constraints on questions (language limited to English and years covered) increased relevance and precision.
- Users' expectations of finding pertinent information tended to be greater than searchers' expectations, as did users' internal knowledge about search problems
- Searchers seem able to classify and distinguish questions without problems.
- Searchers who scored high on language ability (measured by a word association test) were more likely to obtain high levels of relevance.
- Searchers' logical ability as measured by the symbolic reasoning test had no impact on search performance.
- There is wide variety in the strategies different searchers apply to the same problem and surprisingly little overlap among results.
- Searchers whose learning style emphasized abstraction rather than concreteness tended to achieve better relevance and recall.

What are the implications of these findings for the design of intelligent retrieval systems? Systems should attempt to elicit well-defined problems. Problems where users expect to find information are more tractable. Establishing constraints on search problems (especially limits on language and time period) will improve results.

Perhaps certain constraints should be built into the system by default. The ability to classify problems is probably important. The capability to develop a problem context is important. The successful system would most likely include a problem classification and context-building module. A system with linguistic abilities and the ability to reason in abstract terms is more likely to simulate the traits of successful searchers. The relationship between ability to perform well on a word association test and search success argues in favor of incorporating access to a thesaurus or other syndetic structure in an expert system for information retrieval. The ability to apply a variety of strategies to a single problem will most likely improve results. Items which are retrieved by more than one strategy may be more relevant than items which were retrieved by only one strategy.

The studies by Belkin and Windel and those of Saracevic and colleagues are similar in that they both focus on the search process as a problem-solving process. However, they are different because the work by Belkin tends to focus on the interpersonal interaction between client and searcher while the work of Saracevic tends to focus on the internal cognitive states of the searcher and the client. More research in both areas is needed as well as studies that attempt to focus on internal respresentations and attributes along with communicative behavior.

Automated Knowledge Acquisition

Knowledge acquisition is one of the most fascinating aspects of the knowledge engineering process. There are techniques which are intended to facilitate the articulation of expert knowledge by human experts. There are also techniques in which machines are used to extract expert knowledge by analyzing examples provided by experts and inducing the underlying knowledge which is being applied to come up with those examples. Parts of the protocol analysis process have also been automated.

The most famous of automated knowledge acquisition systems is **TEIRESIAS** (named after the blind seer in the Oedipus myth) which was developed by Randall Davis (Davis and Lenat, 1982, p.227) as part of the MYCIN project at Stanford University. TEIRESIAS was designed to aid in the knowledge acquisition tasks of creating and updating large knowledge bases. The program helps the user debug MYCIN's knowledge base of production rules by evaluating individual rules as an expert user interacts with the system.

This is done by means of a focused dialogue. As the dialogue proceeds, the human expert identifies errors in the computer's reasoning. The program finds the line of reasoning or rule that caused the error, presents it to the expert, and allows him or her to modify the knowledge base to correct the faulty reasoning that caused the error. TEIRESIAS maintains meta-knowledge about its own functioning in the form of rule models and schemas. For example, it knows what types of values are typically related to one another in MYCIN rules. Davis's program is also capable of maintaining expectations about the dialogue between it and the human expert. Meta-rules are used to determine which sets of equally plausible rules — which chunks of knowledge — to try next.

Michie (1985) contends that the major problem of knowledge acquisition is the process of getting human experts to articulate their expertise. He hypothesizes that as knowledge becomes more complex, it becomes increasingly difficult to articulate and raises the possibility that the most complex expertise is intuitive in nature and essentially inarticulable.

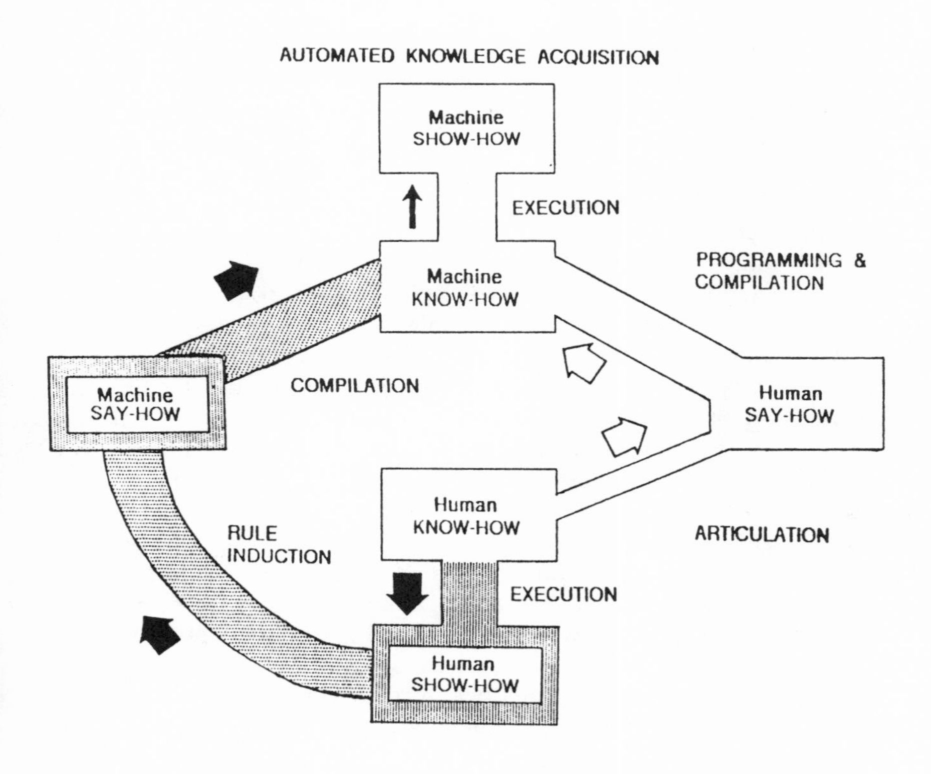

Figure 5.2. Michie's map of overall problem (from Michie, 1986a, used with permission)

Michie therefore proposes machine induction as the most efficient mode of knowledge acquisition. Induction would be used to build the initial version of the knowledge base, which an expert would then be able to edit. Before we describe machine induction techniques, let us differentiate between deduction and induction.

Deduction is the form of reasoning which allows us to derive facts from rules — to move from the general to the specific. For example, if we have a rule which states that all directories contain addresses, and we know that *Standard and Poor's Corporate Register* is a directory, then we can deduce with a high level of certainty that *Standard and Poor's Corporate Register* contains addresses.

Induction, on the other hand is the form of reasoning which allows us to derive rules from facts — to move from specifics to generalities. For example, given this set of facts:

Title	Category	Contains
Standard and Poor's Register	directory	addresses
Business Periodicals Index	index	citations
Palgrave's Dictionary of Econ.	dictionary	definitions
Ward's Automotive Directory	directory	addresses
Encyclopedia of Assns.	directory	addresses
Predicasts F&S Index	index	citations

we can derive rules such as: If the category is directory then the title contains addresses. It should be apparent that induction is less certain than deduction and that the number of examples has a lot to do with the reliability of rules that can be induced. We might use the same set of examples to induce a rule that states: If the category is index then the title contains citations, or a rule that states: If the category is dictionary then the title contains definitions. However, since there are fewer examples from which to derive our rule about dictionaries, we wouldn't be as certain about its validity. Palgrave also includes citations. Yet a rule that states: If the category is dictionary then the title contains citations just wouldn't make very much sense. Palgrave can also be viewed as an encyclopedia, and if the example relating to that specific title and the fact that it contains citations categorized it as an encyclopedia, then the resulting rule would make more sense. So the quality of induced rules is determined not only by the number of examples but by the categories used in examples.

Ross Quinlan (1979) developed a machine induction technique known as the **ID3** knowledge induction algorithm. It is probably the most famous method for using a machine to induce rules. The ID3 algorithm is designed not only to generate rules from examples but to recognize unusual cases and use them to generate new rules.

When given a set of "training instances," the algorithm selects a random subset which is put into a table of examples. The column headers on the table represent the categories into which the specific variables in the table belong. The last column represents the values that will go into the right-hand side of the rules derived from the table. Examples to examine for new rules are determined by identifying examples that don't match rules which have already been induced.

The ID3 algorithm derives rules from examples by focusing on exceptions to already established rules. Here's how it works:

- A "working set" of examples is selected from a long list of examples and relationships between conditions are identified, moving from broad to narrow categories; the links established in the decision tree derived from the initial "working set" are used to develop the first set of rules.
- The remaining examples are then examined and exceptions to the rules are identified.
- A new "working set" is built from the current working set and the exceptions identified.
- This process continues until all of the examples can be matched to an existing rule — that is, until there are no longer any exceptions to the rules (because each exception has become a new rule)

Machine induction, because it is relatively straightforward, is in widespread use on micocomputer-based expert system shells. To get rules from examples requires a large number of fairly clear-cut examples. Machine induction seems like an especially useful technique for representing knowledge about sources themselves. Building the knowledge base would involve collecting examples of sources along with the questions they had answered, and putting the information about sources, questions, and answers into a table. Given a large enough set of examples, some rules about which sources answer which questions should be easy enough to generate. Compared to other forms of knowledge acquisition, it could be relatively easily implemented and it could take advantage of existing machine-readable databases.

Michie (1985) identifies opacity as one of the major problems of induction rule bases. Complex rule bases generated from large example sets tend to be inaccessible even to the experts who provided the examples. Another problem has to do with the unreliability of rules derived from an insufficient number of examples.

Articulation techniques like interviews and protocol analysis are more analogous to formal teaching. Knowledge acquisition by inducing rules from examples is more analogous to an apprenticeship in which the apprentice learns by observing the expert as the expert deals with individual problems. It isn't always necessary (or possible) for the expert to explain himself to the apprentice. The apprentice will learn by inducing general principles from a large number of specific observations.

Another way to get knowledge into a system is by deriving it from the real world. This method is typically used in expert systems which are connected to sensors and charged with monitoring events, for example, an earthquake prediction system. This technique would be difficult to apply to reference and retrieval systems which are primarily advisory in nature. But there are some possibilities. Citation indexes are a good example of an already established technique for deriving new knowledge from events in the real world. Whenever one author cites another, a decision is being made — a decision about the relationship between the two documents. Citation indexes already contain massive amounts of real world knowledge. "Relevance feedback" techniques (Oddy, 1977; Salton, 1983) also offer some possibilities. Inducing rules from examples provided by users is another way of exploiting real world events to acquire knowledge.

Michie (1984) recommends the use of induction systems in a "knowledge refinery." The purpose of Michie's knowledge refinery would be: "to get knowledge into the machine; to test it; to debug it; to fill gaps; to extend it; to modify it."

Michie (1984) identifies the following requirements for a knowledge refinery:

1. knowledge-engineering software able to make inferences from data supplied, and to retrace and display the lines of reasoning
2. induction modules able to generate rules from examples
3. a good software development environment, e.g., **UNIX** or **INTERLISP**
4. trained knowledge engineers familiar with the above tools
5. one or more experts....

In the library of the future, what we now call the cataloging department may very well assume some of the functions of Michie's knowledge refinery.

Knowledge engineering, whether automated or not, usually involves sorting things into categories. Induction is no exception. The headers at the top of the columns in an induction table represent the categories of things which must be addressed by the rules the induction algorithm will yield. Some likely candidates for a reference system: types of sources, subjects of queries, and types of users.

Repertory Grids

Saracevic and his colleagues relied heavily on the use of psychological measurement techniques in their study of the attributes of searchers. Another interesting use of psychological measurement is the **repertory grid technique**. This technique, which has its origins in the **personal construct psychology** of George Kelly (1955), has been applied to knowledge engineering by Shaw and Gaines (1987) and Boose (1985). It is now one of the most promising methods for machine-assisted knowledge acquisition.

Kelly believes that people organize their knowledge about the world as primitive, bipolar ideas called **constructs**. Constructs can be facts, opinions, feelings, or even heuristics. For example, the traffic crossing construct of most people has two poles. On one pole is the idea: GREEN LIGHT - WALK. On the other pole is the idea: RED LIGHT - WAIT. Constructs are models which are compared to the real world and revised as events dictate. If a person visited a place where cars stopped on green and went on red, it wouldn't be long before she either got hit by a car or revised her construct about traffic lights.

The sum of an individuals constructs about a particular aspect of the world form that individual's **belief system**. An individual's belief system may be organized as a group of constructs known as a **repertory grid**.

The process of building a repertory grid might go something like this. First place a group of reference sources from a domain on a table. Pick three. Ask an expert to put the two which are most alike together and to identify their similarity. Then ask the expert to identify their difference by identifying the quality opposite the quality the two share, or by naming what it is about the excluded item that differentiates it. Each of the individual titles selected for analysis is known as an **element**.

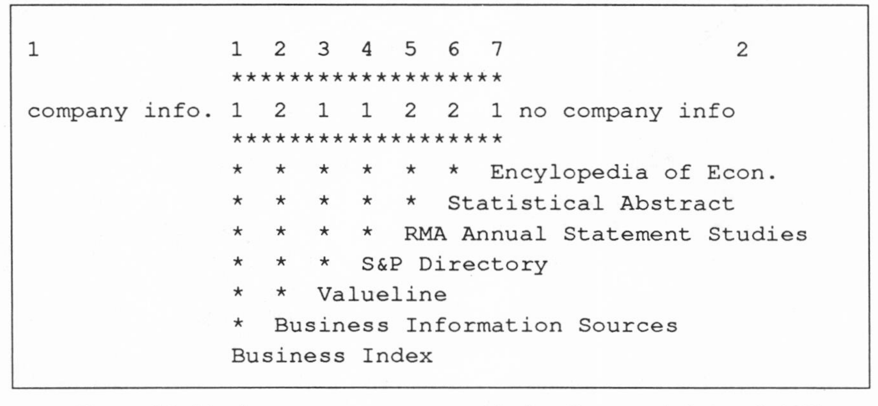

Figure 5.3. Single construct repertory grid after Shaw and Gaines (1987)

```
1               1  2  3  4  5  6  7        2
                ******************
company info.   1  2  1  1  2  2  1 no company info
citations       1  1  2  2  2  1  1 no citations
numeric data    2  2  1  1  1  1  2 no numeric data
                ******************
                *  *  *  *  *  *  Encylopedia of Econ.
                *  *  *  *  *  Statistical Abstract
                *  *  *  *  RMA Annual Statement Studies
                *  *  *  S&P Directory
                *  *  Valueline
                *  Business Information Sources
                Business Index
```

Figure 5.4. Repertory grid with 3 constructs after Shaw and Gaines (1987)

```
1               1  2  3  4  5  6  7        5
                ******************
company info.   2  4  1  1  5  4  5 no company info
citations       1  1  5  5  5  4  2 no citations
numeric data    5  5  1  4  1  1  4 no numeric data
                ******************
                *  *  *  *  *  *  Encylopedia of Econ.
                *  *  *  *  *  Statistical Abstract
                *  *  *  *  RMA Annual Statement Studies
                *  *  *  S&P Directory
                *  *  Valueline
                *  Business Information Sources
                Business Index
```

Figure 5.5. Repertory grid with constructs rated on a 5-point scale after Shaw and Gaines (1987)

Each of the characteristics considered is known as a construct. Constructs are identified by placing opposite elements at opposite poles. The process of developing a repertory grid would involve repeating the process over and over until all of the attributes of the sources contained in the expert's belief system had been identified. As each construct is identified, it can be placed on a grid with other contructs for same group of elements.

Elements can be placed at one pole or the other (Figure 5.3) or a scale can be used to indicate position of an element within a construct (Figure 5.5). For example, consider the **numeric data construct**. *S&P Directory* has a value of 4, indicating that while it has some numeric data (otherwise its value would be 5) it does not tend to fall on the "contains numeric data" pole of the expert's construct. A repertory grid can be used to measure congruity of different sources by covering a number of different constructs (Figures 5.4 and 5.5) A grid could also be used to "fit" sources to problems.

Construct elicitation and analysis have been automated. High-end workstations (what's new?) have been the vehicles for the most impressive efforts in the field. But we expect to see repertory grid systems along with other knowledge acquisition tools move into the micro arena. This technique also lends itself to building knowledge bases from the knowledge of multiple experts by establishing a grid based on the constructs of each expert and then merging the grids with one another. Once a series of grids have been identified, they can be manipulated with powerful analytical tools, including some which are capable of generating rules (Shaw, 1987 and Boose, 1985). The problem with this technique (along with many others, including machine induction) is that it forces a single knowledge representation formalism upon a complex body of knowledge.

Conclusion

We have defined the process of knowledge engineering and described some of the more interesting methods for knowledge acquisition. We know that it is important to separate the knowledge acquisition process from the knowledge representation process. It is also important to avoid letting the formalism which will be used for representing knowledge guide the identification of expert knowledge. It is better to gather the knowledge first and then develop a model for organizing and representing it.

Finally it must be noted that knowledge acquisition should be an ongoing process which doesn't stop when a system is first implemented. Maintaining, debugging, and updating the knowledge base are as important as initial development. A knowledge base is very much like a database or a reference book; it can become dated very quickly. The beauty of expert system technology is the modularity of knowledge bases. As new "chunks" of knowledge within the domain are identified, they must be added to the knowledge base if the system is to remain effective. Knowledge can be added or removed without affecting other knowledge in the system. A knowledge base is built in separate increments.

Recommended Reading

In addition to the items cited in the chapter, the following titles are recommended. The knowledge acquisition process is covered well in three recent books, Kidd (1987), Hart (1986) and Slatter (1987), as well as in a series of special issues of the journal *International Journal of Man-*

Machine Studies (vol 26, nos. 1, 2, 4 and vol. 27, no 2. 1987). Brachman and Levesque (1985) have gathered together an excellent collection of readings on knowledge representation, and the book edited by Bernold (1986) includes papers on different aspects of the knowledge engineering process. Michie is the most forward thinking writer on knowledge engineering topics. Forsyth and Rada (1986) consider machine learning within an information retrieval context. From a library point of view, Belkin is one of the leading researchers on knowledge engineering, and his extensive writings are recommended.

6
Knowledge Representation and Information Retrieval

In developing any expert system, the knowledge engineer is necessarily constrained by the knowledge representation techniques supported by the development tool being used. A good understanding of the data structures involved can avoid frustration and result in a better product.

Knowledge representation implies some systematic way of codifying what is known about some domain. A representation of knowledge should render that knowledge easily accessible and easy to apply via more or less natural mechanisms. No matter what notational system is used, a computer must ultimately be able to store and process the codified knowledge. The following section addresses the knowledge representation criteria which should be considered for library and information retrieval applications.

Criteria for Evaluating Knowledge Representation Schemes

Logical Adequacy

The scheme must have the power to make the distinctions between the general and the specific. For example, if we want to represent the idea that every drug has some undesirable side-effect as well as the more specific fact that aspirin aggravates ulcers, we must be able to use variables of quantification, as is done in predicate calculus. For all (X), if X is a drug, then there exists a Y, such that Y is an undesirable side-effect associated with X.

Heuristic Power

Representations must be constructed to solve problems. Remember the methods discussed in Chapter Two. By formalizing the structures and reducing the variety and richness of natural language to patterns or predicates, we gain considerably in heuristic power. Heuristic power makes it easier to bring the right knowledge to bear at the right time.

Notational Convenience

Most expert systems require the encoding of substantial amounts of knowledge, and this task will not be an enviable one if the conventions of the representation language are too complicated and inflexible. The expert system shell selected should provide an adequate software development environment. Users should expect an adequate full-screen editing capability, an English-like interface that is easy to follow, detailed help messages, and debugging tools in a windowing environment. For an inexpensive example, either **Turbo Prolog** or **First Class** will provide the beginner with a well-designed environment (Ruth, 1988; Borland, 1986).

Inheritance and Properties

Any robust representation formalism must provide a satisfactory mechanism for the inheritance of properties from one class to another. As soon as humans determine that an object is an instance of a class of objects or events, then they draw upon deeper knowledge associated with the class that can be applied to the object under specific scrutiny.

To give a very simple example: Let us assume that we are discussing a pet bird called Tweeter. We know that Tweeter is an instance of the class "canary," and therefore that he is a song bird, lays eggs, flies, has feathers, eats seeds, is yellow in color, of a certain size range, etc. Encoding all such information in the form of rules results in hopelessly cumbersome and unwieldy systems, particularly if no provision is made to inherit from a class to an instance of that class (Charniak & McDermott, 1986).

Contextual Information

We almost always depend on knowledge of the context and general world knowledge to communicate. How to add this type of knowledge to any expert system remains controversial, but all agree that a system of rules does not provide an adequate mechanism for providing contextual information.

Schank makes this point very well with his study of language-generating programs (Schank, 1984). The little, computer-generated stories about Joe Bear make the point very clear. One of the stories begins with Joe Bear threatening Irving with bodily harm if he would not tell him where some food could be found. Even though Irving tells him that there is a bee hive on a nearby tree, Joe Bear continues to threaten him. Reason: Irving had not been programmed to understand that bee hives contain honey.

In the next version of the story, Joe Bear again threatens Irving, who tells him that there is a bee hive on a nearby tree. Joe Bear ambles over and eats the bee hive! Clearly, an additional piece of common knowledge was missing from Joe Bear's database. No one had remembered to tell him that bee hives are food containers. They are not edible.

Numerous efforts have been made to provide this sort of deep understanding through the use of property lists, semantic nets, frames or scripts. In each case, the knowledge representation technique involves linking two or more records together with pointers. The more we attempt to provide the needed context, the larger and more unwieldy the knowledge bases become. It is almost impossible to anticipate all the possible contingencies that can occur, even in a simple act such as visiting a restaurant. For this reason, most succesful expert systems today have focused on in-depth analysis of a narrow, well-structured and specific subject domain. Susanne M. Humphrey's **MedIndex System** for indexing medical journals is a viable example (see below).

Ability to Handle Fuzzy Logic and/or Probability Weightings

In many situations requiring the advice of an expert, there is no clear-cut, simple solution. Rather the expert will draw on his experience and training to determine the best of a number of suboptimal solutions. These need to be ranked according to some consistent weighting scheme and the system should deal with the issue of combined weights. There are both formal and informal methods of handling uncertainty.

Support for a Formal Bayesian Statistical Approach

The Bayesian approach is a mathematically rigorous technique but it requires prior knowledge of the probabilities involved in order to make the calculations. It cannot distinguish between the absence of belief and disbelief because the hypothesis requires the constant relation that the probability of A added to the probability of not A adds up to 1, which can be expressed as the formula: $P(A) + P(1\text{-}A) = 1$(Lindley, 1984).

Support for Informal Methods

The **Dempster-Shafer method** provides a way to measure subjective uncertainty. This technique develops a lower and upper probability for a particular subset of results. The lower value is called the belief function because it represents the conservative amount of probability. The upper probability implies the optimistic amount of probability and is also called plausibility (Shafer, 1976).

Belief functions are another approach to handling uncertainty. **Confidence factors** are used to indicate the degree of certainty the expert has in a given outcome arising from a specified set of circumstances.

This method does not measure the statistical probability but rather the subjective degree of confidence the expert has that certain conditions will yield certain results. Belief functions can be tied in with the interactions between one's value hierarchies and views. For example: MYCIN is an expert system designed to diagnose and recommend therapies for bacterial infections in the blood.

In MYCIN the confidence factor (CF), a number between -1 and 1, indicates the strength of association between the symptom and the cause and also captures how important it is that a diagnosis be considered in therapy selection. A series of rules have been set up to clarify how to handle multiple, conflicting confidence factors (Nau, 1983). A number of other systems have developed similar solutions to the problem of how to handle uncertainty.

Using the MYCIN system approach to uncertainty, let us assume we are trying to establish a fact X, and there are two rules in the system that allow us to conclude X.

Rules:

1. If E and F and G are true then conclude X is true (CF= .8)
2. If R and S and T are true then conclude X is true (CF= .7)

We are given the following facts with the associated CFs.

E	.5	R	.8
F	.3	S	.9
G	.6	T	.7

If we had a CF of 1 that E, F and G are true we can use rule 1 to conclude X with a CF of .8, but clearly we are not very confident of any of the conditions. The rule applied in the case of a conjunction is to take the minimum of the CFs involved.

CF (E) = .5
CF (F) = .3 ===> MIN = .3
CF (G) = .6

Then, using a second rule that the CF for the conclusion produced by a rule is the CF of its premise (.3) multiplied by the CF of the rule (.8) we calculate the CF for the conclusion X

===> .8 x .3 = .24

We repeat the process for R, S, T where X has a CF of .7, using rule 2.

CF (R) = .8
CF (S) = .7 ===> MIN = .7 ===> .7 x .7 = .49
CF (T) = .9

As a result of these calculations we have two results for X, namely .24 and .49. The rule is that the CF for a fact produced as the conclusion of one or more rules is the maximum of the CFs produced by the rules yielding that conclusion.

The maximum of .24 and .49 is .49, and this is declared the CF of X given the conditions described.

Fuzzy Logic

Yet another way of representing uncertain knowledge is **fuzzy logic**. Fuzzy logic was originally proposed in 1965 by Lofti Zadeh, a professor of computer science at the University of California-Berkeley, in an effort to model concepts such as "tall," where there is considerable fuzziness (Zadeh, 1979). Fuzzy logic works by creating partial memberships in a "fuzzy set." If Bob were 7' 2", he would have a 1.00 membership in the set of tall people — that is, full membership. If he were 6 feet he might have a .8 membership, fairly complete and if he were 5' 2", he might have a .05 membership, that is very slight.

Fuzzy logic has been very succesfully incorporated in a number of significant expert systems. The University of Vienna has developed a fuzzy system called **Cardiac-2** to help doctors diagnose cardiac problems. Fuzzy logic is also being used in pattern recognition, enabling electronic eyes to recognize alphabetic characters much faster than prior methods had been able to accomplish that task (Scripps-Howard, 1989).

Truth Maintenance/Nonmonotonic Reasoning

If an expert system has to deal with facts that change over time, it must also have the ability to handle nonmonotonic reasoning. A patron who comes in with an ill-defined search strategy will in many cases modify her request as she begins to discover what is available. The system must be able to withdraw or modify search strategies based on the initial request as the patron changes her strategy. Unfortunately, many of the less expensive, PC-based expert system shells make no provision for truth maintenance (nonmonotonic reasoning) (King, 1987).

Ability to Interface with More Conventional Data Representation Techniques

There is no question that in order for expert systems to be truly useful in libraries, they must be fully integrated with current library automation. They must run on equipment that is compatible with existing machines and must be able to interface with conventional databases already in use.

This means that it is not very practical to buy dedicated LISP machines designed for stand-alone systems, and issues of compatability and integration will be key factors in the purchase decision. More and more we are seeing expert system components integrated into very large systems that also use a variety of more conventional data processing techniques, such as relational database management systems.

In this chapter, we will evaluate knowledge representation techniques offered by the more sophisticated expert systems shells on the market. But since in the future it will be imperative that knowledge and data representation schemes be compatible with one another, we will also have a look at the more conventional data structures currently in use in library systems.

Other Knowledge Representation Considerations

Liebowitz (1988, p.50) identifies these additional criteria to consider when selecting a knowledge representation scheme.

- **Pre-existing format of the knowledge**. For instance if the heuristics are being expressed in the form of rules by the expert when he is explaining the task to the knowledge engineer, then it is easier to leave them in that form.
- **Type of classification desired**. If it is predominantly categorical then production rules are best suited to the task. Most of the decisions should be yes/no decisions.
- **Context dependence** of the inferences required. If a lot of context is required, then it is probably better to go with frames which provides a structured way to show the context of a knowledge structure.
- **Ability to modularize knowledge**. A robust formalism will permit the knowledge engineer to represent domain knowledge in a series of discrete modules.

While it is a relatively simple matter to build a small prototype with somewhat less than fifty rules, it often proves much more difficult to scale it up satisfactorily. By the time the system has grown to over 1,000 rules, it is very difficult to manage the firing order of the rules in any coherent way and more often than not the project is out of control.

Two possible modularization techniques that can be used either together or separately are:

- **Decompose the problem** into smaller subproblems that can be managed more easily and then provide the metarules to control the flow of decision making. (For more details see Chapter Ten.)
- Use more **robust knowledge representation techniques**, such as the frame-based systems or object-oriented programming languages.

Knowledge Representation Techniques

There are three major ways of representing knowledge in an expert system: **predicate calculus**, **production rules**, and **structured objects** which have been referred to in different contexts as **frames**, **scripts**, and/or **semantic networks**. Some of the more powerful expert system shells, such as **KEE**, **ART**, and **KRL** include several knowledge representation techniques as well as adding graphics interfaces, all of which result in a much more powerful environment for developing robust systems.

It should also be noted that some of the larger expert systems have in fact been rewritten in conventional programming languages such as C, because these languages are more efficient and require fewer system resources.

Logic-Based Systems

In Chapter 2 several small, logic-based programs were discussed in some detail and the importance of using standardized phrasings to create patterns was stressed. The idea is to develop stylized patterns or **formulas** that will help to reduce the number of different ways to say essentially the same thing. It is a form of vocabulary control.

Another characteristic of logic-based languages is that all formulas in an internal representation must be unambiguous. A formula is simply asserting a fact about one or more entities. In PROLOG, everything must be explicit and uniquely identified.

It is not sufficient to say "the user borrowed the book," or "he borrowed it." Instead a more stylized form is used: "borrowed user-21 book-223."

Also important is the ordering. In English we can say "the user borrowed the book" or in passive voice, "the book was borrowed by the user." In PROLOG once the order is established then it must be followed consistently. This can become crucial in cases like the English sentence "Mary is Joan's mother," where the possessive case is used to make the relationship clear. In PROLOG we rely on word order to determine who is the mother in "Mother Mary Joan."

In order to express fully the informational content of a single English sentence, it is often necessary to use more than one predicate or formula. Using our earlier example we could elaborate and say, "The mystery novel that was set in the Middle East in the 20th century was borrowed by Mrs Jones."

This would be translated into:

name user-21 mrs-Jones.
borrowed user-21 book-223
instance book-223 mystery-novel
setting book-223 middle-east 20th Century

Deduction

All logic-based languages depend on the ability to draw inferences to derive new facts from those that are given. There are many kinds of inference, the best known of which is deduction. When we derive deductions from true premises we are guaranteed a true conclusion.

All students are mortal
Hector is a student
==> Hector is mortal

The formal system for expressing these inferences is known as predicate calculus because we are calculating the truth of the propositions and what new information can be derived from them.

To make up a formula, we select a predicate to indicate what the function represents, e.g., "borrowed," "setting." Each predicate requires one or more **arguments**. The number of arguments varies according to the need and is described as the **arity** of the predicate.

For example, "setting book-223 Middle-East 20th Century" has an arity of 3, while "borrowed user-223 book 271" and "instance book-223 mystery-novel" both have an arity of 2.

Each of the arguments to a predicate must be filled by a **term**. Terms can be of several different types. **Constant** symbols are used for known information, such as Middle-East, 20th-Century, book-223, etc. Variables, on the other hand, are place holders as in Mother (Ancestor, Person). As the system searches for solutions it will replace the variables with appropriate names derived from the inputs. Functions can also be considered as terms and can be passed as arguments to a predicate; for example, "brother richard (grandfather Person henry)." The system will first find who is Henry's grandfather and then select whichever of Richard's brothers fits the condition given.

In order to be able to derive conclusions from our formulas, our system will also need an **if (condition) then (action)** reasoning capacity. "**If** (age User < 12) **then** (refer User juvenile-literature)." This, of course, implies the use of **connectives**. "**And**" and "**or**" are used to specify more than one condition. "The man must be tall and good looking." "The woman shall be a great cook or rich enough to hire one or both." A "**not**" allows for the exclusion of certain categories: "and not a chemistry major.."

Truth tables and formal logic are used to derive the truth or falsehood of the propositions or axioms being input to the system. Some method also has to be added to allow for **quantification**. It is all very well to say, "If Clyde is an elephant, then Clyde is gray" but this does not permit us to generalize about all elephants.

To do this, two quantifiers are available:

- **universal quantifiers**. These indicate that the statement is true for all instances of X. "All elephants are gray" is formally expressed as: "For all (X), (color X gray) if (instance X elephant)"
- **existential quantifiers**. These are used to convey that there exists some X that meets the given condition.

  "Exists (X), Student (X)

  "paper (X), Exists Y (student Y; wrote Y,X)

This is a very brief and simplified introduction to predicate calculus, which is at the heart of all logic-based languages. For a much more in-depth discussion of the theory, the user is referred to Charniak & McDermott (1986) or other logic texts.

Predicate calculus provides us with rules from making deductions. How does it work? One starts with facts that are known and deduces new facts using rules of inference until at the end one has deduced the fact one wanted. The problem is in a large system, one can go on and on generating useless and meaningless new facts without apparent progress toward the fact one wants.

There are several different kinds of inference that can be made. **Deduction** is considered "**legal inference**" because, given true axioms, the inferences drawn will also be true.

Abduction

Unfortunately, a great deal of the common sense knowledge that enables us to function in our world cannot be obtained using formal logic. Humans often resort to **abduction**.

Given: B is true
and Knowing: if A then B
Infer: A

For example let us take the case:

Given: feels-awful (Jim)
and Knowing: for all (X) if has-hepatitis (X)
then feels-awful (X)
Infer: has-hepatitis (Jim)

While not permissible in formal logic, abduction is a very legitimate and widely practiced problem-solving tactic. We use this technique to make informed "guesses." Then we test our conclusion to see it is correct. This tactic enables us to make progress in solving a problem when little is known with certainty, but a course of action must be selected anyway. There is no guarantee that we will not be led to the wrong conclusion. For example in the case cited above, if there is any likelihood that the patient has hepatitis, the doctor will test for it.

Induction

Another useful technique is induction. Here we study many cases and attempt to derive general principles from these examples. PROLOG was not designed to deal with induction, but a number of packages have been developed that do so quite adequately. The First Class package is typical of these and is based on Quinlan's ID3 algorithm (1984).

For example:

canary(1) is yellow; canary(2) is yellow; canary(...) is yellow;
canary(n) is yellow.

From these examples we conclude:

for all (X) if instance(X, canary)
color (X, yellow)

Production Rules

When dealing with human "experts," it is important to try to select the approach that is most natural to the expert. For instance, if we were to ask an expert how to determine if a person has a cold, he would probably respond: "If the patient has a runny nose, watery eyes, and a sore throat there is a good possibility that she is afflicted with a cold. But on the other hand it might also be an allergy."

The most natural way to encode this heuristic is as a set of IF- THEN rules. Notice also that the expert is using a measure of probability. He is expressing the possibility that if it isn't a cold, it might be an allergy. The decision is not clear cut.

Production rule systems are one of the most popular knowledge representation methods in expert system shells. A production rules system has the following components:

- A **global database** or **working memory** in which the production rules operate. The database maintained in working memory may range from a simple list of facts to a complex relational indexed file structure.
- The **production rules** phrased as follows:

  IF [condition], THEN [action]
- The **control system** which controls the order in which production rules are fired and resolves conflicts if more than one rule is eligible for firing.

Advantages of Production Rules

There are several advantages to using production rules.

- They are a natural expression of **what-to-do** knowledge (i.e., procedural knowledge).
- All knowledge for a problem is uniformly represented as rules.
- Rules are comprehensible units of knowledge.
- Rules are modular units of knowledge, which can easily be added to or deleted from.
- Rules can be used to represent **how-to-do** knowledge (i.e., **meta-knowledge**). This is done with rules about the rules. A metarule is a production rule that controls the application of object-level knowledge.

Disadvantages of Production Rule Systems

On the other hand, production rule systems have a number of significant disadvantages. For one thing, there is no mechanism for showing context dependency. And the globally enforced conflict resolution strategy (mea or lex) will often cause some strange side effects in the firing order of the rules.

There is a good deal more to writing an effective rule-based program than formulating a set of rules that capture the generalizations of the expert and encoding them in a production rule language. Unless the rules have been written with the conflict resolution strategy used by the interpreter kept constantly in mind, often the results will not be as expected. It is usually difficult to predict the outcome of competition between the pattern-directed modules for the attention of the interpreter at each recognize-act cycle. This becomes a critical consideration when adding new rules to the system.

Production rule systems fail to take advantage of whatever explicit structure the domain possesses in terms of taxonomic, part-whole, or cause-effect relationships that hold between objects and between classes of objects. No discipline at all is imposed on the programmer, or on the ordering of the rules. This becomes a major problem as the system grows in size and complexity, resulting in very slow and inefficient systems. With each cycle of the control program, an exhaustive search is performed through all the rules. It becomes almost impossible to ensure consistent performance.

The end-user rapidly loses the ability to follow the reasoning or a trace of the execution as the system increases in size and complexity. Another of the shortcomings of the rule-based systems — particularly MYCIN, used to diagnose over 600 diseases — is that while they can draw conclusions when specific conditions are found to be true, the underlying explanations for such relationships are not encoded. The knowledge being represented is **shallow knowledge**.

Frame-Based Knowledge Representation

One of the important issues in the development of expert systems has been how to connect related pieces of information together in a meaningful way. If I am describing a particular reference book, I should be able to access all the relevant data in one cluster. Regardless of what diagramming technique is used to conceptualize these links, they are all based on a form of indexing. When we find Tweeter in the system, we want all of the information about Tweeter to be accessible from there without having to churn through the entire database looking for other references to Tweeter. This has been accomplished in most systems by adding indexing schemes to the predicate calculus. In this way we can obtain the best of both worlds.

Frames are useful in categorizing knowledge when that knowledge has some underlying structure. If the knowledge can be related to a set of objects or concepts, then at least a portion of the facts contained in the knowledge base can be clustered around those objects or concepts.

For example in a knowledge base dealing with automobiles, frames would permit the clustering of knowledge around each type of automobile. You could look up the information on all Chevrolets without having to scan the entire database. In a knowledge base for reference books, all reference books share certain common characteristics, but then they can be subdivided. A user with a question on biographies would want to search only the subclass of biographical reference tools. This class could be further subdivided into contemporary and historical, American and foreign.

Slots and Fillers

Frames can be considered as collections of related facts that can be treated as a single unit. In one sense, a frame can be considered a record with fields or slots that can be filled in with specific values; e.g., a student transcript will contain a slot for the name, address, phone, and status as well as the grades recorded for each class and the quality point average.

One can use the slots to describe the properties of a given object or class of objects, and in most systems it is possible to specify the range of permissible values in a slot. For instance, a color slot can be restricted to a list — red, brown, blue, or black — or a type such as decimal or logical, or to one of three options — true, false, or unknown. One can specify maximums or minimums.

In some systems, the user is also offered a number of standard facets with the frames, which can be used to enhance or restrict the slot values. One can add prompts if the value is to be sought from the user, and help messages or translations can be provided.

Inheritance

More importantly, inheritance can be managed through the use of frames in a taxonomy that uses an indexed tree structure to pass slot values from the parent to the child. Using frames, it is also possible to group knowledge in discrete chunks.

For instance, we could define a general frame for the class of automobiles, with subclasses/frames for domestic and imported. Each subclass provides additional details not available at the higher level, and is itself a class for the level below in what may be described as a taxonomic representation of information. The class "domestic" may be subdivided into Chevrolet, Ford, and Chrysler. The class of Fords may be further subdivided into the Ranchero and the LTD (Walters, 1988).

By convention, such hierarchies are represented as an upside-down tree structure. The class at the top, automobiles, the broadest class, is considered as the root of the tree while the instances, which each represent a particular case of the class, are considered as the leaves of the tree and placed at the lowest level.

For example my Chevy, Jeff's LTD, and Helen's Ranchero would all be considered as instances of their respective classes (see Figure 6.1).

In some cases, an object can belong to more than one class at a time. A wooden duck decoy belongs to both the class of ducks and the class of wooden decoys and inherits some but not all properties from each.

Problems with Inheritance

It is not always desirable for an object to inherit properties from its parent. Sometimes there are circumstances when inheritance can cause problems. Walters & Nielsen (1988) provide an excellent analysis of the

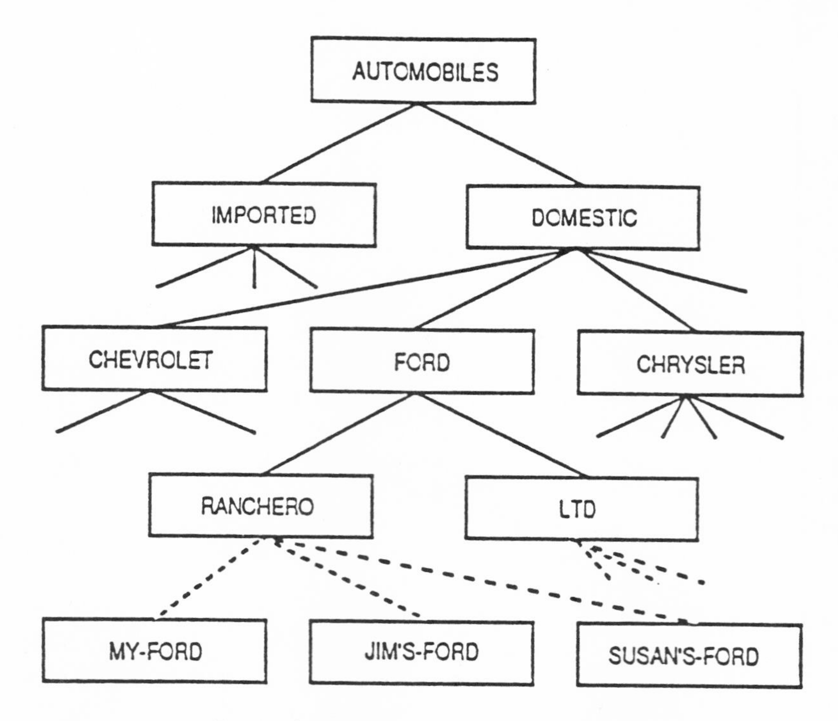

Figure 6.1. A classification tree (Crafting)

Example from Walters and Nielsen

The Passenger Car	1/2 ton truck
1. Carries: Passenger	Carries: Cargo
2. Colors: (restricted to:	Colors: (restricted to:
3. Red, White, Blue, Brown, Green)	Red, Blue, Black, Brown)
4. Cylinders: 6	Cylinders: 8

RANCHERO
Carries: (Passengers, Cargo)
Colors: (Red,Blue,Brown)
Cylinders: 6

Figure 6.2.

complexities involved in managing inheritance. They discuss the Ranchero, which is a half-ton truck that can serve double duty as an automobile. It inherits properties from both classes, but considerable care must be taken in controlling the type of inheritance.

In the first slot (Figure 6.2), "Carries," we have multiple inheritance of the **union** type. The Ranchero will inherit values from both parents, since it carries both passengers and cargo.

In the second slot, "Colors," this is not possible since black passenger cars are not made. Clearly in this case, an **intersection** is required, where only the values present in both categories are inherited. The only colors found in both were red, blue and brown.

For the third slot, "Cylinders," the Ranchero cannot inherit both values — it would have two different engines — nor can there be an **intersection**, or it would not have an engine at all. Two solutions are available. The designer can declare the inheritance to be **null** and make sure that the value for "Cylinders" is entered whenever the Ranchero class is described, or the designer can determine which value will be inherited and specifically code this information. In this case the Ranchero has a six-cylinder engine, a property it inherits from automobiles.

To distinguish between hierarchical or member/class relationships and the whole/part relationships, different predicates have been designated and the terms for these generic predicates have become part of the jargon. The **isa** predicate and the **instance-of** predicate indicate different aspects of the **parent/child** relationship so critical in inheritance. This is not to be confused with the **whole/part** relationship described by the has-a predicate. **Has-a** is complemented by **contained-in**. We can say the Ranchero has-a gasoline tank, and that gasoline is contained-in the Ranchero's gas tank.

Sometimes it is necessary to constrain the facets that can be inherited. Some useful predicates for establishing constraints are **derives-from**, **not-member-of**, or **exclusive-member-of**. Standard predicates can also be used to add restrictions (e.g., **instance-of:domestic**).

As we have seen, slots can be used to store values, or basic facts, and also frame relationships. They can also be used to accommodate procedures or rules, and in some cases whole rule sets.

Special Uses of Frames: Semantic Nets

The systematic use of networks for knowledge representation begins with Quillian's seminal article on language understanding in 1968 (Quillian, 1968), wherein he proposed understanding on a deeper, semantic level. He stressed the importance of real world knowledge in language understanding, and suggested that the relevant aspects of human memory could be modelled in terms of a **semantic network of nodes** representing concepts, and **arcs** representing the relationships between concepts. Quillian also set out to develop a processing model for the retrieval of semantic information from such a memory.

Knowledge is organized around the objects being described with pointers to related objects or frames. Each object is considered as a node in a graph, while the relations among them are represented by labelled arcs. A semantic network is a collection of nodes and arcs where a variety of different relationships can be encoded. We use the "**isa**" predicate to indicate that the desk is a piece of office furniture, i.e., isa (desk, office-furniture).

Many other relationships can also be expressed by suitably chosen predicates such as: office **ispartof** suite, computer **hasa** CPU, CPU **contained in** computer, and so forth (Rogers, 1987).

These semantic nets are often portrayed as diagrams on paper, but in the computer the same frame structures are used, with pointers to link related frames together. These networks are used to represent specific events or experiences and are convenient when a great deal of context-dependent information is needed.

Scripts

A script is a special kind of frame used to describe a stereotyped sequence of events in a particular context. One might well develop a script for a typical reference interview that involves retrieving company-specific information. Then the computer would match the actual interview being conducted with the script to determine what had been omitted, to suggest alternate strategies, and to provide helpful information to the user. The stereotypical frame would have various typical tracks such

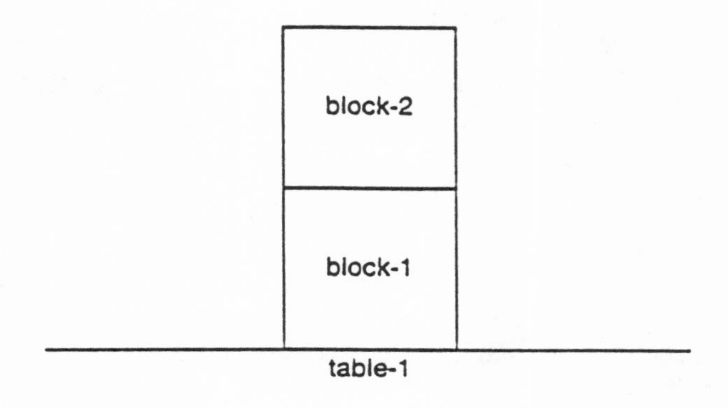


```
(inst table-1 table)                    ; table-1 is a table.

(inst block-1 block)                    ; block-1 is a block.
(color block-1 yellow)                  ; It is yellow
(supported-by block-1 table-1)          ; and supported by the table.

(inst block-2 block)                    ; block-2 is a block.
(color block-2 red)                     ; It is red
(supported-by block-2 block-1)          ; and supported by block-1.
```

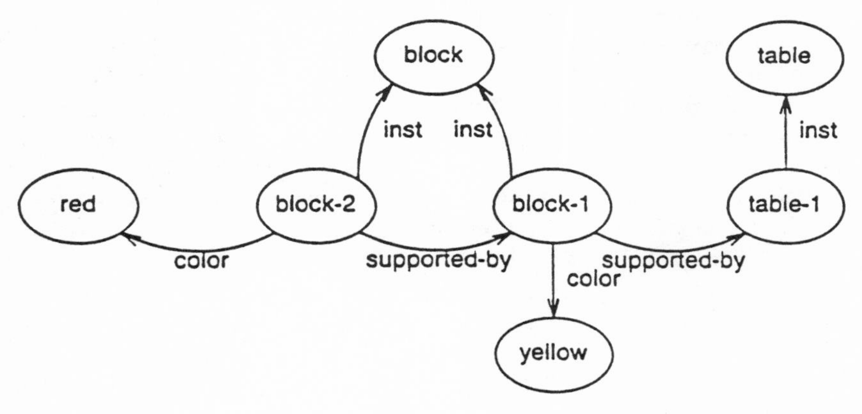

Figure 6.3. Semantic network

---

as (a) Fortune 500 company, (b) public company, and (c) closely held company. It would have scenes dealing with financial information, ownership, history, etc. A tools slot could be used for the different reference tools and so forth. Scripts are most helpful when there are many causal relationships between events.

Applications of Frame-Based Systems

By the late 1970s, artificial intelligence researchers were beginning to experiment with reasoning systems using detailed causal models. In the field of medical informatics, Dr. Glen Rennels, although impressed by the medical causal models of pathophysiology, determined that doctors do not depend on mechanistic models. More typically they will cite the literature, mentioning data from clinical trials and other research reports.

Dr. Rennels set to work to develop a consultant program that bases its advice on the content of articles drawn from the clinical literature. His first effort, the **Roundsman** project, focused on breast cancer management, but can be viewed more generally as a general approach to any domain where empirical data are crucial in expert decision making. His primary goal was to model the process of reasoning from the clinical trials literature (Rennels, 1987).

In order to accomplish this, he had to have a means of interpreting the applicability of a published study to a specific clinical situation. Frames were chosen as the organizing principle for the Roundsman project. Each clinical study is represented by a frame with slots to indicate the characteristics of the study population, including the different demographic strata represented, as well as a **comparison of interventions (COI)** data. The COI contains experimental data comparing one intervention against another and reporting the outcomes of each treatment strategy. For example, COI 1 might pertain to overall survival at five years, whereas COI 2 might pertain to recurrence-free survival at ten years. It would be of little value to the clinician if all Roundsman did was provide a statistical skeleton of experimental data. Each COI also includes "distance metric knowledge," which is used to evaluate the clinical relevance of the statistical results within the context of a particular patient and treatment.

The Roundsman project is significant because it bases its knowledge and expert advice on an understanding of the structure of the clinical literature. Roundsman uses its understanding of the literature to make inferences about how an article might relate to the clinical problem which a physician faces (Rennels, et al., 1986).

Another application of a frame-based system in the medical world is the **Medindex System** developed for interactive knowledge-based indexing of the medical literature (Humphrey & Kapoor, 1988).

Medindex is still under development. The system uses a frame language, **Cframer**, written especially for NLM in **Sun Common LISP**. It is designed for use by trained MEDLINE indexers. Indexers are prompted to enter MeSH (Medical Subject Headings) terms as slot fillers for completing document-specific indexing frames. The values placed in frames representing specific documents are derived from generic frames in a knowledge base.

The knowledge base consists of facts about the terminology used in MeSH, together with rules for applying them to indexing medical documents. Knowledge base frames correspond to the terms in the MeSH thesaurus and the slots in the frames are the relations or facets. Frames are connected into a complex hierarchy so that slot values can be inherited when appropriate. Slots contain executable procedures, which are invoked automatically as needed. Two types of relations are recognized: **Children** and **Inherits-From**.

While any slot is being filled in the indexing frame, the indexer may request a hierarchical display of the restrictions (permissible fillers) for that slot as inherited from the knowledge base.

For example, here is the representation for **bone neoplasms**.

```
DISEASE
SLOTS:   Inherits-from      (VALUE    Medical Subjects)
         Children           (VALUE    Bone diseases/Neoplasms)

      Anatomical Structure
      Etiology
      Complication
      Age-of-Onset
      Procedure
      Process

NEOPLASMS  Inherits-from      (VALUE    Disease)
           Children           (VALUE    Neoplasms by site,...)

NEOPLASMS BY SITE
SLOTS:          Inherits-from      (VALUE    Neoplasms)
                Children           (VALUE    Bone Neoplasms)
       .... (inherits slots from DISEASE)

OTHERS
        Metastasis-To
        Secondary-From
        Complication
        Histologic Type
```

Not only are slots inherited in this hierarchical structure, the system also supports internal retrieval. A frame can call procedures associated with a slot which return values from other slots in the same frame or values from slots in other frames. The children slot value includes a path name, making it possible for a term to have different children, depending on its location in the hierarchy. For example, the hierarchies for **Bone and Bones** will differ within different contexts. The children associated with the term will differ depending on whether the context is **Muskoskeletal System** or **Connective Tissue**.

Muskoskeletal system	Connective Tissue
Bone and Bones	Bone and Bones
Facial Bones	Bone Matrix
Leg Bones	
Femur	
Fibula	
Tibia	

Constraints in Developing Expert Systems for Information Retrieval

One of the major constraints that information specialists must deal with is the way in which existing electronic knowledge is stored. Knowledge-based information retrieval systems must manipulate information that is already stored in very large databases using conventional knowledge representation techniques. It would be misleading to present knowledge representation techniques that are peculiar to knowledge engineering while omitting the many other schemes that have served and continue to serve us well.

If we are to understand how expert systems might interact with the existing electronic store, then we should be aware of some of the representation formalisms that are already so well established in the field. Therefore this section will provide a brief overview of each of the following representation/indexing schemes. Many of these schemes rely upon mathematical and statistical analysis of terms appearing in source documents. They are described here without mathematical details, simply to give the reader an awareness of their existence, and a basic sense of how they work.

- relational database management systems
- keyword indexing
- KWIC/ KWOC/PRECIS programs
- N-grams

- The Connection Machine/parallel processing
- hypertext
- object-oriented programming

Relational Database Management Systems

Currently, most library OPACS are using some form of relational database management system, or a network system. These are particularly well designed to supply processing of sets of structured records that all adhere to the same basic record format (MARC) with minor variations. Each file of records is sorted by one or more elements of the record, such as **book number** or **author**. This element is known as the **key** to the record. If the key is known we can quickly and efficiently move to its location in memory to retrieve the full record.

But, quite often, the user will want to access the record by some other characteristic, e.g., all the books about auto repair or books published by Addison-Wesley. Relational database management systems enable multiple key access by using a variety of data structures.

The simplest of these is the **linked list**, in which each record carries a pointer to the address of the next record in the chain. The last record can then be made to point to the first if so desired. Clearly, people want to be able to traverse the records in both directions, selecting either the next record or the previous record. To accomplish this, a second set of pointers can be added to each record pointing to the previous record in the chain.

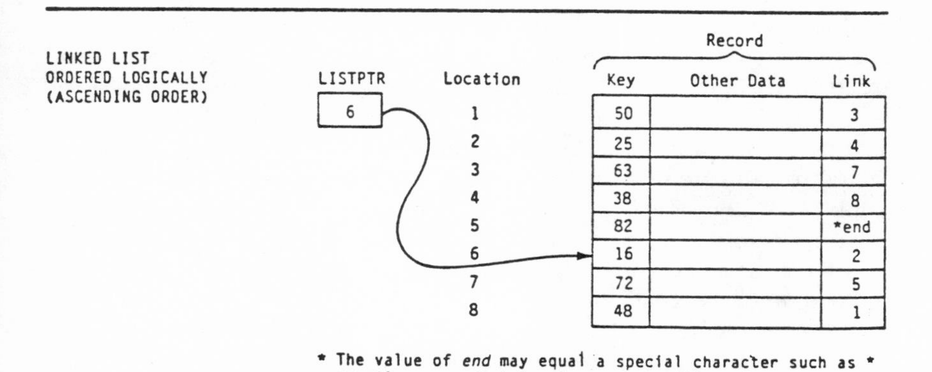

Figure 6.4. Linked lists

Linked lists can become very cumbersome when there are multiple access points in each record. Another option is the inverted index. In the file shown in Figure 6.5, the records are sorted by social security number in the primary list. In order to enable the user to find a person by name, a small, inverted index is created by last name and sorted. There are only two fields in the inverted index: the names and a pointer to the location of the actual record. If Karen Caldwell's record is required it is searched for in one of the indexes which will provide the record location required — in this case, record location 10.

Most relational database management systems use B+ trees for indexing records in very large files. By using a two-level directory for the inverted index, they can speed up retrieval and find the required records more efficiently. In Figure 6.6, the user is searching for Bill. Bill comes before Connie, the first entry, so the user follows the pointer from Connie to the first record in Connie's subgroup, no. 50. Bill follows Anton but is before Bob. The user follows Bob's pointer to the first record in Bob's set which is Barbara. From Barbara, each record is reviewed until the entry for Bill is found.

The reader is referred to standard texts in relational database theory for a fuller description of the physical data structures involved (Kroenke, 1988).

The most important feature of relational database management systems is that two or more flat files (i.e., ones that have no repeating groups) can easily be related to each other by joining them on a common link, such as the user number. Then the information in both records can be accessed and manipulated as if belonging to one.

For example, every library has a set of records for patrons that include the borrower number, name, address, and other particulars. Likewise for every book there is a complete MARC record including unique book number and in a third file is maintained information on books that are in circulation. In a database management system, all that is needed in the circulation record is the unique book number and the user number, date borrowed, and date due. The three files are quite independent of each other and are maintained separately. But when needed they can be combined. For instance, the system can readily generate overdue bills by linking, or "relating," the three files together. Each book record is linked with the user name and address and combined with the date borrowed and date returned as shown in Figure 6.7.

The advantage of relational database systems is that they can process sets of records and perform repetitive tasks very well. They can also support numerous inverted indices for keyword access, but they are not well suited to dealing with complex sets of conditions and the heuristics which are the hallmark of expert systems.

PRIMARY LIST

	SSN (Key)	Name	Division	Pay Grade	Years Service
1	242533209	SMITH, JOHN E.	SALES	12	10
2	284627452	BAKER, JOSEPHUS	SUPPLY	8	3
3	322113789	JOHNSON, MARY L.	SALES	10	3
4	357821603	EMORY, JAMES R.	SUPPLY	7	1
5	379428917	WASHINGTON, JUDY H.	D.P.	8	1
6	426720412	ORACLE, DALEY D.	D.P.	11	4
7	448536821	YOKUM, ABNER	SALES	10	5
8	484696353	BRAUN, FRITZ R.	PERSONNEL	8	2
9	512128256	LANE, LOIS	PERSONNEL	9	6
10	569032184	CALDWELL, KAREN	D.P.	9	2

INVERTED INDEX

Order Field	Record Identifier
BAKER, JOSEPHUS	284627452
BRAUN, FRITZ R.	484696353
CALDWELL, KAREN	569032184
EMORY, JAMES R.	357821603
JOHNSON, MARY L.	322113789
LANE, LOIS	512128256
ORACLE, DALEY D.	426720412
SMITH, JOHN E.	242533209
WASHINGTON, JUDY H.	379428917
YOKUM, ABNER	448536821

(a) Using record key values

Order Field	Record Location
BAKER, JOSEPHUS	2
BRAUN, FRITZ R.	8
CALDWELL, KAREN	10
EMORY, JAMES R.	4
JOHNSON, MARY L.	3
LANE, LOIS	9
ORACLE, DALEY D.	6
SMITH, JOHN E.	1
WASHINGTON, JUDY	5
YOKUM, ABNER	7

(b) Using record locations

INVERTED INDEX ON DIVISION

Division	Locations
D.P.	5,6,10
PERSONNEL	8,9
SALES	1,3,7
SUPPLY	2,4

Figure 6.5. The inverted index

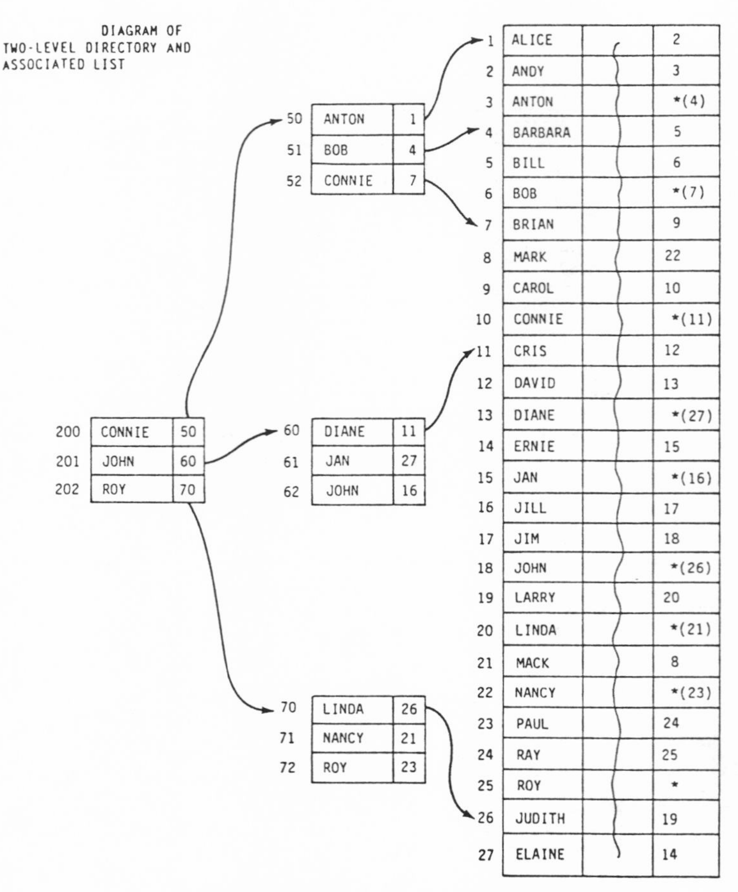

Figure 6.6. The B+ Tree indexing structure

Despite this, it is important to recognize that there is nothing to be gained by recoding all the information from relational databases into the form of **PROLOG** predicates, rules, or frames which are processed much less efficiently. Rather, we need to develop interfaces between the two technologies so that we can have the best of both worlds. A number of such knowledge-based database systems are currently under development and testing, and certainly this technology holds considerable promise for library applications (Abarbanel & Williams,1986, Ceri, Gottlob & Wiederhold, 1986).

Keyword Indexing Systems

Keyword indexing systems are still the mainstay of information retrieval systems dealing with large volumes of text. Designed to work with any

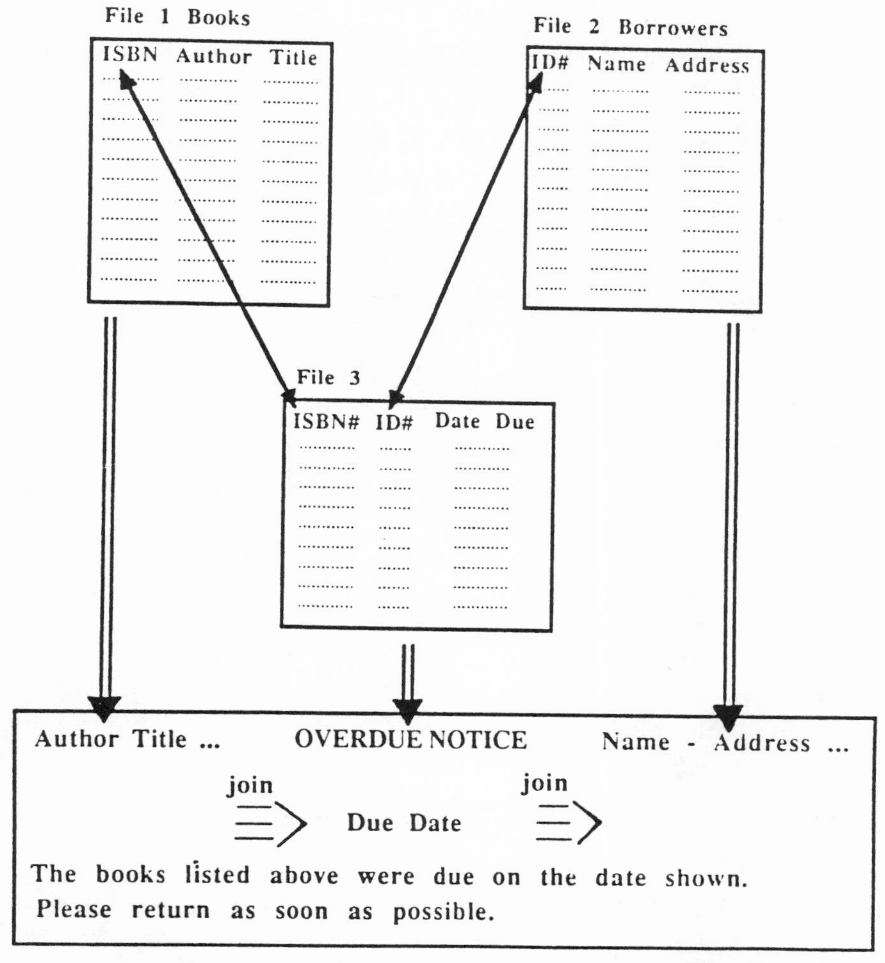

Figure 6.7. Relating three files

---

free-form textual information included in the record, keyword systems index every unique word in the title and other selected fields, including the abstract or table of contents where available, thereby providing a much larger number of access points for the record. Most systems provide Boolean searching capability with AND, OR, and BUT NOT. Also supported is proximity searching, which allows the searcher to specify that terms appear within a given number of words from one another, or in the same sentence or paragraph.

This is accomplished by building inverted indices, listing each word individually along with the document number in which it appears. If an intersection is desired, it is a simple matter to compare the two lists and select only the documents appearing in both lists. In full-text databases, every individual word is listed, with the exception of common words, such as "the," "an," "every," "another," etc., which appear on a stop list.

In most library OPACS, separate, inverted indices are maintained at least for the authors, the titles, and the subject headings. Most of the current generation of OPACs can maintain multiple indices derived from a variety of different fields in the MARC record. Keywords from different fields can be combined at search time.

Keyword Indexing

Keyword	record #	paragraph#	sentence #	word #
Artificial	111	1	1	1
Intelligence	111	1	1	2
and	*stopword			
the	*stopword			
design	111	1	1	3
of	*stopword			
Intelligent	111	1	1	4
Systems	111	1	1	5

By rapidly locating the identification numbers of the desired items in the much smaller inverted indices, the user can readily go on to retrieve the full documents from the database. Keyword searching is still considered to be the most effective technique for searching large databases. However, its major drawback is the fact that its user has no effective means of browsing the collection. This is a particular problem, for the user has no way of knowing what terms will work best in a specific collection. The best that can be done is to retrieve a large set of materials and then let the user rank their relevance. And there is no way to discover what has been missed.

Keyword indexing is considered a brute force approach to searching, since it makes no pretense of applying any intelligence to the search process. Instead, it relies on the speed and power of the machine to search for any and all occurrences of the keywords in question.

If the user requests materials on "expert" AND "systems," a quick scan for the two terms in the inverted index will show all the relevant record numbers

Expert 111145 222232 333532 444121 555321 888321: 6 hits

Systems 111146 333213 444122 666312 777433 999111 98713: 7 hits

The first entry, record 111145, and 111146 shows clearly that the two words are in the same document and in the same paragraph and sentence.

The system will compare both lists, retaining the matching record numbers, 111, 333, and 444.

Over the years many experimenters have attempted to add intelligence to this process in a variety of different ways, but for the most part, all they have succeeded in doing is adding considerably to the cost of indexing and impeding the retrieval process, without any significant gain in precision or recall.

One approach being offered by a number of vendors today, including Info-DB, combines the features of relational database management systems with full-text keyword indexing of designated fields. In this way different library files, such as circulation and the OPAC catalog, can be "related," while at the same time providing keyword access to titles, subject headings, and other selected fields. Again, this involves the use of pointers, linked lists, and chunks of text.

In the future, we may see OCLC offering us the same structured MARC records but also including the capability to search and view the full text of the documents we select. The **Electronic Publishing and Information Delivery Project** at OCLC is involved in a number of such experiments. Particularly exciting is a joint venture with G.K. Hall Publishers to create a database of over 100 full-text books in the **Twayne's United States Authors Series**. Each of the books will be browsable through its table of contents, back-of-the-book index, and text. There will also be a searchable body of associated literary criticism, theory, and biography. The creation of the **Electronic Manuscript Standard**, which was originally developed by the Association of American Publishers (AAP) Electronic Manuscript Project, will encourage future developments in this area (Kurdyla, 1988).

KWIC and KWOC Indexing

As a variant on these techniques there are the permuted keyword listings of titles, of both the KWIC (keyword in context) and the KWOC (keyword out of context) variety, as well as the much more sophisticated

	SSN (Key)	Name	Division	Pay Grade	Years Service
1	242533209	SMITH, JOHN E.	SALES	12	10
2	284627452	BAKER, JOSEPHUS	SUPPLY	8	3
3	322113789	JOHNSON, MARY L.	SALES	10	3
4	357821603	EMORY, JAMES R.	SUPPLY	7	1
5	379428917	WASHINGTON, JUDY H.	D.P.	8	1
6	426720412	ORACLE, DALEY D.	D.P.	11	4
7	448536821	YOKUM, ABNER	SALES	10	5
8	484696353	BRAUN, FRITZ R.	PERSONNEL	8	2
9	512128256	LANE, LOIS	PERSONNEL	9	6
10	569032184	CALDWELL, KAREN	D.P.	9	2

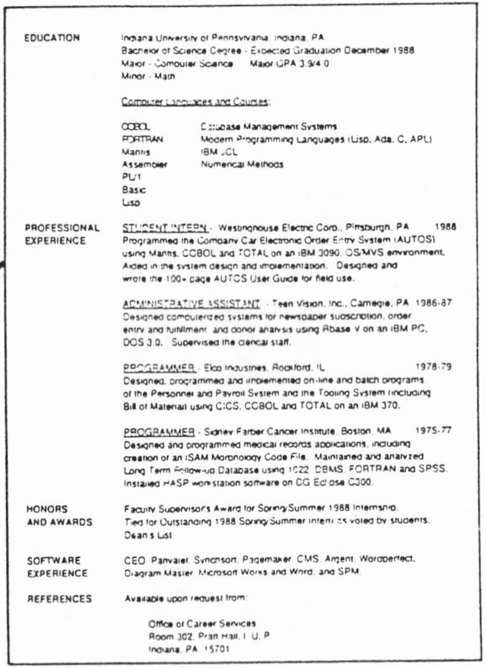

EDUCATION
Indiana University of Pennsylvania, Indiana, PA
Bachelor of Science Degree - Expected Graduation December 1988
Major - Computer Science Major GPA 3.9/4.0
Minor - Math

Computer Languages and Courses:
COBOL — Database Management Systems
FORTRAN — Modern Programming Languages (Lisp, Ada, C, APL)
Mantis — IBM JCL
Assembler — Numerical Methods
PL/1
Basic
Lisp

PROFESSIONAL EXPERIENCE
STUDENT INTERN - Westinghouse Electric Corp., Pittsburgh, PA 1988
Programmed the Company Car Electronic Order Entry System (AUTOS) using Mantis, COBOL and TOTAL on an IBM 3090, OS/MVS environment. Aided in the system design and implementation. Designed and wrote the 100+ page AUTOS User Guide for field use.

ADMINISTRATIVE ASSISTANT - Teen Vision, Inc., Carnegie, PA 1986-87
Designed computerized systems for newspaper subscription, order entry and fulfillment, and donor analysis using Rbase V on an IBM PC, DOS 3.0. Supervised the clerical staff.

PROGRAMMER - Elco Industries, Rockford, IL 1978-79
Designed, programmed and implemented on-line and batch programs of the Personnel and Payroll System and the Tooling System (including Bill of Material) using CICS, COBOL and TOTAL on an IBM 370.

PROGRAMMER - Sidney Farber Cancer Institute, Boston, MA 1975-77
Designed and programmed medical records applications, including creation of an ISAM Morphology Code File. Maintained and analyzed Long Term Follow-up Database using 1022 DBMS, FORTRAN and SPSS. Installed HASP workstation software on DG Eclipse C300.

HONORS AND AWARDS
Faculty Supervisor's Award for Spring/Summer 1988 Internship.
Tied for Outstanding 1988 Spring/Summer intern as voted by students.
Dean's List

SOFTWARE EXPERIENCE
CEO, Panvalet, Syncsort, Pagemaker, CMS, Argent, Wordperfect, Diagram Master, Microsoft Works and Word, and SPM.

REFERENCES
Available upon request from:

Office of Career Services
Room 302, Pratt Hall, I. U. P.
Indiana, PA 15701

Figure 6.8. Combining a relational database management system and full text retrieval

PRECIS strings which attempt to convey the inter-relationships of the keywords in the given strings. In the KWIC system, a different entry is made for each word in the title except for a few stop words. The rest of the title is attached to the entry word, which is rotated to the first position. In KWOC indexing, the title is left intact and not rotated. The entry word is added to the front. There are a number of variations on these two basic techniques.

These techniques were specifically designed for use in printed bibliographies or online search systems that assist the user in recalling a title that is only vaguely remembered. Users can enter their search terms and pull up the permuted listings of all the titles in which the term has been used. This provides a limited but useful form of browsing because the user can then determine what titles are relevant without actually searching the whole database.

KWIC: Key Word in Context.*

KEYWORD CONTEXT
Knowledge-Based Systems: Expert Systems Made Easy. Crafting
Systems: Expert Systems Made Easy. Crafting Knowledge-Based
Expert Systems Made Easy. Crafting Knowledge-Based Systems
Systems Made Easy. Crafting Knowledge-Based Systems: Expert
Made Easy. Crafting Knowledge-Based Systems: Expert Systems
Easy. Crafting Knowledge-Based Systems: Expert Systems Made

*After permuting all the terms for each entry the entire file is sorted alphabetically.

KWOC: Key Word out of Context.

Crafting	Crafting Knowledge-Based Systems: Expert Systems Made Easy.
Knowledge-Based	Crafting Knowledge-Based Systems: Expert Systems Made Easy.
Systems	Crafting Knowledge-Based Systems: Expert Systems Made Easy.
Expert	Crafting Knowledge-Based Systems: Expert Systems Made Easy.
Systems	Crafting Knowledge-Based Systems: Expert Systems Made Easy.

Made	Crafting Knowledge-Based Systems: Expert Systems Made Easy.
Easy	Crafting Knowledge-Based Systems: Expert Systems Made Easy.

PRECIS Strings

A technique favored by the British National Bibliography, **PRECIS strings** involves building a string to describe the contents of the book, carefully coded to convey the roles and relationships of the terms being used. While such strings perform a bit better than simply permuting the title, developing the strings is labor intensive and therefore the technique has not been widely adopted. Its main value is that it produces a printed bibliography for human consumption that lists a descriptive PRECIS string for each item (Austin, 1975).

For example, a book on *Wind Damage to Crops in East Anglia* would be coded by an indexer as follows:

(0) East Anglia
(1) Crops
(2) damage (w) to (v) by
(3) wind ✔

The codes can be interpreted as follows

0 ==> Location
1 ==> Key system: Object of transitive action
2 ==> Action/Effect
3 ==> Agent of transitive action

The check (✔) means a lead term.
$v and $w are used as connectives to link two terms in a phrase.
$v connects to the next lower term....damage by wind
$w connects to the next higher term...damage to crops.

Using these codes, the following entries would be generated in the printed bibliography:

1. East Anglia
   Crops. Damage by winds
2. Crops. East Anglia
   Damage by winds
3. Winds. East Anglia
   Damage to crops

N-grams/Statistical Clustering

In sharp contrast to the PRECIS approach, which focuses considerable effort on capturing the deeper meaning of the relationships between words, the **N-gram** technique relies completely on the brute force supplied by the machine. The approach differs from traditional methods of indexing because the content of the text is characterized by counting the occurrences of a fixed, finite number of selected index word fragments (N-grams), ignoring those that fall entirely within longer index N-grams (Mah & D'Amore, 1985). Every text segment can be described as a vector of N-gram counts and a measure of the similarity of two text segments in their content can be defined as an inner product of their respective N-gram index vectors. The similarity measure can be scaled with respect to its significance.

The effectiveness of this technique has been demonstrated in a number of applications, but particularly in an electronic mail application set up to classify incoming messages and to mark unusual ones automatically so that the recipient does not have to read all of them.

N-gram technology is based on two key ideas:

1. Short word fragments can be selected to make up a fixed but complete set of index terms for text.
2. It is possible to develop a multinomial model of N-gram occurrences in text that permits the scaling of numerical text similarity measures according to significance.

An N-gram approach overcomes some of the problems with Boolean conditions on keywords by using scaled similarity measures based on N-gram counts instead.

There are some obvious disadvantages, the most important of which is the need to set clustering thresholds to achieve satisfactory clustering. If set too high, there will be no clusters; if set too low, one huge cluster will result with little or no discrimination.

Also, and perhaps more significantly, the N-gram approach to text analysis discards a great deal of information, even more so than a keyword indexing approach. It would definitely be a poor fit for an application such as legal searching, where it is important to make exact matches of extended phraseology. For example, An Estimate of Wind Damage to East Anglia Crops will yield: esti wind dama east angl crop.

An application that demonstates an appropriate use of N-gram indexing is the **EMIC (Electronic Mail Indexing and Classification System)**, which handles electronic mail in the same way that secretaries handle old-fashioned hardcopy office mail. It offers the following functions:

- **MATCH** will watch for particular types of incoming messages and put these aside for later review. A set of standing profiles consisting of a set of scalar weights assigned to particular N-grams defines what **EMIC** is to watch for.
- **DETECT**: If a new message that matches a given profile is sufficiently different from others in the same category it is deemed unusual, and the system will notify someone immediately.
- **GROUP** will collect messages not being watched for and sort these by content.
- **FILTER/REVIEW** will search for particular messages in old mail and highlight the portions of retrieved messages that are of special interest. To support full text, partial inversion is balanced with complementary search reduction techniques based on the special characteristics of N-gram indexing. **EMIC** does not perform as well as full-text searching with special hardware but is much more efficient and cost effective than full inversion indexing.

Messages are clustered according to similarity of content using a variant of something known as the minimal spanning tree algorithm.

Other Automatic Indexing Techniques

For years, automatic indexing has been the Holy Grail of automated systems which information scientists have sought. There is now an impressive body of information retrieval literature that deals with methods for computing the similarity between a document and a query for retrieval purposes. Many methods of calculating similarities have been presented. Some of the better known methods are:

- The **inverse document frequency method** (Sparck Jones, 1972). The inverse document frequency method assigns a higher weight to terms that occur in fewer documents than to terms that are more widely used. It is considered that the fewer documents in which the word appears the higher the discrimination power of the term. The similarity measure between a document and a query involves comparing the sum of the weights of the query terms in the document.

- The **cosine method** (Salton and McGill, 1983). The cosine method involves calculating the cosine of the angle between the query and the document when they are both represented as vectors.
- The **binary independence model** (Yu and Salton, 1976; Robertson and Sparck Jones, 1976). In this technique, weight is assigned according to a formula that balances the probability that a relevant document has a given term and the probability that an irrelevant document also has the term. This technique supposes *a priori* knowledge of these probabilities. These have to be estimated from other parameters.
- The **nonbinary independence model** (Yu and Lee, 1986). In addition to the probabilities described in the binary independence model, the term frequency of each term in each document is also taken into account.

As computers have become cheaper, faster, and very much more powerful, there has been considerable renewed interest in statistical techniques such as the ones cited above.

Massively Parallel Systems: The Connection Machine

There has been a great deal of publicity about parallel processing and the speed and power it can deliver to information retrieval. **The Connection Machine** builds on the work on term weighting for document retrieval that was briefly described above.

The Connection Machine (Stanfill & Kahle, 1986) provides a massive brute force capability. The system can search 64,000 full-text documents simultaneously for a 100-term vector. Since very few readers are interested in developing a 100- term vector to describe their information need, this is accomplished by first retrieving some records and asking the reader to rank the most nearly relevant. Then the system will develop a 100-term vector from the articles deemed most relevant. While very impressive in terms of raw power, this system assumes that the reader has chosen the best and most appropriate terms the first time and is completely satisfied with the ones being marked as relevant. It also assumes that the database selected for searching is the most suitable.

Another parallel approach that is considered artificial intelligence filters the natural language of the user through a massive morphological analysis. Synonyms are located and then submitted for searching in any full-text database requested (Dudek, 1987).

One example of this approach is the **METAMORPH** system being marketed by Thunderstone Inc. For example, given a subjective sentence like, "Have there been any recent power struggles in the Middle East?" the METAMORPH software will find passages such as "Tension between the U.S. and Iran increased yesterday when mines were found floating in the Straits of Hormuz," or "Students at Tel Aviv University clashed with bakery truck drivers making deliveries on the Sabbath." METAMORPH's power is derived from an engine consisting of an English-language morpheme matrix containing in excess of 250–500,000 entries. This engine works in concourse with very fast pattern-matching algorithms as it retrieves information from the full-text databases (Thunderstone, 1988).

These technologies are very exciting and certainly open up major new opportunities and research questions. The approach here is to completely eliminate the middle man and do away with all forms of indexing or structure. Indexing and structured records are considered unnecessary in these systems. Clearly, there is an urgent need for more powerful systems to deal with the ever-increasing quantity of material to be searched, particularly in full-text systems handling voluminous paper flows, such as the intelligence data pouring into the CIA on a daily basis.

However, most users are very uncomfortable with this total dependence on the brute force of the machine and the bird's eye view provided. There is no way to gain a perspective of the whole collection or the distribution of documents on different topics. Readers using these systems will never know what was missed, nor is there an opportunity to browse — to exercise serendipity. Despite their raw power, such systems are counterintuitive.

Future systems will undoubtedly combine these very powerful searching machines with intelligent front-end systems to guide the reader in setting up a search strategy, modifying the search interactively, and evaluating results. Much further research is needed on how to take advantage of this power for improved delivery of information services.

Hypertext/Hypermedia

As parallel computing pushes out the boundaries of what is possible, other technologies are having a major impact on the user interface. With more powerful workstations, high-resolution screens, windowing, icon-driven menus, and the mouse, we can begin to be much more creative about the types of interfaces provided for library researchers. A generation ago we were all resigned to dealing with card catalogs. Now even online OPACS seem slow and cumbersome, and there are a host of new problems we didn't even know existed.

Elaine Svenonius has identified the "**Humphrey Clinker**" problem of retrieving too many records from a bibliographic database (OCLC, 1988). A search in OCLC by author/title key "smol,hump" retrieves over 100 bibliographic records, each of which represents a version or edition of Humphrey Clinker. This set cannot be reduced by subject or facet or type, since all the records represent essentially the same book. Svenonius has concentrated on developing a hierarchical ordering scheme that will enable the user to define sets based on work, text, typesetting, subedition, imprint, and reprint. Testing of her scheme will focus on whether these sets will achieve satisfactory and automatic clustering.

In fact, the Humphrey Clinker problem is part of a more comprehensive problem, namely, how generally to display records in large retrieval sets and avoid "cognitive overload." Hudson & Walker (1987) from the University of California reports that the average subject search by a skilled user in the University of California OPAC yields over 181 citations, results which he describes as uncomfortably large. Lynch also says additional problems include lack of understanding of the classification system and the sheer size of the database. As we improve subject access and hence the number of records retrieved, this problem is going to become increasingly more significant.

Fortunately, **hypertext** offers a solution for displaying hierarchical orderings of the type described by Svenonius. Hypertext, an idea originally proposed by Ted Nelson, was first implemented at Xerox PARC as NOTECARD, a system for authors to keep track of bibliographical references and footnotes for a paper. Essentially, **NOTECARD** is designed to graphically display unstructured chunks of text, the sort of information one would put on a 3 x 5-inch card, in a series of linked displays. The user can connect any two cards together and create an almost unlimited series of such links.

Let us take, for example, an article on information in Grolier's encyclopedia. One might decide to consider each paragraph in the article as a chunk of text. These chunks would be linked together in a single, linked list. When the last paragraph is encountered, the reader could ask for the next chunk and be automatically linked to the first one. A different linked list would be developed for an article on libraries. What makes the hypertext system so useful is the ability it provides to then place additional links between the records, such as a link from the word libraries in the first article on information to the article that deals with libraries.

The reader can use these links to go forwards and backwards in the article being examined, or follow a link to a related topic. The richer the network of links, the more powerful the browsing capability.

Shortly after the introduction of hypertext, researchers realized that the chunks could also be used to manage graphics and sound. hypertext became **hypermedia**.

Hypermedia has been popularized by **HyperCard**, the Apple Macintosh version of a hypertext system, which was released in the third quarter of 1987 and is now being given away with every new Macintosh sold. PC based versions are **OWL**, available from Guide and **HYPERTIES**,

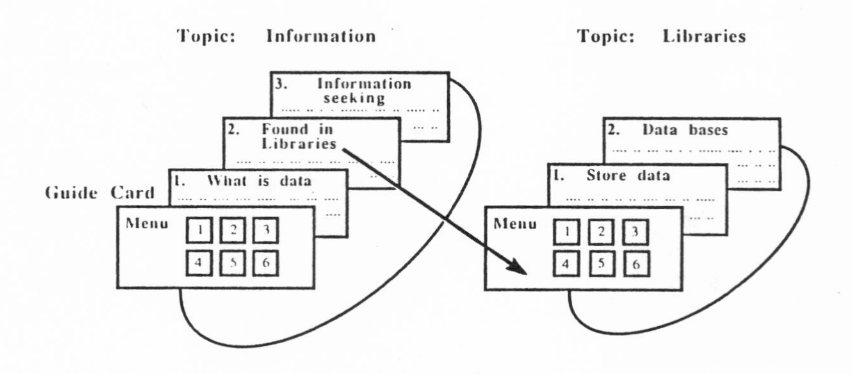

Figure 6.9. Hypertext linking chunks of text

available from Cognetics, Inc. **KRL** from Knowledge Workshop is one of the better known hypertext programs for Sun or Apollo workstations, both of which are often used for expert system development.

Hypermedia provides the ideal tool for mounting and displaying bibliographic tools such as encyclopedias, Dewey and LCSH subject headings, and reference tools that can serve as guides to other information sources.

The **Emperor I** project began in 1985 and was designed to demonstrate the application of videodisc technology to a complex humanities project, presenting and interpreting one of the most important and early historical/archeological periods of Chinese history. The site and artifacts recorded on videodisc are from the period of the first emperor of China, about 2,200 years ago. The videodisc system exemplifies the union of the computer, audio in two languages, text, and video in a single medium.

This system was adapted to run on HyperCard and had its debut at the Macworld Exhibition in Boston in August 1988. For the first time, the Project was able to deliver any of the chosen multimedia information — still pictures, moving video, audio in both Chinese and English, music, chunks of descriptive text, expert commentary, and database information as well as full text at speeds not previously possible. Here was a seamless environment where a researcher could easily gather and link information from different storage media and sources to obtain his or her own desired information package (Chen, 1989).

The Emperor I project is an excellent example of what can be accomplished by combining many different media in a retrieval system that permits the user to move freely about as needs or interests dictate. But it is focused on gathering material on a specific topic. The same technology could well be applied to a collection of tools designed to assist in navigating the world's recorded literature.

Until now, however these hypermedia systems have generally been designed to function in small domains. Particularly in the medical world, we have seen a plethora of hyperbooks. But very few have addressed the problem of creating hyperlibraries (Frisse, 1988).

There are reasons for this. For one thing, the creation of effective, large-scale hyperlibraries will involve far more than the creation of a simple collection of modular hypertext books.

In most hypermedia systems, links are used to interconnect individual frames into networks or structures or related cards. Each link is a directional type connection between a source card and a destination card. Links are anchored by an icon at a specific location in the body of the source card but are anchored to their destination card as a whole. Clicking the mouse on the link traverses the link, retrieving and displaying the destination link.

To help in managing larger systems of notecards, browsers are provided that contain a structural diagram of a network of cards. Browsers support two levels of editing. The user can edit individual cards, or the user can edit the underlying structure of a network of notecards by carrying out operations on the nodes and edges in the browser diagram without making corresponding changes to the underlying notecards structures. There are also fileboxes, which are specialized cards that can be used to organize or categorize large collections of notecards. Every notecard must be filed in a filebox.

Halasz (1988), from Xerox PARC, discusses the workstation version of NOTECARDS and suggests seven issues for the next generation of hypermedia systems. He points out that hypermedia systems have performed very well for the tasks for which they were designed:

- **small authoring systems** and notetaking by one or a few people
- **display-oriented navigational tasks** centered around a single display used to represent the structure being studied

- **online interactive presentations**. Here the user is often given navigational instructions as he makes a guided tour of the tutorial material.

However, hypermedia systems have not done as well in situations where there is a large, unfamiliar, heterogeneously structured network, such as traditional library databases. Users tend to get "lost in hyperspace." A possible solution is to provide a better query-based access mechanism that is not navigationally oriented but rather relies on the standard techniques described above: keyword searching, connectionist approaches, statistical clustering, and last but not least, rule-based searching.

Another issue raised by Halasz is the lack of a computational engine in hypertext. As presently designed, most hypermedia systems in general make no attempt to make inferences from the information stored in the network. Certainly, this would be an interesting avenue to explore, since in many ways it would not be difficult to add an expert system component. The two technologies are a natural fit. As far as the data structures are concerned, hypermedia systems and knowledge based systems utilizing frames of text are both object oriented with nearly identical data models. Each of the technologies is based on the principle of frames with slots that form network structures. The hypermedia system is passive and depends on links and nodes inserted by the user for navigation. The expert system depends on an inference engine that actively uses rule- or logic-based reasoning in conjunction with the information provided by the frames to make inferences and draw conclusions.

Object-Oriented Programming

We have discussed frame-based expert systems and hypertext, both of which use and manipulate **objects** to achieve their goals. The discussion would not be complete without a reference to a whole group of object-oriented programming languages which are particularly appropriate for large applications such as those required for comprehensive information retrieval projects. The earliest and perhaps best known of these is **Smalltalk-80** (Goldberg, 1983 and *Byte*, Special Issue, 1986).

At the abstract level, object-oriented languages consist of associative networks of abstract objects which are manipulated by means of messages passed between them. Each object is capable of receiving messages, initiating messages, and carrying out a variety of tasks relevant to its status in the system (Gallo, Serano & Tisato, 1989). Objects have most of the characteristics of frames, but also have associated with them procedures and procedure calls. Other, more recent object-oriented languages include **ADA**, **Object Pascal**, **C++**, and **Objective-C**.

Concurrent Access in a Networked Environment

An additional challenge is posed by the rapid expansion of networking capabilities and the resulting demand for distributed processing. Users want to be able to dial in to library databases and conduct their searches from their own offices. Not only do the systems in place have to support a much higher volume of traffic, they must be able to support concurrent use in a networked environment.

Project Mercury is designed to demonstrate the feasibility of a large-scale distributed electronic library allowing remote access to text and graphics stored on various media (Arms, et al., 1988).

This project is jointly sponsored by Carnegie Mellon University and OCLC and is already well under way. Users can dial in to the library services from their desktop machines. A **Reference Assistant**, which is under development, will present a menu showing the databases available, augmented by an index to database services. Planned for the future is an expert system that will interact with the user to determine the information need and refine search queries, select and connect to appropriate databases, and perhaps suggest alternative sources of information, such as electronic bulletin boards or other users of the network.

The experiment will focus on testing and developing multimedia capabilities, including full-text searching in a complex environment with networks and servers providing access to multiple databases mounted on a variety of storage media. The search server will use conventional magnetic disks, while the image server will store digitized information using WORM (write once, read many times) optical disks. Typically images will be scanned, digitized, and stored on disk. Part of the plan also involves looking at the possibility of incorporating local databases on CDs. One of the problems to be addressed is the relatively slow access to information provided by the CD ROM medium.

One of the major goals of this project is to monitor the performance of various searching algorithms in a complex networking environment where each user has a desktop workstation, there are a number of larger machines working as file servers, and an intelligent communications network. A different world, indeed, and yet one which every library must begin to think about.

Conclusion

There are now a wide variety of knowledge representation techniques for managing large sets of loosely structured information. It seems clear that no one of these techniques is able to perform all the information retrieval tasks that users are likely to want. Instead we must actively explore ways to provide seamless integration of all these techniques with an acceptable and friendly user interface. We must build on what is already in place and at the same time develop means to harness the new technologies effectively.

The next chapter will discuss a couple of prototype systems whose goal is to enhance existing technologies in order to provide readers with enhanced retrieval capabilities.

Recommended Reading

A good overview of knowledge representation techniques that is not overly technical is provided by Jay Liebowitz in his *Introduction to Expert Systems* (1988).

A number of excellent seminal articles have been collected into *Readings in Knowledge Representation* by Brachman & Levesque (1985), including Marvin Minsky's paper on frames.

Quinlan has given a good explanation of induction-based systems in his article. Answerman from the National Library of Agriculture is an induction-based system developed with First Class (Waters, 1986).

The best treatment of frame-based systems is found in *Crafting Knowledge Based Systems* by Walters & Nielsen (1988). Clearly, they have had a considerable amount of practical experience in designing many different types of expert systems. They share many war stories in the book.

The serious library user interested in actually building a frame-based system will want to examine the work being done by Humphrey and Kapoor at the National Library of Medicine (1986). Another frame-based reference system worth looking at is the Roundsman project implemented by Rennels (1987).

For a more in-depth look at relational database management systems the user is referred to Kroenke's text (1988).

For material on PRECIS see Austin (1975). A totally different approach is taken by the statistical techniques, such as N-gram clustering (Mah & d'Amore) and various automatic indexing advocated by Salton & McGill (1983).

A good analysis of the problems with this generation of hypertext systems is offered by Halasz (1988). A general introduction to object-oriented programming can be found in *Byte* magazine (1986) in a special issue dedicated to the topic.

7

Building a Solid Foundation: A Vocabulary Control System

Standardization and improvement in subject access to recorded information worldwide must be accomplished before expert systems can be truly useful for information retrieval. When that happens, it will become possible to implement expert systems that support vocabulary control and/or mapping natural language keyed by the reader onto terms used in the information system. The systems currently being used resemble a crazy patchwork quilt of indexing techniques and access mechanisms. While monographs are assigned only an average of 1.7 subject headings per volume, flimsy periodical articles of only five to ten pages are allotted thirty to fifty keywords as access points (Micco, 1980). Access to the information in reference books is even more primitive.

The next challenge to librarians is to develop more realistic subject access systems that utilize the capabilities of artificial intelligence and other new technologies. The information explosion is a *fait accompli* and the volume of printed material to be organized, indexed, and stored increases hourly. We can no longer settle for the very skimpy subject access information provided by MARC records and encoded in the Library of Congress Subject Headings (LCSH), even if this is supplemented by numerous subject thesauri for periodical literature.

Problems with Subject Access Today

Michael J. Simonds sums up the current problem of subject access:

> The main problem with subject access is not with the online catalogs themselves. The problem lies with the databases they use....I do not oppose the introduction of elements such as tables of contents into our databases, I believe in the usefulness of keyword searching of titles. These efforts must be recognized for what they are: desperate attempts to overcome the basic inadequacy of access deficient LC MARC cataloging (Simonds, 1984).

Charles Hildreth echoes this sentiment. He maintains that systems design in online catalogs, generally, has still not gone beyond implementing the card catalog in online form, with some online search features tacked on. According to Hildreth, we have only scratched the surface of what is possible in online systems (Hildreth, 1983).

Over the years, a number of user studies have indicated that people were reasonably satisfied with the results of their searches, with 70 percent or better levels of satisfaction being the norm. There are two major flaws with these studies. The average library user is not very sophisticated in the use of computers and has low expectations. Secondly, the average user has no knowledge of what was missed (Bates, 1986a).

Fragmentation of Our Information Store

One peril of having no standard methodology or infrastructure for subject access is the rapidly increasing fragmentation of our information store into multitudes of specialized databases, each with its own indexing scheme, classification, and terminology control. As Raya Fidel (1988) puts it: "The uncoordinated growth of databases is an impediment to on-line searching. Standardization and coordination are required if users are to be able to fully exploit the capabilities of on-line systems." An infrastructure is needed that will serve to guide the end-user to the correct information packages in appropriate databases. There have been a number of efforts to integrate subject access.

- **Superindex**, a database created by merging the indexes of a large number of scientific and technical reference books. There were a number of problems with this approach. Some of the terms in the merged index were too specific; others weren't specific enough. Eventually the database was discontinued.
- A number of experiments in merging thesauri have also been reported in the literature (Wolff-Terroine, 1975; Jachowicz, 1975, Rada, 1986).
- There have also been a number of attempts to devise universal classification schemes (Rigby, 1974; LLoyd, 1972).

But there is still no coherent, well-organized infrastructure that links all information sources in a unified framework for searching. Expert systems may provide the mechanics for implementing computerized support for such an infrastructure. However, careful thought must first be given to the standards and to the flexibility needed to serve a widely diversified user population.

Multiple Thesauri and Indexing Structures

We can no longer ignore the fact that we have many types of thesauri and informal indexing conventions with very few efforts at forming an integrated system out of these disparate tools. Subject access tools exist in widely differing database formats at many different levels of specificity. We need to develop some means to collect, summarize, and display this information in a comprehensive subject access control system. A good analogy is the U.S. highway system. None of us would settle for being handed an alphabetical list of streets in the United States, even if we were told that the mapping system had Boolean searching capabilities, so that if we want an intersection of two streets we can ask for Fifth *and* Bigelow. Continuing the analogy, there would of course be an addendum and if we didn't find what we were looking for in the first list, there would be over one thousand other lists to check!

We know there are maps that summarize the highway system at many different levels of detail, ranging from maps of the superhighways down to census maps showing every house in a block. We expect to be able to select the map that has the appropriate detail, and to have the information displayed in a format that is graphic and easy to understand. Maps also convey a great deal of information in a condensed form. Mileages, types of road surfaces, geographic features, tourist attractions, and many more kinds of data are easily accessible. We demand this level of service from our maps. We should not settle for any less in our subject access control system. Modern computers with their powerful graphics capabilities can now offer at a reasonable price the ability to manage a browsing system of this type.

At present we depend on reference librarians to know and utilize subject access tools, to find out where to look and how to phrase an effective search strategy. The reader comes to the library with a desired search pattern, the reference librarian or reader's advisor has to try to match this pattern with what is found in the collection or to retrieve like materials that will satisfy the need. At present much of the work must be done manually because our automated systems are not yet designed to support subject access effectively.

Lack of Integration in Subject Access Tools

Many subject access tools, whose function is to assist the user in identifying the correct terminology, are not made available online and when they are, browsing is limited. A number of efforts have been made to automate LCSH for online access, but it is still not widely available. Even if it were available, no record is kept of the number of books posted to any given heading and therefore the user cannot glean any idea of the distribution of the literature. The system does provide a limited network of broader, narrowe, and related terms but two problems mitigate against this being very useful. The vocabulary of LCSH is quite restricted, and the syndetic (cross-reference) structure rapidly leads the user away from the subject of interest rather than through it (Sinkankas, 1975; Micco, 1980).

While there are also a sizeable number of periodical databases that offer online thesauri, none of them are in any way connected to LCSH. If a researcher does not find a term in his OPAC, he is left high and dry and will often leave the library with the impression that it has nothing on the topic of interest. Almost all OPACs depend on a direct match with only limited mapping from terms not used to those that are. Nor are stemming algorithms typically in place, or displays of broader and narrower terms. It is difficult, if not impossible to obtain a classified listing, online, of the subject headings in use in a particular subject area, which also shows the number of hits associated with each class. **Grateful Med** is one of the few systems that does try to provide guidance to the researcher in choosing terms by moving into a hierarchical display of the MeSH subject headings (Grateful Med, 1987).

Lack of Public Awareness

Mitigating the development of an integrated subject access system has been the fact that retrieving **some** material on any topic is a relatively simple task. However, finding the **best** information package and **most relevant** material greatly depends on the expertise and dedication of the individual conducting the search. For example, a search of the current **Magazine Index** will likely yield some articles on President Kennedy's assassination, but library professionals know this is neither the best nor the first place to look.

All too often, searches that require a high degree of experience and skill are conducted directly by end-users with no outside help and even less awareness of the options available. Library clients may be searching the wrong type of material or database, and/or using a poor choice of terms. Yet, they find *some* material and leave without realizing the wealth of information they failed to locate.

Cognitive Overload

A corollary problem emerges as our systems grow ever larger. Most of our systems work on the principle that "If a little is good, a lot is better." But now we can deliver so much material that users are overwhelmed by the sheer volume and have few means to narrow the retrieved set except by date and language, because of the lack of specificity in the terminology. Dealing with so much information at once can cause the user to experience "cognitive overload." Refining the search strategy by specifying the reading level, the intended audience, the type of information package, and the scope of the coverage will certainly help to resolve this problem, but this information is not even being captured in our cataloging and indexing processes.

Limited Vocabulary of LCSH

It is unrealistic to implement a vocabulary control or mapping scheme that deals only with the terminology in an OPAC while ignoring all other sources of information and hence vocabulary. Markey has shown that 45 percent of search statements entered by end-users in their OPACs resulted in no retrievals, while only 29 percent of searchers' terms matched or closely matched LCSH (Markey, 1984). A vocabulary control system that fails to find a match in 45 percent of all searches cannot by any stretch of the imagination be considered acceptable. No amount of natural language parsing or expert systems can solve the problem of the very limited vocabulary provided by LCSH.

Byrne & Micco have demonstrated that for a collection of 160,000 volumes, the total number of individual keywords generated from LCSH was only thirty thousand. When table of contents terms for only 6,000 books were added, the vocabulary jumped to 101,559 keywords (Byrne & Micco, 1988).

Traditional Boolean Retrieval Unsatisfactory

A Boolean search using OR makes no distinctions between the document with only one term and the document that contains all the terms listed. They are regarded as equally valuable. Conversely, in an AND strategy using several terms, a document missing only one of the desired terms is completely ignored (Salton, 1984). Slight variations in wording can also result in search failure, in spite of stemming algorithms. For example, a search for "terminal illness" will not find articles dealing with "terminal cases."

Proposed Solutions

An Integrated Subject Access System

There has been much talk about expert systems that can map natural language terms to the controlled vocabulary of LCSH. This will not happen until there is a solid network of interconnected, hierarchically arranged terms to work with, a **rich semantic network**, in the words of Marcia Bates (Bates, 1986a). The solution lies in combining and integrating the many existing subject access tools as well as adding new features to provide better access. New paradigms are necessary.

Unquestionably, we need to enhance present techniques of describing individual information packages as well as linking the different subject access tools together in a meaningful way. They should be placed online for interactive consultation during the search process on an as-needed basis. Users should be able to pop up **Books in Print** or the **Fiction Index** or **Ulrich's Periodical Directory** with the touch of a key. Try to envision a computer screen like the one shown in Figure 7.1. The user, sitting at a workstation using a mouse, could be presented with a screen like this one, which uses icons to indicate the tools available. The lower portion of the screen could carry on a dialog, directed by an expert system component to guide and assist the end-user.

A classified system of thesauri and other subject access tools, such as encyclopedias and dictionaries, could be organized online in a three-tier hierarchy, possibly taking advantage of locally stored CD ROM databases (Micco, 1987).

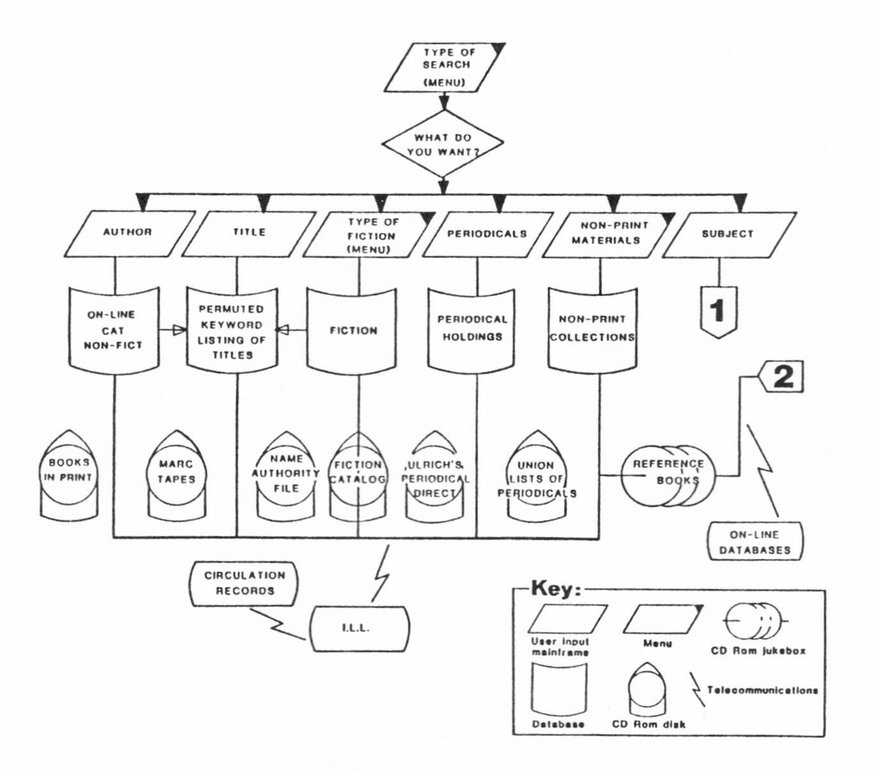

Figure 7.1. An integrated system interface

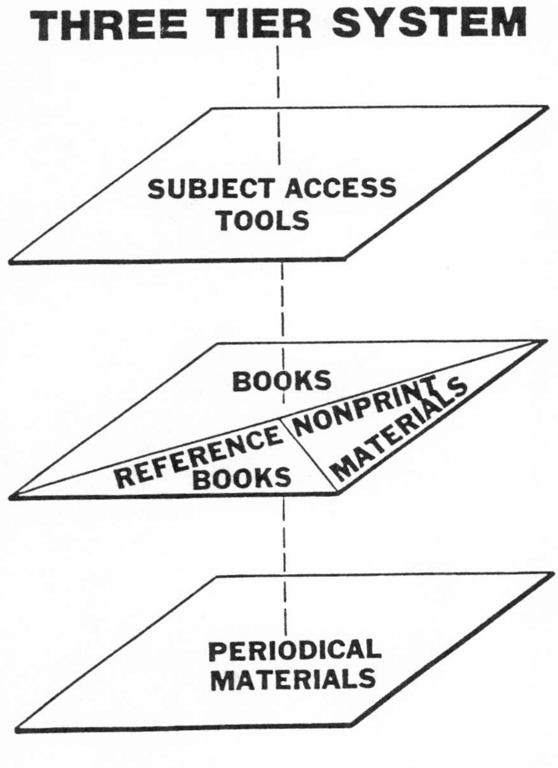

Figure 7.2. A three-tier hierarchy

Subject access tools should be arranged hierarchically by topic and information package type. A thesaurus for a specialized database will be performing at a very different level of specificity than LCSH. The technique is relatively simple. It involves collecting all the desired tools in machine-readable form and cataloging them with a special type of descriptive cataloging, and then assigning classification numbers based on topical coverage. An expert system would guide the user through the search process, suggesting alternatives or other places to try when a search yielded no hits. There is nothing more frustrating than searching for material on a clearly defined topic, such as **anaphora in natural language systems**, and yet being unable to locate any material. Most second generation OPACs simply report 0 hits and the user must start again from scratch, often with little idea of where else to try.

A number of different solutions to the problem of improving subject access have already been proposed, and many research projects are under way. One of the key problems is the considerable gulf that exists between the researchers working on subject access to books and those who work with the periodical databases. It would appear that eventually elements of many of these projects will be combined in new ways to create a new generation of more sophisticated subject access systems.

Linking Multiple Thesauri

A number of groups have focused on linking multiple thesauri in some systematic manner. Carol Mandel summarizes some of the techniques for managing multiple thesauri in online library bibliographic systems (Mandel, 1987).

Logically separate subject indexes. One solution is to maintain logically separate subject indexes and subject authority files for each vocabulary. This would be the cheapest and easiest solution if the infrastructure or road maps provide the necessary pointers to alert the user to the existence of alternative terms and to invoke their use when appropriate. The obvious disadvantage is the requirement for multiple sequential searches when users are interested in materials in more than one collection.

Mixed vocabularies. Simply combining vocabularies can lead to two kinds of problems, vocabulary clashes and degradation of access to specialized collections. Such was the case with Superindex.

Integrated vocabularies. In integrated systems, one vocabulary is mapped to the other with a single master file and a system of cross-references. Roy Rada has developed algorithms for automatically merging thesauri in his work at the National Library of Medicine (Rada, 1986).

Front-end navigation systems or switching languages. Niehoff at Batelle Labs developed a Vocabulary Switching System to experiment with a variety of algorithms from exact matching on lead terms, to stem matches, to exhaustive matching on all possible synonyms and related terms (Niehoff, 1984).

Of all the schemes being tried, those based on artificial intelligence may well hold the greatest promise. Once again, a quote from Mandel:

> There are a wide variety of specialized software packages for thesaurus management in organizations all over the world.... Some thesaurus management systems are designed for the development of multi-lingual thesauri; others are tailored to the handling of facets. Research has even begun on the potential of artificial intelligence in thesaurus software, in this case the use of a high-level "object-oriented" programming language...(Mandel, 1987, p.6).

Linking LCSH with LC Classification Schedules

Other efforts have focused on classification as the solution to the problem of subject access. At the very least, we should be linking subject headings to the relevant classification numbers; they are not the same and provide complementary subject access points. Karen Markey of The University of Michigan is cooperating with OCLC in a major project to link subject terms entered by online catalog users with the library's controlled vocabulary (Markey, 1988).

Phase I of the project involved a preliminary statistical analysis of the machine-readable version of LCSH. Several of Markey's findings show how much remains to be done before even this level of automation can be accomplished. Markey reports:

- LC class numbers occur in only 43.02 percent of records.
- 39.74 percent of all topical headings are orphan headings (with no parents or broader terms).
- 75.75 percent of the records do not bear narrower terms.

Another difficulty is that the indexes to each schedule of the Library of Congress Classification Schedules are not linked to LCSH. For example, **Boots and Shoes** is the heading in LCSH while **Footwear** has been chosen in the classification schedules. Immroth and Daily developed a considerable body of scholarly literature on the schedules and proposed a rigourous grammar for forming subject headings and for chain indexing LCC. These proposals were never adopted, but they provided many useful insights (Immroth, 1971; Daily, 1982).

In earlier work, Markey created a system for online subject access to the Dewey Decimal Classification Schedules and the Relative Index as well as the notes for browsing (Markey, 1984).

Not only are headings in LCSH not linked in any systematic way with the classification numbers in LC, but also the cross-reference structure of LCSH has been severely criticized in numerous studies since its inception (Sinkankas, 1976; Micco, 1980). In fairness it must be recognized that LCSH was never intended as a subject access system — the subject headings were considered as alternate book titles, as a means of supplementing the points of access provided in an author/title dictionary catalog. The **see** and **see also** references would seem to organize subject headings by categories (Daily, 1978) but even there access to the information contents of the books was never a goal. Headings are chosen to be as specific as the topic covered by the book, "but when the heading is broader than the topic, the cataloger should use two specific headings which will approximately cover it" (Haykin, 1951).

There are groups such as the developers of the **AAT** (**Art and Architecture Thesaurus**) who feel that the cross-reference structure of LCSH will never allow adequate online access. They are replacing it with a tree-like indexing structure that can provide linkages between terms which are logical, consistent, and can be displayed in a helpful array. The problem is that building a whole new schedule requires an enormous investment of human time and energy (Petersen, 1983).

MeSH is an excellent example of a very succesful system in which subject headings are linked into a hierarchically structured classification system. This enables users to explode headings and to broaden or narrow searches at will. It is possible to access the system at different levels of specificity (Micco, 1980).

Using Classification Numbers to Sort Retrieved Sets

A quite different, quick-fix approach is suggested by Prabha at OCLC. He is examining the use of library classification schemes to reduce large retrieval sets (Prabha, 1988). Theoretically, library classification schemes collocate books on similar topics. Therefore, by sorting retrieved sets by classification numbers the user will be able to determine the distribution of these items and select a subset.

He suggests as an example: a search for plants might yield one thousand hits. Sorting them by class number, we might find the following distribution:

Science (Q)	450
Geography/Anthropology (G)	100
Agriculture	200
Technology (T)	50
Other	200

Users would then be able to determine more closely their field of interest. This technique could be carried over to database searching. Where periodical titles are classified, the retrieval sets could be sorted by periodicals and then by class number.

These experiments can only be considered as the first steps in achieving a true subject access infrastructure that can provide online the sort of subject access support now offered by the expert reference librarian. No one is yet clear about how to solve the problems involved, but expert systems components will undoubtedly form part of the solution that is eventually adopted.

Using Full-Text Systems

The ability to search in full-text systems was once hailed as the solution to the vocabulary problem. This method allowed the user to go directly to documents themselves to locate a term, thus eliminating any dependency on a controlled vocabulary. However, this approach aggravates some of the problems already identified. Due to the massive storage requirements of full-text systems, the world's literature will be fragmented into an ever increasing number of databases. Without some form of vocabulary control spanning the whole system, it will become impossible to guarantee that the literature being searched contains the desired term.

Nor will there be any way to guarantee that no significant material is being missed. Finally, full-text systems at present offer little support for the grouping and synonym control functions provided by controlled vocabularies.

However, a number of interesting experiments in recent years have suggested that users can negotiate a 100-term vector, specifying the pattern of terms they are interested in. Then the vector can be submitted for searching in full-text systems using fuzzy set theory to obtain approximate matches (see Chapter Six for further discussion).

Certainly the question of vocabulary control in full-text systems is hotly debated. Borgman's studies have shown that even experts vary widely in their choice of terms for an identical search (Borgman, 1986). This would strongly suggest that some form of vocabulary control should be used to guide people to the controlled terms actually being used for indexing, regardless of what term is initially entered in the system.

On one hand, there are many who regard vocabulary control as unnecessary, particularly since parallel processors like the **Connection Machine** can search full-text documents at incredible speeds using 100-term vectors and relevance feedback to make searching more effective.

On the other hand, a number of research studies indicate the value of a controlled vocabulary to provide a grouping function and to suggest terms for searching. Often a searcher has only a vague idea of the terminology in a field. Among the more interesting research is that done by Fidel, who analyzed the behavior of skilled online searchers.

Fidel reports that all the skilled searchers she evaluated relied heavily on thesauri. They consulted a thesaurus for 80 percent of the search keys they selected. When they failed to do so, it was often because there was no thesaurus. Furthermore, she reports that the quality of thesauri and indexing as well as availability greatly affect the selection of search keys. Surprisingly, she reports that the most frequent reason for the selection of a search key derived from the request was the need to enhance recall. The number of moves to increase recall was almost double the number of moves to increase precision (Fidel, 1988).

Encoding the Heuristics of Reference Librarians in Expert Systems

There has been considerable interest in harnessing expert systems to assist in the process of managing vocabulary. Fidel's study represented a serious effort to study and codify the heuristics of expert searchers. She offers the summary of the rules she extrapolated that guide the selection of terms for searching (Figure 7.3).

Other heuristics are used by librarians when searching for a term not found in LCSH (Smith, 1987). New terms frequently appear first in confer-

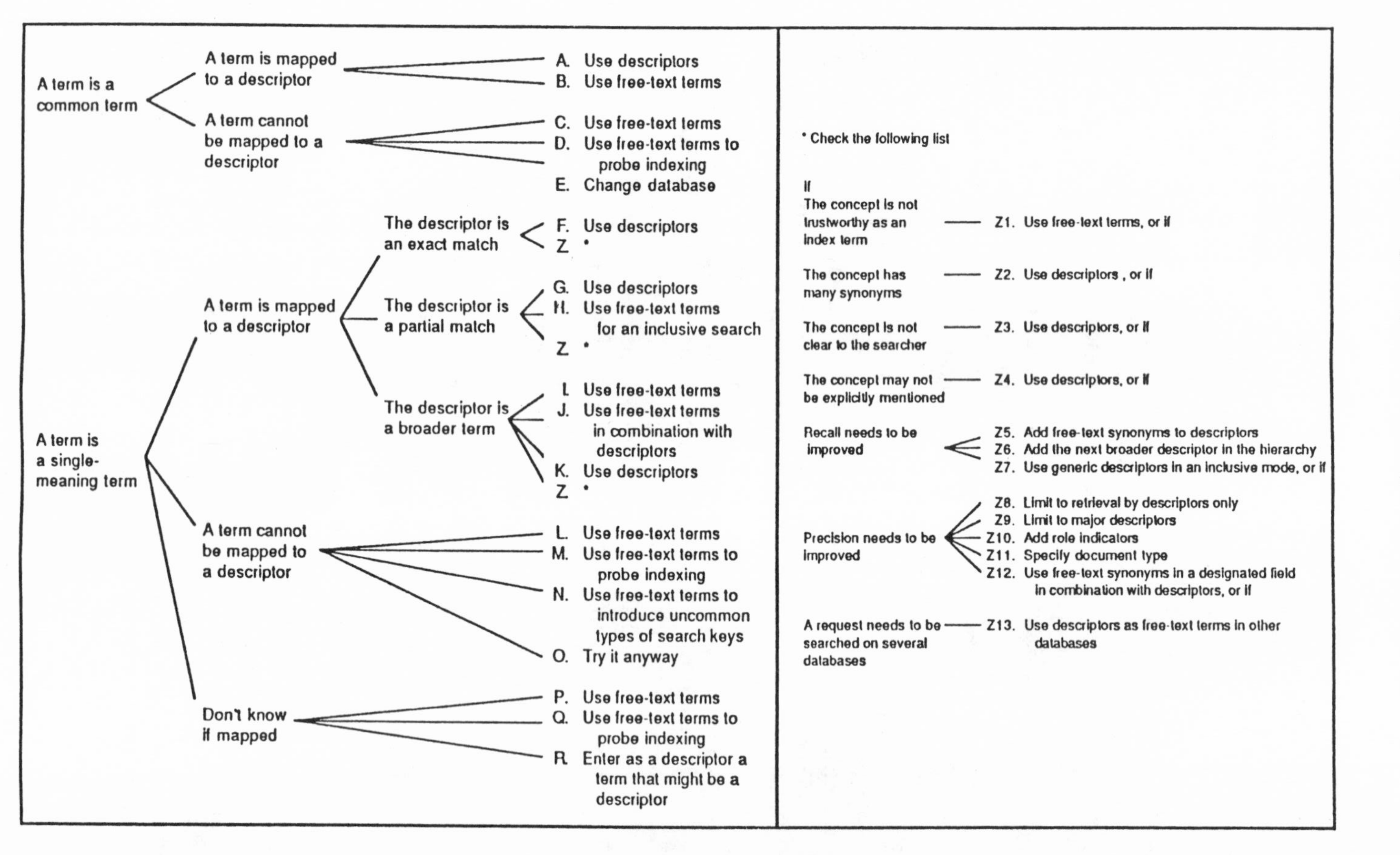

Figure 7.3. Fidel's table of search keys

ence papers or proceedings before shifting to marginal journals. Eventually, new terms show up in the better known, more scholarly core journals. Along the way, a certain percentage of these new concepts will appear in the popular press. Later, a concept that achieves recognition will be used in a book and, if well received, may become the subject of an entire book or conference.

At this stage, a body of literature may emerge that is significant enough to attract bibliographies and review articles. This will begin to have an impact on indexers of online periodical databases, who will consider making the subject a new heading. A concept must be thoroughly established with a significant number of publications appearing before it will receive a new subject heading. It takes even longer to be covered in the classification schedules. Much later, the concept will find its way into textbooks and established reference books, such as encyclopedias. Along the way there is a very high attrition rate because many new terms fail to establish themselves.

Any vocabulary control system that proposes to help the end-user to locate material on a topic of interest must accommodate this slow, evolutionary filtering process. A metarule in the system might evolve in this form:

Step 1. If interested in a subject area, first check the OPAC. If not found, go to the relevant discipline specific databases to check for periodical articles. Then check **Dissertation Abstracts** as well as conference proceedings. If still not found, check the popular press and general encyclopedias. Finally go to topical dictionaries to check spelling, and reference books to check that the terminology is correct.

OR

Step 1. If a specific piece of information is being sought, then check the subject-specific reference books; if not found try the dictionaries then thesauri in the subject area. Newspaper indexes are another place to check. A key determining factor here will also be the type of information being sought, such as an address, a date, information on an event, statistics, etc.

In order for this kind of a system to work in an online environment, all the subject access tools will need to be classified using a hierarchical universal classification scheme, such as Dewey. When a researcher is searching for a particular topic, such as "latch-key children," he will position himself in **sociology** and be given access to the relevant subset of tools. If a thesaurus is selected, the client should be able to browse the entries in the thesaurus while viewing the count of items associated with each term. If a reference book is selected, the client should be given immediate online access to the indices for that reference work and then to the full text of items selected.

Present systems lack a method of connecting the researcher to new concepts by mapping them to well-established terminology. For example, "latch-key children" was an unknown phenomenon ten years ago, but is now the object of considerable research and concern. New concepts such as "latch-key children" evolve gradually. If we are to provide a system that can manage a constantly evolving language, then we must link all different information packages in one integrated system.

The controversy still rages about the advantages of controlled vocabulary versus free text. In the 1960s the **Cranfield studies** reported by Cleverdon (1984) seemed to indicate that free text keyword searching outperformed controlled vocabularies. Many other studies using a great variety of language controls have since been carried out to determine which types of search keys provide the best retrieval. The results have been contradictory, which would seem to suggest that a combination of both free text and controlled vocabularies would offer the best solution. The issue is still unresolved and hotly debated in the literature (Cleverdon, 1984; Lancaster, 1980; Dubois, 1987).

Another controversial issue is the use of phrases as well as keywords. It is argued in some circles that keywords and phrases should be used together. Most OPACs today support both phrase matching on ex-

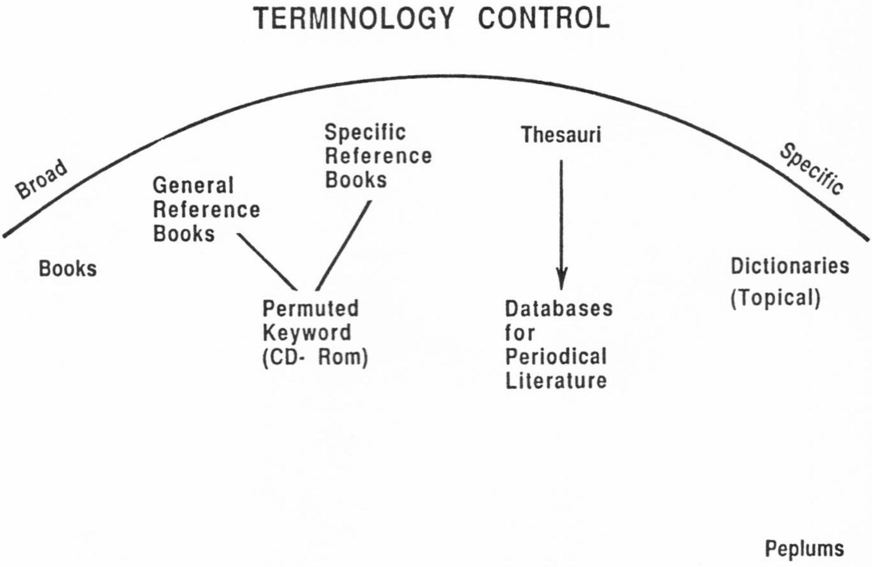

TERMINOLOGY CONTROL

Broad
Specific
Specific Reference Books
Thesauri
General Reference Books
Books
Dictionaries (Topical)
Permuted Keyword (CD- Rom)
Databases for Periodical Literature
Peplums

Figure 7.4. Terminology control system

act Library of Congress Subject Headings and keyword matching. However, these are hybrid systems that do not integrate or link these separate approaches in any useful way during a search (Hildreth, 1989). Most systems do not allow library clients to combine multiple word subject headings with single keywords using Boolean operators.

Bates makes a very important distinction between the **end-user thesaurus** and the **indexer thesaurus** in her seminal article on subject access (Bates, 1986a). She points out that the end-user thesaurus must provide a **dense semantic network** with a huge entry vocabulary that will almost guarantee the user will find *something*. Terms from the end-user thesaurus then need to be mapped to the more controlled vocabulary of the indexer thesaurus and the classification system, because the latter provide an important grouping function.

Building a Taxonomy of Information Packages

Building an infrastructure that will create order and cohesion out of the confusion is a major challenge today. A subject access infrastructure must form part of any solution to the problems which will ultimately be addressed by expert systems and artificial intelligence. This will involve building a taxonomy of information packages, cataloging and classifying each type, and noting contributions to vocabulary control. Books, reference books, nonprint materials, and periodical literature as well as subject access tools should all be integrated in one subject access system. Researchers will need to develop techniques for upgrading subject access at all levels.

Expert systems can contribute considerably to this process. The Dewey, UDC, and Library of Congress classification schemes were designed as shelf ordering systems with only one location for each book. Their main purpose is to group like books together. Subject headings were added subsequently to provide additional access points. In retooling for a computerized world, the classification scheme could provide the infrastructure needed to link the many diverse information packages in a loosely interconnected system. This system will provide dynamic online access to information rather than the bibliographic description of the book.

A researcher interested in a particular subject area should be able to refer to the online classification scheme to obtain a point of entry into the system and to access the appropriate subset of tools (indexes, thesauri, reference tools, and databases). This does not mean to imply that such procedures would be needed for every search but rather that a support navigation system should be available when needed. We have in the past supported only one search strategy — Boolean, brute force keyword searching with post coordination of terms. Yet, we all know there are many different needs to be satisfied and widely varying strategies used by skilled librarians. A known item search differs considerably from a subject search. A reader's advisor performs a different task from that of the ready reference librarian. Considerably more flexibility is needed in our online systems.

One very important system requirement is that the user should be able to move to a listing of relevant subject headings with a count of the number of titles available under each heading and the ability to expand to display these titles if so desired (i.e., a small adaptation of the old shelf list). Two levels of searching should be provided. First the local collection, then the Union Catalog facility offered by OCLC.

This "road map" would then provide the user with information on how a literature is evolving and what the hot topics are. It would also direct users to the most appropriate tools for their subject area search by marking them with special codes or highlighting them in some way.

Improving Subject Access to Books

There are a number of major research projects that have focused on improving subject access to books using one or another of the approaches outlined below.

- Add additional facets to the bibliographic record to provide a better match between the user and the material retrieved.
- Enrich the subject description of the records to provide a richer entry vocabulary.
- Use the records to build a dense semantic network of the type proposed by Bates (1986a).
- Use a variety of techniques to enhance retrieval. These include stemming algorithms (Porter, 1984), spelling correction routines which will search for words that sound like the given term, and synonym control or cross-references as well as term weighting based on the frequency of occurrence of terms. The lower the number of hits the more useful the term becomes as a discriminator and the higher the ranking assigned to it.
- Relevance feedback. If a user identifies a retrieved article as relevant the system can automatically select the LCSH headings assigned to it for further searching. This technique can be of mixed value, due to the wave linking syndetic structure of LCSH which quickly leads the user away from the subject

of interest. A search that retrieved twenty-five books on natural language yielded numerous headings for further searching, very few of which were of interest to the researchers involved as seen in Figure 7.5 (Byrne & Micco, 1988).

Another technique tested in **OKAPI-84** (Hildreth, 1989) was a weighted **quorum** search. If a Boolean **AND** search fails to retrieve anything, the search words are assigned weights based on the frequency of occurrence in the database. Uncommon words are, of course, assigned higher values and the system will search for records which contain fewer than all the words in the query (all words - one; all words - two, ..., all words - n) until the list is exhausted. Retrieved records are assigned a ranking value equal to the sum of the weights of the words by which they are indexed. Records with the highest rank value are listed first in the output. For example, a search for "methods of incineration" will yield the following rankings, because methods has a very high count and would not be considered as a good discriminator.

1. Documents containing both terms: methods/incineration.
2. Documents with the term: incineration only.
3. Documents with the term: methods would not be shown as the count here would be too high and the word would have been added to a stop list.

RANKING OF LCSH HEADINGS AVAILABLE

High Relevance	Relevant	Marginal	Useless
Ambiguity		Artificial Intelligence	
Anaphora			
	Cleopatra		
Discourse analysis			Electronic digital computers—programming
Generative grammar			
	Grammar—Comparative and general —Syntax		Engineering design
Parsing—Computer grammar			English language—Data processing
		Linguistics—Data processing	
Question-answering systems			Interactive computer systems
		Logic—Symbolic and mathematical	
Machine translation			Language and languages
		Machine theory	Languages—philosophy
Semantics			Programming languages—Electronic computers—semantics
			Visual communication

Figure 7.5. Number of LCSH cross-references found valuable by researchers

Different rules are used for known item searches. If a title phrase search produces no match, OKAPI-84 will look for titles containing the individual search words.

Increase Facets Captured in Data Records

Fidel makes a very important distinction in search strategies. The types of moves made by skilled searchers can be divided into two classes: **operational moves** which keep the meaning of a request unchanged but may seek to increase recall or limit a search set which is too large, and **conceptual moves** which actually change or modify the nature of the request. Both are important and need to be considered in designing expert systems to support searching (Fidel, 1988).

There is much more that could and should be done to support operational moves. Every information package should be classified according to its function, intended audience, reading level, and organization. This information should be added to the MARC data and periodical articles, also. Reference librarians use this information intuitively and skillfully to match the user with appropriate material. Even small children will decide on whether they want to read a book based on the size of the print (reading level) and appeal (intended audience). This information or facetting can be very useful in breaking down large retrieved sets to reduce the cognitive overload. An expert system module could perform this matching if the information were recorded in the MARC record.

For example, here is one possible way of representing the facets of a reference work:

ADDITIONAL TAGS RECOMMENDED FOR THE MARC FORMAT

Function:
Overview, research report, history, criticism, ready reference, introduction, analysis, biography, textbook, bibliography, guide to the literature, subject access tool (see below)

Intended Audience:
General Interest, Educated Layperson, Scholarly research, Juvenile

Organization:
Index type= [alphabetical, classified, authors, citations, glossary]

Arrangement : [chronological, facetted, geographic]

Special features: [Illustrations, diagrams, portraits, charts, maps, graphs]

Time period covered:[contemporary, 20th century...]

Geographic qualifiers:[regions, countries...]

Scope: [Comprehensive, General, Narrow]

Databases, in turn, will be classed by subject content and by the type of information packages they contain.

Subject access tools [encyclopedias, indexes, dictionaries, thesauri, bibliographies, concordances] will all be coded as such and made available online to the patrons who can search from a workstation in the reference room.

Enrich the Subject Description of Books: Increase Specificity of Vocabulary

Access to the information contents of books is very restricted. For centuries, librarians have used classified shelf arrangements to group like materials together. Hence card catalogs offered minimal entries about the collection. Because every book is treated as a complete unit, subject headings are selected to reflect as accurately as possible the topic of the whole book or its "aboutness." This has resulted in an average of 1.4 subject headings per OCLC record (O'Neill & Aluri, 1981).

As Fidel has indicated, we need to provide better support for conceptual moves made by searchers. They modify their strategies to achieve better results by narrowing the search that is too broad or broadening the search that is too narrow. This often occurs after a preliminary scouting of the subject area to determine what is out there. Our present subject access systems fail to provide this sort of support.

Clearly there is a need to build a dense semantic network that will increase the specificity of the vocabulary as well as providing a better cross-reference structure. A number of research efforts summarized by Byrne have pointed out that the best performance is obtained from searches using title, author, and if possible abstracts as well as subject headings (Byrne, 1975). One method proposed for achieving this is the addition of table of contents terms to the MARC records (Settel & Cochrane, 1982). An ongoing experiment to enhance the MARC records with table of contents terms for all new acquisitions is reported by Byrne & Micco (1988). The objective is to provide subject access at the chapter level, thereby greatly increasing the specificity of the vocabulary.

Techniques Proposed

In a study conducted at the Australian Defense Force Academy Library (ADFA), several techniques for enhancing subject access in the online public access catalog (OPAC) were evaluated (Beatty, 1985). This research was prompted in part by a need to promote fuller use of the collection. A survey had shown that little more than 20 percent of the collection was circulating. The following methods for improving subject access were considered.

Adding LC headings for each chapter. Librarians considered adding more LC headings to the MARC records, for instance, one for each chapter of the book. This, however, would not solve the problem of a strong American bias in LC terminology or its very slow adoption of new terms. Also upon analysis, the LCSH terminology is not specific enough to be used for the detailed analysis of specialized material.

Adding thesaurus terms to records. Another option was to use thesauri relevant to specific subject areas, such as computing or engineering. However, this is greatly complicated by the different meanings assigned to similar terms in different disciplines. Selecting a general thesaurus would elicit the same problems as using LCSH and the thesaurus would have none of the LCSH's advantages. The principal advantages of LCSH is that about 70 percent of records come with LCSH supplied, and catalogers are already familiar with it.

Writing abstracts for the books being cataloged. This was rejected as being too time consuming.

Building an in-house thesaurus. This also was ruled out as being too expensive and time consuming. Even if this option seemed ideal, the ADFA Cataloging Section lacked the subject specialists needed to provide adequate in-depth analysis of most areas, particularly technical fields.

Adding Table of Contents Terms

Finally, the techniques advocated by Pauline Cochrane and Barbara Settel were used to enhance records by adding table of contents terms to the local subject field in the MARC record. Under the instruction of the Australian National Bibliography, these terms were added to the 653 field, and tagged for four levels of subdivisions reflecting different levels in the table of contents.

Initially, librarians were concerned that not all books would include the needed information, but this proved to be a minor problem. A background study performed on a sample of 179 items showed that 104 contained both a contents page and an index, fifty-two had contents only, three had index only, and twenty had neither. Of the twenty, twelve were fiction, four bibliographies, three indexes, and one a dictionary.

Other Questions

Three other questions had to be addressed before embarking on the actual processing.

Eliminate LCSH? One of the first issues was to decide whether the augmented headings would be used separately or in combination with LC headings. A small trial with twenty-two queries confirmed that the augmented headings would be most useful if available for searching as an alternative to the LC headings. The LC terms would cover the main subject or "aboutness" of the book and the additional terms its information content. The reference librarians were adamant about the use of the Library of Congress subject headings because of the very useful grouping function they perform in controlling vocabulary.

How to structure the augmented headings? The best solution appeared to be entering all headings into a single field. This would include the 653 field for local subjects. Semantic relationships between the terms were preserved. Separate headings were delimited with "@," and subheadings by ",", punctuation, which would not distort the retrieval process. This was done in anticipation of some day using this coding to develop hierarchical displays on the screen.

Use a weighting scheme? Weighting was considered but rejected because of the possibility that it would increase the complexity of indexing by requiring value judgements. Librarians also believed a reliable method was impossible within the constraints of current software (Beatty, 1985; Byrne, 1986).

Procedures Involved in Enhanced Subject Processing

Enhanced subject processing (ESP) is an ongoing project. These are the procedures currently being used. Clerks provide photocopies of the title page, the table of contents and, when needed, the index. In turn, catalogers highlight the phrases or terms they feel should be added to the MARC record. A procedures manual and a standardized approach has been developed to guide the selection of terms.

Finding terms in the table of contents and/or index. The first step involves deciding whether to use the contents page and/or index. The table of contents is preferred, provided that:

- It contains at least one heading for every thirty-five pages of text.
- It largely consists of content-bearing terms rather than whimsical phrases.

- It does not contain a significant amount of repetition. Care was taken to reduce redundancy by entering each term only once per document.

In fact, the table of contents is preferred whenever possible, as it often provides excellent topical headings more concisely than the index. It also indicates the relationship between the parts of the book.

Highlighting the desired terms. The next step involves highlighting the terms from the table of contents that refer to five or more pages of text, or terms from the index referring to seven or more pages. Phrases which are not "content bearing" are omitted. Words may be omitted from phrases if they are not content bearing or essential to the meaning of the phrase. If the tables of contents include the names of authors who contributed articles, neither their names nor the page ranges are highlighted. There are special rules for dealing with various problem cases. For example, when neither the table of contents nor the index provides enough information, the cataloger assigns terms to cover the work's contents.

Coding the terms to reflect levels. Terms are coded for computer input using a hierarchy of codes that reflect the levels on the table of contents page. More than 80 percent of the books coming into the ADFA library are processed in this manner. The following categories are usually excluded:

- Serials. Since the broad topics are adequately covered by the title and the LC headings, including journal titles is unnecessary. Also, the contents of serials are already indexed by standard indexing and abstracting services.
- Fiction.
- Dictionaries, indexes, atlases, encyclopedias, bibliographies without subject subdivisions, collective biographies, directories, and any source where each subject is covered in less than five pages are also excluded.
- Very general works where the author does not address subdivisions of the subject in depth.
- Highly specific items which are often described adequately by title and/or LC headings, like some research reports and computer manuals.
- Library working tools and the library science collection.

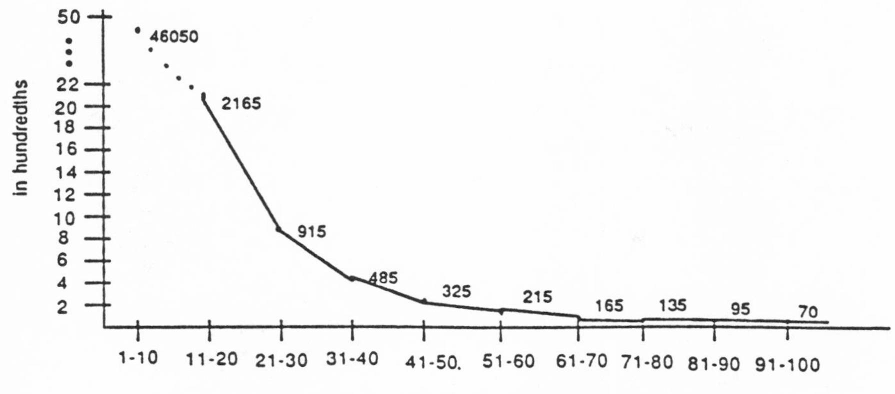

Figure 7.6. Vocabulary distribution

Advantages of ESP

The ESP approach provides the following advantages.

1. Subject access is enhanced by many additional access points.
2. The terminology used reflects the author's wording. This avoids misinterpretation by an intermediary.
3. Access is provided to topics covered by chapter headings and subheadings.
4. Minimum time and intellectual effort is needed for processing.

To further reduce the processing time required, librarians have given some consideration to using an optical scanner to speed up input, but so far none tested can deal with the constantly changing typeface of contents pages and indexes.

Impact on Resources and Workload

Researchers found in analyzing the impact on resources and workload that in an undergraduate campus library of 160,000 titles, the number of distinct keywords in the subject headings for the entire collection amounted to little more than 30,000. With the addition of chapter level terms for only 6,000 books, the number of keywords rose dramatically to more than 100,000 words. This would appear to support the hypothesis that the LCSH vocabulary is quite restricted. It is designed to describe the contents of books or their "aboutness" rather than their information content and lacks the specificity of the chapter level headings. Proper names and jargon are included in this vocabulary, but there are few non-English language terms included. The vocabulary distribution was interesting in that a very large number of words, 89 percent of the words, had less than 10 occurrences. Fifty-eight percent had only one hit.

There is still a question about whether the dramatic increase in the vocabulary size stems from working with a small database. Because there are a limited number of terms related to concepts covered by the ADFA collections, perhaps the vocabulary size will stabilize as the database expands. Vocabulary size certainly has implications for searching. By searching all the low-frequency terms first, the user will pull a small pool of relevant documents much more quickly. An "OR" capability is necessary to ensure that a sufficiently large pool of documents is retrieved.

A controlled study of searches submitted compared the number of documents retrieved with the enhanced entries to the number obtained using LCSH without enhancement. The enhanced entries showed retrieval increased 300 percent. An immediate result of this enhancement was greater utilization of the collection.

The impact these enhancements have had on the workload is not overwhelming. Statistics were collected to determine how much time it takes at each step to add table of contents terms to 200 volumes. Photocopying takes an average of 1.5 minutes per volume. Assigning the terms takes 8.5 minutes, not including the time taken to photocopy the index in the 20 percent of cases where this is desirable. Keying the terms takes

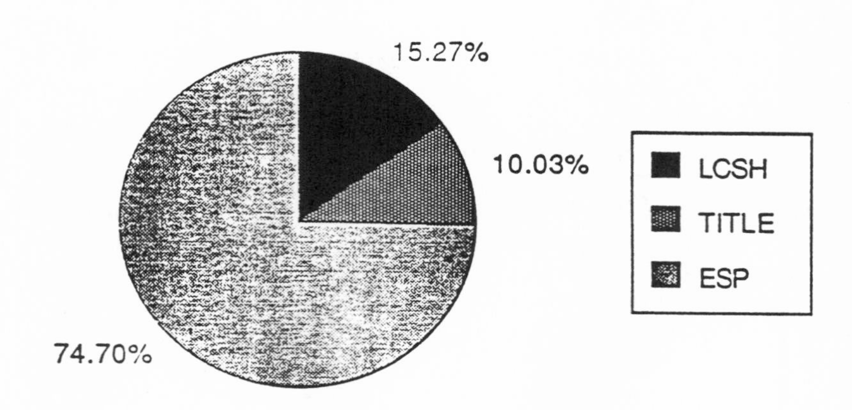

Figure 7.7. Increased retrieval with ESP

the clerical help 10.7 minutes per volume, allowing for proofreading, corrections, and system filing time.

Nor was the impact on system resources as great as researchers had anticipated. Before ESP, the bibliographic database took 244 megabytes of storage. It has increased 14 percent to 279 megabytes but its growth has reached a plateau. The subject authority file increased very rapidly at first but has levelled off at eight megabytes.

The anticipated degradation of response time has not occurred, although occasional problems have been noted if more than two people are keying in ESP data while an Australian National Bibliography tape is being loaded.

Impact on Users

Most of the library users surveyed took the improvement in retrieval for granted or seemed unaware of the changes. Most users viewed the increased information available in the catalog record to evaluate the relevance of items as the major benefit. However, users had some problems with the displays.

The records were generally too long to fit on a single screen. Users had to scroll through far more material than they were accustomed to. Another unanticipated problem occurred with conference proceedings. It seemed that searches on any topic in computer science would pull up one very large set of conference proceedings that took up eight screens because every paper had been given its own entry and the topics ranged widely. This became a major nuisance, and users complained that they knew of that conference and did not want to see it every time they executed a search!

Now that we've seen how a library might go about enhancing subject access by enriching the search vocabulary, let us examine another prototype project for enhancing subject access by improving displays and linking subject headings to a classification scheme.

Creating a Dense Semantic Network or Adding an Expert System Component

A number of researchers report that the majority of subject access points entered by online catalog users fail to match the controlled vocabulary. Users are not familiar with the controlled vocabulary and want related terms to be suggested (Markey & Vizine-Goetz, 1984). Users feel that "**online aids for finding, browsing and selecting controlled vocabulary are imperative.**" User studies reported by Cochrane indicate that the library researchers selected the ability to view a list of words related to their search words more frequently than any other option available to improve online catalogs (Cochrane, 1984).

Additional ammunition in explaining the failure of keyword access can be derived from research on memory and cognition; the verbal context in which a word is learned can be very important in recall. If a word is learned in a particular semantic context, e.g., between two other words, free recall of that word will be much higher if the surrounding words are presented during the recall efforts. (Baker & Santa, 1977).

Psychologists agree that our ability to recall is not nearly as great as our ability to recognize members of a set (Rubin & Kontis, 1983). There is ample proof of this in the research on searching behaviors. Searchers typically have difficulty and will resist being asked to come up with a number of synonyms for their chosen topic. However, when presented with lists of options or facets, they have no hesitation in selecting subordinate concepts for their topic. Librarians accomplish this by browsing through the table of contents of relevant books. An important goal is to provide a similar online browsing capability by utilizing a series of subject area maps, generated from the table of contents terms.

The ADFA experiment has demonstrated the feasibility of enriching the number of keywords per MARC record and thereby providing a larger entry vocabulary on a par with the subject access provided for periodical articles. But it did not provide any sort of user interface to assist the user in browsing. The next logical step involves building an online browser from these enriched records that will serve as an end-user thesaurus of the type described by Marcia Bates.

It is possible for an interface to provide a dense semantic network built up from the table of contents terms linked to the titles, formal subject headings, and classification numbers of books. This should ensure a much denser network than currently exists. It should also make it possible for a user to enter the system succesfully at almost any level of specificity. The researcher would see the distribution of the literature and be encouraged to narrow a search that yielded too many hits, or to broaden one that was too specific. Most importantly, a researcher would be able to select relevant terms from those actually being used in a given subject field.

Several constraints must be imposed on this type of system. The system must be feasible and cost-effective in an existing library environment with off-the-shelf hardware and software. It would have to be interfaced with the OPAC in place and most importantly would have to build itself automatically from the records in each library's OPAC.

A number of experimental OPACs have explored methods of providing better subject access. Among them is **KIM (Knowledge and Information Mapping)**, a prototype system with a graphical thesaurus in which subject maps can be displayed at different levels of detail or focus. The graphics provide inherent cognitive and psychological advantages over linear lists (Hildreth, 1989).

Micco & Rambler are working on a prototype that will add a **hypertext browser** as an option to the OPAC user interface in the Carlyle **TOMUS** system. The MARC records used in this prototype have already been enriched with table of contents terms. The Browser will enable readers to familiarize themselves with the collection by browsing online through the table of contents of relevant books.

When a client enters a keyword, she will be directed to a listing of the different classification numbers in which the keyword is used. In this way, she can quickly determine the emphasis she wants. For example, is there greater interest in a work on economic history classified as history, or is there more interest in the history of economics classified in economics? Once a classification number has been selected, the user can view the subject headings assigned to that class number and from there can quickly move to looking at the book titles and table of contents terms assigned to that heading.

Objectives of System Design

The prototype system described above has been designed to accomplish the following objectives:

To make an online browsing capability available for the end-users, and help them with term selection by displaying the thesaurus described above at many different levels of abstraction. The user should be able browse freely through series of hypertext maps to determine the distribution of the literature and the terminology that is in vogue, before finalizing a search strategy.

To build an online thesaurus that is updated continually and reflects current usage. As each book is added to the collection, the thesaurus (central dictionary) is updated with any new keywords. In this way, the thesaurus accurately reflects current usage of the terminology.

To provide mapping of the author's natural language terms to the Library of Congress subject headings. Every keyword used by the author in the table of contents and title is mappped to the controlled vocabulary of the subject headings and classification number provided for the work. This network of linkages is captured and displayed as a subject area map for the user to browse through. This provides a much denser semantic network to assist users in finding material of interest. They are effectively searching chapter level terms.

To automatically link classification numbers to Library of Congress subject headings. As each keyword for an individual book is posted, it is linked to the subject headings assigned to the book and also to the classification number. In the same way, all subject headings assigned to a particular book are linked to the classification number for that book. In effect, the syndetic structure (cross-references) is built dy-

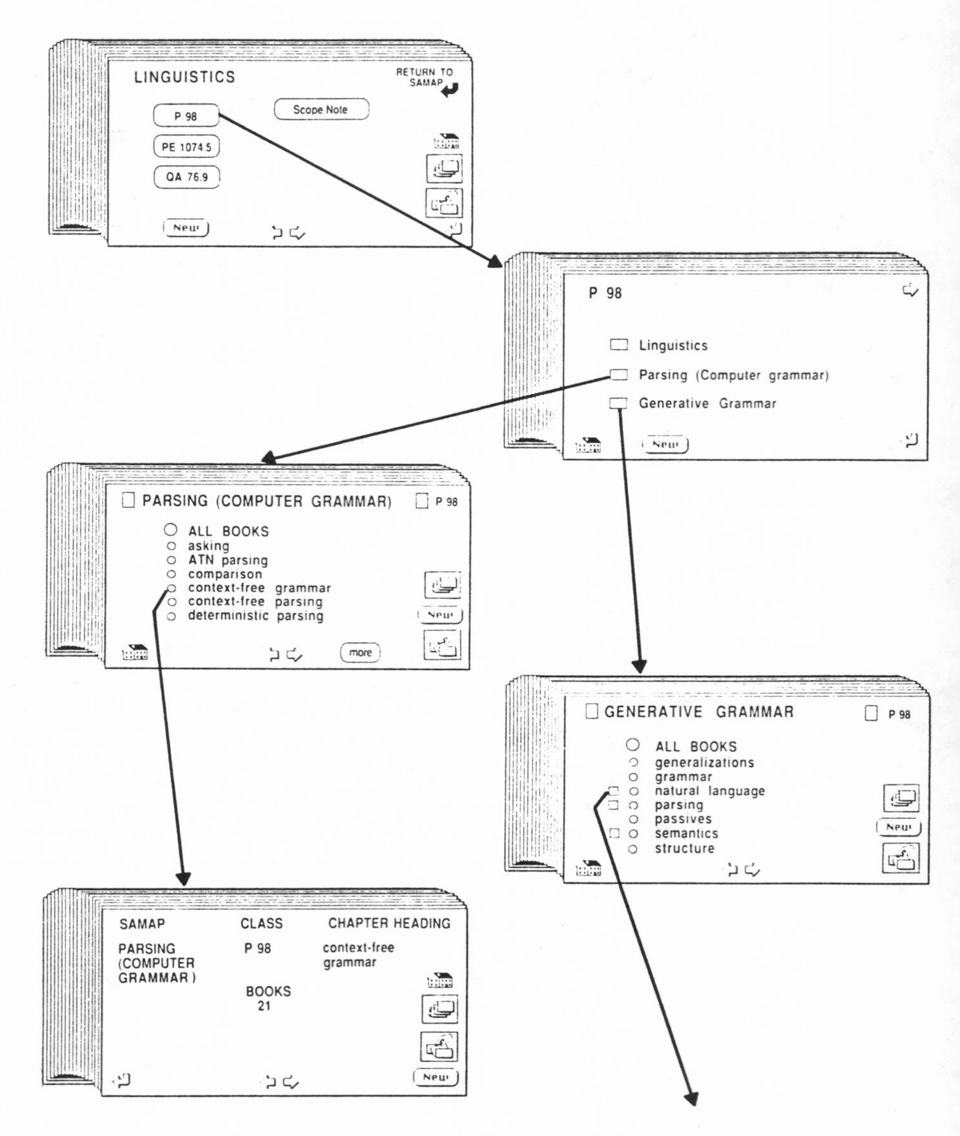

Figure 7.8. Request for information on linguistics

namically and reflects the actual literature as it is evolving. The classification numbers are very important in providing a firm foundation for managing the system of hypertext maps. They also enable the user to quickly eliminate irrelevant material by pruning the retrieved set. The users can immediatedly situate themselves in the section of the classification scheme most likely to meet the information need, while at the same time being made aware of other possible options.

To increase use of the book collection. It is an axiom that in most libraries, only 20 percent of the collection sees active use. Librarians anticipate that the ability to locate chapters on a topic of interest will lead users to books that might otherwise have gone unnoticed. An increase in recall of 300 percent is being reported from the ADFA experiment (Micco & Byrne, 1988).

Demonstration of Proposed System

A small prototype based on a collection of books that deal with the subject "**natural language**" has been developed using an SE Macintosh with **HyperCard** to demonstrate the proposed system design. A HyperCard "stack" corresponds to a Rolodex containing index cards. Each "card" in the stack may be linked to other cards in the same stack, or cards in other stacks. Users of the system can press "buttons" to indicate they want to see the card referred to.

Let us assume a particular user has requested information on "linguistics." The system recognizes via the central dictionary that three subject maps for linguistics exist, each with a different classification number: P98, PE1074.5 and QA76.9 (see Figure 7.8).

It presents these options for the user, providing helpful scope notes which enable the user to differentiate among them.

For years, professionals have discussed the value of linking classification numbers to subject headings, but the logistics and cost have appeared prohibitive. The system proposed above, however, enables these links to be built automatically as the books are being entered into the database. In doing so, this greatly enriches the syndetic structure available. The classification numbers provide a formal infrastructure for organizing the information, while the formal subject headings extracted from the book enable the user to perceive real differences in focus and purpose of actual books in a particular classification number. The table of contents terms provide the enriched vocabulary needed to match natural language terms to the more controlled vocabulary of the subject headings. They are linked automatically to the classification number.

In the case of linguistics, maps appear in three locations in the schedules. **P** deals with **philology and languages** in general, while **PE** deals specifically with English language. **QA**, on the other hand, has to do with technology and computers. If the user selects P98 for further scrutiny, the hypertext links will immediately pull up the classification card for P98, showing three subject headings and hence three subject maps associated with P98 in the schedules. The choices are books on **linguistics**, **parsing (computer grammar)** or **generative grammar**.

The user selects one of these and is linked directly to the subject area map with the chapter headings displayed. The user can decide to look at

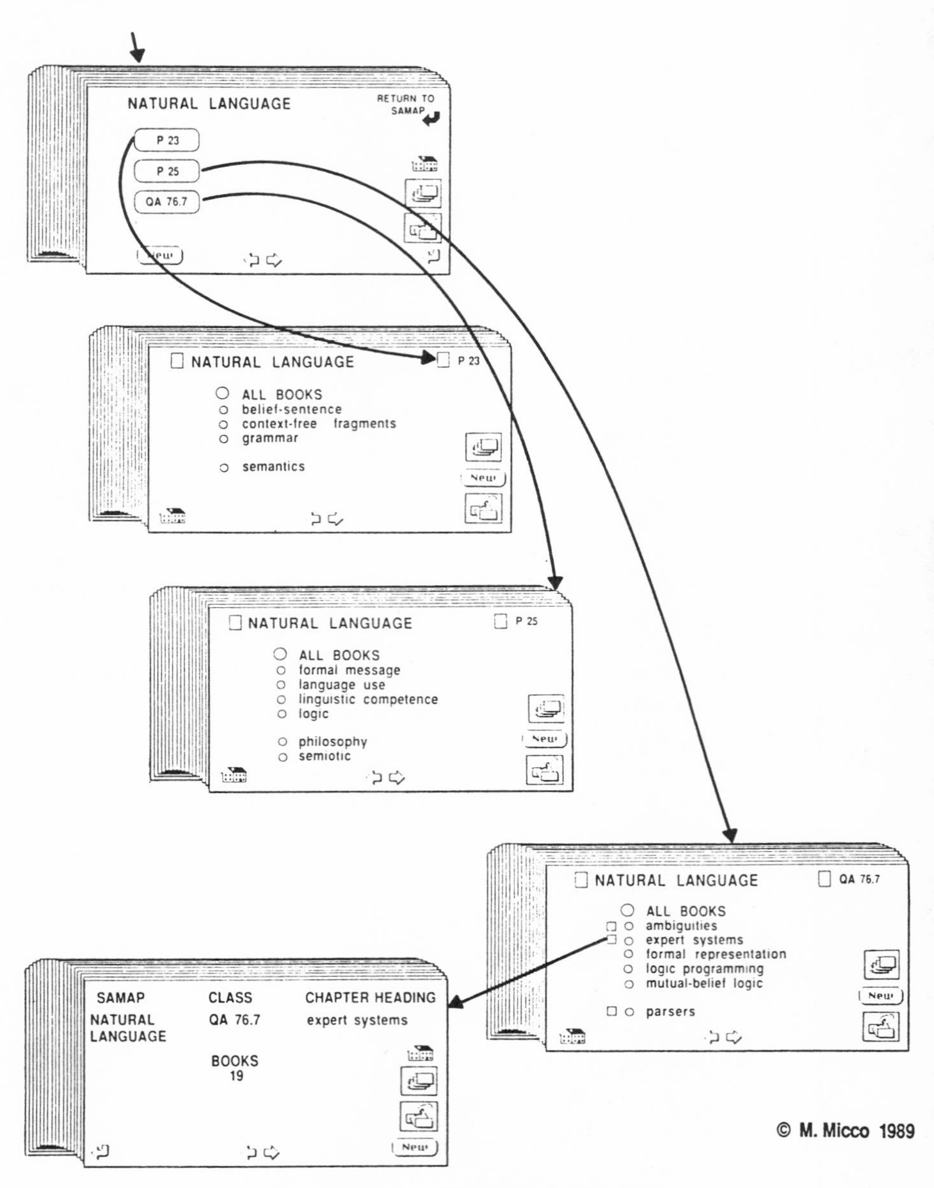

Figure 7.9. Searching for a narrow term: an example of a subject map

all the books in this group or to select a subset, such as the books on parsing (computer grammar) restricted to those with chapters on **context-free grammars**. Once a group has been selected for display, the system will pass the book identification numbers back to the MARC database for retrieval and display under the normal OPAC software control.

Entering a Narrow Term

Someone requesting information on **deterministic parsing** would be directed through the central dictionary, where it is listed as a chapter heading term to the subject area stack as shown in Figure 7.9.

The user would be able to ascertain immediately that this is a chapter in a book on parsing (computer grammar) in class number P98. From here a number of options are available.

1. The reader can work through the neighboring cards dealing with parsing in other parts of the classification schedules. Each card in this stack holds a unique subject heading and classification number combination.
2. The reader can switch to P98 in the schedule to see other books classified here, perhaps selecting generative grammar.
3. The reader can decide to examine the books about parsing (computer grammar) with chapters on deterministic parsing.
4. The reader can explore other chapters on parsing, such as those relating to "context-free grammars," a suggestion drawn from the display of table of contents terms.
5. The reader can cancel the search and start again with a different term.

In this type of display, the user is quickly made aware of the terminology used in books of interest and can modify her search strategy to gain greater precision.

Also, the reader could manipulate book counts to influence the developing search strategy. Every book on parsing that has a chapter on deterministic parsing is counted as it is being posted. These counts can be displayed and manipulated in a variety of ways at different levels of abstraction.

An expert system component could use the counts to determine the strategy to use in a given search. If only one book contained a chapter on "deterministic parsing," the search could be easily broadened to "parsing." Conversely, if thirty to forty books had chapters on the topic, the search could be restricted to some facet, such as the **books that provide an overview**.

As more and more libraries acquire color terminals, the system could rank the chapter headings by frequency of occurrence and then graphically display each map with colored concentric circles indicating the number of hits. The most frequently used chapter headings could be coded yellow in circles closest to the center, next orange, then red. Green or blue could represent less frequently used terms.

Entering a Broader Term

If a user enters a broader term, such as "linguistics," the system will recognize from the dictionary that there are three subject area maps for linguistics, each with a different classification number. It will present the options, providing helpful scope notes to enable readers to differentiate. It should be noted that for years librarians have discussed the value of linking classification numbers to subject headings. This system enables

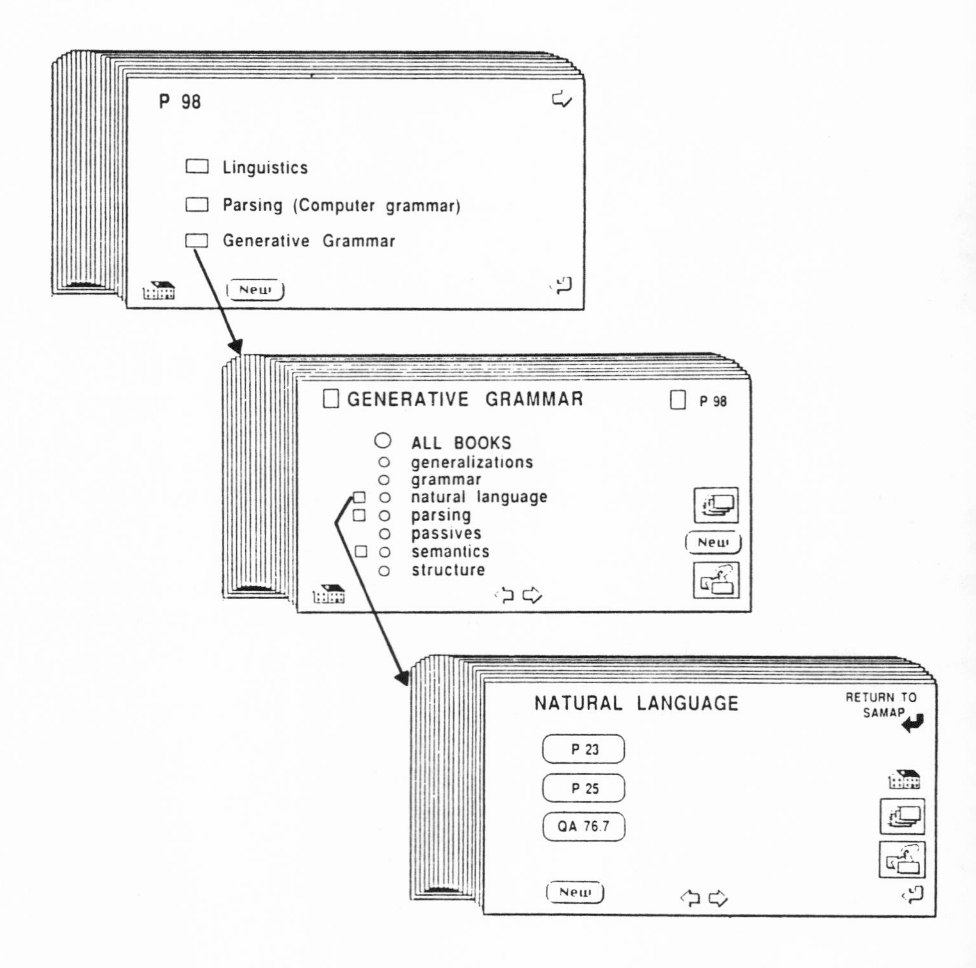

Figure 7.10. Changing to search for a different term

these links to be built automatically as a book is being entered and greatly enriches the syndetic structure available. The classification system provides the necessary underpinnings, while the formal subject headings enable the user to perceive real differences in focus and purpose of actual books in a particular classification number. The table of contents terms provide the enriched vocabulary needed to match natural language terms to the more controlled vocabulary of the subject headings.

One of the difficulties that surfaced in this prototype was the problem of how much information to include in each map, what to post. At first phrases derived from the table of contents were displayed as well as all the individual keywords in each map. This meant that every word appeared twice, and also greatly increased the size of the display. Eventually, it was decided to suppress the display of the keywords and to use only the actual phrases derived from the table of contents and the title in the subject map displays.

Flexibility

At any point, the user can stop the process and return to the initial input screen or backtrack to an earlier decision point or select an alternate path. For instance, if the subject headings displayed on the map for "parsing" proved not to be relevant to his information need, the user could return to the P98 screen and select a different heading, such as "generative grammar."

Upon viewing this display, he might decide to select books with chapters on "natural language." Two symbols appear beside the term "natural language." The circle indicates this is a chapter-level term in the books listed. The square indicates there is also a subject map for whole books on natural language. A third symbol, the triangle, denotes that there is a subject access tool available for online consultation. If the user elects the latter, he will be returned to the data dictionary with a search for books on natural language (see Figure 7.10). The whole search process will begin again with books on "natural language." Again, the user will be prompted to select the classification number that most closely matches his information need.

Scope Notes

The user may also decide to seek help from scope notes which are available from a different hypertext stack. Here, the user will find suggestions about other possible links not yet considered (see Figure 7.11). The user can also elect to browse through the P schedule or skip over to QA76.9.

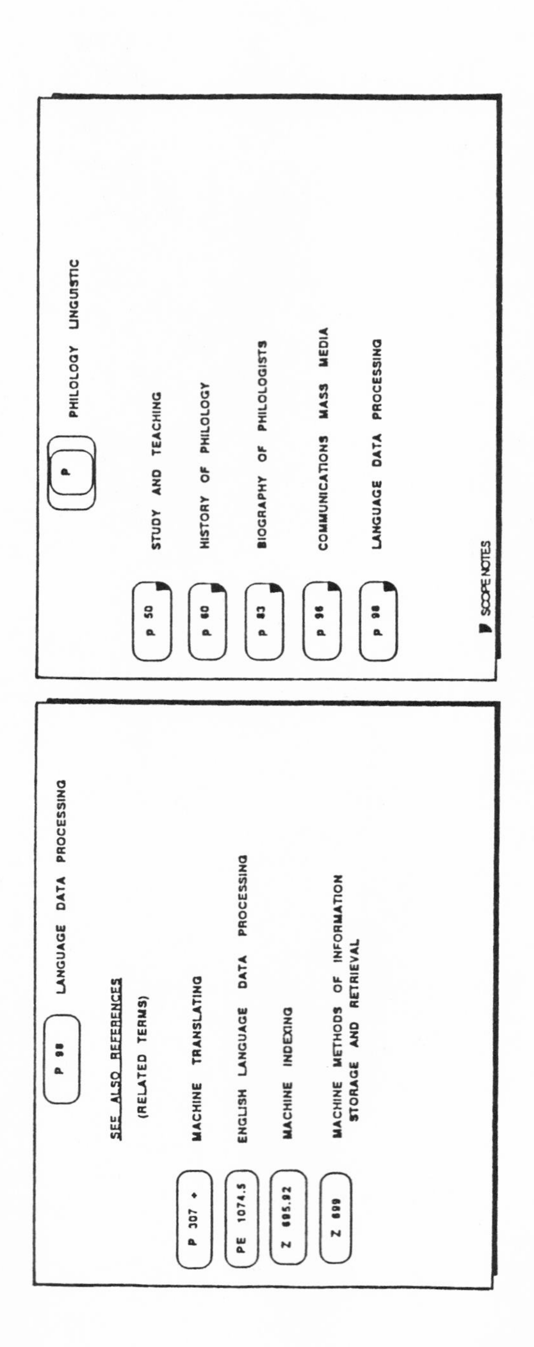

Figure 7.11. Scope notes and guide cards

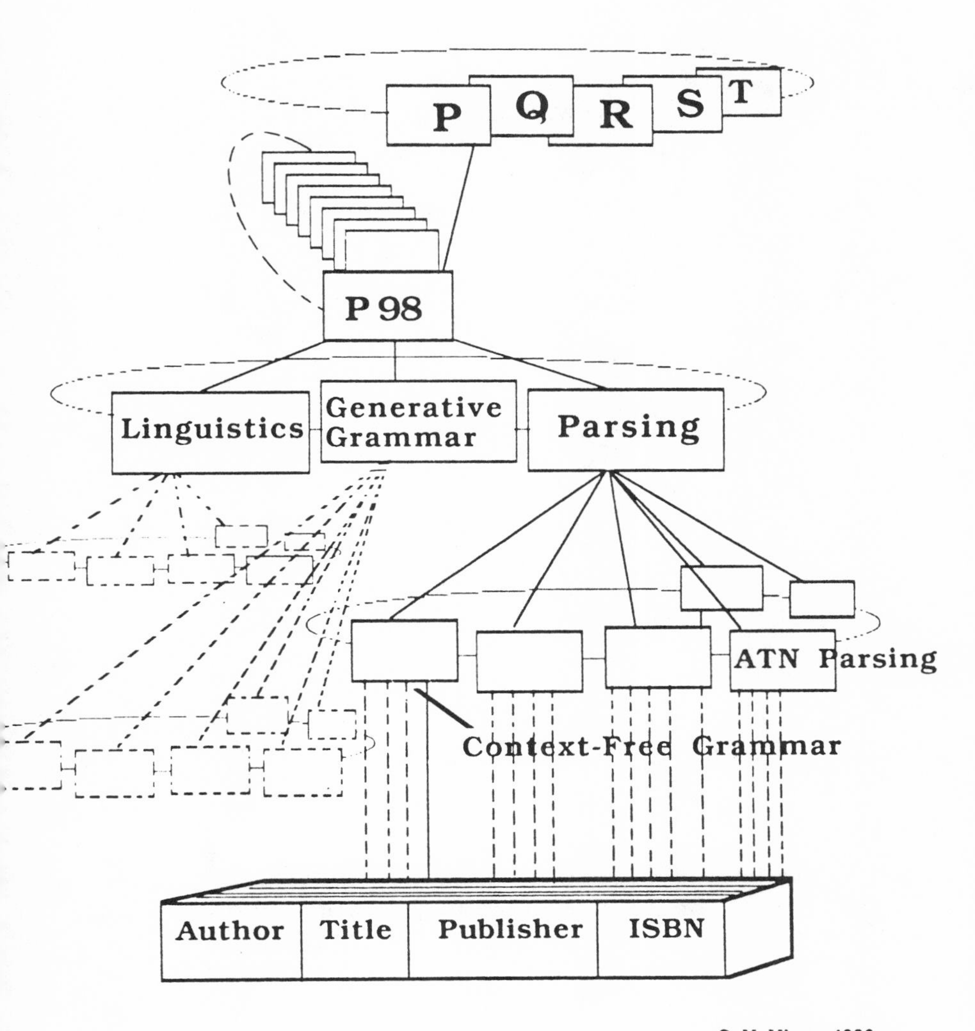

Figure 7.12. Overview of a hypertext stack

Mechanics of the System

The system depends on the power of hypertext to organize, link, control, and display information found in MARC records. A simplified graphic summary of the arrangement of linked hypertext stacks is shown in Figure 7.12. The diagram shows hypertext's ability to provide a much more complex set of linkages between terms than has been possible in earlier systems. The hypertext stacks needed for this system will be built in a hierarchical arrangement to allow the user to view the contents from many different levels of abstraction. The following stacks will support the subject access system described.

1. A **central dictionary** consisting of one card per keyword term will comprise the system's largest stack. Every keyword will be linked to at least one subject map.
2. **Subject maps** form another stack. Each is identified by a unique subject heading and classification number combination. These maps contain all the phrases and associated keywords drawn from the table of contents of the relevant books in the database. This stack will facilitate matching the user's query to the subject headings in the database.
3. The **classification schedule** stack consists of one card for each class number used in the central dictionary. These will be organized in a series of linked lists with a tree-like structure.
4. A stack of **scope notes** consisting of one card for each note will be placed in a separate stack to be accessible when requested by the user.

One of the great advantages of hypertext systems in general is the ability they provide to move freely throughout the system of links at many different levels of abstraction. They also adapt readily to uneven growth patterns, unlike our very rigid linear classification systems, Dewey and LC. If a stack grows too large and unwieldy, it can be subdivided into several smaller stacks, allowing room for expansion.

Improving Subject Access to Reference Books

Present cataloging of reference books can only be described as primitive and virtually useless in providing access to their informational content. This is in spite of much discussion in the professional literature of the need to categorize reference books as types of tools able to resolve different types of information needs.

Clearly the knowledge base of reference tools will need to contain this type of detailed information before one can even attempt to build a useful expert system. Standards for categorizing reference books will need to be established, perhaps using schema such as those proposed by Meredith. Standard schema can then be incorporated in enhanced subject access and hypertext systems such as those discussed in this chapter.

Now that we've discussed some methods for improving subject access — techniques which involve both knowledge representation and an improved user interface — let's move on to a more detailed discussion of the user interface.

Recommended Readings

Problems with LCSH and particularly with its syndetic structure have been identified in a number of studies (Micco, 1980, Sinkankas, 1976), while problems with retrieval in online catalogs have been extensively reviewed by Cochrane and Markey (1984). Mandel has looked at linking multiple thesauri together (1987). A switching language has been proposed by Niehoff (1984). Bates, in a seminal article, proposes a dense semantic network as a solution, while Fidel has carefully analyzed search strategies. An effort to enrich MARC records by the addition of table of contents terms is reported in several articles (Beatty, Byrne, Micco & Byrne).

8

Designing the User Interface

One of the most crucial factors associated with the willingness of people to use computers is the way the software handles the interaction with the person in front of the monitor. Online systems can provide multiple access points and powerful manipulation capabilities. But if the program's communication with its user is defective, then the sophistication, the features, and the power are wasted. The term for the point at which person connects to machine is "**user interface**."

The user interface with which an information seeker interacts may really be a group of different programs distributed among several computers. Part of the user interface may reside in a local workstation, part may reside in the host system computer, and another part may reside on a network. Another part of the user interface is hardware. The devices used for input and output (keyboards, mice, monitors, printers, etc.) have a lot to do with the way the user interacts with the machine. Factors such as display quality make a big difference.

It really doesn't matter which part of the user interface is located on which machine. What matters is the image the set of programs comprising the user interface presents to the user. Development of user interfaces requires knowledge of psychology as much as engineering and programming. Development of user interfaces has been neglected in comparison to advances in storage and processing. Before effective user interfaces could be developed, technological and psychological barriers had to be broken. Just recently, we've begun to see engineers, systems analysts, and programmers turn from purely technological problems and begin paying as much attention to human/machine interaction as behavioral scientists have.

Evolution of Human/Machine Communication

Let's look at the way human/machine communication has evolved. At first, one communicated with the machine by rewiring its circuits. Then people talked to machines in what is known as a batch mode. The person's messages to the machine were prepared in advance, usually as a stack of punched cards. Those messages, at first, were in the form of low-level code which in no way resembled English, or Polish, or Swahili, either. After batch came the online era. The process of entering into a dialogue with the machine online, in real time, is familiar to all of us now. The use of English-like, higher level languages is now routine as well.

The term "user-interface" implies many things, including:

- display control
- input modes (keyboard, mouse, etc.)
- dialogue control (including natural language processing)
- help, explanation, and advice facilities
- mode of interaction (menus, commands, point and shoot)
- transparent query translation

When it comes to expert systems, we must be concerned both with the expert system as a user interface and with the user interface to expert system knowledge bases. In other words, for many retrieval appications the primary purpose of the expert system is to serve as a user interface to one or more databases — helping the user navigate the documentary domain and providing facilities for tasks such as problem definition and query formulation. On the other hand, expert systems themselves are complex programs and sophisticated interfaces are required to create, edit, debug, and interact with them. Most of the expert system development tools feature multiple windows, trace and explanation functions, and high-resolution graphics. Articfial intelligence will continue to influence interface design. Natural language understanding, speech recognition and synthesis, and pattern recognition will all play a role in the interface of the future. It could be argued that, for information retrieval, the expert system is the user interface.

Desiderata

We're asking a lot from the user interface.

1. We want simplicity but we want to perform complex tasks.
2. We want adaptability but we also want the ability to learn new tasks in different contexts without having to relearn the way to interact with the machine. We want to be able to do new things without abandoning what we've already learned.
3. We want graphics but we need text as well.
4. We want menus sometimes and commands other times. And we want to be able to define for ourselves an interaction mode which combines menus and commands.

5. Systems that are designed for beginners don't work as well for experts. The ability to "evolve gracefully" is rare. We want interfaces that will support the needs of novices and experienced users at the same time.
6. Standardization is important (commands and terms should be consistent and formats should be immediately recognizable), but so is the ability to develop customized solutions to local problems. We want standards but we also want interfaces that allow users to develop their own displays and formats.
7. We want a mouse, but we want keys also (not to mention touchscreens, trackballs, joysticks, and eventually voice and eye movement input).
8. We want the ability to jump rapidly from one function to another, from one database to another, from one term or set to another. Yet, we also want the structure needed to be able to zero in on something very specific in a directed way.
9. We want modes of interaction that are natural extensions of the tasks we are trying to accomplish. We want metaphors that will allow us to relate to the computer in a more natural and direct way.
10. We want interfaces that can analyze our behavior and adapt themselves to our personal styles and that can engage us in a meaningful dialogue.

The user interface for an effective expert system will almost certainly be able to do most of the things on our list. The user interface will be based on the way the knowledge is structured in the knowledge base. Options must be presented logically (often hierarchically) and designing a menu or organizing commands into a decision tree is closely analogous to structuring a knowledge base.

An ideal interface will perform different functions during different phases of the process. During the problem definition phase, the interface would focus on controlling the dialogue, and displaying possible terms and term networks. Many displays would be generated by graphically manipulating machine-readable thesauri.

During search execution, the user interface would guide the searcher through the cycles of a search by providing displays of document surrogates and by representing concepts as graphic images. It would also provide functions (for example, strategy triggers, display controllers, filters, etc.) that could be activated by pressing "buttons" and that could control the interaction with the host system in a variety of ways. During the post-search phase, it would assist the user in interpreting results and preparing subsequent iterations if necessary.

Now let's look at some of the key ideas on interface design and examine systems that exemplify those ideas.

User Models

In Chapter Five, we examined the searcher's mental model; now let's examine user modelling and the user's mental model of the information system.

As people interact with the world around them, they build abstract structures in their minds — mental models that influence subsequent thought and behavior. Walter Lippmann (1922), in his classic book on public opinion, described those models as "pictures in our heads." Lippmann recognized that there is a big difference between the reality of the world and the pictures people carry around in their heads. Another important work on this idea is *The Image* by Kenneth Boulding (1956). Boulding describes an "image" people develop in their minds — subjective knowledge based on experience. It is this image and the way in which it is affected by messages from the external world that determines how people behave. Pratt (1982) has written a thought-provoking little book which examines the "image" from a library and information science perspective.

Although people rely heavily upon mental models, few people are able to articulate their mental models. Borgman (1984) reviews the application of mental models to information retrieval. According to Borgman, it is the user's model of an information retrieval system that determines the user's behavior when using that system. Since a person's mental model of an information system is responsible for the way in which that person uses the system, an understanding of the mental models of information systems that people develop should help us develop systems that can be used more effectively.

Just as a people have mental models of information systems, many information systems attempt to build models of the people using them. This process is commonly referred to as **user modelling**. It has long been recognized that information seekers differ from one another and that intelligent retrieval systems will have to incorporate user modelling capabilities if they are to serve a diverse population and accommodate individual differences.

Korfhage (1985) suggests that the system's model of the user can be used in three ways: as a "filter" to remove information that is not congruent with the system's image of the person's information needs; as a query modifier that can be used to develop a query which is more consistent with the system's image of its user; or as a facet of the query — a set of parameters that is factored into every query. According to Korfhage, the user profile generated from the modelling process should include information on the user's subject interests, the user's information-seeking style and experience, the user's expertise within the subject domain, the user's familiarity with the specific system she is using, and a log of the user's activities as she interacts with the system.

Sparck Jones (1986), in a discussion of user modelling, differentiates between static and dynamic user models — that is, models which remain fixed once they've been developed and models which change as the user interacts with the system. We know that information retrieval is a dynamic problem-solving process. A static user model developed at the beginning of an information interaction and not changed as the user changes her image of the problem would be clearly inadequate in an expert system for information retrieval. User profiling for information retrieval must be dynamic — the system's model of the user must accommodate the user who changes her image of the problem as she interacts with the system. The user interface of an expert retrieval system should be nonmonotonic; it should be able to maintain a constantly changing picture of the user and her needs.

Grundy

Rich (1979) developed a system called **Grundy**, which relies upon **user stereotypes** to recommend fiction to people. A stereotype as described by Rich is like the **default frame** discussed in Chapter Three. Information supplied by the user is matched to long-term stereotypes, which are used to associate clusters of characterics with users — characteristics used to infer reading preferences. Grundy engages its user in a dialogue, attempting to identify characteristics that it can match to the novels in its information base.

Words in the user's description of himself evoke stereotypes. For example, if someone describes himself as Jewish, Grundy will assume that he is politically liberal and suggest novels with a liberal slant. Grundy can ask the reader to supply alternatives for words it can't understand. Grundy can also ascertain a reader's likely interests by matching characteristics of novels in its catalog to novels which readers have already read and enjoyed.

System Models

There is a difference between the system's model of the user and the user's model of the system. Norman (1986) differentiates between a **design model**, which comes from the mind of the system designer, and the user's model, which comes from the mind of the user. The point at which these two models come together is known as the system image. The user's model is derived from the **system image**. The system image is the part of the design model which manifests itself to the user. The design model and the user model are both mental models. The system image is partly physical — the nature of the displays, the way the keyboard is used, etc. The system image perceived by the user may indeed be the one intended by the system designer; on the other hand, the system image may not be perceived by the user as it was intended to be perceived. Since the system image has a lot to do with the mental model developed by the user, and since the user's mental model will determine how efficiently she is able to use the system, great care must be taken in designing a system image which conforms to the design model envisioned by the system developer.

Kidd and Cooper (1985) emphasize the importance of a close match at the cognitive level between the user's mental model of the problem and the system's problem representation.

Norman (1983) also describes the mental models people develop to guide them in their interactions with machines. He asserts that most peoples' mental models are imperfect and can be based upon faulty assumptions and "superstitious" beliefs. Mental models also tend to be incomplete and inconsistent. They often include knowledge and beliefs that are uncertain. Uncertainties in a mental model can have an impact on user behavior. People who use several similar systems — for example, an OPAC, one or more CD-ROM databases and online services — have to simultaneously maintain several mental models. Overlapping mental models can increase a user's level of uncertainty and increase the potential for errors based upon confusing different systems with one another. Apparently, the number of mental models a person can maintain is limited in a simlar way to the number of "chunks" of information that can be maintained in short-term memory.

The user interface has a lot to do with lack of acceptance of many computer systems, including expert systems. As Kimura et al. (1986) discovered, doctors who rejected a sophisticated system with numerous features accepted a much simpler system with fewer features. It seems that the **cognitive load** associated with a particular system image will have a great deal to do with the willingness of people to use the system.

Problem Solving Through Dialogue

In most of the discussions of user interfaces, the dominant metaphor has been that of a conversation between two human beings, with the computer assuming the role of one of the participants. The user interface is the means people use to engage the computer in a dialogue.

Coombs and Alty (1984) studied the interactions between computer users and staff at a computer help desk. The most successful interactions were those where the person with the problem did most of the talking and the advisor did not attempt to be too directive. Users were more often dissatisfied with advisors who controlled the structure of the dialogue. The primary purpose of the most rewarding interactions seemed to be the development of a mutually understood problem definition.

Initial lack of focus was not an impediment to successful interaction and, in fact, seemed to be necessary for a successful resolution of the user's problem. In many cases the user was able to devise his own solution; all that was needed was another person with whom to talk through the problem. This shouldn't surprise students of the reference interview; it is the approach suggested by Belkin, Saracevic, and many others. The successful intermediary has to have something more than extensive knowledge of information resources — something analogous to "bedside manner" is required.

Oddy (1977) was among the first to suggest a method for automating the iterative, gradually evolving process of formulating an information problem description. Oddy summed up the central dilemna of information seeking when he said, "It is important to come to grips with the problem of serving a library user who is not able to formulate a precise query, and yet will recognize what he has been looking for when he sees it."

So the information seeker shouldn't be forced to formulate a query in advance. He shouldn't have to predict what relevant documents should look like before he has seen them. Instead, the query should be formulated interactively. As a search progresses, the information seeker's view of his need is influenced by new information as it is acquired, changing his "dynamic understanding" of his need. The search process itself determines its own scope and nature as it proceeds. Oddy developed a system which

> forms an image of the searcher's interest, derived from its world model, chooses references for display according to the state of the image, and modifies this image continuously in the light of his reactions to the displays. The program's world model consists solely of knowledge about the organization of literature (Oddy, 1977, p.5).

Contrast this to the reference librarian's world model, which includes but extends far beyond knowledge of the way the literature is organized. The librarian's model incorporates common-sense knowledge, knowledge about the user, and subject knowledge in additon to knowledge about sources and their organization. The process used by Oddy, which has come to be called **relevance feedback**, is analogous to showing someone a possible "answer" to their query, assessing their response, and using that assessment to determine whether and which other possibilities to present. Not only is the user's image of his need determined by his response to an entire document surrogate, it is determined by his response to terms, authors, and concepts associated with that surrogate.

RABBIT

A more modern version of this approach, incorporating screen windows, menus, highlighting, and a hierarchical knowledge representation scheme is the **RABBIT** retrieval system developed by Tou (1982) and his colleagues. RABBIT aims to address four problems of casual users of database systems (Tou et al., 1982, p.314).

1. The user has incomplete knowledge about the descriptive terms needed to create a query.
2. The user's own intention is only partially articulated.
3. A considerable amount of information is known in the database about any given item, and hence, the presentation of that information needs to be limited or structured in some way.
4. The structure of the database is heterogeneous, with the result that the "shape" of the database changes depending upon where one is in the database.

RABBIT works with a database that is derived from different sources, structured differently in different parts, and that contains information about different types of things related to computers. RABBIT guides its users in formulating a query by using techniques referred to as **descriptive retrieval** and **retrieval by instantiation**. Descriptive retrieval is defined as gradually and incrementally building a query as a series of **partial descriptions**. Retrieval by instantiation involves matching partial descriptions to **examples** derived from the database. The query is developed by analyzing the user's response to a series of successive examples. For example, RABBIT can present the user with a detailed description of a specific computer disk drive and use its attributes and the user's responses to guide the selection of additional disk drives for the user to examine.

The screen is divided into a series of windows that present different views of the search in progress. Users can jump from one window to another and scroll through the information contained in any window. Users can also select commands such as: **require**, **prohibit**, **alternatives**, **describe**, and **new view**.

One window contains a description, in general terms, of the user's current query. Another contains an example that matches the current description. A third window contains the **previous description** supplied by the user, and another includes an index of **matching examples** for the current query. Using RABBIT is an iterative process that allows users to zoom in and out and move freely and easily through the data in different parts of its diverse computer industry database.

Interface Modes

One major aspect of the system image is the way in which the user is expected to communicate with the system. Menus have replaced commands as the grammar of commercial software, and the way in which menus are presented can make them as quick and easy to use as a set of familiar commands. The keyboard is gradually being supplemented by the mouse as a means of interacting with a computer. It is now possible to perform different operations (producing text, drawing pictures, working with the numbers) on the same information entity with a single program. Words, numbers, and images — each of which once had a separate domain in the software world — are becoming just more symbols to manipulate as boundaries disappear. We can't speak of menu- or command-driven systems anymore. Now we must speak in terms of knowledge-driven systems.

NL Menu

Thompson and colleagues (1985) have developed what they describe as a "toolkit for building menu-based natural language interfaces." The user of the system, which is called **NL Menu**, builds a query by selecting words or phrases from menus displayed in different windows on the screen. As the query-building process continues, the choices presented to the user are determined by previously entered information.

NL Menu includes a knowledge base that contains information about the different "parts of speech" used by the system and the ways in which they can be acceptably combined with one another to form logically and syntactically correct statements. It is impossible to construct an "illegal" query with NL Menu because at each stage of the query building process, only acceptable choices based on earlier choices and the constraints expressed in the knowledge base are presented as choices. There are numerous potential menus, but the system will only present menus that make sense within the context of the query as it stands at any given point in time.

In an information-retrieval situation, these concepts could be used to develop menus that reflect the limitations and structure of available databases and query languages. The choices presented to the user would be guided by constraints built into the system. For example, it would be impossible to create a query that contained an illogical heading/subheading combination. Knowledge about which types of queries make sense in a given situation would be built into the user interface. The **CANSEARCH** system developed by Pollitt (1987) and discussed in Chapter Four uses an approach that is quite similar to the approach employed by NL Menu.

Interface Design Issues

Carroll and McKendree (1987) provide an excellent review and critique of interface design issues. One of the dilemmas facing the system designer is the fact that most people want to begin using a new system quickly and are not willing to sit through a tutorial or read extensive documentation. People are not willing to invest the time required to learn advanced features of complex systems. Consequently, once someone has learned to use a system at a minimum level of functionality, he becomes stuck and doesn't learn new features or take advantage of system capabilities that weren't part of his initial learning experience.

With online retrieval systems that change constantly, this tendency has some unfortunate implications. Online searchers who use several systems tend to prefer the one they learned first. The trick is to design a system that is capable of recognizing counterproductive user behavior and suggesting a more efficient interaction strategy.

It seems that the majority of currently available systems do not take user behavior into account. With just a few exceptions, interfaces are based on the intuition of the designer and not on empirical studies of the ways in which people use actual systems.

Knowledge Versus Advice

Carroll and McKendree (1987) suggest that domain knowledge may not be the primary consideration for advice-giving systems. General skills, including knowledge about different tutoring styles and natural language, and the ability to develop a user model may be more important. Just as there are many possible styles of reference interviewing, there are a number of possible advisory styles, but for the current generation of expert systems, it seems that little thought goes into which one is chosen and why.

Carroll and McKendree suggest that it may be more effective to focus on major categories of user problems instead of attempting to build large amounts of fine-grain domain knowledge into a system. For a reference advisory system, as much attention should be paid to the dialogue with the user as is paid to representing knowledge from the domain.

It is important to develop a model of a typical ("normative") user, but it is also important to enable specific users to adapt the interface to their own personal styles. We all know that some people are interested in "answers" only without too much hand-holding, while others are more concerned with a high level of personal contact than they are with the search for information. The ideal system should be able to analyze user responses, infer user's preferred style or skill level, and adjust the dialogue accordingly, in much the same way that a reference librarian does.

Most current systems attempt to provide context-sensitive help. A step beyond context-sensitive help is a system with the ability to initiate advisory functions that haven't been explicitly requested by the user. In some sense, such an adaptive interface could be said to be learning. Many of the principles underlying current thinking on interface design are derived from the study of **intelligent tutoring systems**. The goal of an intelligent tutoring system is to analyze the state of a learner's knowledge, identify gaps, and take steps to provide the learner with a more complete picture. This involves recognizing a learner's misunderstandings and providing explanations to correct them. For this, the system must maintain a profile of the user, infer goals even when they aren't explicitly stated, and shift from one problem area to another as the state of the learner's knowledge changes.

Among the important advisory functions identified by Carroll and McKendree (1987) are:

- **Confirmation dialogue.** We see this a lot in both real life interviewing situations as well as in common programs such as DOS, which make the user verify commands, such as Format. Imagine an online searcher saying to a client, "Are you sure you want to have 467 records printed online?"
- **Control blocking** denies access to specified system capabilities. We see it in programs that allow users to begin at a simple level and only gradually have access to more advanced features. For example, the Wilsondisc system can be set up to operate in a number of increrasingly sophisticated modes. A simple browse mode is the default but Boolean capabilities are available to more advanced users.
- **Automatic correction.** Responses are examined with the user's intentions in mind and automatically "corrected." For example, if an input term is incorrectly spelled, a good system should place the user in an index at a point close to the entry term. In an online environment, if a command is entered incorrectly, the a good system should attempt to infer what the user wants (if necessary engaging the user in a confirmation dialogue) and transmit the command in a syntactically correct form.
- **Protected modes** allow users to see a simulated response to a particular course of action and reverse things if it wasn't

> what they expected. Most expert system shells provide a "What if?" capability that enables users to specify different conditions and view the ways in which the system's inferences change.

One of the dangers of systems that attempt to second guess users is the tendency of users to follow the lead of the system, even in situations where their own first impulse would have yielded better results. Carroll and McKendree warn that if learning is to take place, users should be allowed to make errors and experience the consequences and that small amounts of advice are often more effective than large amounts.

Semantic Approaches

We know from our studies of end-users how important browsing is and the fact that initial queries are likely to be vague and poorly defined. Help facilities for reference/retrieval systems tend to focus on syntax — the form in which queries are presented to the system. Help facilities should also extend to semantics — the contents of queries and the underlying concepts. Knowledge of search vocabularies and natural language is necessary to accomplish this. Systems like the one developed by Brajnik and Guida (1986) represent attempts to provide assistance on a semantic as well as a syntactic level.

The next generation of systems should also be able to diagnose user behavior at a macro level, providing strategic as well as tactical assistance. Rather than analyzing specific commands, patterns of search behavior should be analyzed. The big picture is at least as important as the little details.

One of the earliest attempts to develop a retrieval assistance system capable of diagnosing user behavior that was not producing optimal results was the **IIDA** system developed by Meadow (1982) and his colleagues. IIDA examined user commands and was able to recognize and suggest remedies to such common dysfunctional behavior as "thrashing," or moving from concept to concept with no obvious goal. IIDA was also able to uncover other mistakes made by inexperienced searchers, such as duplicating sets which had already been created.

Documentation for Expert Systems

Perhaps one day we'll see truly intelligent interfaces that require no documentation, but for now documentation is still required and, in this area, expert systems present some unique problems. McGraw (1986) considers the unique requirements of expert system documentation and describes the phases in the expert system documentation development process.

Documentation for online retrieval systems focuses on search commands and commands to output information, with relatively little attention paid to database structure and organization. Documentation for expert systems must also address the domain knowledge incorporated in the system and the way in which it is structured. Expert systems are different because:

- they are nonprocedural
- they are graphically oriented
- they are designed for naive users
- they incorporate large amounts of domain knowledge
- they are developed incrementally (they are always changing)

Access to Underlying Structures

Bates (1986b) outlines some of the problems associated with existing interfaces to online systems:

- There is a **black box mentality**; users aren't allowed to see what is happening in the system in response to their queries.
- All communication with the system must be explicit and syntactically "correct."
- Browsing capabilities are limited.
- Designers assume that searchers and indexers are consistent in describing information needs and documents; this is not the case.

Bates advocates machine-enhanced retrieval systems but underscores the importantance of differentiating between things which computers do well and things which humans do well. We should delegate to computers those tasks which computers do well. For example, repetition, memorization, calculation, and measurement are all done more precisely by computers, and computers don't get bored and make simple mistakes. We can't delegate higher level tasks to computers but we can use the computer to enhance or augment tasks which humans do well. Pattern recognition, application of strategy, and rapid selection from multiple options are all necessary for effective information searching. They are tasks that humans can easily master but which baffle the most powerful computers. Shneiderman (1987, p.76) also provides an overview of human and machine capabilities.

Bates (1986b) contends that the most effective systems will be those that allow users greater access to data and data structures by allowing users to select terms from information displayed on the screen and to ignore terms that are not of interest. Systems that take advantage of the human ability to scan, or take in large amounts of information visually — a capability provided by printed indexes but not by most online systems — is also important. One part of the problem (which we can expect to see reduced as display technology improves) is the relatively low resolution of monitors compared to printed pages.

In an expert system context, it is also important to provide users with access to underlying structures and assumptions. A "black box" system is unlikely to be accepted. Would you take advice from someone who was unable to explain their rationale for giving that advice? There are many in the AI community who contend that the ability to explain one's reasoning is the true hallmark of intelligence.

Expert Explanation

Neches et al. (1985) describe an explanation facility which goes beyond presenting "canned" text or paraphrasing rules in the knowledge base. A typical expert system doesn't provide an explicit rationale within its code nor is canned text likely to adequately address user questions. Neches and his colleagues advocate explicitly incorporating the design rationale for an expert system in the system's code. This approach makes it easier both to generate explanations and to maintain and modify the system.

An explanation-based system was created by establishing a taxonomy of question types likely to be posed by users and developing an explanation strategy for each type of question. Once a user's question is stereotyped and an explanation strategy identified, the answer to a user's question can be derived from the knowledge base. Question types include:

- **questions of justification** , which are answered by explaining why the system is doing or assuming something. For example, an intermediary might justify a comprehensive and expensive search by assuming that a Ph.D candidate would want that approach if dissertation preparation was the final goal.
- **questions of timing or appropriateness** can be answered by describing why a sequence of events is occurring. A reference librarian can usuually explain why it is a good idea to check to see if there are bibliographies or review articles before checking for specific papers and to develop a user profile before formulating a query.

- **questions of definition or function** are answered by explaining a term from the domain or describing one of the system's functions. An online searcher can explain what a **field** is, which fields are available for specific databases, and how different fields are labeled.
- **questions of capability** involve explaining what the system is capable of, and, perhaps more importantly, what the system can't do. Answers to these questions are derived from the system's meta-knowledge. For example, a business reference librarian might have to explain to a client why it might not be possible to find extensive financial data on a privately held company.

Anticipating User Behavior

Philip Smith and his colleagues (Smith, P.J. et al., 1988, Krawczak et al., 1985) at Ohio State University are developing an adaptive interface for searching the environmental pollution literature included in the **Chemical Abstracts** database. It is a good example of an interface which attempts to focus on semantic as well as syntactic concerns and which employs a design model based on user behavior. The goal is to help users formulate and clarify concepts in the domain while compiling a list of keywords for each concept which are matched to pollution documents indexed in Chemical Abstracts.

Smith (1988) advocates predicting possible user errors and ambiguities and alerting the user about "potential misunderstandings." **EP-X**, the system being developed is based on the "Do as I intend" or "Do what I mean" approach described by Norman (1986) and used by Teitelman and Masinter (1981) in a version of **LISP** which anticipates user input and attempts to type ahead of the user, using the context supplied by earlier statements to guess what the next statements will be and to correct mistakes. Smith supports a similar approach. "Another sense in which the computer can do as the user intends is by detecting inputs that would normally be treated as errors, but that can still be interpreted properly."

PaperChase (Cochrane, 1982), a commercially available system for searching the medical literature, does this by accepting misspellings and spelling variants. The EP-X system can infer higher level goals by examining the "sequence of inputs." For example, if a user expresses an interest in a large number of freshwater fish, EP-X might broaden the search by incorporating all freshwater fish in the strategy.

"Thus, an intelligent system should be monitoring user behavior for evidence of goals, and upon detection of a goal, should try to apply its repertoire of tactics in order to assist the user."

Smith (1988) contends that expertise in the subject domain of the information seeker is required of an effective intermediary. He has attempted to build this subject knowledge into his system by identifying six types of frames that can be used to describe documents relating to environmental pollution. As the system is used, the user is presented with clarifying information based upon the system's understanding of the concepts from the domain in which he is interested. The hierarchical relationships between expressed concepts and concepts that have not been expressed but may be implicit are derived from the frames describing the types of documents in the database. If the user enters an ambiguous term, the system seeks to resolve the ambiguity by presenting the user with the different options suggested by the term. If the user enters a broad concept term, he is presented with a list of narrower concepts that may also be of interest. If the user enters a term that is equivalent to the slot label of a frame, he is presented with a list of possible filler values for the slot.

The approach is also modeled after the "answers first" approach described by O'Malley (1986) and also by Owen (1986). The goal of the system is to help users ask the right questions — a complex process that involves engaging the user in a dialogue to teach him what he needs to know to ask appropriate questions.

EP-X is similar to NL-Menu in the way in which options for "legal" choices are presented to the user. Concepts related to different aspects of environmental pollution are organized in broad categories such as:

ANALYTICAL TECHNIQUES
GEOGRAPHIC LOCATIONS
ORGANISMS (that accumulate pollutants)
POLLUTED MEDIA (lakes, rain, sludge, soil, etc.)
SOURCES (of pollutants)
REMOVAL/TREATMENT PROCESSES

Within each concept are narrower concepts. For example, in the **organism** concept, there is a **fish semantic primitive** which is linked to a **freshwater fish** concept which may include a concept such as **brook trout**. A window on the screen is used to display **available concept hierarchies**. For each concept, a **concept definition** can be displayed in a window on the screen. The concept definition, like a **scope note** in a thesaurus, is intended to reduce ambiguity. For example, **New York State** as a concept is differentiated from **New York City**. Synonyms for chemical names are provided in definitions, as are scientific names of organisms.

In another window, the keywords associated with concepts selected by the user are displayed. Another window displays an **interpretation** of the current status of the search, including the number of documents in the system's working memory, and the Boolean formulation which caused them to be retrieved. A final window, the **document display** window, presents the user with abstracts of documents in the current working set.

EP-X uses its semantic knowledge to display pruned hierarchies. It is possible to display all of the possibilities in a category upon request but the default is to use context knowledge to display only those choices which make sense under current circumstances. For example, in a search on acid rain when the **sources of pollution** category is displayed, only those sources contributing to acid rain will be shown. The pruned hierarchy guides the search by limiting possible search facets to those which make sense within the network of relationships between pollutants, treatment methods, and types of pollution in the system's knowledge base.

Recognition Versus Recall

Another important aspect of the system image is the way in which information is presented to the user. People are much more likely to be able to recognize something than they are to recall something. If someone asked you to list the names of all the fish you knew, you would probably have a difficult time. But if you were presented with a list like this:

TROUT
FLOUNDER
OSTRICH
FORK
BASS
PERCH
GUPPY
SHARK
SPOON

it would be fairly easy to recognize the names of fish. Every reference librarian has experienced the disoriented feeling that comes when the reference stacks are shifted. It is because recognition rather than recall is the method being used to locate items on the shelf. There is a difference between users approaching a system with a preformulated query (recall) and users approaching a system to learn what is available (recognition or browsing). The preformulated query is explicit; each term has to be specified as well as the ways in which they will be combined logically or in proximity.

In a hierarchical browsing system, the "children" of a superordinate class concept are implicit and don't have to be specified. Specific subtopics of a broader class should be accessible without having to specify their individual names. When we say **fish**, we get **trout** as well. It should also

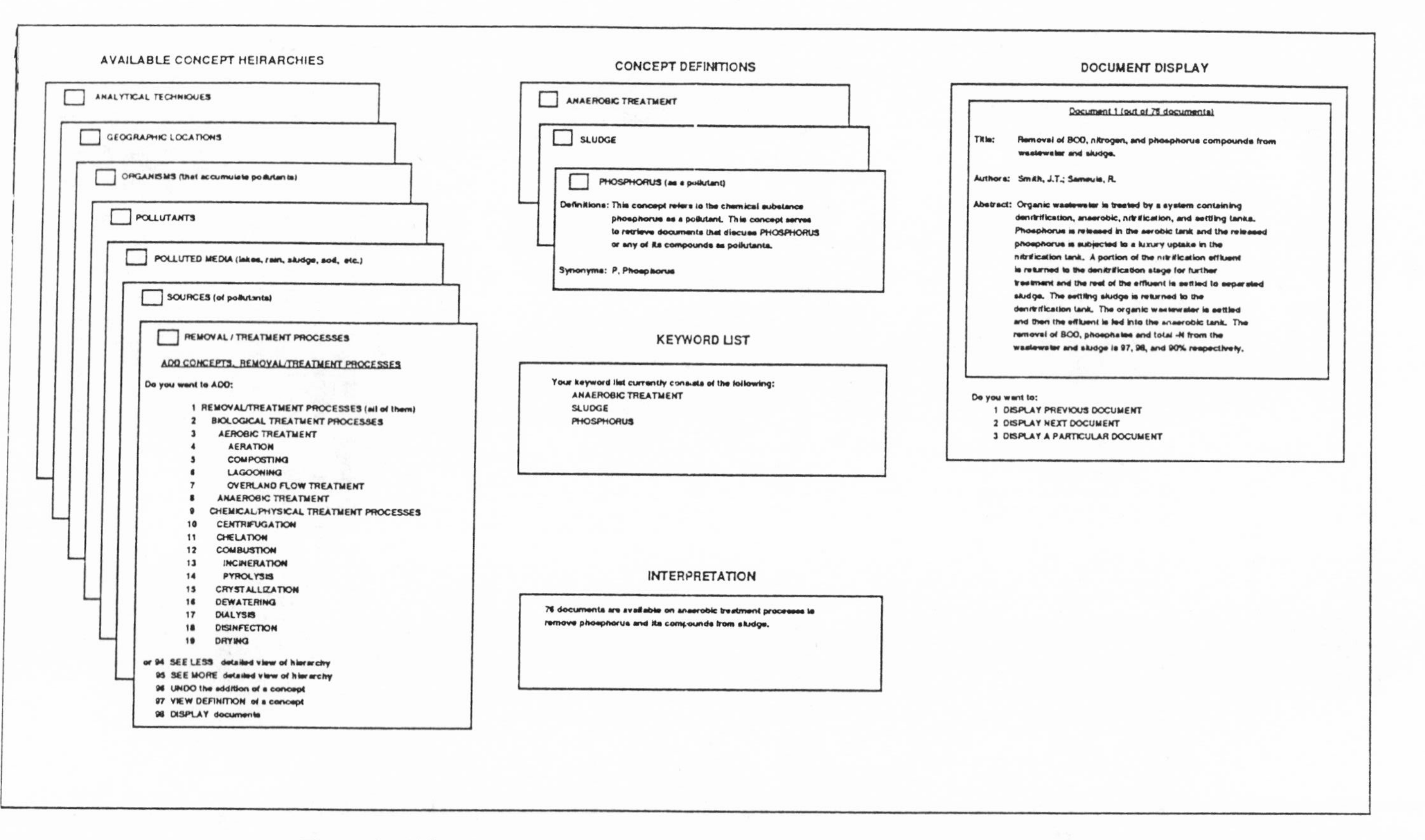

Figure 8.1. The EP-X System uses windows to display facets of a search (from Smith, Shute, Chignell, and Knowczak, 1988).

be possible to move from narrower to broader categories. When we say **nutmeg**, we should be able to establish the conditions under which we'll accept **spices** as well. The prototype hypertext system described in the last chapter is one of many attempts underway to address the fact that humans are more likely to recognize than they are to recall.

Browsing and purposeful fact retrieval lie at opposite ends of a spectrum. At one end is totally free-form browsing; at the other end is a concerted search for a specific data element. In the middle are different degrees and combinations. Often they can be stereotypes for institutions or client groups. For example, **deciding on a topic for a term paper** might suggest a browsing mode, while **looking for the gross national product of Peru** might suggest a more formal strategy. The modality of a browsing system has a large educational component, while that of a fact retrieval system is more task-oriented and analytic.

Hypertext

Hypertext, a method of dynamically linking associated pieces of information together with one another and presenting information in a nonlinear way (first described by Bush, 1945, and reviewed by Conklin, 1987), is essentially a sophisticated form of browsing.

Marchionini and Shneiderman (1988) contrast hypertext with traditional, index-based information retrieval systems. Hypertext systems will require different types of design and generate different types of mental models. Such systems will require more computing resources but will reduce the "cognitive load" on the user. Designers may attempt to build hybrid systems that permit the "direct manipulation" and browsing capabilities of hypertext but which also support features like Boolean searching, truncation, field delimitation, and adjacency operators. Designers will have to make tradeoffs. The system that is easy to use (low cognitive load) will lose some of the capabilities of traditional command-driven systems. The system with a large repetoire of sophisticated commands will place greater mental demands on the user.

While it has the potential to reduce cognitive load, hyperterxt, can become confusing and the user can easily become lost within tangled networks of concept relationships. Effective browsing and hypermedia systems will provide maps showing the nodes and arcs and indicating to the user where she is in the system and where she has been.

An Electronic Encyclopedia

Weyer and Borning (1985) describe an electronic encyclopedia that integrates text, still images, video and simulations in a concept network; users of the encyclopedia can navigate the concept network and custom design their own "articles" on topics of interest. In addition to browsing, which is the primary mode of interacting with the electronic encyclopedia, Weyer and Borning envision a user interface that incorporates four other metaphors: **models**, **tours**, **filters**, and **guides**.

Evolving Systems

The traditional focus of information retrieval systems has been on purposeful, analytic retrieval of specific items. There is evidence that users (including professional information intermediaries) behave quite differently, relying upon serendipity, visual cues, hunches, loose associations. The way in which most electronic IR systems present information does not support that type of behavior pattern.

Commercially available systems do not do this very well but progress is being made. OCLC, a number of integrated system vendors, and database producers like the National Library of Medicine are all experimenting with new approaches to browsing and display. It is only a matter of time before we see browsing capabilities added to OPACS (online public access catalogs) and other commercial systems.

OCLC's **Advanced Interface Management** (AIM) (Dillon et al., 1987, 1988) project is experimenting with a "prototyping environment" for a new generation of user interfaces. Special emphasis is placed on searching and displaying full-text databases like books. The **D display language** provides facilities for developing interfaces to full-text and bibliographic databases, taking advantage of multiple windows, icons, high-resolution displays, and alternative input devices.

Other research underway at OCLC is focusing on the relationships between windows and menus, and developing a menu-driven online catalog. Experiments are being conducted on a search system that features high-resolution display of full text. A hypertext-like interface is used to move through full-text databases. Part of the project involved collecting data by means of verbal protocols from scholars in the academic community. Research has also begun on an online catalog which uses "target records" to retrieve additional records which are somehow associated and may be of interest.

Experimenting with new display technologies is a high priority at OCLC. The **Graph-Text** (Hickey, 1988) project aims to develop effective displays that combine text, graphics, tables, and equations. The *Kirk-Othmer Encyclopedia of Chemical Technology* is one of the source texts for this project. Another project, **Information Display**, is experimenting with advanced display technologies.

Object-Oriented Programs

The type of programming required for an iconic user interface is known as **object-oriented programming** (see Chapter Two). Symbols and the programs needed to manipulate them are viewed as parts of information entities known as **objects**. For example, when using **Microsoft Windows** or an **Apple Macintosh**, whenever a **Paint** object is dragged into the workspace, the paint function becomes active. Moving a written document into the workspace puts writing and editing capabilities in the hands of the user.

The traditional type of programming involving commands, statements, and a formal syntax is known as **function-oriented programming**. Emphasis is on program modules that perform specific functions, such as word processing, spreadsheet analysis, or communications. Procedurally oriented, structured programming languages encourage the development of procedures that perform different tasks and function as separate modules within a single big program. Object-oriented programs use primitive objects to build more complex objects and allow the passing of messages from one object to another.

Project HYPERCATalog

Project **HYPERCATalog** (Hjerppe, 1986) is a project underway at Linkoping University (Sweden) to develop a catalog in which navigation and browsing are the primary modes of interaction. Hjerppe argues that the traditional library catalog is designed primarily for the librarian, not the user, and that even OPACS that have evolved from traditional catalogs have retained limitations that are related to the physical constraints of the old card catalog. In other words, the amount of information which can fit on a card, and the linear arrangement of cards, are among the primary determinants of the ways in which information is organized and displayed in computerized systems. HYPERCATalog is intended to overcome some of the limitations inherited from other formats. According to Hjerppe (1986), HYPERCATalog is intended to:

"• support browsing and navigation...

- have a much higher degree of internal structure than traditional catalogs
- have alternative means for presenting and illustrating structures, information, and relations
- have tools for establishing relations and following "trails"
- be dynamic in nature, not only growing in number of records
- provide each user with the ability to specify, and save, his views of the library, enabling it to be enriched by the use that is made of it
- have models of users available, both stereotyped and individualized...

- contain more and other information than present catalogs, especially in terms of links and relations between fields, records, and files, and facilities for utilizing this
- in addition to providing information on individual items also have information on collections" (Hjerppe, 1986, p.213–14)

CALIBAN

Frei and Jauslin (1983) describe a system which is intended to overcome the problems inherent in command-based information retrieval. With command-based retrieval, the machine is a "one-state machine" (once a command has been entered and executed the machine returns to its single state). The **CALIBAN** system screen is divided into three windows: an information window, a command window, and a message window.

The information window contains both information structures (e.g., thesauri) and information items (e.g., bibliographic records). The command window contains "a structured set of available services" as well as the currently active service. The message window contains system messages primarily designed to assist the user, including a display of the mouse pointing device with the currently available functions of its buttons indicated. The information window can display thesaurus sections graphically or textually.

The command window displays commands hierarchically as services and subservices. Only those services which are currently available show up on the graphic display. A mouse can be used to highlight a command and activate it. Commands which have irrevocable results (e.g., deletion) require use of the keyboard. It is possible to use the mouse to select items by browsing a graphically displayed (tree) index structure. It is also possible to formulate an explicit query by filling in a query formulation template; specific terms can be moved directly from a structural display into one of the blanks in a template. The user is also given a chance to specify the importance of individual terms by assigning them weights; this is done by "coloring" more important terms darker on the screen. Users define "virtual information items;" templates which are instantiated as specific items from the database are matched with desired attributes.

Machines used to talk to people by means of teletypewriters. The printed word was the first way the machine talked to the person. Then came the display monitor, which remained largely unchanged for several years. Now there are high-resolution displays filled with crisp graphic images. Printing technologies have also changed. The machine which once relied upon a language of numbers, and now uses a language of words, is beginning to learn a language of images.

Imagine being able to put a document representation on the screen, highlighting relevant terms including author, keywords language, and pulling in other records having similar patterns of descriptors. Imagine being able to insert links, connecting documents to one another, links activated like "magic buttons." Now imagine, a powerful microprocessor, running a program which will (behind the scenes and totally out of mind) statistically weight the cumulative effect of the links and pull in other documents with a similar "shape."

Virtuality

VISICALC, which presented its users with a computer screen that closely resembled the accountant's spreadsheet whose functions it was designed to perform, is widely acknowledged as one of the first programs to exhibit the qualities which Ted Nelson (1980) calls "virtuality." Now the majority of successful microcomputer programs incorporate features related to the concept of virtuality. Programs that reflect human behavior are much more likely to encourage their users to become immersed in a virtual world.

STEAMER

Another famous program, **STEAMER** (Hollan et al., 1984), uses graphic color displays, including an instrument panel as the interface for an intelligent training system in the field of ship propulsion engineering. **STEAMER**, by using an instrument panel and different views of a steam plant in its interface, attempts to match mental models which are already available within its domain. The screen is divided into several windows which:

- allow the user to select views of the steam plant with differing levels of detail, ranging from an abstract schematic to a detailed flow diagram of a specific subsystem; over one hundred diagrams are available
- allow the user to control the operation of various aspects of the operation of the plant and view the results of decisions
- allow the user to modify the mathematical simulation which drives the displays
- allow the user to cause malfunctions to various parts of the plant and view the way in which the simulation responds

STEAMER also includes a graphic editor, which can be used to develop new views of the steam plant. An important concept underlying STEAMER is the "interactive inspectable simulation." Users are presented with graphic simulations of steam propulsion processes employed in Navy ships. Users of STEAMER have access to many views of a ship's propulsion plant, at many hierarchical levels. Actions taken by users result in immediate feedback as the events resulting from those actions are simulated on the display. Users of the system learn about shipboard steam plants by moving through a virtual world, but the virtual world also provides views that aren't possible in the real world.

For example, it is possible to see liquid flowing through a pipe. In STEAMER, if a pump is working, it is displayed as green; if not, it is red. Part of the expertise of a propulsion engineer involves the ability to respond to the **sound and feel** of the steam plant. The close match between the virtual world of STEAMER and the real world of a shipboard steam propulsion plant allows novice engineers to experience situations which, in real life, would be dangerous or rare, while retaining much of the "feel" of an actual plant.

Direct Manipulation Interfaces

A closely related concept to virtuality is the idea of **direct manipulation** (Shneiderman, 1987, Norman, 1986). Although most people recognize one when they see one, a direct manipulation interface is a hard thing to define. Definitions are subjective. A direct manipulation interface provides the user with a natural and direct way of interacting with the computer. Rather than having to memorize complex commands and adhere to a formal syntax, computer users can interact directly with the machine at the level of the tasks they are trying to accomplish. The actions required to accomplish a task are readily apparent and there is immediate feedback to commands issued by the user.

Direct manipulation interfaces present many advantages. Less knowledge of syntax is required. Remembering commands isn't important. Different ways of manipulating symbols are represented as icons on the screen — a file cabinet, a paintbrush, a waste basket. A mouse or joystick is used to move the user of the system into applications and files. Everything is more intuitive. The user doesn't have to know the difference between programs and data or worry about where either is located. No detailed knowledge of paths and directories is needed. Nor is it necessary to have a detailed knowledge of database structure.

A direct manipulation interface is easier on the eyes as well. Windows appear on the screen offering lists of options. At different times, different programs or files (represented by windows and icons) become active. Shneiderman (1987) characterizes direct manipulation interfaces as those which are based on simple responses to visual commands and not on prior knowledge of a formal syntax.

Among the features of direct manipulation interfaces outlined by Shneiderman (1987) are:

- use of **analogy**
- each step building upon previous steps ("**incremental operation**")
- commands can be **easily reversed**
- commands are initiated through a **physical response** to a display
- advance knowledge of commands and syntax are not required
- commands are easy to learn without documentation
- "**graceful evolution**"; the system can be adapted to meet the needs of more advanced users
- "**graphic form**"

Unfortunately, most commercial retrieval systems fail to incorporate the design principles embodied in direct manipulation interfaces. Usually, there are lots of commands to keep track of. Typing becomes a crucial skill to have. Some commands require a complicated syntax. There can only be one thing at a time happening on the screen, and usually the action is limited to one line at a time. Contrast this approach to CALIBAN, RABBIT, and EP-X.

Metaphors

Carroll and Thomas (1982) discuss the established psychological premise that people learn new things by relating new knowledge to previously existing structures. Remember frames, scripts, and stereotypes? Existing metaphors can be used to help people interact more easily with computers. System designers whose primary concerns used to be technical are now confronted with such fuzzy tasks as developing metaphors.

People with little computer experience tend to use metaphors borrowed from some other domain. In the case of research systems, one of the most common metaphors is "the library," with its card catalog and printed indexes. But OPACS and online retrieval systems typically do not incorporate metaphors drawn from the card files and printed indexes which preceded them. There is a fundamental difference in the way in which an online database and a printed index are used, even if both contain the same information. The printed index presents more information more clearly; the online database can be traversed more rapidly.

Carroll and Thomas (1982) suggest that system designers should attempt to identify metaphors which help naive users learn new systems by allowing them to refer to already existing knowledge structures. A good system would enable its users to select metaphors that are appropriate to the task at hand and reject those that are counterproductive. The request and fetch metaphor employed by OPACS and online systems may be counterproductive; it brings to mind a library with closed stacks.

The system image presented to the user should match her metaphorical representation of the task to be performed, even if what is actually going on in the computer is quite different. The **Query-By-Example** and **Office-By-Example** systems developed by Zloof (1982) are good examples of this philosophy. So is the iconic user interface pioneered at **Xerox PARC** and popularized with the Apple Macintosh.

Carroll and Thomas (1982) provide the following advice to designers who wish to take advantage of the human tendency to interact with the world in metaphorical terms:

- Use metaphors that are naturally related to the way the system works and the task the system is designed to accomplish.
- Avoid metaphors that have an inappropriate emotional tone.
- Do not mix metaphors from different domains; choose metaphors which complement one another.
- Avoid misleading metaphors; don't assume that people will interpret a metaphor the way it was intended to be interpreted; try to anticipate how people will react to a metaphor.
- Establish the limits of a metaphor.
- Be aware that the metaphor which is suitable for beginners may not be appropriate for advanced users; a good user interface will "evolve gracefully."
- Exciting metaphors can be used to increase motivation. Game-based metaphors can make work seem like play. For example, think of an information system which treats a search as a treasure hunt.

Office-By-Example

Zloof (1982) describes a powerful, object-oriented environment called Office-By-Example (OBE), which takes as its metaphor the forms used in a typical office environment. The purpose of the software is to enable people who aren't familiar with computers to develop their own applications. One of the basic premises of the system is that it is easier for people to specify what they want the computer to do by providing an example than it is by issuing a command. In information retrieval, this would be analogous to asking people to provide the imaginary title of the book or article that would meet their needs.

Users of OBE build complex applications by using primitive objects supplied with the software and working with template forms called skeletons. Users design their own screen displays, search hierarchical and relational databases, send and receive electronic mail, create graphics, and do word processing by manipulating and creating business objects that are analogous to already familiar business forms, letters, and reports. Users are able to establish "trigger" conditions which take prespecified actions when certain conditions are encountered. In an online search context, this is equivalent to letting users design their own mode of interaction with different responses from the host system triggering different display formats, filtering mechanisms, even search processes (e.g., Boolean versus vector). Function keys are used to activate simple operations such as **erase**, **move**, **locate**, and **zoom** which behave differently depending upon the context in which they were activated.

Problems with Metaphors

Some metaphors have almost become cliches. In the business world, the **desktop metaphor** is a prime example. We're all familiar with office objects that correspond to things people do in offices. There is usually a trash can (How many people keep a trash can on their desktop?), an assortment of file folders, a variety of tools such as pens and paintbrushes, and sometimes a telephone. When metaphors work, they can be very effective. But metaphors have their limits. One can reduce the computer screen to a virtual world by means of icons and other graphic metaphors. But, for many tasks, the computer can perform much more complex operations than can be represented with "physical objects" in the virtual world. And the association between the icons displayed on the screen and the data and commands they represent may not be intuitively obvious.

Idiosyncratic Systems

Nicholas Negroponte, director of MIT's futuristic Media Lab, talks about "idiosyncratic systems." The idea of idiosyncratic systems grew out of the **Soft Architecture Machines** project (Negroponte, 1975). The aim of the project was to use artificial intelligence to allow people to design environments that meet their personal needs. The book describing the project is as much about computers as it is about buildings. According to Negroponte, people shouldn't have to adapt their styles to buildings and computers. Computers and buildings should adapt to the needs of the people using them.

One of these days it will be possible to superimpose an expert retrieval interface upon existing information services. A user-defined interface will serve as a translator between a variety of "native" computer languages and the information seeker's own self-defined style. All commands, queries, and displays would be translated into an unique langauge invented by the person using the retrieval system.

WYSIWIS

Stefik et al. (1988) describe **WYSIWIS** (What You See Is What I See), an interactive display system for meetings. The WYSIWIS concept was developed at the legendary Xerox PARC as part of a larger project called **COLAB**. COLAB is intended to augment the exchange of information during meetings. Each participant in a meeting has a graphic workstation connected to a network. Each workstation has a **chalkboard** on which currently active information is displayed, an area called a **stampsheet** where different chalkboards can be stored as icons, and **implements** which serve a variety of functions and which are stored in a **chalktray**.

A search workstation could employ a similar interface schema. Search concepts could be labelled and put in something like a stampsheet, and implements could be developed to perform different search functions. Different functions, perhaps reflecting the tactics described by Bates and others, would be represented by icons. A search workstation would thus display implements to do things like **zoom**, **display**, **explain**, **filter**, etc.

It's hard to predict when we'll see the impact of object-oriented programs on reference and information retrieval. As we've seen, there are many experimental projects underway, but few commercial systems. The success of desktop publishing and the increasing popularity of multifunction, high-resolution workstations may be harbingers of a new approach to search software. Think of the possibilities. Wouldn't it be nice to be able to see displayed in a window thesaurus terms associated with records which you indicated an interest in by clicking a mouse? Wouldn't it also be nice to be able to drag terms from the thesaurus display into windows representing different facets of your search and to be able to delimit or combine the results in each window?

Maybe someday we'll see prerecorded search strategies delivered to the online system through windows. Maybe we'll see icons which, when activated, will adapt the search software for specific databases. Customized help windows and menus would be designed to exploit the unique characteristics of each file. New ways of displaying search results should be just around the corner. Already, multiple windows are a feature of just about all of the experimental projects. Wouldn't it be nice to see a list of all the sets, terms, and postings displayed in a small window at the corner of the screen at all times? Already, we can open several communications sessions at the same time and simultaneously view different databases in separate windows on the screen. As standards for the transfer of graphic symbols are developed, the big database vendors will get into the act.

Sensory Metaphors

Fields and Negroponte (1977, p.56) discuss the "clues" people use to locate information:

> Perhaps the most powerful non-symbolic clue for finding data is location, the "it's there..." clue. In our daily life, the information we deal with is mostly on paper and we put that paper at particular locations for later retrieval.
>
> In my office, I locate files where they are in the filing cabinet, not by an alphabetic organization. I locate books by where they are on my shelves, rather than by a subject matter grouping. I have as many tables as I can squeeze into my office, and each is covered by piles of paper. The piles are in particular places, and individual documents are at memorable heights within each pile. To be complete, location as a clue to finding data is augmented by iconic appearance. Location gets me close to the book I want, but its tall skinny blue binding helps me locate the exact book that I am looking for.

To take advantage of people's reliance upon locational clues to find information, Fields, Negroponte, Herot, and colleagues have developed a database system that allows users to "fly through the information space." Many of the system's capabilities reflect the capabilities provided by paper, but additional capabilities that reflect the computer's ability to simulate a virtual environment are also available. Herot (1980) describes the use of **spatial data management** with a database that contains information about ships. Information about ships is presented graphically and users of the system retrieve and organize information by positioning it in a **graphical data space** using a joystick. Users can select a variety of different views of a fleet of ships. It is possible to examine a **world-view map** or to zoom in on a specific ship for greater detail. Images are stored on an optical disk and it is even possible to request a picture of a particular ship's captain.

Colors are used by the system to carry information in a similar way to the way in which colors are used in the STEAMER system. Different colors are used to indicate the readiness of different ships in the fleet. Similar concepts are beginning to show up in document retrieval systems. Remember how CALIBAN allows the searcher to assign greater weight to important concepts by shading them? Spatial Data Management is just one of the interesting projects developed at the Media Lab (Brand, 1987). It should be noted that OCLC is a major sponsor of the Media Lab. Other Media Lab projects will be discussed in Chapter Eleven.

Owen (1986) compares the sensory experience of using a book to the sensory experience of using a computer. Computer interaction tends to be more purposeful and goal-directed. As we have seen, the current generation of information retrieval systems require the information seeker to know what he is looking for and to approach the information seeking task in a purposeful way.

But we also know that the behavior of someone browsing through a book is less purposeful and precise. Many of the locational cues are tactile and visual; the browser is not focusing on specific pieces of information but upon a gestalt made up of the thickness of the pages, the location of items on pages, and visual cues for relating items to one another. Much of the information is acquired incidentally rather than deliberately. In print systems, such as library stacks, serendipity leads to many discoveries.

Owen has developed a system called **DYK** (Did You Know). DYK is designed to teach users about system capabilities by allowing them to learn as a "displacement activity" when they become tired of the task they are working on. The idea is to take advantage of the human knack for absorbing information indirectly. In a similar way, information systems of the future will be designed to encourage serendipitous discovery.

Research on all aspects of the user interface is accelerating. New hardware and larger memories have made possible sharper displays and totally different ways of communicating with the machine. Behavioral scientists have begun to study the human-machine communication process in terms of the way humans process information. New visually oriented, more intuitive systems are being developed. Perhaps science fiction can provide us with a glimpse of the future.

OVERDOCS

Vernor Vinge, a mathematician and science fiction writer, has written a science fiction detective novel, *Marooned in Real Time* (Vinge, 1986). The action takes place among the few survivors of an unknown catastrophic event referred to as the **singularity**. The book is a cross between a hard boiled detective story and techno-future science fiction.

The book is set in the distant future during a time when people can transport themselves forward through time, but not backwards. The world is divided into **high techs** and **low techs**. High techs are people who were transported into the future from a technologically advanced era. Low techs are people who were transported from a less technologically advanced era in the more distant past. Low techs are at the mercy of high techs who brought their technology with them to the future. The hero of the book is a low tech, who was stranded in the future by a criminal who he was about to apprehend in his former life as a police detective.

The hero is asked by the leader of the high techs to investigate a murder. For his investigation, he is given access to massive databases spanning thousands of years. He is assisted in his investigation by his own personal intelligent interface, which is called an **overdoc**. The overdoc augments his search capabilities and allows him to move through the data space in a way which is similar to the Spatial Data Management system.

Among the capabilities provided by the overdoc are:

- the ability to link diverse passages to one another heuristically, identifying relationships that are not readily apparent
- the ability to adapt the search process to the searcher's line of inquiry
- a variety of display formats, including holographic images of original documents
- the capability of being customized as it's being used

Despite the fact that the murder happened thousands of years before the investigation, and was probably committed by a high tech, the hero is able to use the information in the databases to track down the culprit. He is also able to identify the miscreant who stranded him in the future.

Marooned in Real Time is a challenging and thought-provoking book that reflects its author's mathematical background. Unlike much of science fiction, it is quite plausible, especially to someone who is familiar with current developments in the design of retrieval interfaces.

Recommended Reading

The best two books on the user interface are the text by Shneiderman (1987) and the collection edited by Norman and Draper (1986). Carroll and McKendree (1987) offer the best critical review of interface design issues. Hendler (1988) focuses on the user interface for expert systems.

The book edited by Gentner (1983), although it deals with issues broader than computer systems, provides a fascinating glimpse of the ways in which people use models to represent their knowledge of the world. Its coverage ranges from the navigation skills of south seas islanders to the work habits of physicists.

Hildreth often writes on interface issues from a library point of view and his work is recommended. Bates and Cochrane also write frequently on library interface design topics and are both cited frequently in the bibliography. Carroll and Thomas (1982) emphasize the importance of metaphors in interface design. Conklin (1987) provides a thorough overview of hypertext. Foley (1987) and Bolt (1985) provide intriguing looks at the interface of the future.

9
Developing a Microcomputer-Based System

Now that we know some of the basic principles of expert system design, we should also know that building an expert system is a complex task requiring a major commitment of time, money, and skill. One of the questions that might come to mind is whether or not it is worthwhile to experiment with developing one's own expert system. Developing an expert system is not an easy or an inexpensive undertaking. Should the average librarian even bother to try? What is to be gained from the experience?

Why a Toy System?

There are those who argue that expert system development should be left to professionals and that the development of "toy" systems is a waste of time. While we recognize that expert system development is a challenge that is beyond the scope of many, we also contend that there are benefits to be gained from developing one's own modest expert system and that there are many librarians who are up to the task. In this chapter, we will attempt to answer some of the questions of neophyte expert system developers by taking a case study approach.

First of all, let us assume that expert systems developed in-house by most libraries will fit into the category of expert systems referred to as "toy" systems. Toy systems are characterized by a limited search space. A rule-based toy system would probably have a knowledge base of less than 100 rules. Toy systems typically address extremely narrow domains of limited complexity. Toy systems are not as robust as their more sophisticated cousins. It is relatively easy to push a toy system to the limits of its capabilities, and a toy system is unlikely to "know" when it is approaching its limits. It is rare to find a toy system that contains large amounts of meta-knowledge. A toy system is unlikely to know what it knows. And the conflict resolution strategies employed by toy systems, if present at all, tend to be primitive.

Given these limitations, it is still possible to learn a great deal by developing one's own system. And locally developed, microcomputer-based systems can and have addressed real needs (Gupta, 1988b). There are real benefits to be had by developing a system within a library. Staff will acquire experience with expert system technology, preparing them to evaluate commercial systems that will become available in the coming years. Working on a system is the best way to develop realistic expectations about what is and what isn't possible. Finally, a locally developed expert system can serve as a medium through which specialized knowledge can be shared among members of the staff and between experts on the staff and clients. The development process itself necessarily involves the codification and transfer of expertise, much of which had previously been unexpressed. Even if the system itself is disappointing, the development process will contribute to a greater understanding of the expertise of the librarians involved.

There are already a number of small-scale reference systems under development in libraries. A domain must be sufficiently complex so that expertise is required to move within it. But a domain must be limited enough to be easily manageable. This is especially true of micro-based systems.

Expert systems for reference functions tend to take a subject approach. An interesting project at the micro end of the scale is **Answerman**, a prototype system being developed at the National Agricultural Library in Beltsville, Maryland (Waters, 1986). One of the components of Answerman that has already been implemented is **AquaRef**, which deals with information sources in aquaculture. AquaRef is a classic example of a system that tightly focuses on a manageably narrow subject area. Samuel Waters, in his article on the system, encourages librarians to "think big but start small." Answerman is one of the most notable examples of what can be accomplished with modest goals, a microcomputer, and a little imagination.

So the goals for a locally developed expert system shouldn't be too ambitious. And it is important to recognize that the final product will have limitations. But it should also be recognized that despite the drawbacks and limitations, developing a toy system can be a rewarding experience. Let us begin our case study by establishing some ground rules.

Modest Goals

First of all, our goals should be modest. We shouldn't attempt to clone librarians. Even if we had all the time in the world, an army of skilled knowledge engineers, and the most powerful of supercomputers, we would be sorely disappointed if we expected to be able to develop a system which functioned at the level of a real human expert. Some things are best left to humans. A general reference interview, for example, is a complex social interaction with a significant affective component. Such a task is clearly beyond the scope of currently available technology. The more successful library systems have focused on ready reference questions and tutorials.

Another ground rule relates to the extent of the knowledge engineering project for a toy system. A major knowledge engineering project is a full-time job. Many hours are required from both a human expert and a skilled knowledge engineer who is equally at ease with techniques from computer science and from the social science. It is not the kind of thing one does between reference questions. So a small, locally developed system should attempt to take advantage of existing knowledge and try to identify knowledge which has already been expressed in some form. On the other hand, even a toy system should attempt to meet real needs. The trick is to identify a narrowly bounded domain where human expertise is scarce but not so scarce that some of it hasn't already been partially recorded. Part of the knowledge engineering for a small, in-house expert system might very well involve extracting from a large body of recorded knowledge only those chunks of knowledge which would be most useful within the local environment.

Even with modest goals and limited expectations, there are some roles for which small expert systems are well suited. Remember that since our system will most likely function within a tutorial modality and will be designed to provide advice rather than answers. Such a system would most likely be referred to clients by a reference librarian in much the same way that clients are now referred to literature guides, indexes, and bibliographies. A small expert system might realistically provide one or more of the following services.

- consultation within narrow subject domains
- specialized instruction for difficult-to-use sources
- dynamic descriptions of reference sources
- database selection assistance and "hooks" to external databases
- assistance with development of user and institutional profiles

These possible roles for a toy system will be discussed in greater detail within the context of our case study.

Hardware and Software Ground Rules

Now let us establish some hardware and software ground rules for our hypothetical system. Microcomputers are the most widely available form of computers being used in libraries. Microcomputers are also the most accessible computer technology both in terms of ease of use and availability for development projects. Therefore our system should be built using standard microcomputer components. Right now (1989) most of the micro-based expert system development market centers around DOS-compatible PCs but the situation could change, so we won't focus on a particular type of hardware. Let's establish as our absolute minimum a system with at least 640K of RAM, at least a 20-megabyte hard disk, and a modem. Additional memory of both types would be highly desirable and could mean the difference between success and failure.

A substantial amount of development work is also being done on high-end workstations, but such workstations aren't normally found in libraries, so the workstation as a development vehicle lies beyond the scope of our modest goals. However, the distinction between workstations and PCs is beginning to blur as PCs based on more powerful chips achieve greater market penetration. More ambitious projects will become feasible in the near future. PCs based on Intel's 386 chip should provide the hardware capabilities for some fairly sophisticated expert systems. Speed and the ability to address large amounts of memory will make possible much larger and more complex knowledge bases.

The software on which our system will be developed should be reasonably priced microcomputer-based shell software rather than an AI language, such as **LISP** or **PROLOG**. Both hardware and software should interface easily with industry standard off-the-shelf products. Hardware and software are evolving at such a rapid pace that any specific recommendations would quickly become dated. Therefore, we won't spend too much time discussing specific pieces of hardware or programs. Later on, we will discuss the selection of software development tools in general terms, as well as considering what to look for in a shell program for a small system.

Selecting a Domain

Now that we have laid out some ground rules for the development of a small advisory system, let us address the issue of domain selection. For a small system especially, it is important to identify a well-bounded domain for which a limited number of information resources are available. The domain should also involve a subject area where there are frequent numbers of relatively unambiguous reference questions. But the subject area should be specialized enough so that human expertise is scarce.

Uncertainty should apply within the domain. For any given question, there should be a number of possible sources for the answer. The human expert might be identified as the person who is most easily able to select the most promising sources from a group of possibilities which seem equally plausible to a nonexpert. Think of this as the equivalent of developing rules with similar conditions but different certainty factors. Sources within our domain would probably also cover a variety of formats, precluding the use of a single finding tool, such as an OPAC or periodical index. Such a domain might be shallow but would require the kind of broad knowledge of different sources in different formats that human experts possess.

Finally, although it is desirable to begin with a narrowly bounded domain with a relatively small search space, it would be nice if the domain covered by the system could be scaled up as the system becomes more sophisticated. In other words, the domain should be easily factored. System development would begin with a subdomain of the larger problem area with additional subdomains added as development proceeds.

Is there a domain which would be suitable, given the constraints we've established, for a small-scale project? Obviously general reference wouldn't work. Too large of a search space, too much complexity, and more uncertainty than most large-scale systems now deal with. An intelligent front-end to online databases wouldn't be feasible, either. Natural language capabilities that are beyond the scope of today's micros would be required.

Our hypothetical system, like most microcomputer systems, will probably be rule-based. Imagine how many rules it would take for general reference or a natural language front-end. If general reference or a front-end won't work, is there some more specialized domain that will? What we need is some aspect of reference where knowledge is easily represented as rules. And the results of the conditions expressed in our rules should be as straightforward as possible.

Business Reference as a Domain

There are many possible areas of specialization for small system development. As our example, let us use business reference as practiced in an academic library. There are several reasons why it is a good candidate for a small-scale advisory system. It is an area in which human expertise is limited but for which clearly indentifiable human experts exist. Business reference can be intimidating for those who haven't had experience with the specialized kinds of information involved. In most libraries, there is a subject specialist to whom the generalists and people with humanities backgrounds appeal when help is needed on a tricky business reference question. A small expert system has the potential to transfer some of that specialist's knowledge to his or her less specialized colleagues.

Although they can be difficult to answer, business reference questions tend to be less ambiguous than other sorts of reference questions. Unlike many types of questions, it is usually possible to recognize the answer to a business question when one has found it. Answers to questions are often facts which can be answered by using ready reference sources. There are "right" answers. And there are a limited number of core business reference sources. They are expensive but they can be identified and categorized. There is much overlap but there are fine distinctions as well — distinctions which are learned from experience. For any question there are multiple possibilities, but there are also best choices. Sources also come in a variety of formats, so there is no single access route to business information. Books, the contents of a number of reference works, periodicals, newspapers, government publications, and specialized financial reports are all used frequently, as are a fairly large number of electronic databases.

To a certain extent, knowledge in the field has already been codified. In many institutions, some attempt has already been made to transfer the knowledge of business reference experts by developing inhouse publications. Libraries serving business clientele generally have handouts on topics ranging from company analysis to marketing research. There are also a number of commercially published guides to locating business information — probably more than for any other field. Additionally, there are guides to other types of sources which are important to business research, including such things as statistics sources, or special issues of journals, many of which contain business-related information. Taken together, all of the various types of guides represent an already existing core of knowledge about business reference sources. Since it is not our goal to undertake a major knowledge acquisition project, the large body of already codified business reference knowledge is an important consideration.

Business reference, while it is a complex activity involving a large search space, can nevertheless be factored into smaller areas. Traditional subcategories of business reference include areas such as company information, industry information, management, marketing, economics, and business law. Certainly, there is much overlap among categories and a number of possible schemes for organizing types of business information. But it is relatively easy to establish categories and to further subdivide those categories. For example, a search for company information could be further narrowed by determining whether the inquirer needed directory information, financial information, statistical information, market/product information or narrative description. And each of those categories could be further subdivided. Industry information could be factored in a similar way, with the additional possibility of including sources for a specific industry, such as the computer industry or the automobile industry.

Types of business information can be factored and organized into categories. Sources of business information can also be factored and organized hierarchically in terms of the types of questions they can be used to answer. The factorable search space associated with business reference makes it possible for us to begin with a relatively narrow subdomain of the larger domain. Thus we can achieve our goal of beginning with a small domain and gradually scaling up. Perhaps we could begin

Business Information Tangled Hierarchy

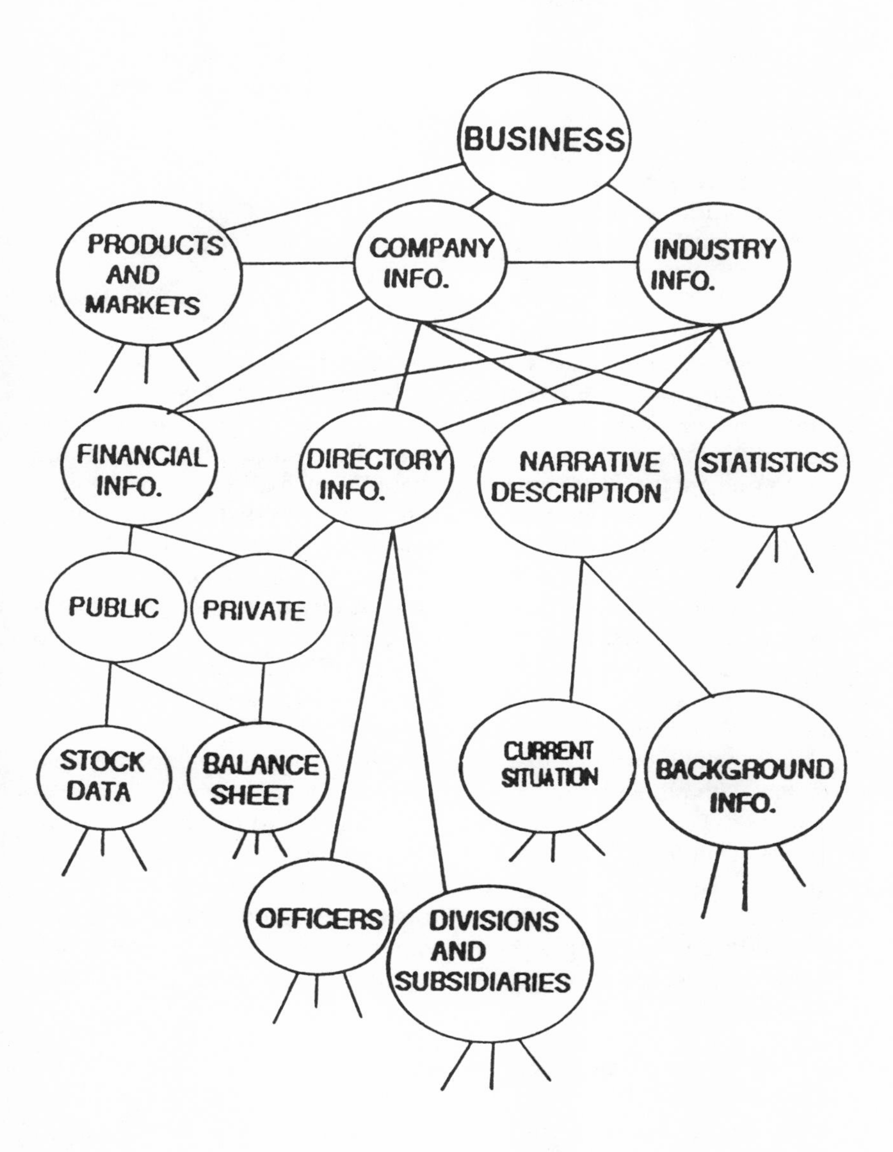

Figure 9.1. Business information is not easily categorized.

with a knowledge base of sources on company information and eventually add an industry information knowledge base.

General Design Principles

Now that we've identified a problem area and some ground rules, let's outline the general design principles we'd like to follow. The following three basic principles will guide the development of our system.

1. **modular structure**
2. **incremental development**
3. **explanation facilities**

Modularity

A well-designed expert system, even a toy system, will be modular and expandable. Our hypothetical system will be modular in several respects. Separate knowledge bases will be developed for separate facets of the broader domain. It will be possible for separate knowledge bases to be linked to one another, passing along what is known about the problem at hand to related knowledge bases. A **company knowledge base** may be linked to an **industry knowledge base**, and a general industry knowledge base may be linked to a knowledge base for a specific industry.

Another area in which modularity will be designed into the system is the separation of facts, rules, and explanatory text. Explanations should be able to be tailored to the context of the problem being solved. The inference engine, itself separate from the knowledge base, should be able to address facts, rules, and explanations independently.

A final example of modularity will be the ability of the expert system to interact with other computer programs, including commercially available software. For example, our expert system should be able to read to and write from local database files by interacting with commonly used programs, such as **dBASE**. If necessary, the system should be able to acquire information about the domain from those local databases. Our system should also be able to invoke communications programs which will be used to connect the user to a number of external electronic information resources.

Incremental Development

Since we won't have large amounts of time to devote to system development, we will attempt to build our system in small increments. We will begin with the least ambiguous subdomain, develop a small knowledge

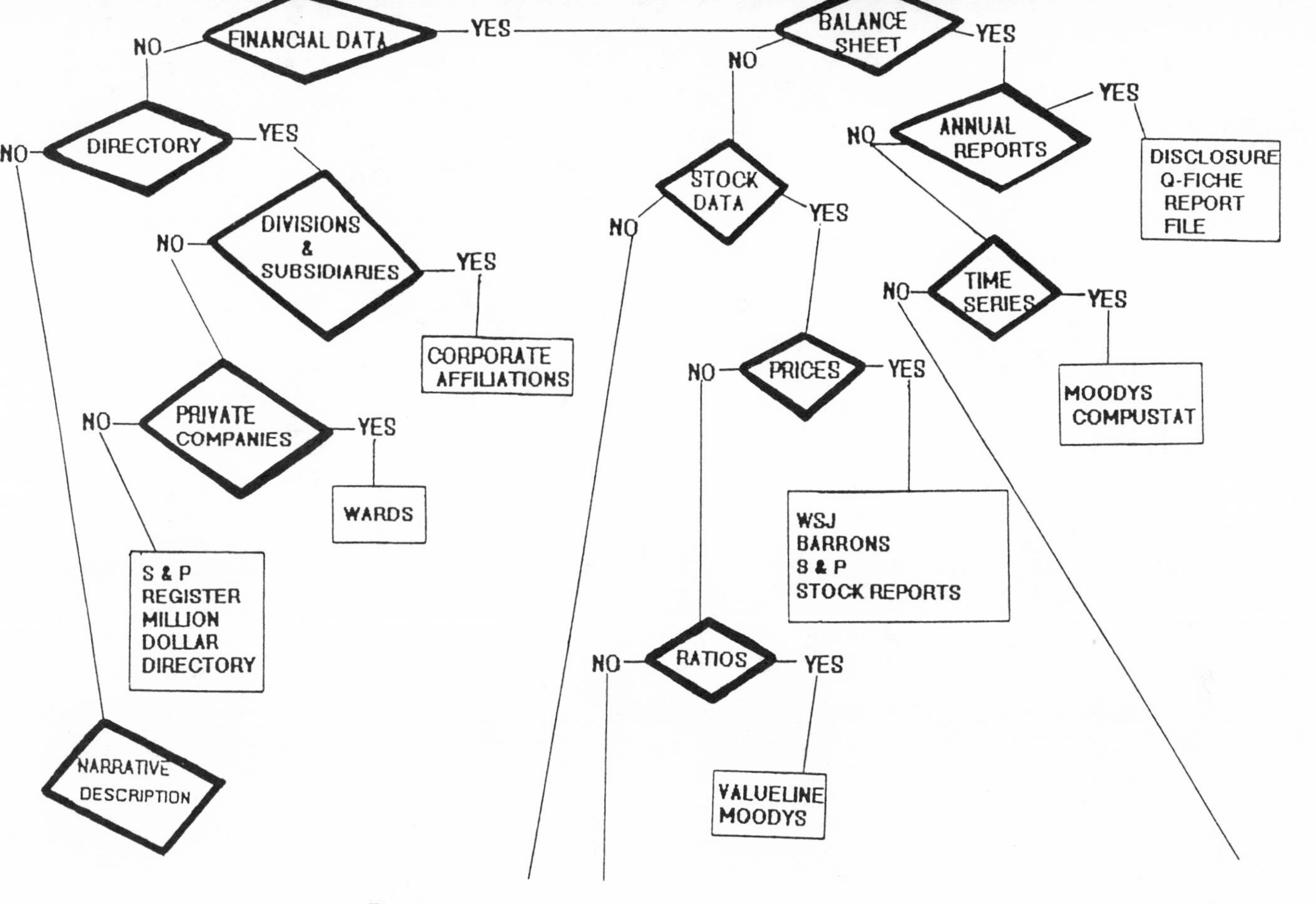

Figure 9.2. Company information decision tree

base, and refine it until it makes similar recommendations to those which would be made by our human expert. In this case we'll start by building a company information knowledge base. Next we'll add a general industry information knowledge base and a series of smaller knowledge bases for specific industries. After that, we'll add a **marketing knowledge base**. For our small system, we'll focus on those areas where there are concrete answers to specific questions, rather than on more ambiguous areas such as management, economics, or business law.

Cupello and Mishelevich (1988) discuss three stages of expert system prototype development. The first phase is a **demonstration prototype**. The demonstration prototype will be used to demonstrate expert system technology to constituents and to gain acceptance within the organization. The demonstration prototype can also serve as a proof of concept system for the capabilities the final system is anticipated to embody. The system resulting from this phase of development will have limited depth and capabilities.

The second phase of a development project involves building a **full prototype**. The full prototype demonstrates all of the capabilities of the final product but it is not yet ready to be delivered to its final users. The final stage of the process is the development of a **deliverable system**. A deliverable system is characterized by a polished user interface, adequate documentation, and acceptable response time. Even a deliverable system will require much debugging and constant maintenance. Cupello and Mishelevich estimate a development time of three to six months for a **demonstration prototype**, six months to a year for a **full prototype**, and eighteen months to two years for a **deliverable system**. Altogether, it is estimated that a relatively small system would take a minimum of three to four years total development time.

There are several advantages to an incremental approach to expert system development. This approach reinforces the idea of expert system development as a learning process. As the project moves forward those involved gradually learn more about the dimensions of the problem the system is being designed to address. Project participants also become more familiar with knowledge representation techniques which are appropriate within the domain. Once a demonstration prototype has been developed, it is easier to identify desired capabilities that the final system should have. Developing one's own system is also a good way to gradually become more aware of development tool capabilities.

An expert system project might begin with a public domain or inexpensive rule-based shell. Once that tool has been mastered, a more sophisticated rule-based shell could be used. As each tool was mastered and its limitations identified, it would become easier to select and learn tools that more adequately addressed problems of system development within the domain. Eventually, it would be necessary to use a tool that permitted the development of run-time, stand-alone expert systems which could be compiled and distributed independently from the development tool.

If the different phases of development were successful and administrators, colleagues, and clients became convinced of the value of an expert system within the domain, it would become easier to acquire the financial and administrative support necessary to move beyond toy systems. At some point, it would probably be necessary to move from a relatively simple, rule-based shell to a more sophisticated development environment that supports a wider variety of knowledge representation formalisms.

Explanation Facilities

The final design principle involves building explanation facilities. The system should be able to provide an explanation of why any particular rule fired and the assumptions underlying any of its recommendations. The system should also be capable of explaining why it is pursuing a particular line of questioning. Among the specific explanation facilities our system should have are the ability to explain the use of particular sources it is recommending and the ability to use a dialogue to guide its users through a search strategy within the domain.

In order to ensure a relatively transparent system, rules should be kept fairly simple. It is important to avoid asking the user unecessary questions as the system chains backward through its rules looking for conditions associated with desired results. To maintain the simplicity of the system and enhance its tutorial modality, the number of OR'ed conditions within each rule should be kept to a minimum.

Project Management

Now that we have selected a domain and identified some of the basic design elements of our system, let us briefly discuss some of the more practical aspects of managing a development project for a small system. Identifying feasible problems and selecting appropriate domains are among the most important preliminary steps. Serious projects usually begin with several possible problem areas to address. The field is gradually narrowed down to a few promising candidates. If, during the early stages of development, an insurmountable obstacle is encountered, the development effort can be shifted to another problem area.

It is also important to establish a budget and project timetable fairly early on in the process. For our small project, the major budget categories will be hardware and software, but a larger project would include lines for categories such as training, consultants, documentation, and maintenance. Cupello and Mishelevich recommend building a contingency fund into the budget for unanticipated expenses. The budget for a typical expert system is hundreds of thousands of dollars. For our toy system, a realistic figure, excluding personnel costs, could be in the range of $10,000. Once the system reached the implementation phase, additional hardware and software would be required for each installation.

The budget for a toy system might look something like this, although it is possible to experiment with toy systems with a substantially smaller budget (Alberico, 1988).

Budget for Small Expert System

Category	**Cost**
Hardware	
386 PC clone with 2MB RAM, 40MB hard disk, VGA monitor, dot matrix printer, 2400 baud modem and optical disk drive	6000.00
Development software	
micro-based shell capable of generating runtime systems, linking to applications software, and including limited graphics and hypertext capabilities	1500.00
Other software	
communications with script language, database management, text editor, utilities	1500.00
Supplies	300.00
Contingency	700.00
Total:	$10,000.00

Another early part of the development process is establishing a project timetable. Development can't begin immediately. It is important to identify sources of expertise and to do some preliminary knowledge acquisition. After gaining an idea of the kind of knowledge that applies within the domain, it is necessary to select a development tool. Some of the criteria for selecting a shell program will be addressed later in this chapter. It is also necessary to select and purchase hardware and additional software with which the shell will interact.

Project participants must be identified and trained, both within the domain and in using the development tool selected. Key players should include a person who is comfortable with computer programming and an expert in the domain. The skills and commitment level of project participants are the single most important factors in determining the success of the project. Since large amounts of time will be required from both the knowledge engineer and the domain expert, administrative support is crucial. Cupello and Mishelevich recommend cultivating an "executive champion" within the organization. Much of the early development work will be a learning experience for the knowledge engineer and the domain expert. The early system will go through several iterations before a development strategy is established and serious work begins.

The timetable should therefore include plenty of time for the project participants to learn to use the shell selected and to become comfortable working with one another. Other milestones should be set for purchase of hardware and software, and implementation of each of the capabilities which the system is planned to include. A proof of concept approach involves establishing the validity of each of the system's desired features before moving on to develop a new feature. The final milestones would involve testing the system as a complete entity with many inter-related parts and field testing it with users. User acceptance is the acid test for any system.

We've already selected a domain and made the vague statement that our system should have a **tutorial modality**. Now let's look at some of the capabilities we might want to include and, more specifically, what we mean when we say tutorial modality.

First of all let's consider where the knowledge for our system is going to come from.

Reference Librarians as a Knowledge Source

One source of knowledge is the reference librarian. For our case study, what we need is an expert business reference librarian with a strong commitment to instructing users — someone who will supply us with both the business reference knowledge we need for our domain and the instructional strategies we need to develop a system with a tutorial modality.

A good part of reference work involves recommending the best of many similar tools, and switching from one information format to another. Each tool has its own organizational structure and access language, neither of which are familiar to most clients. Hence the need for the reference librarian to serve in a largely instructional role. The reference librarian plays the role of mentor and gatekeeper — recommending sources and courses of action, instructing clients, and interpreting some rather arcane schemes for handling information. Technology has been applied to many of the problems of information access faced by reference librarians, but so far the problems associated with recommending sources and instructing clients have resisted technological solutions.

There are still large classes of information which are not easily (or cheaply) accessible to the uninitiated. Reference works, especially, tend to fall outside the scope of bibliographic utilities and the current generation of integrated library systems. Access to the contents of and services provided by most reference sources is simply not possible at the level of the MARC record. Providing access to the types of information contained in print and electronic reference works has remained the job of the reference librarian.

Reference librarians have always focused primarily on helping clients use locally available resources. The growth in importance of bibliographic instruction is evidence of that focus. Recommending and interpreting specialized sources of information is a big part of the job. Within every subject field, core resources are consulted frequently. So our knowledge acquisition efforts will focus on locally useful knowledge identified by reference librarians and recorded in in-house publications.

Bibliographies, pathfinders, workbooks, and locally developed instructional material are all designed to help users navigate small domains within much larger collections. Most are attempts to compensate for deficiencies in larger, more globally oriented systems, such as OPACs and online utilities. The goal of our development project is to add new interactive tools to the repertoire of user aids created by reference librarians. Small advisory systems such as printed handouts can reinforce the reference librarian's role as mentor and instructor. Such systems can also be used to interact directly with OPACs, bibliographic utilities, online databases, and CD-ROMs.

Another of our goals is to enhance access to information at the local level while continuing to take advantage of already established global information systems. Therefore our system won't be designed to operate in a vacuum. The capability of interacting with already existing information systems should be built into our system.

In-House Publications as a Knowledge Source

Expert system technology may be less threatening to reference librarians if expert systems are viewed as another form of user aid, an interactive handout that can contain descriptions of information sources as well as rules for using them. Librarians consult handouts prepared by other librarians who have more expertise in the subject area being considered. Clients also use locally prepared handouts to help them with research in specialized subject fields. A locally published guide is a distillation of a reference librarian's knowledge about sources within a specific domain. Small systems, like our prototype, can be expected to function in similar ways.

It seems logical that another of the major sources of knowledge for our system should be the handouts that are already available in such profusion in so many libraries. One of our first knowledge acquisition steps would be to gather all of the in-house publications related to business reference and attempt to derive rules from them. The goal is to take advantage of rules that are implicitly stated in the text of our publications, while also using the text itself to present users with explicit advice.

The difference between an expert system and a handout is that an expert system is capable of acting upon the advice that is typically found in a handout and developing a search strategy for the client. Imagine a pathfinder that can modify the path it recommends as a student interacts with it. If handouts are already in machine-readable form, inexpensive expert system shells can be used to design systems which incorporate rules for recommending specific tools and links to explanatory text.

Once a rule "fires" and a source is recommended, descriptive and instructional text for the recommended source can be displayed or printed. Annotations can be electronically cut and pasted directly from existing in-house publications.

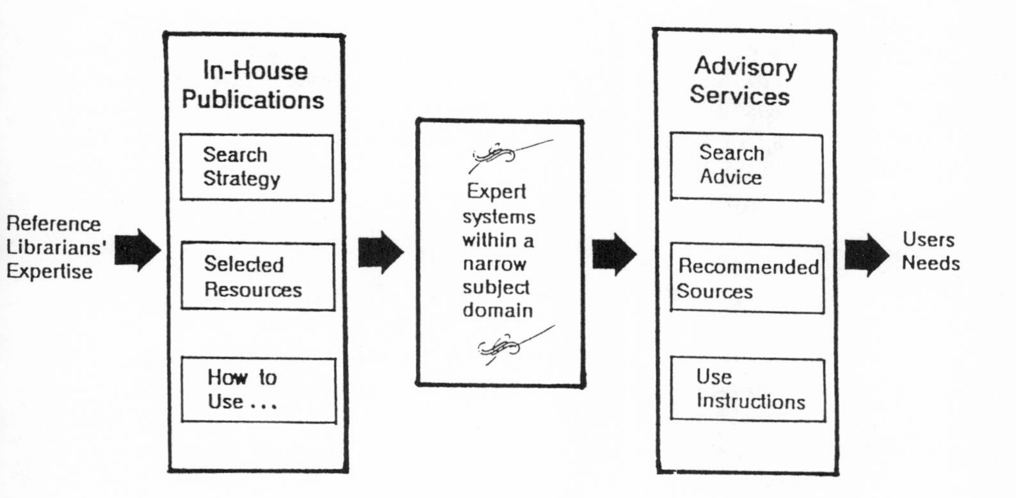

Figure 9.3. Expert systems as instructional media

Guides to the Literature as a Knowledge Source

Another source of knowledge for our small tutorial system will be the core "meta-level" reference works frequently consulted by practitioners within the domain. In this case, knowledge from titles such as Daniells' *Business Information Sources*, Wasserman's *Statistics Sources*, *Guide to Special Issues and Indexes of Periodicals*, and similar titles would be built into the system. At the very minimum, the reference librarian(s) participating in the project should be asked to look at the reviews and guides to the literature in the domain and identify those which are most useful in the local environment. A larger level of involvement would include tasks like analyzing contents of sources and adding rules to describe business-related government publications, serials, and trade literature.

Database Documentation as a Knowledge Source

A final source of knowledge for our system will be the documentation supplied with the electronic resources to which our system will connect. Therefore, our system will include knowledge derived from the DIALOG "bluesheets" for the business databases we plan to build hooks to, and from the documentation supplied with the COMPUSTAT database to which our system will connect. Knowing, for example, which databases had a searchable **market share** field might influence the advice or actions generated by our system.

We won't have room on our computer to include too much knowledge about the way our OPAC is organized (e.g., the LCSH), but we might want to incorporate some knowledge about the use of our OPAC within narrow aspects of our domain. For example, if the user is being connected to the OPAC for a search on "multinationals," we could either directly advise him to use the LC Subject Heading "international business enterprises," or advise him to consult the LCSH "red books" before continuing. We could also easily help the client perform keyword searches using standard LC subdivisions for different types of reference sources (e.g., directories, encyclopedias, maps, concordances, etc.).

Review of System Specifications

Now that we have an idea of where the knowledge for our advisory system might come from, let's review some of the goals of our project.

Our system will be advisory in nature. It will function as an "electronic pathfinder," including knowledge about a highly select group of core sources. Special attention will be paid to sources that can provide the client with access to additional information. The potential for direct links to electronic databases will be possible. Subject coverage will be limited and the focus will be on teaching clients to use information resources recommended by a human expert. Our system will recommend specific reference works. It will describe the contents of the works it recommends. The way it is organized and the sequence of menus presented to the client will attempt to teach search strategy by walking the client through the search process. The text presented to the user will provide explicit advice addressing the ways in which specific information sources are typically used.

A major effort will be made to address needs not met by larger systems or OPACs. Rather than being comprehensive, our system will filter out peripheral material. It will focus on the needs of specific client groups. It can be designed around frequently recurring assignments if necessary. We won't be describing reference sources in abstract terms. We will be working backwards from reference questions. Our system will be designed to reinforce the advice given by business reference librarians. We may even decide to use it in conjunction with library instruction.

Our advisory system will attempt to serve many of the same functions served by in-house publications, including being available when reference librarians aren't. The cost of printing has always had a chilling effect on the length and number of handouts published in many libraries. A domain advisory system would only generate descriptions of those specific sources that were pertinent to the information problem at hand. Annotations could be as long or as numerous as required by the subject domain. One by-product of a reference expert system is a custom-designed handout based on each user's specific needs.

But initially our system won't be as easily or as widely distributed as the publications it aims to supplement. Nor will it be as available as reference librarians typically are. At first the knowledge bases we develop will require dedicated workstations, workstations with access to an OPAC, a CD-ROM, and an assortment of online databases. Eventually knowledge bases will come to be distributed less expensively and more efficiently than handouts. Small advisory systems will be made available over data networks. Then our knowledge bases will be available for many more hours and at many more locations than reference librarians.

Our system will attempt to develop user profiles at a primitive level by creating rules that recommend different sources to different user categories. Once again it would be crucial to draw upon the expertise of skilled practitioners when devising rules. For example, we might have two different rules for a subject area; one for a freshman marketing student and another for a faculty member doing research for a book. If the topic were market research, the rule for the student might recommend and describe one of the basic printed sources. The faculty member's rule might activate a communications script, connecting her to the **Predicasts** database and allowing her to specify her own delimiters while supplying appropriate codes and downloading results.

Selecting a Development Tool

Now that we've determined *what* we want to do, we'll need to start worrying about *how* we're going to do it. Our first concern will be the capabilities of the shell we select. To get an idea of some of the features of well-designed shells, we'll compare the two major categories of expert system development tools, shells, and languages. The choice for those interested in creating an expert system lies between a shell (there are dozens of them now) and a scaled-down version of an AI programming language. PROLOG and LISP are the two main contenders, although more conventional languages such as **C** and **Pascal** are also used for expert systems.

Most shells fall somewhere between applications programs and programming languages.

Shells, like programming languages, may be used to develop applications that meet a specific developer's needs. Unlike programming languages, shells may be used efficiently by those with limited programming experience. There is, however, a tradeoff between ease of use and flexibility. Capabilities that are available to programmers using languages such as LISP or PROLOG are sacrificed with shells. Most shells are somewhat more than simple applications programs but somewhat less than full-blown programming environments. An expert system shell is to expert system applications what a programmable database manager such as dBASE is to database management applications

The decision to purchase a shell or a programming language will be influenced by the same kinds of factors that influence just about any application versus language purchase decision. For most tasks, it's easier to buy a software solution off-the-shelf than it is to develop one yourself. Not only is it easier to buy and use someone else's program, it's cheaper. The applications program that seems more expensive at first glance will almost always end up being cheaper when the costs of development, debugging, and maintenance are added to the purchase price of a programming language. So a shell program will be our choice for a development tool. But it is important to realize that there are more than a few knowledge representation schemes that aren't easily supported by the majority of shells on the market.

The programming language we'll examine is **Turbo PROLOG** from Borland International, probably the least expensive and most widely distributed AI language for micros. We've already used it for a number of examples in earlier chapters. The shell we'll examine is **VP-Expert** from Paperback Software, another inexpensive and widely distributed piece of software. Each program is the product of a large, California-based discount software house, and the two are comparably priced.

How does one go about comparing these two different types of software? First of all, let's limit our comparison to expert system development. The AI language can be used for other applications, including natural language processing and dynamic databases, but let's leave those capabilities alone for now, even though there is potential for some interesting library applications. How can we go about comparing these programs when it comes to expert system development? Why not examine them in terms of the architectural components of a typical expert/consultation system?

Knowledge Representation with Small Tools

Since it is the knowledge base that lies at the heart of any expert system, let's examine knowledge base capabilities first. The first issue to examine is whether there are constraints on the way knowledge can be represented. The knowledge bases created with inexpensive shells typically take the form of **If...Then** rules. Such constraints can be limiting for some types of real world knowledge. But If..Then rules are easy to understand

```
                    VP-EXPERT - RULES


RULE 2 A
IF   need=address OR
     need=phone_number OR
     need=list OR
     need=name
THEN
     tooltype=directory;

         .
         .
         .
         .

RULE 7
IF   topic=company AND
     tooltype=directory OR
     feature=SIC_codes OR
     feature=executives_vital_statistics
THEN
     source=Standard_and_Poors_ Register;
```

Figure 9.4. VP-Expert rules

INDUCTION TABLE

topic	need	source
company	balance_sheet	Moodys
company	annual_rpt	Qfiche
company	ratios	Valueline
company	analysis	Valueline
company	historical	Moodys
company	officers_names	Standard_and_Poors
company	address	Standard_and_Poors
company	phone_number	Standard_and_Poors
company	jl_articles	Business_Index
company	newspaper_articles	Natl_Newspaper_Index
company	trade_jl_articles	Funk_and_Scott_Index
industry	ratios	Troy
industry	ratios	Key_Business_Ratios
industry	ratios	Robert_Morris
industry	analysis	Industry_Surveys
industry	SIC_codes	SIC_Directory

Figure 9.5. Induction table

and work with. Unlike AI languages, many shells provide a facility for developing rules from examples. VP-Expert can derive rules from a list of examples called an induction table. A knowledge base comprised of rules is easy to develop with most shells. To get more complex and open-ended knowledge structures such as frames requires a more powerful computer and a much more expensive shell.

On the other hand, AI languages such as PROLOG can support an almost infinite variety of different types of knowledge structures. PROLOG can be used for relational databases, it can represent knowledge as lists, or it can represent knowledge as rules and frames. Turbo PROLOG is a declarative language with procedural capabilities. Knowledge representation is its great strength. The possibilities for representing knowledge are much greater with an AI language than they are with a typical shell.

Turbo PROLOG allows the system developer to establish **domains** in which knowledge objects are defined. **Predicates** are used to describe relationships between objects, and **clauses** are used to assign values to the objects defined in domains and predicates. It is the clauses section of a PROLOG program which contains the rules and facts of an expert system. It is there that the relationships established in the predicates section are instantiated as specific examples. With PROLOG, one could develop a descriptive language for reference sources.

Unlike pure declarative languages, Turbo PROLOG is a typed language, like Pascal, in which data types must be defined before they can be used. Defining a domain establishes the data types a Turbo PROLOG program will use. A domain could be defined for describing reference works in terms of their attributes, and another domain could be defined for describing reference works in bibliographic terms. Predicates could be used to describe relationships between different objects and domains. Clauses could be used to describe specific reference works in terms of both their attributes and bibliographic descriptions. Such a knowledge base could be queried to provide a list of bibliographic descriptions of reference works that had desired attributes.

Maintenance will become an important issue as our system matures. The manner by which knowledge may be added or deleted from the knowledge base is important. Both Turbo PROLOG and VP-Expert provide editors that make it relatively easy to update and maintain a knowl-

```
                    PROLOG - COMPLEX OBJECTS


domains
    subjectlist=subject*
    featurelist=feature*
    refbook=refbook(title,subjectlist,featurelist)
    bibl=bibl(author,title,publisher,place,date)
    author=author(lastname,firstname)
    subject,feature,title,publisher,place=symbol
    lastname,firstname=string
    date=integer
```

Figure 9.6. PROLOG complex objects

```
              PROLOG DOMAINS, PREDICATES, CLAUSES


domains
     subjectlist=subject*
     refbook=refbook(title,subjectlist,tooltype)
     bibl=bibl(full_title,place,publisher,date,location)
     feature,subject,title,tooltype,place,publisher,
     date,location=symbol

predicates
     tool_is(tooltype,feature)
     desc(refbook)
     try_this(title,bibl)

clauses
     tool_is(directory,addresses).
     desc(refbook("S&P",[business,companies],directory)).
     try_this("S&P",bibl("Standard and Poors Register",
     "NY","Standard and Poors", 1987,"HF5035 P66")).
```

Figure 9.7. PROLOG domains, predicates, clauses

```
PROLOG PREDICATES and CLAUSES

predicates
    try_using(symbol)
    it_is(symbol)
    positive(symbol,symbol)
    negative(symbol,symbol)

clauses
    it_is(a_directory) if
       positive(do_you_need,a_list);
       positive(do_you_need,phone_numbers);
       positive(do_you_need,addresses),!.

    try_using("Standard and Poors Register") if
       it_is(a_directory),
       positive(is_topic,companies),!.
```

Figure 9.8. Rules implemented in PROLOG

edge base. Both editors can mark and move text and are accompanied by debuggers that can spot syntax errors.

It should be possible to link related knowledge bases to one another, making it possible for one knowledge base to invoke another. Both shell and AI languages can be made to link knowledge bases to one another, but as with most tasks, connecting knowledge bases to one another is much easier to accomplish with a well-designed shell.

Inference Capabilities

Our next point of comparison is the inference engine. It is the inference engine that determines which rules fire and how, and it is the inference engine which determines the line of "reasoning" pursued by the computer during a consultation. The efficiency of the inference mechanism will determine the kinds of questions presented to the user and the sequence in which they appear. Response time is determined to a large extent by the quality of the inference engine. Although there are many possible approaches, a good inference engine will avoid unnecessary lines of inquiry and backtracking.

As we've seen in earlier chapters, access to the underlying mechanisms of a system is important. The developer should have the ability to view the assertions made by the user and the inferences derived by the system. Any development tool should provide a trace function which allows the user to view the contents of the system's working memory as well as the rule currently being tested. Development software also needs to provide the capability of suppressing those displays.

Another useful capability is the ability to change the operative assertions during the middle of a consultation, to take a "what if" approach. This is easy with most shells but beyond the skill of novices with a language such as PROLOG. Yet, another consideration is the degree of control allowed. PROLOG seems to have the definite edge here, but once again it takes a fair amount of skill to get a PROLOG program to perform the way you want it to. PROLOG employs a construct known as a "cut" to eliminate unnecessary backtracking, but working with cuts can be tricky even for experienced programmers.

A long-term goal is a deliverable system. Any system that requires its users to purchase commercial software can't be thought of as deliverable. The development tool we choose should be able to generate an independent executable or run-time program. This is relatively easy with PROLOG. When a PROLOG program is linked and compiled, the parts of PROLOG needed to run the program become part of an .EXE file — a program which can be run without PROLOG being available. PROLOG is a development language, not an end-user product. Royalties aren't a problem to be faced by PROLOG developers who want to sell their expert systems.

VP-Expert, unlike more expensive shells, does not provide the capability to generate run-time, executable expert systems. However, there is a note in the manual instructing those interested in run-time versions of their applications to contact the publisher for a redistribution agreement, for which a fee is charged. Therefore VP-Expert, while inexpensive and useful for early phases of prototype development, wouldn't serve our long-term purposes. Our system must eventually be implemented in a run-time version that we can distribute easily on disk and via electronic mail. The ability to compile royalty-free run-time versions of our system is crucial at the deliverable system phase of development.

User Interface Capabilities

When it comes to the user interface, the contrast once again is between ease of use and level of control. As was mentioned earlier, good development tools can display the logical basis for the direction a consultation is taking at the same time the consultation itself is occurring on another part of the screen. VP-Expert makes it possible to display an explanation of the reasoning underlying a rule with something known as a **BECAUSE** clause. The shell program will also automatically generate and neatly format menus for the user. It can even recommend questions to ask in a consultation based on pieces of information required at various points during the reasoning process. VP- Expert also permits the creation of windows in which text can be displayed, and now also supports limited graphics and hypertext development.

```
                    VP - EXPERT CONSULTATION

You will be using the JMU company/industry knowledge base.
Press any key to begin the consultation.


Indicate whether you are interested in company or industry data:

   company                  industry


Are you interested in a specific type of information:

   not sure                 financial      narrative description

   directory                nonfinancial statistics


Are any of the following types of financial information of interest:

   not applicable           balance sheet          annual report

   SEC rpt                  10 K                   ratios

Enter to select    END to complete    /Q to Quit    ? for Unknown
```

Figure 9.9. VP-Expert consultation

Turbo PROLOG, especially when purchased with the set of companion programs, Turbo PROLOG Toolbox, also supports user interface design. Pull-down menus can be easily created. And sound can also be incorporated. PROLOG can also be used for natural language processing. One of the sample programs accompanying Turbo PROLOG is a geographic knowledge base that can be queried with a natural language interface. PROLOG supports a variety of screen design capabilities, including windowing, color displays, and reverse video.

Disadvantages of Languages

PROLOG can do a lot of things but PROLOG has to be told how to do everything. All capabilities must be explicitly declared. LISP is even more declarative, with few built-in procedures. Those at ease with thinking in Boolean terms will probably find it easier to learn PROLOG than many

```
                    VP-EXPERT TRACE FUNCTION

If timeframe is crucial to your request, enter the time period in
which you're interested.
Otherwise, enter: DOES NOT MATTER.

DOES_NOT_MATTER           current_2_months          current_year

past_year                 past_5_years              historical

time_series

Are you interested in one the following specific industries?

If not, enter:  NOT APPLICABLE

NOT_APPLICABLE       computer        automobile        hotel
```

```
industry_type=computer AND          topic=industry CNF 100
timeframe=does_not_matter OR        need=analysis CNF 100
timeframe=current year OR           need=comparisons CNF 100
timeframe=past_year OR              timeframe=past_year CNF 100
timeframe=past_5_years              source=Industry_Surveys CNF 100
THEN                                source=Moodys_Fact_Sheets CNF 100
source=DataPro CNF 100
Finding industry_type

Enter to select    END to complete    /Q to Quit    ? for Unknown
```

Figure 9.10. VP-Expert trace function

standard languages, but it's still an intellectual challenge. And it takes about 50 times as much time and work to develop a PROLOG application as it does to develop an expert system with a shell.

It is the built-in user interface and special purpose inference engine that give shell programs their advantages. Shorter development periods are the rule. It is possible to get a prototype system up and running quickly. Ease can be deceptive. Whether a shell or a language is used, developing and maintaining a meaningful knowledge base is the real challenge.

```
A SIMPLE PROLOG PROGRAM

DOMAINS
  refbook=refbook(title,subject,tooltype)
  bibl=bibl(full_title,place,publisher,date,location)
  title,subject,tooltype,full_title,place,publisher,location=symbol
  date=integer

PREDICATES
  desc(refbook)
  try_this(title,bibl)

CLAUSES
  desc(refbook("S&P",companies,directory)).
  desc(refbook("Business Index",business,index)).
  desc(refbook("Palgrave",economics,encyclopedia)).
  desc(refbook("Daniells",business,literature_guide)).

  try_this("S&P",bibl("Standard and Poors Register","NY",
            "Standard and Poors",1987,"HF5035 P66")).
  try_this("Business Index",(Business Index","CA",
            "IAC",1988,index_table_7)).
  try_this("Palgrave",bibl("The New Palgrave: A Dictionary
            of Economics","NY","Macmillan",1987,"HB61 N49 1987")).
  try_this("Daniells",bibl("Business Information Sources","Berkeley"
            Univ.Cal.Press",1985,"Z7164 C81 D16 1985")).
```

Figure 9.11. Simple PROLOG program

PROLOG is harder to learn than a shell because a layer of system development understanding must be added to an understanding of problem solving within the domain. The advantage of a shell is its built-in functionality. The disadvantage is the limited design flexibility associated with a structure which comes two-thirds complete. AI languages offer a high level of control but demand a high level of commitment. This is especially true when it comes to developing a workable user interface and tailoring the inference engine to the knowledge base.

Interaction with Other Software

An important design criteria for our project is the ability of our system to interact with other software. Most of the better shell programs provide this capability (including VP-Expert). PROLOG and LISP programs can call applications programs (a tricky process), and communications capabilities can be built right into LISP and PROLOG programs (an even trickier process). As usual, the language can be much more flexible but the shell is much easier. Since this is such an important capability for our system, a shell is preferrable.

```
PROLOG - SPECIFYING GOALS


Goal: desc(refbook(Title,business,Type))
Title=Business Index, Type=index
Title=Daniells, Type=literature_guide
2 Solutions

Goal: desc(refbook(Title,companies,directory)) AND
    try_this(Title,Bibl)
Title=S&P
Bibl=bibl("Standard and Poors Register","NY",
          "Standard and Poors",1987,"HF5035 P66")
1 Solution

Goal:desc(refbook("S&P",Topic,Type))
Topic=companies, Type=directory
1 Solution

Goal:
```

Figure 9.12. PROLOG — specifying goals

Shells can be used to control interaction with other programs. A shell can also be used to call text files, and talk to database management or communications software. An essential feature of the development software we select will be its ability to permit interaction with electronic information sources. At a minimum, we'll want something which can pull text files off our hard disk and call and run concurrently with a communications package. It wouldn't make sense to put our annotations describing the sources our system will recommend into our knowledge base. It would be more efficient to store our explanatory and descriptive material in text files on the workstation's hard disk and to present them only when needed. Nor would it be practical to incorporate information that is already available in electronic format into our system. It would be more efficient to have our system go out and retrieve electronic information when it's needed.

The software on our system would vary from one domain to another. For example, a financial resources expert system would probably provide a spreadsheet interface to handle numeric data. The same system might also include a CD-ROM containing numeric financial data plus software to search the CD-ROM. There will be variations, but one would expect the following categories of software to be represented in a small reference workstation.

- an expert system shell
- programmable communications or search software

- a CD-ROM search engine
- local database management software
- a macro processor
- a word processor/text editor

Connectivity

Programmable communications software will be almost as important to our project as a good expert system shell. It is possible to use such software to develop communications programs called scripts. Expert system rules can activate communications scripts, logging on to online files, connecting to the local OPAC, or connecting to local numeric files on academic computing systems. Besides acting as gateways to a variety of electronic formats, scripts can contain "filters" for limiting the number of acceptable retrievals, limiting a search by date, language or source, even modifying a strategy based upon output.

The shell we select should be able to activate a simple batch file if certain conditions are recognized. The batch file in turn would run a communications script that would connect to the electronic source matching the conditions in a rule. The script might then walk the user

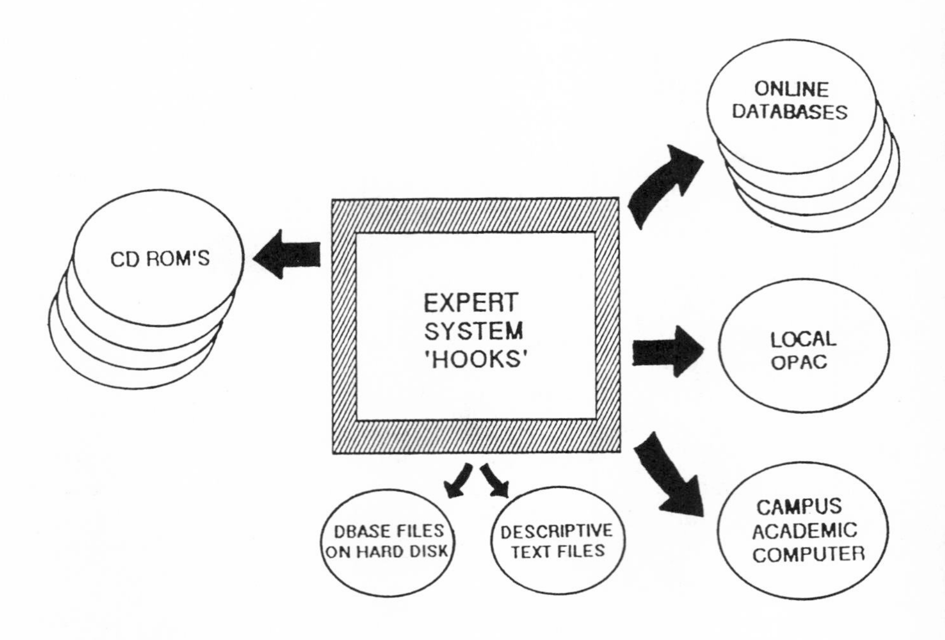

Figure 9.13. Hooks to external information sources

through a simple search, even supplying necessary codes and search protocols. Once the search was completed, control would shift from the communications script back to the shell program and the consultation would resume.

Filters

Filtering is a concept that is central to our small-scale, highly selective system. Here we are again, back to the plumbing metaphor. Remember the computer is a medium. And it is a medium whose properties can be changed. Our workstation can be made to limit the information which is passed to it, and to transform the information which is passed through it.

Just as information is filtered on the production end of the publishing/research cycle, it is filtered at the consumption end. The professional searcher who acts as an intermediary performs a filtering function. The search interview is a way of separating from a narrative stream those concepts, terms, and limits that will control the amount of information allowed to flow from the source being tapped. Delimiters such as time period covered and language, when combined with a subject query, form a screen through which can pass only that which is wanted.

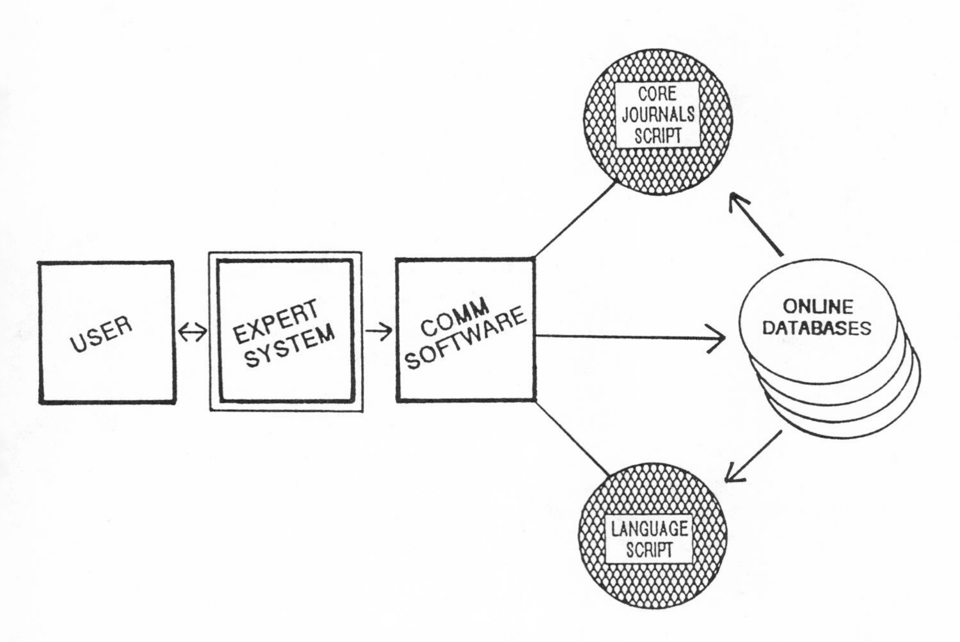

Figure 9.14. Filters

The process of selecting a database can be thought of as a way of establishing a pipeline to an information pool. Some pools are small but rich in the type of information being sought; others are broad and deep. Should the searcher use a database on the coffee industry, or explore the depth and breadth of a file such as **ABI/INFORM**? Before the pipes are connected, decisions must be made concerning the nature and amount of information that will reach the filter. Rules for making these decisions, from selecting a particular database to the kind of output which is acceptable, can be built into an advisory system.

Imagine a rule which indicated that marketing information was of interest and that local core sources should be emphasized.

A simple statement like this:

(ADA CSA DIM ADR JCR JMK JMR PRJ SAL).SO.

when incorporated in a communications script can be used to make the INFO (ABI/INFORM) database on BRS function as an index to nine selected marketing journals, filtering out all other information. Each of the three-letter journal codes is a hole in a filter, allowing only references to the journal it represents to pass through.

In actual practice, the process would work something like this.

1. The expert system would call the communications software when conditions arising from the consultation indicated an online search was appropriate.
2. The communications software would run a script.
3. The script would include filters, determined by conditions established within the consultation.
4. Filters would establish constraints on the search.
5. Constraints would conform to user profiles, budgets, core sources, and educational objectives for the system.

Developing and Testing a Prototype

Once a suitable shell has been purchased, it's time to begin the task of developing a prototype system and testing each of its capabilities. Our methodology will be to test each phase of the project before moving on to the next. Desired capabilities will be added incrementally. Each capability will be thoroughly tested before development begins on the next capability. Even after testing each component, we'll expect an unpredictable result when we put the whole system together. We'll test each of the individual modules, but we'll still have to field test the whole system.

Test One: Codification

Our first test will be our ability to formalize knowledge within the domain. We'll use it to see what kind of a handle we can get on representing expertise about business reference. We'll start with a rough framework of rules representing each of the four major treatments from our decision tree. Initially, we'll create four or five rules for each of these categories on company information:

- financial information
- statistical information
- directory information
- narrative description

For each category, rules will represent sources at different levels of the hierarchy of the decision tree. For example:

narrative description	Narrative description
writing a paper	developing a portfolio
current topic	investment advice
BPI	Valueline

Each rule will include clauses representing facets of the source it indicates. Rules won't be too simple, nor will they be too complex. We'll consider ourselves successful if we can get our rules to fire in the sequence we expected. We'll also need to make sure that the conclusions presented by our set of rules make sense to our domain expert. If they don't we might have to rethink the representation scheme we've chosen.

Test Two: Explanation

The next capability we'd like to prove is the linking of rules to explanatory text. To pass this test, we'll have to be able to put text on the screen when a rule fires. The text we display should include a bibliographic description and an annotation. The annotation should match the context of the rule that triggered its display. That is, a rule that recommended Moody's for company history would be linked to a different annotation than a rule that recommended the same source for balance sheet data. Preferably, the text will come directly from an already existing publication.

It should be possible to link more than a single screen full of text to a rule, and the user of the system should be allowed to control the display of text. At the very minimum, the user should be able to page from one screen of text to the next. Finally, we'll want our system to print in addition to simply displaying text.

Test Three: Hooks

Passing this test requires that we first accomplish a series of subgoals, each of which is necessary for a different type of hook. Our first task will be to develop a small batch file (operating system program) which can be called when a rule fires. The batch file should perform some simple DOS task, for example, typing the contents of a file, and then return to the advisory system consultation.

Our next task involves making our system interact with a dBASE (or compatible) database. We'll want to demonstrate two capabilities before we move on. Our system should **get** the contents of a field from a dBASE record and **put** it into a knowledge base. A rule will be written to trigger the interaction. Conversely, another rule will be used to put some information into a dBASE record.

The next task in this category involves using our shell to call and run a simple communications script. The script wouldn't have to be elaborate. It could be as simple as a PROCOMM command file which logged onto an online vendor, selected a database, and logged off. Similar scripts could be developed to connect to the OPAC and to a campus minicomputer, which might contain business-related numeric databases such as COMPUSTAT or some of the ICPSR statistical files. Upon exiting the script and the communications software needed to run it, the user should be returned to the consultation.

The final task in this category would be building a link to a CD-ROM database and the software needed to search it. We would be satisfied if we could connect our user to a CD-ROM (**Business Periodicals Index** perhaps, or **Compact DISCLOSURE**). A simple connection to the native mode of the host CD-ROM would be sufficient. We could assume that users of the system are already able to use the CD-ROM without mediation from our advisory system. However, our advisory system would recommend when to use the CD-ROM, make the connection, and, when the CD-ROM search was completed, return to the consultation.

Test Four: Filters

Most of this test will involve working with our programmable communications software. The first thing we'll do is write a script that limits results to articles contained in a select group of journals. Separate filters could be created for marketing journals, trade journals, financial media, etc.

Once our simple filter is created, we'll attempt a more complex filter for user profiling. This filter will refer students in introductory classes to descriptions while connecting faculty and grad students to online databases.

Our final filter will be designed to recognize the number of postings yielded by a subject search and take action to modify strategy based on the number of postings (Alberico, 1987)

Test Five: Query Building

Our next step also relates as much to our communications software as it does to our shell. We'll use our OPAC for this test. There may be situations where we'll want to connect our user to our OPAC and build a simple search to meet some need identified in the consultation. This task could be accomplished by a rule which calls and runs a communications script. Consider this rule.

If topic=company AND
need=narrative description AND
desc_type=company history THEN

RUN OPAC COMPANY HISTORY SCRIPT.

When it fired, the first thing it might do is ask the user for all of the possible names of the company he is interested in. Then the script would perform a keyword search designed to find company histories in the OPAC and substituting values supplied by the user for dummy variables in the script.

Test Six: Linked Knowledge Bases

This test will relate to linked knowledge bases. There are two things we want to accomplish here. The first is to have certain conditions transfer control from the knowledge base currently being used to a new knowledge base. The second is to pass along all that is known about the problem at hand to the new knowledge base.

Let's say we are involved in a consultation with a general industry knowledge base. We already know that industry information is of interest, that current information is needed, and that the client's primary focus will be market and product research. Once we determine that the computer industry is of specific interest, we can pass along all of those facts plus the assertion that the general source, *F&S Index*, might be helpful. The second consultation won't have to begin at square one. It can incorporate facts that are already known and almost immediately recommend sources, such as the DataPro reports.

Test Seven: Dialogue Control

Our shell should let us design our own screens and menus, determining what to put on the screen and where to put it. To successfully pass this test, we'll have to demonstrate those capabilities. We'll also need to demonstrate that we can control the sequence with which menus are presented and ensure that the user isn't forced to respond to redundant or unnecessary questions. This isn't as easy as it sounds. To a large extent, the pace and sequence of the dialogue will be determined by the way our rules are put together. For example, this rule

> If topic=company AND
> need=financial information AND
> financ_type= balance sheet data OR
> need=narrative description AND
> desc_type=company history THEN
> MOODYS

would probably result in confusion because it would cause the typical backward chaining system to attempt to find out both what kind of financial information was of interest and what type of narrative description was needed. The user who specified one or the other earlier in the consultation would be asked an unnecessary question. It would be more efficient to have two rules for recommending *Moody's*.

> If topic=company AND
> need=financial information AND
> financ_type=balance sheet THEN
> MOODYS

> If topic=company AND
> need=narrative description AND
> desc_type=company history THEN
> MOODYS

Not only would this approach be more likely to present the client with a sequence of questions more similar to a typical search strategy, when either one of the rules fired the client could be presented with an annotation relating to his specific need, either balance sheet data or company history. If rules are organized properly, it is possible to embed a search strategy in the dialogue of the consultation. If the sequence of menus presented to the user makes logical sense to the domain expert and if there are few unnecessary questions, then we'll consider this test successful.

Test Eight: Hypertext

Many shells support hypertext. If the shell we've selected supports hypertext, we will attempt to demonstrate hypertext capabilities in our system. Hypertext can be used to allow clients to explore concept networks within the explanatory text associated with specific reference works. For example, when a source such as *Robert Morris Associates Annual Statement Studies* is recommended, a description of the financial ratios included in the source would appear. The names of specific ratios, such as **quick ratio**, would be highlighted within the explanatory text. Clicking a mouse on a highlighted term would cause a definition and discussion of that term to appear in a separate window on the screen. In this case the user would see a definition of quick ratio, an explanation of how that ratio is calculated, and a discussion of how that ratio can be used.

Test Nine: Graphics

More sophisticated shells also include graphics capabilities. Once again, if our shell supports graphics, we will attempt to demonstrate that capability in our prototype. One of the best ways graphics could be used would be to display a graphic of a floor plan of a library showing the locations of sources likely to be recommended by rules in the knowledge base.

Putting Everything Together

Our final system might not pass all of these tests. Nor is it likely to include each and every one of the capabilities described. Developing such a system would involve overcoming some tough (but not insurmountable) programming barriers. Some features, especially those involving connections to online databases, might be abandoned for financial reasons.

Individual libraries interested in experimenting with their own advisory systems will need to develop their own desired capabilities, and their own methods for testing those capabilities. Any system, large or small, will need to be field tested and debugged. And any system will need to be maintained by both adding new knowledge and deleting knowledge that is no longer useful.

Finally, once all the separate modules have been spliced together and the whole system has been tested to the developer's satisfaction, it will need to be field tested with other librarians and clients. Field testing will reveal flaws that would not be apparent to those deeply involved in the design of the system.

To call a small system like the one described in this chapter an expert system is stretching the truth a bit. But systems such as the hypothetical system we've described will become increasingly common. Librarians will benefit from the experience of building their own advisory systems. Systems like the one we've described can be widely distributed, serving as another medium for knowledge transfer. Clients can receive customized advice without time pressure. Nevertheless, we shouldn't think of small advisory systems as anything more than electronic pathfinders. The concerns involved in designing a larger system will be discussed in the next chapter.

Recommended Reading

Waters (1986) and Parrott (1986, 1988) have been the most influential writers on library advisory systems in the United States. Forbes Gibb (1985) has edited a book describing some of the more interesting projects in the United Kingdom. Richardson (1989), P.F. Anderson (1988), and Aluri (1988) provide reviews and critiques of the library literature. Articles about small advisory systems in libraries are beginning to appear in ALA journals, especially *Information Technology and Libraries* and *College and Research Libraries. Computers in Libraries* and *Library Hi Tech* also often contain articles of interest.

There are also a number of practical discussions of advisory system development, many of which have already been cited. Harmon and Maus (1988) is recommended. Gupta and Prasad (1988) have edited two books of readings which give a broad overview of development considerations.

10
Methodologies for Designing Large Expert Systems

As the library world begins to take on larger and more ambitious expert systems projects, it will become increasingly important to apply sound software engineering principles to manage complexity efficiently and to be able to verify that systems perform to requirements. The need to formalize our methodologies for building and testing such systems has also become more critical.

The methodology proposed here borrows from existing software engineering methods but also draws upon techniques specifically designed for knowledge-based systems.

Requirements Analysis

Before development work is undertaken, it is important to have clearly defined in a formal and structured way what is expected of the system. The following steps are important parts of the requirements analysis process.

Selection of a Clearly Constrained Problem

The usefulness of an expert system is maximized when it is designed to perform a task that occurs frequently, requires a high level of skill, does not require an inordinate ammount of time, and where the expertise is not readily available. Diagnosing bacterial infections, configuring computers, tutoring in electronics, and determining cable maintenance problems are examples of recurring tasks where expert systems have been successfully applied and used. For reference services, providing a ranked list of sources to satisfy a given information need seems well within the scope of what is possible with today's technology.

Certainly in many libraries, no reference librarian is available during the off-peak hours and patrons might prefer an expert advisory system to no help at all. The goal then is to deliver scarce expertise to sites where it is needed. There is also the intriguing possibility that users could dial in from their home or office to consult the expert system. If further assistance were needed, they could simply be connected to a real reference librarian whose image would appear on the screen with a telephone hook-up to the reference desk. An important issue in requirements analysis is to determine who is to be helped and to clearly specify what sort of help can be provided.

Identification of the Expert and Expertise

Expert systems are built by encoding the skills of an expert decision maker in order to make her expertise available to novices in the same field. A crucial first step in building any expert system is obtaining the support and cooperation of an expert, defined very simply as someone with over ten years of experience who is recognized as an expert by her peers. This may involve introducing the expert to the technology and helping her to overcome feelings of resistance at the thought of being replaced by a mere machine. One of the most successful techniques for gaining the full cooperation of the expert, is encouraging her active involvement early in the process of building a small prototype.

At least one other expert should also be available for independent validation of the system. Only in this way can the designer guarantee a reasonably robust system that will be acceptable to other professionals. It is often difficult to get experts to agree on how to handle a given problem. By combining the skills and insights of several experts, the system becomes both stronger and more acceptable to the average user.

Communication on the Role of Expert Systems

A clear understanding of the role of the expert system is a crucial factor in the eventual success or failure of the enterprise. It must be seen as helpful by those who will eventually be asked to use it, and it must fit into their world. People have difficulty accepting or evaluating what they do not understand. An important task during the requirements analysis phase of development is to introduce clients to expert systems technology. This can be accomplished in two ways:

1. Building a small prototype of a selected module with a subset of the test cases. This will do a great deal to demystify the process, will enable the expert to visualize more clearly what her contribution needs to be, and will result in more realistic expectations as well as the development of a system that is truly useful.

2. Educational seminars. In these seminars, other applications can be demonstrated and evaluated, preferably by those involved in using the proposed system.

The more commercially successful expert systems are serving as tools to assist skilled professionals with complex decision-making tasks or diagnoses. Very often what is required is sorting through a complex set of conditions, and eventually ranking a number of possible solutions.

Expert systems do not replace but rather complement the professional by offering a second expert opinion that will either confirm the professional's opinion or offer other possibilities to explore. Because in many cases they bring together the expertise of several different domain experts, they can enrich the professional's own experience base. In these days when people may be sued for poor judgment, expert systems provide an extra level of confidence.

An expert system also offers the unique advantage of harnessing the power of the computer to process data and carry out complex tasks rapidly and accurately. In many cases, an expert system is able to bring together and place at the professional's fingertips information from a wide variety of disparate sources. Very often collecting the needed information for decision making is acknowledged as a complex, frustrating, and time-consuming task. The very act of designing an expert system forces a re-evaluation of the knowledge involved and often leads to significant improvements in making that knowledge available electronically.

Analysis of the Present System/Information Sources

Active observation of the expert in her normal working environment can provide many useful insights in clarifying system requirements. Just as important can be a careful scrutiny of the information sources actually consulted during the decision-making process. Very often what the expert says she does doesn't match what actually happens in real working conditions. Nevertheless, it is clear that experts utilize a wide variety of information sources in their decision making. Very often one finds that little attention has been paid to the organization and integration of these sources.

In some cases the data are difficult to collect and analyze since decisions are based on subtle, almost unrecognized sensory input. One classic example is the case of the expert cheese maker responsible for evaluating the quality of the cheeses he inspected. The odor of the cheese was a critical component of his judgment, but even he was unaware of it, focusing rather on the feel of the cheese when he pressed his thumb into the shell.

The librarian who unconsciously assesses the educational level and hence the reading skill of the user by subtle differences in speech patterns, dress, mannerisms and choice of terms will often deny that those factors have an influence. Research data from experiments in which the same search query was presented by different stereotypical users indicate otherwise.

In other cases, such as ready reference, there are masses of data to be organized coming from many different data sources. In the reference room the librarian must deal with a very broad range of topics, requiring many different outcomes, to satisfy a varied set of clients. Filtering and summarizing this data is essential before any satisfactory matching can occur between the client's need and the material in the collection.

It must also be recognized that in present day reference rooms, librarians are handicapped by a work environment which has not yet been fully automated. If all the information sources used were to be made available online at one workstation with a master menu to front an integrated system, work would be speeded up and productivity would be increased immensely.

Collection of a Comprehensive Set of Test Cases

The collection of a comprehensive set of test cases has been proposed as the best method of clarifying system requirements. If possible and appropriate, test cases can be sorted into groups with common characteristics. For example, in a reference sources selection system, questions on biographical tools form a distinct group quite separate from those on art-related topics. Each group can be treated independently as a distinct **build**, and can form the basis for a simple working prototype. Each individual reference book can be treated as a separate **thread**. The complete module for biographical tools can be built and tested for its ability to deal with the test cases involving biographical data without involving other modules. In each case, it is a question of matching the user input with the information known in the system.

After several modules have been built and tested separately, then they can be combined and the necessary metarules written to determine which module or modules to consult for a given search. The complete set of cases will be very important in the final testing and validation of the system logic. The **test suite** can be added to, as problems are identified and corrected. Each time a change is made to the system, the test suite can be run in batch mode to ensure that nothing unexpected has been affected by the change. Finally after some modification, the test cases chosen can also serve as training projects for novice users.

Before any design work can be undertaken, the expert, the managers, and the knowledge engineers will need to negotiate the purpose and scope of the expert system. Often test cases help considerably to clarify the issues involved.

Feasibility

A feasibility study is a management study of technical, operational, and economic factors to determine whether or not the project warrants continued investment. A serious effort is made to assess the true costs involved. Cost estimates should include both personnel and time involved and the cost of equipment, software, and supplies. It is also important to categorize the operational and economic benefits that will be derived from the system.

Many factors affect the cost of a project. Not only must one consider the actual costs of developing and testing the system, there also needs to be an analysis of the true cost of installing and running the system. For a reference system, this would involve determining how many workstations to supply in the reference room where the system would be available to the public, as well as the ongoing maintenance expenses and activities for each workstation.

Cost considerations can be subdivided into five major categories.

- **Hardware and software costs.** Sufficient equipment must be made available for the people working on the project. The cost of installing working systems in the reference room must also be considered. This will introduce software and hardware compatibility issues also. One of the difficulties will be finding hardware and software that will provide the capabilities that are needed and still interface with existing library equipment.
- **Facilities and overhead costs.** Project personnel need adequate work space and support systems. The installed system will also require space, furniture, supplies, electrical, and telecommunications hook-ups to mention just a few.
- **Personnel.** The actual amount of time needed to complete the project is influenced by project complexity, skill levels, work habits, and supervisor/staff interactions. These are difficult to project with accuracy. Yet salaries are often the major development cost. The skill levels and training of programmers must be considered. In many cases, they will be unfamiliar with the tools they will be working with and there must be time for training and for the needed learning curve.
- **Project complexity.** This can have a significant impact on costs. It can be evaluated in two ways: first by noting the amount of coordination required among separate system modules, and second by the amount of documentation required to describe the interactions of system components with one another. Project complexity can be determined by analyzing an activity graph of the project schedule.
- **Project methods and tools.** Project management can have a profound effect on productivity. Managing includes setting project standards for key activities such as systems analysis and design, documenting requirements, keeping track of

changes, developing and administering validation and verification activities, and general organizational issues.

Failure to do this competently can result in greatly increased development costs.

Cost Estimation

There is little literature on cost estimation techniques for large expert systems. Yet, cost estimation is an important part of the requirements analysis. There are a number of different cost estimation techniques for regular data processing projects that can be adapted for use with expert system projects.

- **Using analogies.** Costs can be based on experience with other similar projects. Quite apart from the difficulties inherent in such an approach, there are few library-oriented expert systems in production at this time. There is not much of an experience base upon which to draw.
- **Using work breakdown structure.** This method divides the project into tasks or work units. The cost of each unit is estimated from similar units already completed where costs are known. This method overlooks the costs of connecting separate tasks into a working whole, the need for communication between groups, training, and understanding the underlying design. These additional costs have to be factored in with "guesstimates."

  In his classic essay, *The Mythical Man Month* (1975), Brooks warns about oversimplifying the hidden costs of complex systems. He makes a convincing argument that increasing the effort (number of man hours) put forth on a project does not guarantee faster progress because it geometrically increases the complexity of the interactions.
- **Cost per unit of measurement.** For many years, the number of lines of source code has been used as an estimate of project size and as a basis for estimating project cost. Each activity or module is estimated in terms of lines of code and the total price for the project has been calculated by multiplying the estimated number of lines of code by a previously determined cost per line. For expert systems, little literature is available on the true development costs of any system. The literature on existing systems has tended to view development time in terms of person years.

- **Using parametric equations.** Researchers have attempted to isolate factors that contribute to the difficulty and complexity of a project and hence influence the cost. From these they have generated sets of equations that describe the relationships between different factors and cost. Putnam (1978) has generated a model that relates the number of lines of code to the development effort and the time it takes to complete the project.

Others (Brooks, 1975; Yourdon, 1982) have broken down the activities involved in project development such as **planning**, **coding**, **unit and integration testing**, **system testing**, and **implementation**. They have considered how differences in the distributions of these activities may be attributed to project complexity or difficulty.

Boehm (1981) investigated the variation in effort for different types of projects. From a study of thousands of projects, he isolated a number of factors that can be used to measure complexity and can serve as multipliers. These, taken together with the cost of modules and subsystems in terms of lines of source code instructions, can be used to estimate project

Parameters for which there are Multipliers

System Parameters:
- Required reliability
- Size of the data base(s)
- Complexity of the system

Hardware Parameters:
- Constraints on execution time
- Constraints on storage
- Volatility of the virtual machine
- Response time

Personnel Parameters:
- Ability of the analysts
- Ability of the programmers
- Experience with the application
- Experience with the hardware
- Experience with the programming languages, development tools

Project Parameters:
- Use of modern programming practices
- Use of development tools
- Existence of required development schedule

Figure 10.1. COCOMO model (Pfleeger, 1987)

costs. The **COCOMO** (Constructive Cost Model) derived from his research allows the systems analyst to lower the cost by adjusting some of the system requirements, after determining possible tradeoffs.

Figure 10.1 lists some of the project parameters for which there are multipliers in the COCOMO model (Pfleeger, 1987, p.67).

The Design Process

System design is determined by the separate modules and intermodular interfaces needed to satisfy a specified set of requirements (DeMarco, 1982). Using an approach known as **functional decomposition**, the designer begins with a high-level view of the system and then divides the system into modules, listing the inputs and outputs of each module, how the data is transformed or used within each module, and the data stores that will be utilized by each.

Process Flow Diagrams

The **requirements specifications** list the entities or objects of the system and how they are related to each other. In particular the data elements involved are listed. In large systems, a **data dictionary** is often used to keep track of the characteristics of the various data elements and to show where they have been used.

Diagrams are very useful to show the flow of decision making through the system. In any large expert system, the knowledge engineer must extrapolate the different stages in the overall flow of the thought processes involved. These should be summarized in a pictorial form to aid communication with project participants and clarification of system objectives. A model of the expected or routine processing pattern should be developed before exceptions are addressed. A number of graphic methods have been proposed in the software engineering literature, features of which can readily be adapted for expert systems design (see Figure 10.2) (Jackson, 1983; DeMarco, 1982).

Most people resort to chunking when managing a complex decision-making process, breaking the task down into manageable subtasks.

Part of system design involves asking the expert to verbalize the thought processes applied in dealing with a number of the test cases already collected. As part of the protocol analysis, the knowledge engineer attempts to extrapolate the five or six major subtasks involved and diagram them. Techniques for protocol analysis were discussed in Chapter Five. The end result of the protocol analysis will be a diagram of a script such as the often-quoted Restaurant Script of Roger Schank (1984).

The diagram will be used as a focal point for further clarification and negotiation with the expert. Very often in this process it turns out that the

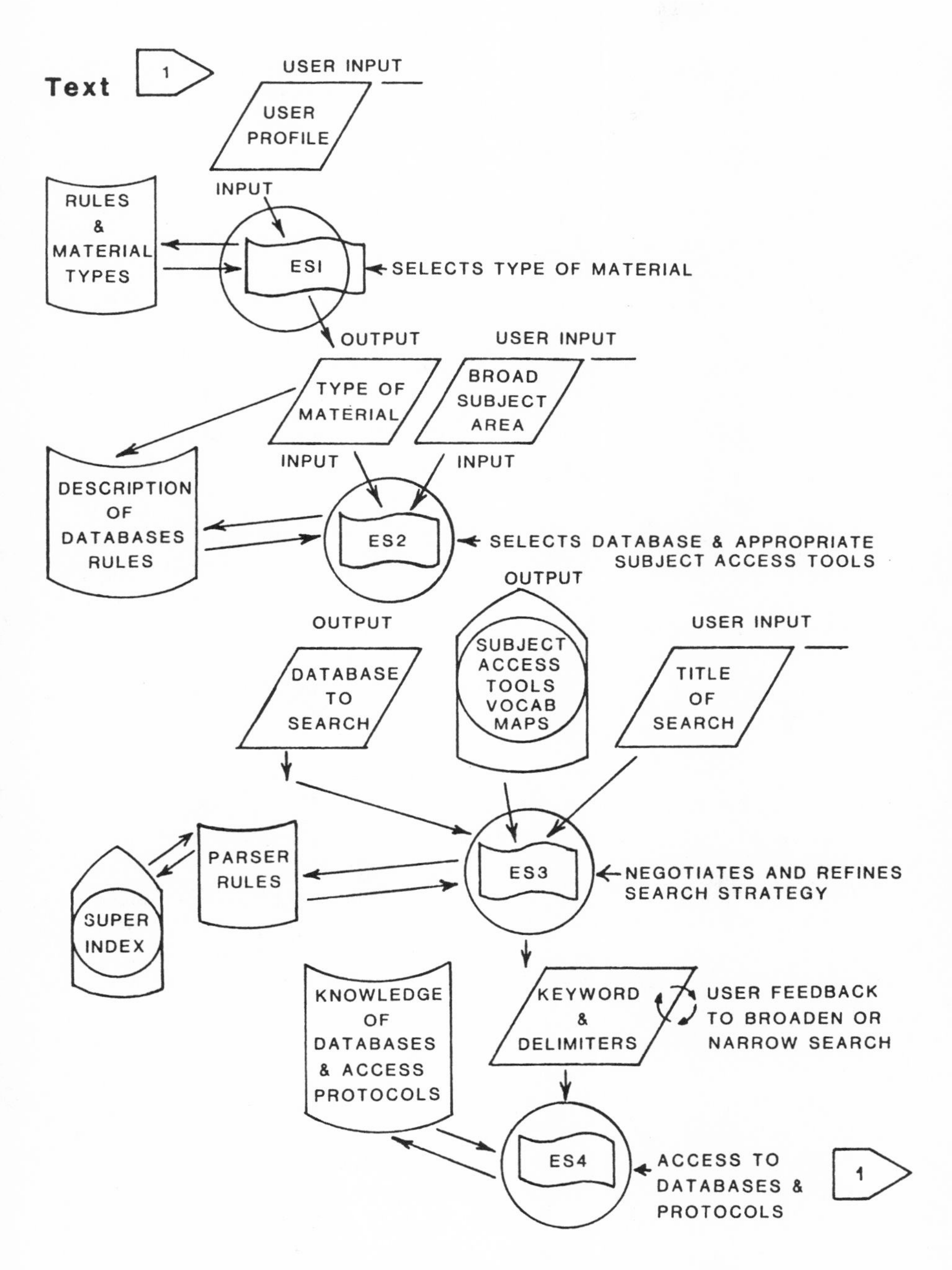

Figure 10.2. Process flow chart of a reference interview

the expert makes decisions so rapidly and with such familiarity that she has difficulty explaining the heuristics or the logic being applied. Diagramming the expert's thought process helps to refine and clarify the process and serves as a communication tool between the expert and the knowledge engineer, and can help to decompile the expert's compiled knowledge. Another difficulty is that the expert will frequently skip stages that are considered unnecessary for the situation under review. In developing the diagram, the knowledge engineer is first seeking a comprehensive script and then developing the heuristics that will determine when a stage can be skipped.

Let us consider how a diagramming technique can be applied to the reference interview. See Figure 10.2

After analyzing numerous protocols, the reference process was broken down into the following six stages, each of which will obviously form a module in the expert system being planned.

Stage 1. Select Type of Material

The expert first assesses the type of user, neatly fitting him into a small number of stereotypes, while also drawing on prior knowledge of this particular client. These stereotypes form a very important role in determining the first choice of type of material to look for.

Stage 2. Extrapolate the Broad Subject Area Involved/Select Databases and Tools

From there, the expert extrapolates the broad subject area involved. Is this a biography question, an art question, or something else? This categorization serves the twofold purpose of evoking knowledge of specialized tools and aids in a particular subset of the data as well as reducing the search space. Another important check that is made is for history on previous searches of a similar nature. This information is then used in helping to determine the most appropriate databases for searching, a task which is completed in Stage 4.

Stage 3. Transform the Request into a Valid Search Strategy

No simple task, this involves parsing the input to extract the key concepts and then ranking them to give priority to high discrimination terms. Based on prior knowledge of what is in the databases selected, the expert will adjust strategies that are too broad, or broaden ones that are too narrow. Clearly, at this stage active negotiation with the user is part of the process to ensure that the search strategy being developed reflects the actual information need while at the same time obtaining the best possible match with what is available in the collection. Specialized vocabulary control tools may be consulted.

Stage 4. Submit the Search Request for Searching in Appropriate Databases

With electronic databases this involves an awareness of passwords, account numbers, and search protocols. Once the actual search is in progress, the expert may modify the strategy several times, particularly if the user is present during the process. Cost is a major consideration at this stage and the expert utilizes many strategies to limit the cost of searching that have little to do with ensuring the most effective search.

Stage 5. Evaluate Results

Not all of the protocols analyzed included this stage. But in some cases experts did manipulate the results in a variety of ways to render the output more useful. Using relevance feedback from the user, the expert may begin again with a strategy modified by knowledge gained from the original search.

Stage 6. Add Insights Gained About the User and the Strategy Used to a History/Experience Knowledge Base

In all cases, the experts added the knowledge gained from the search to their experience base in several different forms. First, there is the knowledge gained about the particular user and his information needs. Second, there is the knowledge gained about the particular problem presented and the solutions found. Finally, there are the insights gained about the contents of the databases consulted.

One of the goals of machine learning is to develop programs that can add continually to their knowledge base. Certainly in this case, consciously maintaining and updating user profiles is not technically difficult. Likewise, the use of search fragments is already well established. The expert might well be given the option of adding a particular search fragment to an online database of such search fragments. In the same way, frames for each of the databases in use could be updated with keywords indicating their strengths and weaknesses.

Identification of the Knowledge Bases Required

At each separate stage identified in the process flow diagram, different knowledge sources are involved. These have to be categorized, organized into machine-readable form and then integrated, sometimes by building specialized interfaces. Clearly, the expert system will need to interface with whatever database and software are being used to manage MARC records. A variety of different knowledge representation techniques will be used to adapt to the data in the system. Another important task will involve identifying appropriate inputs and outputs for each module and ensuring that these are available when needed for continued processing. As databases and inputs and outputs are identified, they are added to the process flow diagram.

For example, the first module deals with selecting the type of material best suited to the information need. In actual practice most of this information is gleaned by the expert without directly asking the user. This is not possible when a machine has to collect the data. Therefore the interface would have to be designed to collect the user profile information that will

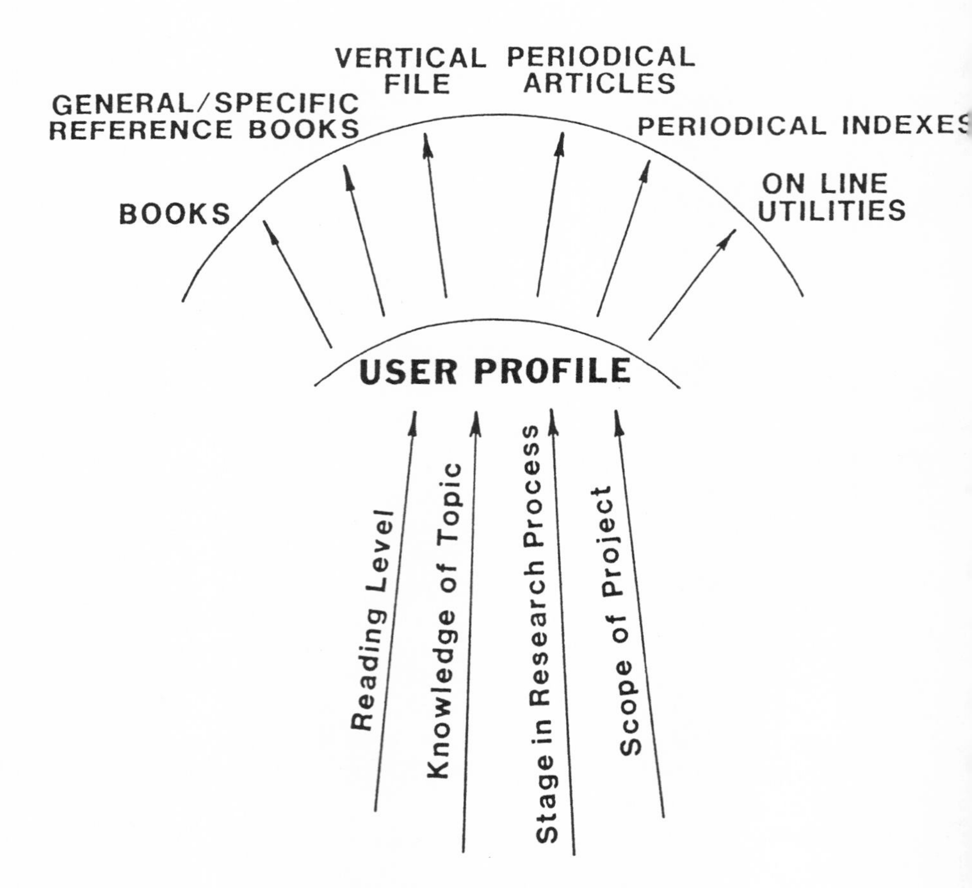

Figure 10.3. First expert system module

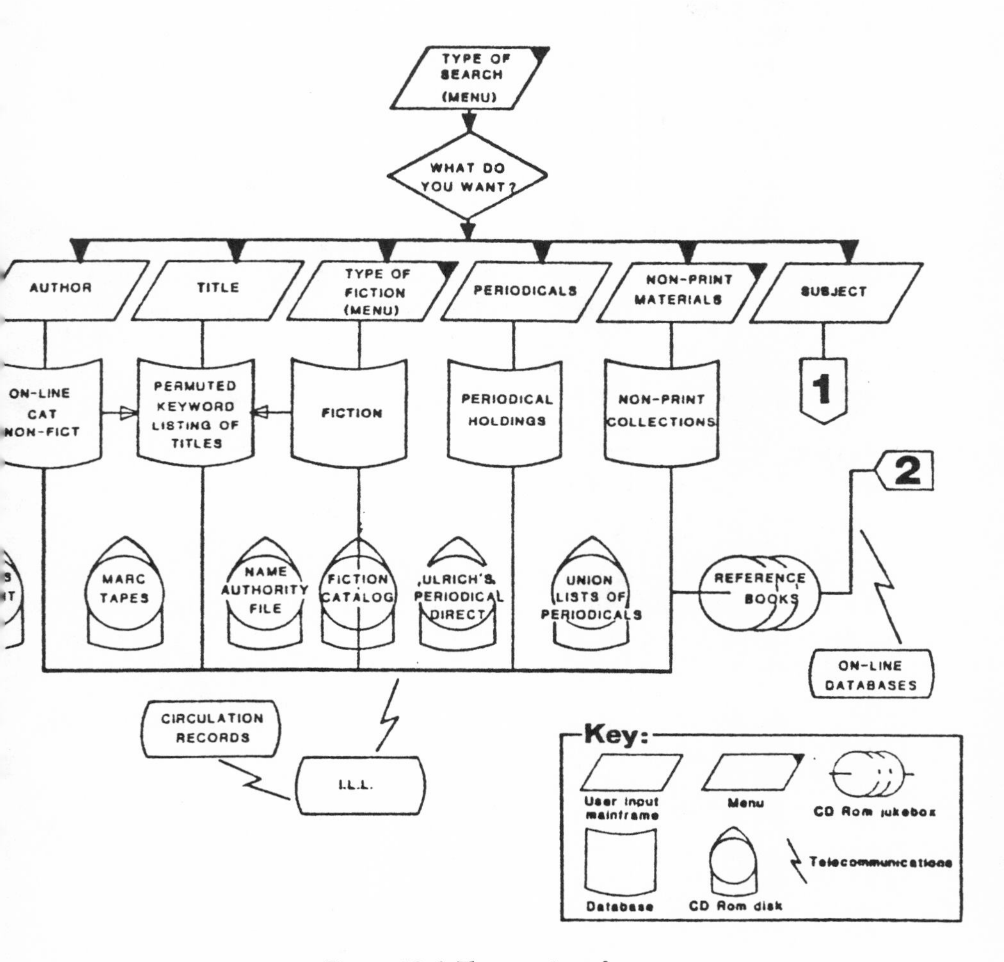

Figure 10.4. The user interface

be used subsequently by the system. The user would be asked for various inputs, such as their knowledge of the topic, what is an acceptable level of reading difficulty of the material, the scope of the project, and the stage in the research process. Time frames and deadlines can also be significant in formulating the search strategy. A set of heuristics in the first module will then determine where to begin the search process.

It goes without saying that if we write rules to match the user's selected reading level with the material in the collection, that records for items in the collection must be coded to reflect the reading level, intended audience, and purpose as materials are being processed. Chapter Seven provides a more detailed discussion of this problem.

User Interface Design

A well-designed user interface is crucial to winning acceptance for the system. The user interface must build on the methodology currently in place, so that there is a natural transition for both users and the expert. Likewise and for the same reason, the interface should use terminology that is familiar in the domain the system proposes to address. Here, the knowledge engineer is responsible for familiarizing himself with the discipline-specific terminology and for avoiding buzzwords from knowledge engineering. However, this does not mean to say that new technologies, such as mouse-driven pop-up menus, icons, and graphics interfaces, cannot be utilized.

In Figure 10.4, we present a proposal for an icon-based view of a front end to an OPAC catalog. By using icons a great deal of information can be condensed on a screen in the form of a menu.

If the user is interested in viewing any of the options, all he has to do is click and point to move himself down to a more detailed screen for the option selected. For instance, if the user were to elect to do a subject search, he might well be shown a pop-up menu like the one in Figure 10.5 that would ask for the broad subject area of interest, information the system will use to narrow the search space by selecting a subset of the appropriate tools and databases.

Functional Decomposition

The high level description covers what goes into the system, how the data will be used or transformed, and what results are produced as well as what the user interface should look like. Once this top level design has been completed, the process of decomposition is initiated. The top level is refined and redefined as a more detailed set of modules. In turn each of these second level modules is broken down and redefined in a third level of detail. The process continues until a set of primitive modules is defined where each module performs on exactly one cluster of rules. A system can be described as modular when each activity is performed by exactly one module.

Formal Specification of the Model

In any large system, it is important to have a systematic, formal design if more than one person is working on the project. In this way consistency can be enforced and standardization maintained. The formal document

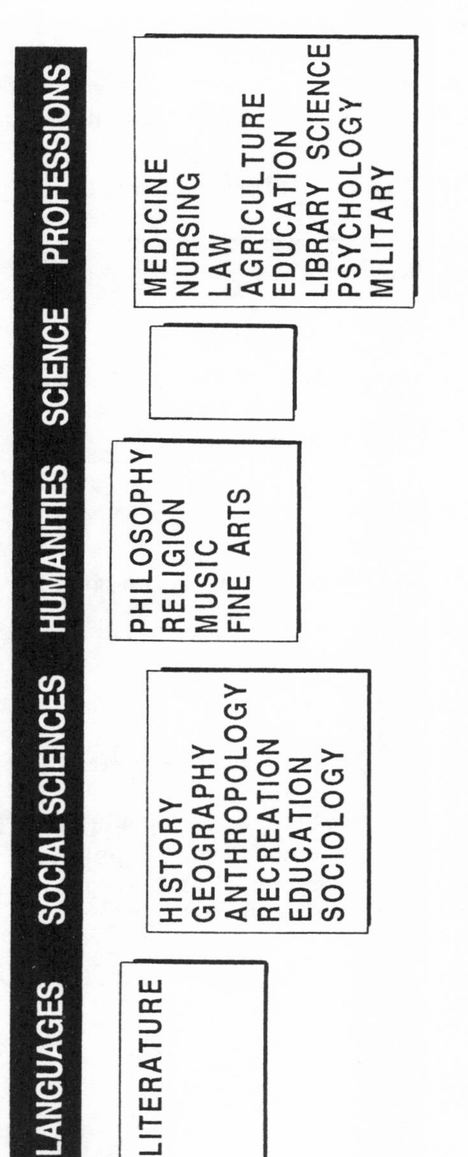

Figure 10.5. Selecting the broad topic of interest

serves as a contract with the funding agency and also as a guideline to the programmers as they go about their work. It greatly minimizes conflicts and unforseen difficulties in merging different modules and makes modifications much easier to plan.

A number of formal specification languages have been developed to simplify the process. Every variable must be clearly defined and its relationships spelled out. Interactions between modules must be clarified and metarules established to guide in conflict resolution. Equally impor-

Type of material selector

Inputs

Read? : reading level
Topic? : knowledge of topic
Stage?: stage in research process
Scope?: scope of project

Outputs

Out! : Type of material recommended

Rules

If (Read? = child and Topic? = unfamiliar and
Stage? = beginning)
⟶ (Out! = encyclopedia)
If (Read? = layman and Topic? = unknown and
Stage? = beginning and Scope? = major)
⟶ (Out! = books)
...

The following symbols are used
? input ! output
If (condition) ⟶ (action)
(then)

Figure 10.6. Example of Z specification of a function

tant is a clear statement of the problem constraints and system capabilities. The advantages of using a formal specification language are that it imposes a certain discipline on the project staff and standardizes the documentation for the entire system.

One specification language that is based on the conventional mathematical notations of ordinary logic and elementary set theory is the **Z specification language** (Hayes, 1987). Z allows a judicious mix of informal prose with precise mathematical statements and can be neatly represented in schema notation. A schema in Z consists of two parts: the **declarations part**, where the different variables used in the schema are declared, and the **predicate part**, where the properties that belong to and relate to the variables are set forth. The schema is placed in a box with a line separating the declarations part from the predicate part. A **schema calculus** provides rules for transforming and combining schemes to generate other schemes. Generally, one schema is used for each module in the system.

Quite a number of large expert systems have been specified using the Z specification language Oblitey (1988). This method has been adapted to a library application as shown in Figure 10.6. Notice that all inputs and outputs for each module are clearly identified. Then the rules that will impact these variables are outlined. This makes for well-documented systems and helps to catch errors.

Other work done using the Z specification language includes the projects of the **Programming Research Group** at Oxford University.

Software Quality Assurance

The overall goal of acceptance testing is to certify that the expert system is performing its specified function at an acceptable level of expertise and properly interacting with the total system. As steps in this process, the system will go through **verification** (testing the threads on the micro level), **validation** (testing the builds as an interacting world on the macro level) and **approval** (assessment by at least one independent expert).

Verification

Verification is concerned with the logical correctness of the program. It is generally accepted that, at this time, testing for absolute correctness is presently unfeasible with any sizeable program. What can be achieved is verification that individual threads are performing correctly in accordance with the design specifications.

It is much more cost effective if testing is built in at each stage of the design process. It will also be more rigorous if performed by an independent test organization. Much less effort and time are needed to detect and correct design errors early in the development life cycle. One method of formalizing these activities is suggested by Deutsch (1984), who recommends the use of threads in developing the system. Each unique case with all its identifying characteristics is considered as a complete thread. Threads that deal with similar instances are grouped into a build with a complete set of test cases to ensure that the necessary fine distinctions have been made.

For example, in the case of a plant identification system, one could consider as a "thread" the rules needed to identify a pine tree. The rules will be split into several subgoals. The first subgoal deals with determining the type of plant. A pine is obviously a tree; therefore a rule is needed to help to distinguish trees from vines and shrubs.

If stem is woody and position is upright
  and one main trunk is yes
Then type is tree.

Another subgoal helps to identify the class.

If type is tree
  and broad and flat leaves is no
Then class is gymnosperm.

The last set of rules deals with the plant family. At this point, it becomes apparent that there are a number of trees belonging to the gymnosperm class. A rule is needed that will help us to distinguish the pine tree from other gymnosperms:

If class is gymnosperm
  and leaf-shape is needlelike
  and pattern is random
Then family is pine.

In this way one thread is completed and can be added as a test case to the database. Obviously, the task is far from over. Rules must be added to distinguish the various kinds of gymnosperms, e.g., cypress, bald cypress, etc. For instance

If class is gymnosperm
  and leaf shape is scalelike
Then family is cypress.

Finally **stubs** will be added for the cases when the plant is not a tree, or the class is not gymnosperm.

Once this is completed, we in effect have a "build," a working system that can stand alone but is going to become a module in a larger system. Each time that a different gymnosperm thread is added to this build, it will be necessary to thoroughly test all existing cases to ensure that the new rule does not conflict with any existing ones and does effectively provide the discrimination that is needed. As the build gets larger, it is often necessary to rearrange the groupings of rules and to introduce additional subgoals. Occasionally, too many unnecessarily fine distinctions are introduced and rules can be collapsed or pruned. Each thread must be represented by a test case and should be drawn from the software requirements specifications.

Validation

Once several different builds have been completed, it is possible to move from testing on the micro level, for each individual thread in a build, to testing the interactions of the different builds to ensure that the system performs consistently and correctly. Here at the macro level, the testing will focus on the decision tree being used to determine which build is appropriate to the problem at hand. If the plant is of the type "vine," it will not be relevant or necessary to look at any of the rules differentiating various trees. As the number of builds increases, the system can become increasingly cumbersome and inefficient, not to mention incorrect if the design has not been carefully thought out.

Experts typically have difficulty verbalizing the process of selecting one build over another, often using a variety of subtle clues to guide them. At the macro level, the focus is on identifying the factors with the highest discrimation power that can assist in deciding which build to select. Humans consistently use classification schemes or hierarchically ordered choices to guide them in this process of narrowing or pruning the search space. We have found that while this underlying decision tree may be functioning at the subconscious level when the expert is analyzing the problem, the same expert will have no hesitation in critiquing a formal decision tree presented for examination. An essential part of the validation process is to have an independent expert thoughtfully examine this decision tree expressed in the form of meta-rules.

Here we are moving from deterministic rules, spelling out in great detail precisely what decisions can be made from the facts available, to reasoning from axioms or underlying models of decision making. It is in this stage of the process that the expert often draws upon: world knowledge, previous experience, axioms or first principles, and seeking a second opinion.

World Knowledge

A key factor in validation is ensuring that all the relevant and useful world information is being made available to the expert system. Here are some of the different types of world knowledge that should be incorporated in a reference system.

- The user profile will play an important role in decisions made about the type of material to be retrieved. These profiles need to be stored and consulted during the retrieval process.
- At present few formal mechanisms exist for capturing and storing successful search fragments. Fragments for frequently recurring searches should be part of any reference system.
- Many of the tools librarians use are not automated and hence cannot at present be consulted online. We need to develop a whole new approach to categorizing reference books by type, function, and services provided and for making that information available electronically. The work of Meredith (1976) represents one possible approach.
- We have already pointed out in Chapter Seven the need to add facets to the MARC record as well methods for enriching MARC records with table of contents terms.

In the reference query, the librarian is drawing upon knowledge of user stereotypes, as well as specialized knowledge of information resources in the collection. Also part of the reference librarian's world knowledge is the ability to recognize a large number of terms and to determine where they fit in the organizational framework provided by whatever classification schemes are in use locally.

Previous Experience

When in doubt, experts frequently fall back on previous experience of what is likely or probable — a best guess methodology. Validation must subject to rigorous scrutiny the probability weightings being applied to best guess strategies, particularly when dealing with complex, multifaceted requests. The best protection from error here is to clearly list the possibilities in ranked order by the probability of successful retrieval, thus leaving the final judgment to the person ultimately responsible. Having at least one independent expert examining the weightings is very useful in the design process.

Axioms or First Principles

In any discipline, there are certain basic principles or axioms that can be encoded as metarules. These can serve as constraints on the system. For example, in categorizing reference works, the key features must be extracted and then matched against a given search pattern in order to make a positive recommendation.

Todd (1986) has shown in his research that it is not sufficient to simply identify the key features. Basic design principles must be applied to constrain the possible combinations of these features, and particularly one must examine the primary purpose of a reference work before recommending it for a particular query. For example, the *Encyclopedia of Associations* does contain addresses but it is not the place to look for Jacqueline Kennedy's current address. Setting up constraints on possible combinations can provide significant help in making a positive identification and/or in eliminating unlikely possibilities.

Seeking a Second Opinion

When in doubt, experts will frequently seek an opinion from a colleague or discuss the problem with someone else. Part of validating an expert system is ensuring sufficient checks and balances. One of the most important is keeping the human actively involved in the loop by utilizing adequate explanation facilities.

Explanation Facilities

In any system, part of the validation process involves ensuring the robust behavior that is necessary for user acceptance. Part of this robust behavior involves the explanation facilities built into the system. The system must be able to justify its findings in a way that is comfortable and easily understood by the independent expert who is part of the testing team charged with validating the system. The jargon must be familiar to the discipline of the user population. The system must be capable of making explicit the reasons for accepting or rejecting uncertain propositions. How was the value of <x> deduced, and/or what factors led to <x> conclusion? This can be accomplished in a variety of ways.

A simple tracing of the rules. This is standard in almost all systems but cannot be considered as the only tool needed. Traces are cumbersome and do little to reveal the deep reasoning that has been built in.

Canned text. This works well for definition questions but is difficult to maintain.

Forming sentences that draw on the facts known about the case. These can be helpful to summarize the reasoning process.

List of the possibilities considered in ranked order. Such listings provide a quick and convenient tool for the independent expert to check the outcomes, but do nothing to explain how these results were obtained.

Some sort of deep reasoning capability is considered desirable. A reference system should be able to specify: why/why not reference book X. In order to make a positive identification, the key features of each reference work should be assigned weightings based on their importance in answering certain types of information needs (positive reasons). Also stored with this information are key features that would enable one to determine that the reference work under consideration was not suitable for a given type of query (negative reasons). This information is, of course, reinforced by the information coming from other

Biography and Genealogy Master Index
was recommended because:

Positive Reasons:	Level
Is good if the person is not known	.9
Indexes over 1000 books of collected biographies	.8
Has good American coverage	.7
Picks up most new biographical sources	.6
Updated annually	.4
Has esoteric coverage such as occult	.35

Negative Reasons:	
Does not cover people in the news	.9
Has very little periodical or serial material	.83
Names are not standardized and can appear in several forms	.8
Has multilistings for each individual	.75
Primarily North America	.69

Figure 10.7. SIRATAC Cotton Management System

sources. Upon request, the list of features that have been positively identified and the weightings assigned can be obtained together with any other supporting evidence. Conversely, in response to the why-not question, the system can list the negative reasons in descending order.

The reference librarian consulting the system is interested in a ranked list of possible sources and may want to know why a particular selection was made. If a favored source is missing from the list he may well want to ask, "Why not a particular source?" One popular technique first advocated by Clarke (1987) in the **SIRATAC Cotton Management System** is to develop for each book in the system positive reasons for using it as well as negative ones. Weights are attached to each of the possibilities, thus making it possible to rank relevant reference works. This technique can be readily adapted for reference works, as shown in Figure 10.7.

Using a form sentence of the following type, the system could take the information in the frame and present a Why Not explanation to the user.

WHY NOT?

Form Sentence:

<conclusion> was not recommended because it **<negative reason 1>**, **<negative reason 2>**, ... **<negative reason n>**. These considerations outweighed the fact that **<positive reason 1>**, **<positive reason 2>**, ... and **<positive reason m>**.

Actual Explanation Produced.

The Biography and Genealogy Master Index was not recommended because **it does not cover people in the news, has very little periodical or serial meterial (.83)....** These considerations outweighed the fact that **it is good if the person is not known, indexes over 1,000 books of collected biographies...**

What-if capability. It is also very helpful to provide a what-if capability that allows the validation team to explore and test the sensitivity of the analysis to changes in incoming data.

Truth Maintenance

At present, every system seems to have a different approach to **consistency checking** and **truth maintenance**, particularly with non-monotonic reasoning (i.e., the search stategy is modified while it is in process). The key issue is that as new knowledge is acquired, system performance must be modified to reflect changing conditions. From the point of view of validation, there are a number of concerns.

- New information may make previous inferences incorrect.
- Inconsistencies may develop between old and new inferences.
- Intermediate solutions may be less than optimal.

Approaches include carrying **multiple worlds** representing the various options available, **poisoning** or deleting each as a rule is found that negates that possibility (**ART** or **KEE**). Another technique is to provide **when...then....demons** that fire when certain preconditions occur and over-ride other logic.

For example: The user wants a list of parks with boating and white water rafting in the Northeast sector. Further into the search it is discovered that they want to stay a week and hence the availability of overnight accommodations is a critical consideration. They also have a pet dog. A metarule could be written as follows:

> When overnight accommodations are required, then move the user into a different module that determines the budget for the trip, the number of adults involved and the type of accommodations preferred.
>
> The presence of pets will also impose constraints on the choices that are possible. A different group of sources will be consulted and suggestions drawn from the original request may well prove unsuitable.

More difficult and yet probably as important is the provision of techniques for refining and upgrading the existing rule base as well as adding new information.

Approval

One of the problems in validating expert systems is establishing realistic performance standards, since it is not possible to achieve complete accuracy. At best one can require that the system perform as consistently and as well as independent experts in blind tests, both in the standard tasks that it is designed to handle and on the boundaries of its knowledge when the unexpected occurs. This should be the *sine qua non* of all acceptance testing.

Just as important is ensuring that independent experts in the field can use, understand, and agree with the system's findings. If the system is cumbersome to use, deals with a trivial task, or is unreliable in its findings, then it will not meet with user approval. Rigorous field tests under actual working conditions with end-users are a must.

More standard verification procedures identified in software engineering should also be applied. These include checking the validity of the input data, testing with typical input, and asking an independent expert to verify the logic. It is also important to check the system operating under extreme conditions, with overloads, equipment malfunction or failure, and combinations of catastrophic events. Last but not least there should be testing for system security. This is especially important for library systems that provide access to expensive, external online databases. Proper provisions should exist for maintaining audit trails to detect tampering.

Constraints and Limitations

Another aspect of acceptance testing is the testing of system limitations. How would an ideal reference system handle multifaceted problems with overlapping subjects of equal weight, such as "The Economics of History"? What about uncertainty created by the failure to identify any relevant source? Is system degradation abrupt, or worse, misleading? The danger of using probability weightings and printing out the likelihood of a source being useful is that the system is limited to its knowledge base and cannot intuitively sense when some new edition contains significant changes. Provision will have to be made for ongoing maintenance. Will the librarians be able to adjust the rules, do fine tuning? If so, then how can consistency be maintained when more than one copy of the software is circulating? These issues need to be addressed and adequate provisions made for handling such situations.

Statement of System Limitations

Unrealistic expectations are a very common problem faced by most developers. Therefore, a clear statement of system limitations should be developed during system evaluation and testing. Typically most expert systems degrade rapidly when pushed to the edges of their knowledge. Careful documentation and testing, as well as a written record of cases in which the system has failed to perform at expert levels, can provide the basis for continued growth and development as well as alert users to the need for human intervention at those trigger points.

Conclusion

A formal design methodology as well as verification and validation tests need to be planned and implemented as an integral part of the system development process from the very first thread. Not only must there be concern for verification of the logic involved but also for the proper interactions of the different modules. The user interface presented is a major determinant of user acceptance. Another important aspect of the verification/validation process is assessing the provision for ongoing maintenance and upgrading of the system.

Recommended Reading

There is not much published on the subject of how to cost an expert system project. The November 1985 issue of *IEEE Transactions on Software Engineering* includes papers on AI software engineering (Bobrow, 1985, Subrahmanyam, 1985). Brooks's study, *The Mythical Man Month* (1975), deals primarily with traditional software engineering, but still provides very useful insights.

There are a number of software engineering texts that review the different programming techniques, including DeMarco (1982) and Jackson (1983). Yourdon (1982) is considered one of the leaders in software engineering circles and should not be overlooked.

For background material on formal specification languages, the user is referred to Hayes (1987) and Oblitey (1988).

The SIRATAC Cotton Management System (Clarke) is an excellent example of a good technique for providing adequate explanation facilities for the end-user and could readily be adapted to the library scene.

11
The Future of Expert Systems and Artificial Intelligence in Libraries

This chapter will attempt some forecasts about where the technology is headed. Along with our forecasts, we will present a few scenarios of what may be in store for libraries. In its short history, artificial intelligence has had humbling failures and modest successes. It is a field that has been almost as impressive for its spin-offs as it has for its actual accomplishments. Among the technologies that are completely or partially derived from AI research are windowing, object-oriented programming, graphics workstations, fourth- and fifth-generation languages, and software development environments. The list could easily go on for a few pages.

The research that spawned these developments originated in a surprisingly small number of institutions at labs whose primary focus has been AI research. Among the more notable research centers are MIT, Stanford University, Carnegie-Mellon University, and Xerox PARC. Simply observing the research originating at those institutions provides a fair idea of what the future might hold.

In this chapter we'll try to keep our predictions within the boundaries of what can be realistically expected from current technology. But it is more than likely that by the year 2000, we will have had fundamental advances that couldn't have been predicted as having evolved from today's technology. Thus it is easily possible that the next generation of AI technology will bear little resemblance to what is currently available. Consider biological computers, for example. Eric Drexler (1986) posits a biologically based nanotechnology where molecular machines will revolutionize the technological landscape. For less down-to-earth forecasts than ours, look to science fiction. Authors Vernor Vinge and William Gibson are especially recommended.

The AI Marketplace

Many of the technologies on which our predictions are based have already migrated from the labs to the marketplace. For economic reasons, libraries aren't usually on the cutting edge when it comes to expensive, largely experimental technology. AI is far more prevalent in industry and in government (especially the military) than it is in libraries. But there are encouraging signs. Developments from other sectors are finding their way into library applications, and library-related research and development is increasing.

Libraries are in a position to learn from the failures of pioneers in other fields and to apply this technology in a public, socially beneficial atmosphere. The potential is enormous. After all, libraries and AI share the same primary concern: recorded knowledge.

After decades of research, a substantial AI marketplace is finally beginning to emerge. Commercial AI software and hardware was virtually nonexistent ten years ago. In 1981, the AI marketplace was estimated to be worth under $100 million. By 1990, sales are projected to exceed $4 billion per year (Barber, 1986). The AI market will have increased by a factor of forty in less than ten years. A recent Arthur D. Little report projects a $50–$120 billion a year AI market by the year 2000, with AI accounting for 20 percent of the entire computer industry. Of all the AI categories, expert systems is the fastest growing (an 86 percent growth rate over the past seven years) and by far the largest in total sales (cited in Wenig, 1988). Equally impressive growth is forecast for the international AI market. A recent U.S. Department of Commerce study projects a $10.6 billion AI hardware and software market in Japan by 1995.

Presently the greatest segment of the expert systems market is in the sales of shells and languages. We have yet to see a large number of "turnkey" expert systems. But turnkey systems will eventually enter the expert systems market. When that happens, we can expect turnkey system sales to eclipse shell and language sales just as the applications programs have eclipsed programming language in the traditional software arena. Field-tested, market-ready systems will give expert system sales a tremendous boost.

Computers themselves are becoming exponentially more powerful and less expensive. Software development is becoming more streamlined, thanks largely to techniques arising from AI research. Entire governments, following the lead taken by Japan with its Fifth Generation project, are gearing up to invest heavily in AI development. Within a decade AI will become one of the dominant sectors of the computer industry.

Right now, AI is far from mature, but the field is changing rapidly. One milestone we've recently crossed is the development at Carnegie-Mellon University of a chess-playing computer program, Deep Thought, that has attained Master status. Chess is a game with an incredibly large search space. A program with the ability to solve problems in such a large search space indicates that experimental efforts can be scaled up to handle complex, real world problems.

A burgeoning market for business, government, and scientific AI products will give rise to a consumer market. There will eventually be a flourishing consumer market with AI techniques being used in a diverse range of hardware and software products. All kinds of specialized programs will also become available for libraries. Functions such as indexing, cataloging, database searching, and records management will be addressed by commercially available expert systems. Electronic reference works are being introduced and there will be development environments created especially for work within library and bibliographic environments.

Trends in AI Software

One of the central issues in the AI marketplace will be user acceptance. Even systems that were considered successful in their experimental phases can be rejected by the people for whom they were intended. Acceptance will come slowly, and only in areas where the expert system promises to assist rather than replace human experts. But there will be a gradual assimilation of AI technology. The number of commercial AI programs is increasing steadily, and as AI becomes more familiar, it will gain greater acceptance.

Development Environments

Expanding markets will push the need for efficient, inexpensive development tools. After all, expert systems are just another form of computer software, and software development is still a time-consuming, expensive process. But development tools of the future will reduce the time needed to develop an expert system and, for the first time, move the development process from the realm of the software engineer to that of the domain expert. Software will evolve to take advantage of recent dramatic advances in hardware capabilities. Almost all commercial software will incorporate approaches first taken in AI reasearch. New programs with AI capabilities will run only on the new generation of more powerful machines. The current trend has been to "enhance" programs originally developed for less powerful machines. The new generation of software will be qualitatively different, having been originally designed to work with far more powerful computers.

New knowledge representation languages will emerge, but AI programming languages are notoriously difficult to follow, so shells and other software building tools will become the norm. Software development tools will enable those who are not expert programmers but who are expert in something else to develop their own knowledge bases.

Shells

Shells that now occupy the lion's share of the expert systems marketplace will become even more popular. Shell programs will make it easier to gather, encode, and use expert knowledge. Shells will become more sophisticated, but it will take awhile before systems come equipped with domain specific knowledge. After awhile, though, it will become difficult to tell the difference between a development shell and a market-ready knowledge base. The two will come bundled with one another. The importance of system maintenance and modification will convince users of knowledge bases to look for capabilities found in shells, and shells which already incorporate large amounts of domain specific knowledge will become commonplace.

Hybrid Systems

One outgrowth of the work on shells for specific domains will be an increase in hybrid systems that combine different representation formalisms. Hybrid representation schemes will allow much greater flexibility than simple rules allow, including inheritance and graphic representation. In PC environments we'll see rule-based systems supplemented by systems employing other schema, especially frames and scripts.

Modularity

Modularity, already a major concern, will become even more important. Architectures are already becoming far more complex but they are also becoming more modular. Expert systems are designed to easily accommodate new knowledge. The future will bring more potential to port knowledge and inference procedures from one system to another. Declarative and object-oriented languages will become more popular and will result in even greater portability and modularity. In the future, we'll be able to piece together software systems from separately available components just as we now build hardware systems with a number of separately purchased elements. Innovation will heat up competition in the expert system shell marketplace with concomitant price reductions. But the high end of the market will go up. Users wanting advanced user interfaces, hybrid representation schemes, and connectivity will be willing to pay the price for innovation.

Object-Oriented Approaches

Object-oriented approaches will become the norm. Most programs will be graphically oriented. Data and the instructions for manipulating them will be bound together as objects that can exchange messages with one another. Data structures will become more abstract and more symbolic. Developers will have more freedom to devise their own ways of representing data and knowledge.

Development environments will include sophisticated display and view, trace and editing facilities. Innovations from AI development software will find their way into commercial products in the form of intelligent help facilities, graphical representation of program functions, and the exchange of messages among multiple display windows.

Scenario: Libraries Develop Their Own "Navigation" Systems

More flexible development tools will result in the introduction of "navigation systems" designed for specific library domains. Many of the initial products will have their origin in research now underway in medical informatics. Medical expert systems will help clinicians and researchers search, evaluate, and organize the medical literature. Development efforts will occur in individual libraries with the support of the national medical establishment.

The National Library of Medicine and other government agencies will provide the leadership role in distributing and encouraging the use of expert system development tools for medical applications. Development tools for medical libraries will allow the local creation of knowledge bases for specific client groups. Early efforts will focus on the clinical literature. Shells will be designed to take advantage of existing databases, bibliographic standards, retrieval systems, vocabularies, and syndetic structures.

A great emphasis will be placed on modularity and the easy exchange of information. Medical libraries will acquire shells and use them to develop locally useful guides to subsets of the medical literature. Each medical specialty will have its own shell, and each shell will come with large amounts of domain knowledge, including subject headings, tree structures, and standard handbooks, texts, and review articles. But the shells for different medical specialties will be similar enough to one another so that the learning curve for development of each new specialty "navigator" will become shorter.

Because there will be a high degree of standardization, it will be possible for libraries to distribute and support systems developed in other libraries and research labs. Domain experts at specific institutions will also develop and distribute their own systems. Standardization will center around knowledge representation schemes now being derived from the Medical Subject Headings and tree structures, but we'll also see new representation standards, many of them derived directly from the medical literature.

Enormous bodies of highly organized and interconnected knowledge will spring up around single diseases. A cancer knowledge network for example, would provide access to clinical studies, experimental results, patient histories, tumor registries, statistical files, and other knowledge bases for related fields, such as biochemistry, and pharmacology. Eventually, development tools for other library domains will be introduced. Fields where there is economic potential — such as law, chemistry, and engineering—will be first. In the more distant future, every library will maintain its own unique collection of databases and knowledge bases while also being part of wide bandwidth international communication networks.

Hardware Trends

Hardware will achieve even greater importance. We will finally see desktop computers capable of taking advantage of advances in artificial intelligence research. An important hardware milestone was the recent introduction by Intel of a million-transistor chip. One of the major hardware trends will be "embedded" systems — systems in which the functions the computer is to perform are built into the hardware. Military research will be the major impetus for embedded systems, but eventually we will see things like "smart" microwave ovens, television sets, and alarm clocks.

The "intelligent terminal" of today won't seem so smart when compared to the terminals of the future. Public access terminals of the future will have expert systems embedded into their hardware. Now there are missiles with navigation capabilities built into the hardware. Before too long, we should have intelligent terminals with a more benign navigation capability built in. Imagine an OPAC terminal with the LC Subject Headings burned into a ROM chip, which can guide the user through a search. Just as we can now purchase chips with different type fonts for our printers, in the future we'll be able to purchase ROMs with search vocabularies and subject knowledge for different databases. Printed thesauri will be replaced by onboard electronic thesauri. Before searching a particular database, we'll plug the appropriate ROM chip into our expert system workstation.

But embedded systems won't be the big hardware story. The most important hardware trends will be the downward migration of artificial intelligence technology to PCs and the widespread commercial introduction of parallel processing.

Downward Migration

We are already seeing the move of AI technology from specialized workstations and minicomputers to PCs. Until recently, much of the AI research done in the United States was done on LISP workstations whose circuitry was specially designed to accommodate LISP, which has been the dominant AI development language in the United States. But the bottom is beginning to fall out on the LISP workstation market. Even if a successful application can be developed on a LISP machine, there will be few potential clients willing to pay the $50,000 to $100,000 dollars required for hardware alone.

There is a vast market for AI that will run on PCs, and with the introduction of high-end PCs we should see a dramatic increase in the number and variety of PC-based AI tools. LISP won't predominate in the nineties as it did in the sixties, seventies, and eighties. Other languages such as PROLOG, and even more traditional languages such as C and Pascal will be increasingly used to implement AI applications.

The IBM/XT and AT are still the dominant machines in the library PC market. It is possible to experiment with artificial intelligence on these machines, and shell software and AI languages are available, but hardware capabilities do impose limits on what is possible. Right now there are a number of modest efforts underway within individual libraries. As more powerful machines move into libraries, more sophisticated, do-it-yourself efforts will be possible, but most library-related AI will continue to originate in government and academic research labs and the commercial sectors.

Parallel Processing

One of the areas in which hardware and software will move forward in tandem with one another is parallel processing. A parallel computer has separate processors working in concert with one another instead of a single processor handling problems as a sequential series of steps. In a parallel computer, each processor is responsible for a different aspect of the problem. Problems are solved in parallel, nonsequentially.

Parallel computers will begin to be used in library applications during the nineties, and many of those applications will involve artificial intelligence. In information retrieval systems, for example, each processor will be responsible for keeping track of its own set of documents, greatly reducing the processing time required for complex queries to large databases. Dow Jones has already begun to experiment with parallel processing for information retrieval from large, full-text databases (Waltz, 1988).

Parallel processing also promises to increase the efficiency and reduce the downtime of transaction systems like those used in libraries. Vendors of integrated library systems are already beginning to explore **parallel architectures** and **redundant computers** as ways of making systems more efficient. Before the end of the next decade, we will see many commercially available systems that reduce downtime by redirecting workflow to other processors if one part of the system goes down (Hurley, 1988).

There will be a new emphasis on hardware, but whole new classes of software will also evolve to take advantage of parallel processing. Each processor can have its own process, or subproblems can be passed from one processor to another until one says, "I'll handle this one." We will see new computer architectures, new ways of organizing system components for optimum performance. Computer operating systems will evolve to accommodate parallelism (Torrero, 1985). Among the alternatives to sequential processing are to link processors in tree structures (shades of knowledge engineering), to arrange them three dimensionally to form cubes, or to form them into networks with links determined by the flow of data through the system. It is this data flow architecture which has been adopted by the Japanese for their Fifth Generation project.

Distributed processing will make it possible to share problem-solving tasks among interconnected but physically remote computers. New operating systems will accommodate large-scale interaction among different types of computers. Databases and knowledge bases themselves will be distributed among and shared by a number of machines. Programs will also be shared and distributed. Already it has been demonstrated that the collective power of a series of mini-computers can equal the power of a sophisticated supercomputer.

VLSI and Analog Computers

Another hardware trend will be increased **Very Large Scale Integration** (VLSI). The million-transistor chip is just a beginning. Eventually we will see electronic components replaced by optical components. **Ultra Large Scale Integration** (ULSI) will appear in the nineties, with analog computers replacing digital computers for special applications, especially those involving pattern recognition. Parallelism and VSLI will evolve concurrently, with VLSI making it easier to coordinate the activity of many small processors, and to increase speed.

Optical Computing

Optical computing will bring increased power, speed, storage capacity, and miniaturization. CD-ROM is just the first of many revolutionary developments to be ushered in by advances in optical technology. Transistors will be replaced by transphasors which respond to light rather than electricity. Transphasors will be able to respond to a number of different light intensities with a number of different output signals. A signal transphasor can exhibit more than the two logical states possible with a digital device, increasing the possibility for parallel processing and creating a potential for a new generation of analog machines.

Crystals will be used to store massive amounts of information in very compact spaces. Already there is a technology called **spectral holes** that makes it possible for a device the size of a refrigerator to hold the entire contents of the Library of Congress (Jenkins, 1986). Access speed is a problem with the current technology but the storage capacity is already there.

New Input/Output Technologies

Increased use of new input/output technologies ranging from eyeball tracking to entire rooms becoming computer terminals (Bolt, 1985) to super high-resolution, three-dimensional holographic displays will change the way that user interfaces are designed. New input/output applications will evolve to take advantage of advances in display technology and the pattern recognition capabilities of parallel computers.

Optical character recognition (OCR) will be done with analog machines and parallel processing, as will speech recognition and information retrieval from large full-text databases. Parallel approaches to information retrieval view it as an iterative, interactive process (Stanfill and Kahle, 1986). The information seeker is presented with a list of possible sources to critique. Items that are identified by the user as relevant are then analyzed and patterns are identified. Patterns are then used to compile a new list for the user to critique. Eventually the system is able to derive from its interaction with the user a pattern of document attributes that satisfy the user's needs. The approach is essentially statistical. Documents that are statistically similar to those identified as relevant are considered good possibilities.

Parallelism will also improve speech recognition and voice synthesis capabilities. It should be noted that both **HEARSAY-II** and **HARPY**, two of the most famous speech recognitiion systems, were tested by giving them verbal instructions to retrieve abstracts of computer science documents. Current systems are still largely speaker dependent and have limited vocabularies. Along with VLSI and parallelism will come the increased raw computing power and speed needed to accommodate multiple speakers (male or female) and to include a large vocabulary (10,000+ words). Before long, systems will also be able to recognize and respond to speech in real time.

A combination scanner/communicating printer will also be standard equipment. Text and images will be easily exchanged and captured, and access to just about anything on the network, including video images, will be effortless. Each workstation will have a variety of data jacks that can be cabled into broadband and fiber optic networks.

Digital video interactive (DVI) technology will give rise to a new generation of multimedia workstations. At first CD-ROM will be on every machine but it will eventually be supplanted by other technologies, including DVI. Knowledge bases will probably be distributed on high-capacity WORM disks. A read/write medium would be needed for customization and maintenence. If the knowledge base is to remain "alive," someone must have write access. Besides WORM disk drives, there will be archival optical memory with capacity measured in gigabytes. And there will still be hard disks, superfast hard disks in the two hundred plus megabyte range.

The core memory of the typical system will match that of today's most powerful minis. Sixteen megabytes will be the bottom of the line for most knowledge-based software. Parallel processing will be possible and there will be special processors for different kinds of workstations. ROMs for all purposes will be bought, sold, loaned, and traded. With the exchange of a few plug-in ROM modules, it will be possible to change a medical research workstation into a legal or literary research workstation.

Scenario: The Information Retrieval Workstation

The device sitting on the desktop (or stashed in the briefcase) of the scholar of the future will bear little resemblance to the PC of today. It will still have a keyboard and a monitor, and most cetainly a mouse as well. But the scholar will be able to talk to it and it will be able to talk back. It will also have a graphic interface that will allow scholars to manipulate graphic symbols representing complex tasks and information objects. Its high-resolution display will offer text that is nearly as crisp as the printed page and will support high-quality color graphics along with motion and still video. Scrolling and "paging" capabilities will be similar to those of the printed book. It will be possible to display graphics, text, and video all at the same time.

A verbal dialog will be used along with the keyboard and mouse to issue commands to the workstation and to move through the information environment to which the workstation connects. Vocal interaction will be at a basic level. For example, a researcher might scroll through text simply by saying, "Back up three pages."

Visual metaphors will predominate when it comes to searching for information. Graphics languages will be used to display images of information in the database. Color will be used more extensively to convey information. Interactive video will be incorporated in workstations. GE has a system that provides advice on diesel locomotive repair and that is linked to a videodisc. When a repair technique is being explained, it can be simultaneously shown in video (Bonissone & Johnson, 1984). In medicine, video will become standard equipment on tutorial and clinical workstations, which will be able to simulate on video all sorts of procedures and conditions. Eventually there will be holographic images. Then we'll be approaching the Vicaritron depicted in the Woody Allen movie,

Sleeper. A clinical interaction might include the following dialogue.

CLINICIAN:	"Show me me the abstracts of the most highly cited papers on fungal graft infection, plus anything that matches my profile and deals with fungal graft infections and cardiac surgery."
WORKSTATION:	Displays abstracts of requested documents, stopping when commanded to.
CLINICIAN:	"Show me the video of the procedure described in the paper by Bartle Riordan."
WORKSTATION:	Displays high-resolution video on part of the screen, abstract of the paper of interest in a smaller window, and a list of possible vocal commands in another.
CLINICIAN:	"Give me a closup of the aorta. Rotate it that way [pointing with mouse]. Okay."
WORKSTATION:	Freezes image of aorta on the screen.
CLINICIAN:	"Put the images of my patient's aorta on the screen next to it."
WORKSTATION:	Displays image from text alongside image of patient's aorta.
CLINICIAN:	"Hmmm. Get me a color print, a holo, and a slide. Also download the video and the full text of the documents I've chosen. That's all, thank you."

Assimilation of AI Technology in Libraries

Library-related AI development will proceed along three parallel paths.

- integrated library systems
- PC-based consultation systems
- front-ends to databases

The library market for AI will begin with AI technology incorporated in other computerized systems now being marketed to libraries. OPACs will include AI capabilities. Intelligence will be more distributed on future generations of integrated systems. Workstations will take over many of the tasks now left to minis. OCLC and other utilities will require high-end workstations as terminals. The increased availability of powerful workstations will result in increased experimentation with independent, locally developed systems.

Integrated library system vendors are now beginning to experiment with AI approaches, and we should see the first intelligent OPAC products introduced during the coming decade. Online utilities, including OCLC, supermarket vendors of a variety of files, and large, full-text database producers will introduce front-ends with varying levels of intelligence. The electronic mail systems used by libraries will also incorporate artificial intelligence technologies. Small-scale projects will abound with individual libraries taking advantage of easy-to-use development tools and customization capabilities provided by integrated systems, online vendors, and bibliographic utilities.

Integrated Library Systems

Expert system and AI technology will be incorporated in many integrated library systems. Emphasis will be on the user interface and intelligent browsing. Software will run on large machines linked to numerous terminals. But workstations with graphics and windowing capabilities will also be required to use many integrated systems. A major impetus for development in this area will come from national libraries such as NLM and NAL. But there will be many corporate and academic projects as well. OCLC will also play a lead role and OCLC's requirements will soon lead many libraries to purchase high-end microcomputers.

In integrated library systems, record keeping and data management will be emphasized less. Many of the inventory control problems will be solved. Attention will shift to human factors. Modules for manipulation of data, for creation of searcher profiles, and for enhancement of existing records will become common features of integrated library systems. Later in the decade, there will be turnkey products within specific domains. Intelligent tutoring systems will be widely used in specialized domains such asmedicine and law. We will see a number of cooperative efforts from ILS vendors and database vendors. Online databases will be routinely available from OPAC's.

We will also see joint academic and corporate ventures. For example, project **Mercury**, a joint venture of OCLC and Carnegie-Mellon University (Turner, 1988) aims to develop a prototype electronic research library. An AI program called a **reference assistant** will help researchers identify and connect to appropriate databases. A variety of bibliographic, reference, and full-text files will be available.

A cosponsor of the project is the American Association for Artificial Intelligence. In fact, the AAAI already maintains a user-supported AI database at CMU which members may search over electronic mail networks. Developments in the integrated library systems market will follow the general shift in emphasis from **archiving** to **access**.

PC-Based Consultation Systems

PCs, which are now on the verge of becoming commodity items, will become ubiquitous. PC-based consultation systems will be developed locally by many libraries and will find a large audience. PC systems are now under development at a number of places (Aluri, 1988; Waters, 1986; Vickery, 1987; Richardson, 1989; Vedder et al., 1989). Microcomputer systems will focus on narrow domains and perform many of the functions discussed in Chapter Nine. At first they will be more likely to be consulted by practitioners than clients and will function in a primarily tutorial modality. The technology won't really catch on until there is widespread use of high-end micros and more sophisticated shell programs — both events that are almost sure bets for the near future.

In reference, emphasis will be on providing assistance in specialized subject domains. Focus will be on local collections, and reference expert systems will resemble pathfinders and other in-house publications. Consultation services will be designed to help users exploit the rapidly growing information store. There will be a movement to integrate all categories of finding tools and source texts within a subject domain. Expert systems designed to link to OPACs, CD-ROM files, and other external databases will begin to appear.

In cataloging, PC-based systems will concentrate on narrow, specialized areas and unusual formats such as musical scores and maps. Small subsets of the **AACR2** (Anglo-American Cataloging Rules) will be encoded in knowledge base for use by paraprofessionals. Collection development systems will be less visible, and will focus on developing profiles derived from rules in collection development policies. There will also be expert systems designed to assist libraries in developing approval plans.

Libraries will share advisory systems with one another. There will be shareware bulletin boards where electronic pathfinders will be widely distributed and exchanged. Clearinghouses such as LOEX will emerge to keep track of and make available advisory systems developed by libraries. Library instruction will rely more heavily on locally developed intelligent tutoring modules, and library workbooks will be replaced by electronic analogs.

It will be possible to go to the library and check out a small advisory system to teach yourself about something or help you explore the literature of a specific subject field. Money will be saved by maintainting the inventory of reserch guides electronically rather than in print. Libraries and researchers will also maintain "guides" with online vendors, just as SDI profiles are now maintained.

Front-Ends to Databases

Front-ends to databases are widely used now. Martha Williams (1986) and Linda Smith (1987) provide good reviews of current progress. There are even a number of commercially available systems, although most of them aren't truly knowledge-based. The experimental, knowledge-based systems discussed in Chapter Four (Brajnik Guida, and Tasso, 1986, Croft and

Thompson, 1987, Marcus, 1986, Meadow, 1982, and Pollitt, 1987) will evolve into commercial systems. Knowledge- based front-ends will soon enter the marketplace, perhaps being developed and sold by database vendors.

Emphasis will shift from query formulation to knowledge navigation. Instead of formulating queries in a batch mode like the current generation of front-ends, the new generation of front-ends will interactively assist searchers by presenting them with knowledge maps of database domains. Expert systems will be used as **guides** to help select and search databases and as **filters** to enforce search constraints. Front-ends will follow the shift from bibliographic to numeric and full-text databases. In fact, knowledge-based front-ends will be *required* to effectively search large, unstructured databases.

Distributed Expert Systems

An intriguing possibility is the distributed online expert system. Just as we now dial up and consult online databases, we may one day be able to dial into and consult with expert systems. And it is almost certain that expert systems will help us navigate and interact with large, online databases. Database vendors will share the market with knowledge base vendors. Often databases and knowledge bases will be specifically designed to work together with one another.

In addition to communicating with remote knowledge bases, expert systems will be able to communicate with one another. Imagine a knowledge network consisting of many expert sytems connected to one another. In the future there will be sprawling networks, spread across vast distances yet accessible to individual researchers at many locations.

Cooperating expert systems will be linked to one another and share problem-solving tasks. Interconnected but physically remote computers will solve problems by exchanging knowledge with each, drawing upon its own data and knowledge bases to add to the common knowledge pool. Any node on the network will be able to benfit from the knowledge contained in the whole entity.

Knowledge representation standards will begin to emerge. Already the Japanese are working on standards for knowledge representation and have established **PROLOG** as their standard AI research and development language. The standard-making process will be at least as painful as the process of developing bibliographic and data communication standards, and there will be periods of great confusion.

In addition to serving as front-ends, expert systems will be able to interact with databases for other purposes, using them for problem solving and deriving knowledge from them to update and maintain knowledge bases.

Scenario: Knowledge Networks

After awhile knowledge networks will proliferate. There will be networks for every domain imaginable, and many of them will be connected to one another. Local libraries will serve as switching centers and intelligent nodes. Scholars will be able to dial in and consult locally maintained data and knowledge bases. Personalized guides based on locally maintained profiles will help scholars move through the network, switching from one remote source to another as needed. Downloading and high-resolution printing will be handled to a large extent by individual institutions at nodes on the network. The network itself will keep track of royalties, access charges, and value- added fees that will be automatically billed to scholars who have been authorized to use remote resources.

There will be a seamless transition from one resource to another and scholars using the network needn't be aware of which node is supplying them with the information they need. Exchange agreements between institutions at different nodes will be commonplace. Personalized expert systems will provide easy navigation from one information or knowledge format to another. There will be a greater emphasis on "composite documents." Citations, text, images, and video will all be located with and delivered by the same medium. Scholars will be able to search for information on a given topic, filter output through a profile, and from the core sources identified derive a knowledge base that can be locally maintained and queried in a variety of ways.

Knowledge Refineries and Libraries

Some say that it is the only realistic way to overcome the knowledge acquisition bottleneck (Michie, 1986). Others say it will never work. The goal of machine induction research is a system that can induce rules from examples provided by experts. This capability would eliminate the time-consuming and difficult task of knowledge interviewing. Other automated knowledge acquisition tools will evolve from currrent efforts based on the **repertory grid technique** for identifying **constructs** and **belief systems** (Shaw and Gaines, 1987; Boose, 1985).

Machine acquisition of knowledge from documents will become more common. The first documents converted to machine-usable knowledge bases will be technical manuals, and things such as parts lists. Ford, for example, uses a frame-based system to keep track of its inventory (Fikes and Kehler, 1985) Eventually we will see reference works and finally full text encoded in ways that emphasize use of the knowledge they contain. The **Hepatitis Knowledge Base** was built by hierarchically organizing the contents of seminal articles on hepatitis diseases (Bernstein, 1980). Zarri

(1985) developed a representation scheme for knowledge contained in works on medieval French biography, and the *Handbook of Artificial Intelligence* has been encoded in PROLOG (Fox, 1987).

At the 1987 American Library Association conference in San Francisco, Nils Nilsson (1987), one of AI's founding fathers, predicted that expert systems will eventually become clients of libraries. Libraries will provide the raw source material for expert system knowledge bases. Citation analysis and other techniques will be used to derive knowledge for knowledge bases. The Hepatitis Knowledge Base has already shown how a knowledge base might be derived from the published literature. And there is research directed toward automatically extracting knowledge from printed texts. Once OCR technology is perfected, we will be able to scan the contents of documents, convert them to machine-readable form, and use natural language processing to extract meaning from them. We can then re-encode information derived from documents, placing it into knowledge bases.

Expert systems will be able to request from libraries texts in digital form, which will be transformed and incorporated in domain knowledge bases. Clients will be able to interrogate texts in the digital library and create their own texts. The system will correlate pieces of knowledge from separate sources and draw inferences based on evidence gathered from a variety of different places — creating new knowledge from old. Clients will use expert systems to evaluate texts and identify knowledge that matches their needs. Systems will support subject searching, as well as bibliometrics and other concensus techniques. There will be a great deal of research and development directed toward understanding the relationship between the different parts of a text and the relationships among documents. Entire literatures will be mapped out as document networks. There will other network research also.

Eventually there will be "knowledge refineries" (Michie, 1986) whose purpose is to acquire and encode knowledge within specialized domain. Knowledge libraries will have some characteristics of publishing houses, some characteristics of libraries, and some characteristics of software development shops. On the library scene, knowledge refineries will most likely begin with special libraries of one sort or another serving as clearinghouses for the codification of knowledge within their areas of specialization.

Neural Networks

Neural networks are systems that simulate the biological processes of the human brain. Neural networks are designed to simulate the links between neurons in the brain with the firing of individual neurons determined by the pattern and intensity of inputs from neighboring neurons.

Successful systems have already been developed in a number of areas, including bond analysis and assembly line quality control (Kinoshita, 1988).

Neural network research is highly interdisciplinary, occupying the point at which psychology, neuroscience, computer science, and mathematics intersect. Based on new models of the way in which humans process information, neural network research is also referred to as **distributed parallel processing**. Like the human brain, a neural network operates on several parallel levels simultaneously. Many processors share problem-solving tasks and patterns of activation are more important than the task being addressed by any individual processor (Sejnowski, 1988).

Although neural networks are modeled after the human brain, it is presumptuous to suggest that they'll ever duplicate, replace, or even truly function like the human brain. One of the problems of neural networks is their opacity. Neural networks seem to work, but no one is quite sure how or why, and it is impossible for a neural net to explain to its users how it arrived at a decision. Because explanation facilities aren't built into neural nets as they are for expert systems, it is unlikely that they'll be accepted by users for applications where interaction is involved.

Parallel approaches lend themselves to machine learning. One capability of a neural network is the ability to "learn" by analyzing the spreading activation of processors as they respond to a set of stimuli. We can expect to see the introduction of experimental information systems that will be capable of analyzing many inputs, recognizing patterns, and reorganizing themselves for more efficient operation. Theoretically, a neural network, when provided with a large enough group of examples of successfully resolved reference queries, could learn which sources are likely to pay off for different types of queries. A neural network could also theoretically be trained to catalog a book by comparing words extracted from parts of its text to existing catalog records for other works. Books with similar patterns of content words would be assigned to the same class.

Information Space

It is arguable that the user interface is the most important predictor of the likelihood that a system will be accepted by its intended users. Certainly, user interface research is proceeding at a frenetic pace. Some of the most exciting and futuristic research going on now relates to user interface design. Before too long, we can expect to see revolutionary developments arising from user interface research.

Models and Metaphors

Knowledge representation techniques will be used to develop information systems which are capable of **user modeling**. Systems will maintain user models which will guide the manner in which computers interact with users. A classic example of the application of AI techniques to user modeling is the **Grundy** system which was developed by Elaine Rich (1979) to recommend popular fiction to readers. By the end of the decade user modeling capabilities should be commonplace in information systems. In the future there will be a great deal of research directed toward identifying appropriate **metaphors** for computer interfaces.

Technological advances such as high-resolution displays and object-oriented programming have opened up new possibilities in user interface design. Graphic interfaces will continue to increase in popularity. Remember the **STEAMER** program (Hollan et al., 1984) discussed in Chapter Eight. The user of STEAMER operates within a "virtual world" with screen displays bearing a close correspondence to the functions the system is designed to control.

Browsing and Hypertext

While none of the major bibliographic utilities or online supermarket vendors now offer a graphic user interface, we can expect to see commercial systems introduced in the near future. The browsing metaphor will become more common in the nineties. Users will be allowed to browse through information electronically. Systems will help users navigate by presenting them with hierarchically organized information.

Hypertext will allow users to establish their own pathways through library catalogs and to link related items to one another. System designers will also build cross-references into electronic reference works (Weyer and Borning, 1985). Hypertext will first show up in CD-ROM applications but will eventually become available in OPACs and online systems. **Project HYPERCAT** at Linkoping University in Sweden has as its goal the development of a hypertext online catalog where navigation and browsing are the primary modes of interaction (Hjerppe, 1986). Eventually similar features will be available from integrated library systems, and specific libraries will be able to modify navigation capabilities to suit local needs.

There will be an increased emphasis in providing users with access to underlying knowledge structures. Multiple windows will allow the simultaneous display of facets of the user's query, document representations, and concept hierarchies (which will often be based on existing thesauri). Online query systems of the future will resemble **CALIBAN** (Frei and Jauslin, 1983), which is designed to encourage browsing while providing users with point-and-shoot access to a variety of services.

Retrieval through dialogue will receive new attention. Systems like **RABBIT** (Tou et al., 1982) employ artificial intelligence knowledge representation techniques to guide users through large, only partially structured databases.

There will also be a greater emphasis on using a single, intelligent interface to connect users to different types of electronic information. The **CODER** system developed by Fox (1987) provides intelligent access to what are called "composite documents." In addition to bibliographic records, users can search full-text databases and electronic mail messages. Traditional data representation schemes will be married to newer knowledge representation schemes. Our representation formalisms will no longer be limited to specific formats.

Adaptive Interfaces

As systems provide more access to more types of information, **cognitive overload** will become a significant problem. Unstructured databases will be especially hard to handle. It will be difficult for users to maintain mental models of more than a few different information systems. One solution to cognitive overload will be the development of **adaptive user interfaces**. Adaptive user interfaces, which will evolve largely from research on intelligent tutoring, will adjust themselves to the style of particular users. Adaptive interfaces will be **nonmonotonic** — that is, they will be able to change their image of the user and the problem as the situation changes.

Remember how the **EP-X** System (Smith, P.J., 1988) attempts to anticipate user errors and infer user goals even when they aren't explicitly stated? Higher level goals are inferred by examining the "sequence of user inputs." The system maintains an image of the user and tailors its responses to user behavior. Similar natural language approaches will become widespread. Retrieval systems will be less literal than they are now, more forgiving, and more open to ambiguity. Contextual knowledge will assume greater importance.

Virtual Computers

We have had the storage capacity and computing power to handle full-text databases for several years now. One of the main impediments to greater user acceptance has been the lack of high-resolution displays. As a display technology the printed book is still far superior to the typical desktop computer. But high-resolution displays are becoming available. And interfaces will evolve to take advantage of high-resolution displays.

OCLC has mounted one of the major research efforts in display technology. Its **Advanced Interface Management** (AIM) (Dillon, 1987,

1988) project has as one of its goals the development of a "prototyping environment" for a new generation of user interfaces. The project puts a special emphasis on searching and displaying full-text databases.

When one stops and thinks about it, one of the goals of projects such as AIM is to make the electronic records function enough like the graphic record so that people will be willing to use databases in addition to books. What we're talking about here is an interface that will make a full-text electronic database appear more like a book — a **virtual** book. Display technology is only one of the issues to address when designing interfaces that preserve the properties of books while providing the advantages of electronic files. In addition to visual data, people respond to other sensory and tactile information. When we use a book, we're aware of the thickness of the pages, the visual and spatial relationships among different pieces of information, and the physical location within the book of specific passages and parts.

Spatial Data Management

One of the first people to suggest the idea of using locational and sensory cues to find information was Nicholas Negroponte (Fields and Negroponte, 1977), now director of MIT's famous **Media Lab**. Many of the Media Lab projects (Brand, 1988; Bolt, 1985) involve advanced interface design. Remember that OCLC is one of the Media Lab's sponsors and that sponsors are given the opportunity to commercialize technology developed at the Lab. We can expect to see a much less pedestrian interface from OCLC in the future.

One of the more interesting projects to originate with Negroponte's futuristic ideas is something called **spatial data management** (Herot, 1980). Negroponte proposed an interface in which a joystick is used to "fly through an information space."

Among the other pioneering projects at the Media Lab is the **eyes-as-output project**. The goal of the project is use a technology known as **eyeball tracking** to follow the user's gaze and respond to voice input related to the thing the user is looking at. It should be possible for a user to ask, "What's this mean?" as he glances at a word on the display and receive a spoken explanation from the computer, which was able to tell what he was referring to by following the movement of his eyes. Eyes-as-output is like hypertext married to speech recognition and synthesis. Think of the implications for electronic reference works.

Put-that-there is a Media Lab project that seeks to widen the communications channel between human and machine by accepting multiple parallel inputs. A user can point to objects on a wall-sized display and move them from place to place simply by saying "Put that there." The computer is able to respond at once to the spoken command and to a sensor mounted on the pointing finger. Imagine being able to move documents around so simply. Think about being able to conduct an online search by moving terms from one part of the display to another.

Artificial Realities

As it turns out, there is a fair amount of research that focuses on bringing a fuller sensory experience to the user interface. **Artificial realities** are being developed by using alternative input/output devices including mice and joysticks but moving beyond to exotic technologies such as voice input and "eyeball tracking." Foley (1987) describes a group of futuristic devices whose goal is to bring artificial reality to human computer interaction.

According to Foley, an artificial reality is based on:

- **visual imagery** that corresponds to the real world
- **behavior** of images that simulates real world behavior
- **interaction** that mimics the user's interaction with the three-dimensional physical world where the user interacts with the computer "by moving, pointing and picking things up, by talking, and observing from many different angles."

NASA is experimenting with interface devices that go well beyond the traditional keyboard and monitor. Instead of a monitor, there is a head-mounted display. A high-resoultion display panel is mounted in a helmet worn by the user. The display has sensors that are able to determine when the user is moving her head and adjust the display accordingly. As the user turns her head, her perspective changes on the three-dimensional images projected in the helmet. As with STEAMER, commands and guages can be superimposed on the display. The "reality" displayed in the helmet can also respond to vocal commands.

While wearing the helmet, the user can also wear specially equipped **datagloves** which further add to the illusion of reality. Datagloves allow the user to manipulate objects in the display by moving her hands and fingers. Tactile feedback devices and sensors are used to simulate the sense of touch. Pressure pads mounted in the glove allow the user to "feel" the objects in the scene responding to her touch. Imagine being able to sit in a room on earth and, using artificial reality technology, manipulate objects in space, using the spacecraft as a surrogate for one's own body. And the whole while *feeling* as if one were in space.

Another device known as a **joystring** was developed to provide its users with force feedback. A joystring could be used to simulate the feel of pulling a book from a shelf, for example.

Someday researchers will be able to use shell software to develop personal "constructs" reflecting their preferred approach to information problem solving and interaction. Some will choose visual metaphors, others plain text, and others more exotic modes of interaction.

William Gibson's book *Neuromancer* has become a cult classic of the cyberpunk science fiction genre. One of the main characters in the book is an "AI," which interacts with (and manipulates) the human characters. Another major character is a "ROM construct" incorporating the personality and technical skills of a long deceased master hacker.

In *True Names*, another classic by Vernor Vinge, characters interact with one another within a totally electronic environment. But it is an electronic environment with a high level of sensory stimuli. The characters use their electronic skills to simulate a richly detailed fantasy world. They assume fantastic personas and populate their corner of the network with all manner of props. In reality, they are rather prosaic people, jacked into the network from data sets hidden in their homes. Who knows, someday ordinary people may be able to use their imaginations to develop elaborate, highly personal metaphors based on visual imagery and sensory experience. And those metaphors will operate within the ethereal world of **cyberspace**.

Implications

Let's get back down to earth and discuss some of the implications of these developments for libraries.

Education of staff will become a major issue. There are several reasons why it will be desirable for librarians to learn about AI technology. Librarians will need to know what is realistically possible and what is not. Learning about expert systems will have the side benefit of helping us define what constitutes expertise within our field. Identifying appropriate domains for expert systems will become an important activity. The use of expert systems within sufficiently well-bounded domains will result in expanded services and some shifting up to higher levels of responsibility for staff.

Recommending and evaluating systems for end-users will become more important. Most turnkey expert systems will be beyond the financial reach of individuals, so purchase decisions will be left to institutions such as libraries. User acceptance is critical. Users won't accept systems that don't come highly recommended from the people charged with purchasing and maintaining them. Once systems are purchased, they'll need to be implemented and maintained. And clients will need to be taught to use them.

Special libraries will be the first to be confronted with the decision about whether to buy the latest medical, legal, or business expert system, just as they are now confronted with the task of selecting databases to load on their local computers. And like databases, knowledge bases will be expensive, especially at first.

The purchase of workstations and design and equipping of buildings will need to take into account current technological developments. Connectivity doesn't come easy in old or poorly planned buildings. Will there be special rooms where people can "fly through the information space" of different disciplines? Will there be rooms which themselves are highly interactive, sensory, terminals connecting people to virtual worlds? Will equipment designed for verbal interaction need to be kept in soundproof rooms? Expensive equipment and buildings beyond the financial reach of individuals will be purchased by institutions such as libraries. It's not too soon to start thinking about what those buildings might look like.

Eventually we'll come round to looking at these things as **knowledge artifacts** and the computer as a mere medium. One day expert systems might become so commonplace that they will be considered another knowledge mass medium. There are those (Collins, 1985; Stefik, 1986) who suggest that expert systems will revolutionize knowledge transfer just as the introduction of printing did. CD-ROM has already given us electronic reference works. And though medical practitioners have been reluctant to rely upon systems such as **MYCIN**, those same systems are more acceptable when presented as reference works. People will realize that expert systems aren't clones of human beings, but human artifacts just like books. It won't happen overnight, but by the next century there will be vast interactive knowledge archives available from broadbandwith networks. It's not too early to start thinking how we might evaluate, organize, and provide access to this new knowledge medium.

Expert systems are bound to provide new career opportunities for librarians. Knowledge engineering will become a growth employment field. The knowledge acquisition process has a lot in common with the reference interview. There will be a great demand for people with the interviewing skills needed to acquire knowledge from human experts. And knowledge representation, like cataloging and indexing, involves the classification and description of knowledge — often using similar hierarchical schema.

Social and Ethical Issues

As the technology matures, technological concerns will give way to legal, social, and ethical issues. Pressure will increase for standardization. Lack of acceptance (and blind faith overacceptance) will both become issues. There are a host of legal issues, and litigation will increase in the field before it decreases. Liability is a problem; so is intellectual property.

Anyone who thinks the copyright situation is a mess now should think for awhile on the implications of commercial knowledge bases. Complexities include knowledge bases derived from multiple experts as well as a large body of published literature. Factor in ROM chips (which most likely are patented) and shells, and you get a confusing situation.

Who owns the knowledge? Who gets royalties? Do the domain experts get a piece of the pie? The system developer? The publishers of the source literature? The designer of the ROM chip? The developer of the shell?

There are also questions about the transformation of knowledge: what are the implications of deriving expert systems from the printed literature? What is appropriate, and what is not? ~~Pool~~ (1982) speaks of the canonical text. As texts are electronically transformed, what are our obligations to source documents? Should some documents be frozen in time as permanent records for posterity? Or is it more desirable to maintain a constantly changing knowledge store with the knowledge base being frequently modified to reflect new information? How many versions of an electronic knowledge base should there be, and how should they be differentiated from one another?

What is the value of value-added services? When can something which started out in one form be considered to have been transformed into something else? And how do we measure the value of the transformation?

Finally, there are the philosophical and religious issues that we've deliberately avoided in this book (Dreyfus, 1986; Weizenbaum, 1976). Can machines be considered "intelligent" in the same sense as humans? Will it ever be possible to get common sense into a machine? Should there be limits on things machines should do? As technology pushes forward, these questions will become less academic. And it will be impossible to understand the full implications of these questions without some kind of understanding of the technology itself. We hope this book has explained the technical aspects of artificial intelligence well enough to help the reader confront the issues of the future and make decisions based on rational understanding.

Recommended Reading

Speculating about the future of AI and expert systems has become a popular pastime. Given the number of scenarios being put forth, how does one separate promising possibilities from groundless musings?

Anything by Minsky, Feigenbaum, Hayes-Roth, Michie, or Stefik is worth reading. Among AI's futurists, they combine powerful imaginations with the technical background needed to determine what is really possible. Other recommendations include Brand (1987), Negroponte (1975), Grimson and Patil (1987) and Torrero (1985).

The July 1989 issue of the *Communications of the ACM* is devoted to interactive technologies. For social and political analyses, Pool is a recommended author. *AI Magazine* is the most accessible forum for speculations on the future of these technologies. A subscription to this journal accompanies membership in the American Association for Artificial Intelligence, which is well worth joining and among the best ways to keep in touch with what is going on. OCLC's annual research reports are well worth reading for a library point of view, as are reports on the many worthwhile projects being sponsored by the National Library of Medicine (NLM).

Finally, don't forget science fiction. The novella, *True Names* by Vernor Vinge (1987) is especially recommended.

Bibliography

Abrial, J.R. Programming as a mathematical exercise. In *Mathematical Logic and Programming Languages*, edited by Hoare, C.A.R. and Sheperdson, J.C. Englewood Cliffs, NJ: Prentice-Hall, 1985.

Addis, T.R. Expert systems: an evolution in information retrieval. *Information Technology: Research and Development* 1 (1982): 301–324.

Akscyn, Robert M. et al. KMS: a distributed hypermedia system for managing knowledge in organizations. *Communications of the ACM* 31 (7) (July 1988): 820–825

Alberico, Ralph. Shaping the medium with communications software. *Database Searcher* 3 (4) (April 1987): 26–32.

Alberico, Ralph. Workstations for reference and retrieval; part one: the scholar's workstation. *Small Computers in Libraries* 8 (3) (March 1988): 4–10.

Alberico, Ralph. Workstations for reference and retrieval: part two. *Small Computers in Libraries* 8 (4) (April 1988): 4–10.

Alberico, Ralph. Expert systems as interactive user aids. In *Building on the First Century: Proceedings of the Fifth National Conference of the Association of College and Research Libraries,* edited by Janice C. Fennell. Chicago: ALA, 1989.

Alpert, Mark. 500,000 pages on one erasable disk. *Fortune* 118 (Jan. 2 1989): 98–101.

Aluri, Rao. Expert systems for libraries. *Library Administration and Management* 2 (2) (March 1988): 91–94.

Amori, Richard D. NL/template: an approach and tool for building practical natural language interfaces, in Association for Computing Machinery 1985 ACM Annual Conference. *Proceedings* (1985): 309–317.

Anderson, James D. Indexing systems: extensions of the mind's organizing power. *In Information and Behavior*. 1. Brent, Ruben D. (ed.) New Brunswick, NJ: Transaction Books, 1985: 287–323.

Anderson, P.F. Expert systems, expertise, and the library and information professions. *Library and Information Science Research*. 10 (1988): 367–388.

Aragon-Ramirez, V. and Paice, C.D. Design of a system for the online elucidation of natural language search statements. *Advances in Intelligent Retrieval: Informatics* 8 (1985): 163–190.

Arbanel, Robert M. and Williams, Michael D. A relational representation for knowledge bases. In *Proceedings from the First International*

Conference on Expert Database Systems, edited by Larry Kerschberg. Reading, MA: Benjamin/Cummings Pub. Co., 1986.

Arms, William Y. et al. Mercury: an electronic library. In *Annual Review of OCLC Research, July 1987–June 1988.* Dublin, OH: OCLC, 1988: 36-37.

Austin, Derek W. Differences between library classifications and machine-based subject retrieval systems: some inferences drawn from research in Britain, 1963–73. *Third International Study Conference on Classification Research.* Bombay (January 1975).

Baker, L. and Santa, J.L. Semantic integration and context. *Memory and Cognition* 5 (1977): 151–54.

Barber, Gerald R. The personal computer as a delivery vehicle. In *Expert Systems and Knowledge Engineering,* edited by T. Bernold. NY: Elsevier, 1986: 195–198.

Barr, Avron; Cohen, Paul R.; and Feigenbaum, Edward A. (eds.) *Handbook of Artificial Intelligence.* Los Altos, CA: William Kaufmann, 1981.

Barr, Valerie. Exploring expert systems. *Computer (IEEE)* 21(11) (Nov. 1988): 68–73.

Bartschi, Martin An overview of information retrieval subjects *Computer* 18 (5) (May 1985): 67–84.

Bates Marcia J. (1979a) Information search tactics. *Journal of the American Society for Information Science* 30 (July 1979): 205–214.

Bates, Marcia J. (1979b) Idea tactics. *Journal of the American Society for Information Science* 30 (1979): 280–289.

Bates, Marcia J. An exploratory paradigm for online information retrieval. In *Intelligent Information Systems for the Information Society,* edited by B.C. Brookes. Elsevier North-Holland, 1986: 91-99.

Bates, Marcia J. The fallacy of the perfect thirty-item online search. *RQ* 24(1) (Fall 1984): 43–50.

Bates, Marcia (1986a) Subject access in online catalogs: a design model. *Journal of the American Society for Information Science* (37:6) (January 1986): 357–375.

Bates, Marcia J. (1986b) Terminological assistance for the online subject searcher. In *Second Conference on Computer Interfaces and Intermediaries for Information Retrieval.* Alexandria, VA: Defense Technical Info. Ctr., 1986: 285–293.

Beatty, Sue. An experiment in enhanced subject access. *Cataloging Australia* 11(4) (December 1985): 86–95.

Belkin, N.J. and Windel, G. Using MONSTRAT for the analysis of information interaction. In *Representation and Exchange of Knowledge as a Basis of Information Processes,* edited by H.J. Dietschmann. Elsevier North-Holland, 1984: 359–382.

Belkin, N.J., Hennings, R.D. and Seeger, T. Simulation of a distributed expert-based information provision mechanism. *Information Technology* 3(3) (1984): 122–141.

Belkin, Nicholas and Vickery, Alina. Interaction in information systems: a review of research from document retrieval to knowledge-based systems. (Library and Information Research Report Number 35) London: British Library Board, 1985.

Belkin, Nicholas. What does it mean for an information system to be intelligent? In *Second Conference on Computer Interfaces and Intermediaries for Information Retrieval.* Alexandria, VA: Defense Technical Info. Ctr., 1986: 97–106.

Belkin, Nicholas J. and Croft, W. Bruce. Retrieval techniques. In *Annual Review of Information Science and Technology* 22, edited by Martha E. Williams. NY: American Society for Information Science/Elsevier, 1987: 109–145.

Belkin, Nicholas J. On the nature and function of explanation in intelligent information retrieval. In *Annual Review of OCLC Research, July 1987-June 1988.* Dublin, OH: OCLC, 1988: 61–62.

Bell, Colin and Jones, Kevin P. Back–of–the–book indexing: a case for the application of artificial intelligence. In *Informatics* 5. *Analysis of Meaning.* London: Aslib, 1979: 155–161.

Bell, D.A. An architecture for integrating data, knowledge, and information bases. In *Advances in Intelligent Retrieval: Informatics 8.* London: Aslib, 1985: 240–257.

Bellardo, Trudi. An investigation of online searcher traits and their relationship to search outcome. *Journal of the American Society for Information Science* 36 (4) (July 1985): 241–250.

Benson, D.A. et al. Developing tools for online medical reference works. In *MEDINFO 86* edited by R. Salamon, B. Blum, M. Jorgensen. Elsevier North–Holland, 1986: 558–559.

Benson, Dennis A., et al. A microprocessor–based system for the delivery of full–text, encyclopedic information. In *The Information Community: An Alliance for Progress. Proceedings of the 44th ASIS Annual Meeting.* American Society for Information Science, 1981: 256–259.

Benson, James and Maloney, Ruth Kay. Principles of searching. *RQ* 14 (4) (Summer 1975): 316–320.

Benyon, D. and Murray, Dianne. Experience with adaptive interfaces. *Computer Journal* 31(5) (October 1988): 465–473.

Bernold, Thomas (ed.) Expert systems and knowledge engineering. NY: Elsevier North–Holland, 1986.

Bernstein, L.M., Siegel, E.R. and Goldstein, C.M. The hepatitis knowledge base: a prototype information transfer system. *Annals of Internal Medicine* 93 (1) (July 1980): 165–222.

Bernstein, Lionel M. and Williamson, Robert E. Testing of a natural language retrieval system for a full text knowledge base. *Journal of the American Society for Information Science* 35 (4) (1984): 235–247.

Binkley, R. David and Parrott, James R. A reference–librarian model for computer–aided library instruction. *Information Services and Use* 7 (1987): 31–38.

Biswas, Gautam, et al. Knowledge–assisted document retrieval: I. The natural language interface. *Journal of the American Society for Information Science* 38 (2) (1987): 83–96.

Biswas, Gautam, et al. Knowledge assisted document retrieval: II. The retrieval process. *Journal of the American Society for Information Science* 38 (2) (1987): 97–110.

Bivins, Kathleen T. and Erikson, Lennart. Reflink: a microcomputer information retrieval and evaluation system. *Information Processing and Management* 18 (3) (1982): 111–116.

Blair, David C. and Maron, M.E. An evaluation of retrieval effectiveness for a full–text document–retrieval system. *Communications of the ACM* 28(3) (March 1985): 289–299.

Bobrow, Daniel G. If Prolog is the answer, what is the question? Or what it takes to support AI programming paradigms. *IEEE Transactions on Software Engineering* SE11 (11) (November 1985):1401–1408.

Bobrow, Daniel G. and Stefik, Mark J. Perspectives on artificial intelligence programming. *Science* 231 (Feb 1986): 951–957.

Bobrow, Daniel G. et al. Expert systems: perils and promise. *Communications of the ACM* 29 (9) (September 1986): 880–894.

Boden, Margaret A. *Artificial Intelligence and Natural Man.* New York: Basic Books, 1977.

Boehm, Barry. *Software Engineering Economics.* Englewood Cliffs, NJ: Prentice–Hall, 1981.

Bolt, Richard A. Conversing with computers. *Technology Review* (February/March 1985): 35–43.

Bond, Alan H. and Gasser, Les (eds.) Readings in Distributed Artificial Intelligence. San Mateo, CA: Morgan Kaufmann, 1988.

Books are for use: Final report of the Council on Library Resources. Syracuse University: School of Library and Information Studies: Subject Access Project. Director: Pauline Atherton. Syracuse, NY: 1978 ED 156 131.

Boole, George. Studies in logic and probability. *Proceedings of the Royal Irish Academy* 57 (6) (1955).

Boose, John H. A knowledge acquisition program for expert systems based on personal construct psychology. *International Journal of Man–Machine Studies* 23 (1985): 495–525.

Borgman, Christine L. Performance effects of a user's mental model of an information retrieval system. In *Productivity in the Information Age.*

Proceedings of the 46th ASIS Annual Meeting 20 American Society for Information Science (1983): 121–124.

Borgman, Christine L. Psychological research in human–computer interaction. In *Annual Review of Information Science and Technology* 19, edited by Martha E. Williams (1984): 33–64.

Borgman, Christine L. The user's mental model of an information retrieval system. In *Research and Development in Information Retrieval. Eighth Annual In'tl ACM SIGIR Conference.* Baltimore: Assn. for Computing Machinery, 1985: 268–273.

Borgman, Christine, Case, Donald and Meadow, Charles T. Designing an information retrieval interface based on user characteristics. In *Research and Development in Information Retrieval. Eighth Annual In'tl ACM SIGIR Conference.* Baltimore: Assn. for Computing Machinery, 1985: 139–146.

Borgman, Christine, et al. Incorporating users' information seeking styles into the design of an information retrieval interface. In *Proceedings of the 48th Annual ASIS Meeting* 22. American Society for Information Science, 1985: 324–330.

Borgman, C.L. Why are online catalogs hard to use? Lessons learned from information retrieval studies. *Journal of the American Society for Information Science* 37 (1986): 387–400.

Borko, Harold. Getting started in library expert systems research. *Information Processing and Management* 23 (2) (1987): 81–87.

Borland International Inc. *Turbo PROLOG: Owner's Handbook.* Scott's Valley, CA: Borland International Inc., 1986.

Boulding, Kenneth E. *The Image: Knowledge in Life and Society.* Ann Arbor: University of Michigan Press, 1956.

Brachman, Ronald J. and Levesque, Hector (eds.) *Readings in Knowledge Representation.* Los Altos, CA: Morgan Kaufmann, 1985.

Brady, Michael and Berwick, Roberts C. (eds.) *Computational Models of Discourse.* Cambridge, MA: MIT Press, 1983.

Brajnik, Giorgio, Guida, Giovanni and Tasso, Carlo. An expert interface for effective man–machine communication. In *Cooperative Interfaces to Information Systems,* edited by Bolc, L. and Jarke, M. New York: Springer–Verlag, 1986: 259–308.

Brand, Stewart. *The Media Lab: Inventing the Future at MIT.* New York: Viking, 1987.

Brenner, Lisa P., et al. User–computer interface designs for information systems: a review. *Library Research* 2 (1980–1981): 63–73.

Breuker, Joost and Wielinga, Bob. Use of models in the interpretation of verbal data. In *Knowledge Acquisition for Expert Systems: An Introductory Framework,* edited by Kidd, Alison L. New York: Plenum, 1987: 17–43.

Brittain, M. Consensus in the medical sciences and the implications for information systems. In *Representation and Exchange of Knowledge as a Basis of Information Processes,* edited by H.J. Dietschmann. Elsevier North–Holland, 1984: 165–174.

Brittain, Michael. Implications for LIS education of recent developments in expert systems. *Information Processing and Management* 23 (2) (1987):139–152.

Brookes, Bertram C. (ed.) Intelligent information systems for the information society. *Proceedings of the Sixth International Research Forum in Information Science* (IRFIS 6) Frascati, Italy, September 16–18, 1985. Amsterdam: Elsevier North–Holland, 1986.

Brooks, F. P. The Mythical Man–Month. Reading, MA: Addison–Wesley, 1975.

Brooks, H., Oddy, R.N. and Belkin, N.J. Representing and classifying anomalous states of knowledge. In *Informatics 5: Analysis of Meaning.* London: Aslib, 1979: 222–233.

Brooks, Helen M. Information retrieval and expert systems: approaches and methods of development. In *Informatics 7: Intelligent Information Retrieval.* Cambridge: Aslib, 1984: 65–78.

Brooks, H.M. Developing and representing problem descriptions. In *Intelligent Information Systems for the Information Society,* edited by B.C. Brookes. Elesevier North–Holland, 1985: 141–161.

Brooks, H.M. Expert systems in reference work. In *Expert Systems in Libraries,* edited by Gibb, Forbes. London: Taylor Graham, 1985: 36–49.

Brooks, H.M., Daniels, P.J. and Belkin, N.J. Problem descriptions and user models: developing an intelligent interface for document retrieval systems. In *Advances in Intelligent Retrieval: Informatics 8.* London: Aslib, 1985: 191–214.

Brooks, H.M. and Daniels, P.J. Research on information interaction and intelligent information provision mechanisms. *Journal of Information Science* 12 (1986): 37–44.

Brown, Gillian and Yule, George. Discourse Analysis. Cambridge, UK: Cambridge University Press, 1983.

Bruner, Jerome S. Beyond the Information Given: Studies in the Psychology of Knowing. New York: Norton, 1973.

Buchanan, Bruce G. and Duda, Richard O. Principles of rule–based systems. In *Advances in Computers,* edited by Yovits, Marshall C. New York: Academic Press, 1983: 164–216.

Buchannan, Bruce (ed.) *Rule–Based Expert Systems: The MYCIN Experiments of the Stanford Heuristic Programming Project.* Reading, MA: Addison–Wesley, 1984.

Burton, Hilary D. Developing system interfaces for an intelligent gateway to a heterogeneous resource environment. In *Second Confer-*

ence on Computer Interfaces and Intermediaries for Information Retrieval. Alexandria, VA: Defense Technical Info. Ctr., 1986: 295–301.

Bush, Vannevar. As we may think. *Atlantic Monthly* 176 (1) (July 1945): 101–108.

Bylinski, Gene. A quantum leap in electronics. *Fortune* (January 30, 1989): 113–120.

Byrne, Alex. Life wan't meant to be whimsical: painless subject augmentation. *Australasian College Libraries* 4 (2) (June 1986): 83–90.

Byrne, Alex and Micco, H. Mary. Improving subject access in an OPAC: The ADFA experiment. *College and Research Libraries* (October 1988).

Byrne, Alex and Micco, Mary. Improving subject access in an OPAC: The ADFA Experiment. Unpublished manuscript.

Byte 11 (8) (August 1986). Special issue on object–oriented languages.

Canas, Alberto J. and Safayeni, Frank R. and Conrath, David W. A conceptual model and experiments on how people classify and retrieve documents. In *Research and Development in Information Retrieval. Eighth Annual In'tl ACM SIGIR Conference.* Baltimore: Assn. for Computing Machinery, 1985: 282–287.

Carbonell, Jaime G. et al. On the design of biomedical knowledge bases. In *MEDINFO 86*, edited by R. Salamon, B. Blum, M. Jorgensen. Elsevier North–Holland, 1986: 37–41.

Carroll, John M. The adventure of getting to know a computer. *Computer (IEEE)* 15 (1982): 49–58.

Carroll, John M. and McKendree, Jean. Interface design issues for advice–giving expert systems. *Communications of the ACM* 30(1) (January 1987): 14–31.

Carroll, John M. and Thomas, John C. Metaphor and the cognitive representation of computing systems. *IEEE Transactions on Systems, Man, and Cybernetics* 12 (2) (March/April 1982): 107–116.

Case, Donald et al. Information seeking in the energy research field: The DOE/OAK project. In *Proceedings of the 48th Annual ASIS Meeting* 22. American Society for Information Science. (1985): 331–336.

Cercone, Nick and McCalla, Gordon. Artificial intelligence: underlying assumptions and basic objectives. *Journal of the American Society for Information Science* 35 (5) (1984): 280–290.

Ceri, Stefano, Gottlob, Georg and Wiederhold, Gio. Interfacing relational databases and Prolog efficiently. In *Proceedings from the First International Conference on Expert Database Systems*, edited by Larry Kerschberg. Reading, MA: Benjamin/Cummings Publishing Co., 1986.

Chamis, Alice Yanosko. The usefulness of switching vocabularies for online databases. In *Proceedings of the 48th Annual ASIS Meeting* 22. American Society for Information Science. (1985): 311–314.

Chamis, Alice Y. Selection of online databases using switching vocabularies. *Journal of the American Society for Information Science* 39 (3) (1988): 217–218.

Chan, Lois Mai. Library of Congress classification as an online retrieval tool: potentials and limitations. *Information Technology and Libraries* 5 (3) (September 1986).

Charniak, Eugene and McDermott, Drew. *Introduction to Artificial Intelligence.* Reading, MA: Addison–Wesley Pub. Co, 1986.

Chen, Ching–chih. The first emperor of China's ancient world uncovered: from Xian to your electronic screen. *Academic Computing* 3 (7) (March 1989): 10–14, 54–57.

Clancey, William J. *Knowledge Based Tutoring: The GUIDON Program.* Cambridge, MA: MIT Press, 1987.

Clark, K. L. and McCabe, F. G. *Micro–PROLOG: Programming in Logic.* Englewood–Cliffs, NJ: Prentice–Hall International, 1984.

Clarke, Ann and Cronin, Blaise. Expert systems and library/information work. *Journal of Librarianship* 15 (4) (October 1983): 277–292.

Clarke, Matthew. Explanations and the SIRATAC cotton management system. In *Proceedings of the 3rd Australian Conference on Applications of Expert Systems.* Sydney, Australia: Expert Systems Group, 1987.

Cleverdon, Cyril W. Report on the testing and analysis of an investigation into the comparative efficiency of indexing systems. Cranfield, England: College of Aeronautics, ASLIB Cranfield Research Project, 1962.

Cleverdon, Cyril W. and Aitchinson, Jean. Report of a test of the index of metallurgical literature of Western Reserve University. *Journal of Documentation* 18 (1962): 80–88.

Cochrane, Pauline A. for Howard L. Bleich and Gary L. Horowitz. "Friendly" catalog forgives user errors. *American Libraries* (May 1982): 303–306.

Cochrane, Pauline A. and Karen Markey. Preparing for the use of classification in online cataloging systems and in online catalogs. *Information Technology and Libraries* 4 (June 1985): 91–111.

Cochrane, Pauline A. *Improving LCSH for Use in Online Catalogs.* Littleton, CO: Libraries Unlimited, 1986.

Coelho, Helder. Library manager: a case study in knowledge engineering. In *Intelligent Information Systems: Progress and Prospects.* Chichester, England: Ellis Horwood, 1986: 33–53.

Cohn, Anthony G. Deep knowledge representation techniques. In *Expert Systems 85. Proceedings of the 5th Technical Conference of the British Computer Society.* Cambridge Univ. Press., 1985: 299–306.

Collen, Morris F. Online full–text medical literature retrieval. In *MEDINFO 86,* edited by R. Salamon, B. Blum, M. Jorgensen. Elsevier North–Holland, 1986: 553–557.

Collins, H.M., Green, R.H., and Draper, R.C. Where's the expertise?: Expert systems as a medium of knowledge transfer. In *Expert Systems 85. Proceedings of the 5th Technical Conference of the British Computer Society. Cambridge Univ. Press,* 1985: 323–334.

Conklin, Jeff. Hypertext: an introduction and survey. *Computer (IEEE)* 20 (9) (Sept 1987): 17–41.

Conklin, Jeff. A survey of hypertext. MCC Technical Rpt. STP–356–86, Rev. 2. Austin, TX: Microelectronics and Computer Technology Corporation, 1987.

Coombs, M.J. and Alty, J.L. (eds.) *Computing Skills and the User Interface.* New York: Academic Press, 1981.

Coombs, Mike and Alty, Jim. Expert systems: an alternative paradigm. *International Journal of Man–Machine Studies* 20 (1984): 21–43.

Crecine, John P. The next generation of personal computers. *Science* 231 (Feb. 28, 1986): 935–943.

Croft, W.B. and Thompson, R.H. An overview of the I3R document retrieval system. In *Second Conference on Computer Interfaces and Intermediaries for Information Retrieval.* Alexandria, VA: Defense Technical Info. Ctr., 1986: 123–134.

Croft, W. B. and Thompson, R. H. I3R: A new approach to the design of document retrieval systems. *Journal of the American Society for Information Science* 38 (6) (1987): 389–404.

Croft, W. Bruce. Information retrieval by plausible inference. In *Annual Review of OCLC Research, July 1987–June 1988.* Dublin, OH: OCLC, 1988: 65–66.

Crouch, Wayne M. The Information Interview: A Comprehensive Bibliography and an Analysis of the Literature. Syracuse, NY: ERIC Clearinghouse on Information Resources, 1979. ED180 501.

Cupello, James M. and Mishelevich, David J. Managing prototype knowledge/expert system projects. *Communications of the ACM* 31 (5) (May 1988): 535–541.

Daily, Jay E. The grammar of subject headings: a formulation of rules based on a syntactical and morphological analysis of the Library of Congress list. Ph.D. dissertation, School of Library Service, Columbia University, 1957.

Dalenoort, G.J. Design of a self–organizing documentation system. In *Representation and Exchange of Knowledge as a Basis of Information Processes,* edited by H.J. Dietschmann. Elsevier North–Holland, 1984: 111–128.

Dalenoort, G.J. Solving problems with the help of machines. In *Intelligent Information Systems for the Information Society,* edited by B.C. Brookes. Elsevier North–Holland, 1986: 83–90.

Daniels, Penny J. The user modelling function of an intelligent interface for document retrieval systems. In *Association for Computing Ma-*

chinery. 1985 ACM Annual Conference. Proceedings. ACM, 1985: 162–176.

Danilowicz, Czeslaw. Users and experts in the document retrieval system model. *International Journal of Man–Machine Studies* 21 (1981): 245–252.

Davies, R. (ed.) *Intelligent Information Systems: Progress and Prospects.* Chichester, England: Ellis Horwood, 1986.

Davis, Randall. Knowledge–based systems. *Science* 231 (1986): 957–963.

Davis, Randall and Lenat, Douglas B. *Knowledge–Based Systems in Artificial Intelligence.* New York: McGraw–Hill, 1982.

Defude, B. Different levels of expertise for an expert system in information retrieval. In *Research and Development in Information retrieval. Eighth Annual In'tl ACM SIGIR Conference.* Baltimore: Assn. for Computing Machinery, 1985: 147–153.

DeMarco, Thomas. *Controlling Software Projects.* New York: Yourdon Press, 1982.

Dempster, A.P. Upper and lower probabilities induced by a multivalued mapping. *Annals of Mathematical Statistics* 38 (1967): 37–41.

DeSalvo, Daniel A. and Liebowitz, Jay. The application of an expert system for information retrieval at the national archives. In *Expert Systems in Government Symposium,* edited by Karna, Kamal N. Washington: IEEE Computer Society Press, 1985: 464–473.

DeSolla Price, Derek. Towards three–D chips and orbiting archive super libraries. In *Application of Mini– and Micro– Computers to Information, Documentation, and Libraries,* edited by C. Keren and L. Perlmutter. Elsevier, 1983: 557–560.

Dietschmann, H.J. (ed.) *Representation and Exchange of Knowledge as a Basis of Information Processes.* Amsterdam: Elsevier North–Holland, 1984.

Dillon, Martin, et al. Advanced interface design for library retrieval systems project. *Annual Review of OCLC Research* (July 1985–June 1986): 8.

Dillon, Martin. Advanced interface management. *OCLC Research Reports* (1986–1987): 1.

Dillon, Martin. D: a design language for retrieval system interfaces. In *National Online Meeting: Proceedings – 1987.* Medford, NJ: Learned Information, 1987: 111–118.

Dillon, Martin. Advanced interface management. In *Annual Review of OCLC Research, July 1987–June 1988.* Dublin, OH: OCLC, 1988: 3–4.

Doszkocs, Tamas E. Natural Language processing in information retrieval. *Journal of the American Society for Information Science* 37 (4) (1986): 191–196.

Doszkocs, Tamas E. Natural language processing in intelligent information retrieval. In *The Range of Computing. 1985 ACM Annual Conference. Association for Computing Machinery,* 1985: 356–359.

Doyle, John B. How experts scan journals: implications for expert systems in text retrieval. In *MEDINFO 86*, edited by R. Salamon, B. Blum, M. Jorgensen. Elsevier North–Holland, 1986: 540–544.

Drexler, Eric K. *Engines of Creation.* New York: Anchor, 1986.

Dreyfus, Hubert L. and Dreyfus, Stuart E. *Mind Over Machine: The Power of Human Intuition and Expertise in the Era of the Computer.* New York: Free Press, 1986.

Dubois, C.P.R. Free text versus controlled vocabulary; a reassessment. *Online Review* 11(4) (August 1987): 243–253.

Duda, Richard O., et al. Model design in the PROSPECTOR consultant system for mineral exploration. In *Expert Systems in the Micro–electronics Age*, edited by Michie, D. Edinburgh, Scotland: Edinburgh University, 1979.

Dudek, Virginia. PC natural–language text–retrieval package brought out by Thunderstone Software Corp. *MIS Week* 8 (August 1987): 1.

Dym, Eleanor D. (ed.) *Subject and Information Analysis*. New York, NY: Marcel Dekker, 1985.

Eastman, C. M. The use of logic programming in information retrieval experimentation. In *Productivity in the Information Age. Proceedings of the 46th ASIS Annual Meeting* 20. American Society for Information Science (1983): 58–59.

Eisenberg, Michael. *The Direct Use of Online Bibliographic Information Systems by Untrained End–Users: A Review of Research.* Washington: ERIC, 1983. ERIC ED 238 440.

Ellzey, Roy S. *Data Structures for Computer Information Systems*, 2nd ed. Chicago, IL: SRA, 1989.

Enser, P.G.B. Experimenting with the automatic classification of books. In *Advances in Intelligent Retrieval: Informatics* 8 (1985): 66–84.

Ericsson, Karl Anders and Simon, Herbert. *Protocol Analysis: Verbal Reports as Data.* Cambridge, MA: MIT Press, 1984.

Erman, L.D., Hayes–Roth, F. and Reddy, D. R. The HEARSAY II speech understanding system: Integrating knowledge to resolve uncertainty. *Computing Surveys* 12 (2) (1980): 213–253.

Evans, Nell S. Feasibility study of an expert system reference librarian; final report. Report of a research grant sponsored by the Texas Library Association. College and University Libraries Division. August, 1987.

Expansion Programs Int'l. Inc. *Thunderstone Software Reference: Knowledge Management Through Text Understanding.* Cleveland, OH: Expansion Programs Int'l. Inc., 1988.

Feigenbaum, Edward A., Barr, Avron and Cohen, Paul R. (eds.) *The Handbook of Artificial Intelligence.* Vols. 1–3. Stanford, CA: Heuristech Press/William Kaufmann, Inc., 1981–82.

Feigenbaum, Edward A. and McCorduck, Pamela. *The Fifth Generation.* Reading, MA: Addison–Wesley Press, 1983.

Feigenbaum, Edward A. Artificial intelligence: A status report. In *Next Generation Computers*, edited by Edward A. Torrero. New York: IEEE, 1985: 94–99.

Feigenbaum, E.A. Toward the library of the future. *Long Range Planning* 22 (Feb. 1989): 118–123.

Fenly, Charles and Harris, Howard. Expert systems: concepts and applications. *Advances in Library Information Technology.* Issue Number 1. Washington, DC: Cataloging Distribution Service, Library of Congress, 1988.

Fennell, Richard D. and Lesser, Victor R. Parallelism in artificial intelligence problem solving: a case study of HEARSAY II. Tutorial on Parallel Processing. New York: IEEE Computer Society, 1981.

Fidel, Raya and Soergel, Dagobert. Factors affecting online bibliographic retrieval: a conceptual framework for research. *Journal of the American Society for Information Science* 34 (3) (1983): 163–180.

Fidel, Raya. Do user charges affect online searching behavior? In *Productivity in the Information Age. Proceedings of the 46th ASIS Annual Meeting* 2.0 American Society for Information Science (1983): 132–134.

Fidel, Raya. Request–related criteria for the selection of search keys. *1984: Challenges to an Information Society. Proceedings of the 47th ASIS Annual Meeting* 21. American Society for Information Science (1984): 141–143.

Fidel, Raya. Online searching styles: a case–study–based model of searching behavior. *Journal of the American Society for Information Science* 35 (4) (1984): 211–221.

Fidel, Raya. Individual variability in online searching behavior. In *Proceedings of the 48th Annual ASIS Meeting* 22. American Society for Information Science (1985): 69–72.

Fidel, Raya. Moves in online searching. *Online Review* 9 (1) (1985): 61–74.

Fidel, Raya. Toward expert systems for the selection of search keys. *Journal of the American Society for Information Science* 37 (1) (1986): 37–44.

Fidel, Raya. Extracting knowledge for intermediary expert systems: The selection of search keys: a final report for NSF grant IST 85–09719. Seattle, WA: GSLIS–University of Washington, 1988.

Fields, Craig and Negroponte, Nicholas. Using new clues to find data. In *Proceedings of the Third International Conference on Very Large Databases.* New York: IEEE, 1977: 156–158.

Fikes, Richard and Kehler, Tom. The role of frame–based representation in reasoning. *Communications of the ACM* 28 (9) (September 1985): 904–920.

Firebaugh, Morris W. Artificial intelligence: A knowledge–based approach. Boston, MA: Boyd & Fraser, 1988.

Fischler, Martin A. and Firschein, Oscar. *Intelligence: The Eye, the Brain and the Computer.* Reading, MA: Addison–Wesley Pub. Co., 1987.

Flores, Fernando, Graves, Michael, Hartfield, Brad, Winograd, Terry. Computer systems and the design of organizational interaction. *ACM Transactions on Office Information Systems* 6(2) (April 1988): 153–172.

Foley, James D. Interfaces for advanced computing. *Scientific American* 257 (October 1987): 127–135.

Forsyth, Richard and Rada, Roy. *Machine Learning: Applications in Expert Systems and Information Retrieval.* New York: Halsted Press, 1986.

Fox, Christopher. Future generation information systems. *Journal of the American Society for Information Science* 37 (4) (July 1986): 215–219.

Fox, Edward A. Expert retrieval for users of computer based message systems. In *Proceedings of the 49th Annual ASIS Meeting.* 23. American Society for Information Science. (1986): 88–95.

Fox, Edward A. Analysis and retrieval of composite documents. In *Proceedings of the 48th Annual ASIS Meeting* 22. American Society for Information Science. (1985): 54–58.

Fox, Edward A. Composite document extended retrieval: an overview. In *Research and Development in Information Retrieval. Eighth Annual In'tl. ACM SIGIR Conference.* Baltimore: Assn. for Computing Machinery, 1985: 42–53.

Fox, Edward A. A design for intelligent retrieval: The CODER system. In *Second Conference on Computer Interfaces and Intermediaries for Information Retrieval.* Alexandria, VA: Defense Technical Info. Ctr., 1986: 135–153.

Fox, Edward A. Development of the CODER system: A testbed for artificial intelligence methods in information retrieval. *Information Processing and Management* 23 (4) (1987): 341–366.

Frei, H. P. and Jauslin, J. F. Graphical presentation of information and services: A user oriented interface. *Information Technology: Research and Development* 2 (1983): 23–42.

Frei, H. P. and Jauslin, J. F. Two–dimensional representation of information retrieval services. In *Representation and Exchange of Knowl-*

edge as a Basis of Information Processes, edited by H. J. Dietschmann. Elsevier North–Holland, 1984: 383–396.

Frenkel, Karen A. The next generation of interactive technologies. *Communications of the ACM* 32 (7) (July 1989): 872–881.

Friis, Siv. Tools for user prototyping. In *Intelligent Information Systems for the Information Society*, edited by B.C. Brookes. Elsevier North–Holland, 1986:71–82.

Frisse, Mark. Searching for information in a hypertext medical handbook. *ACM Communications* 31(7) (July 1988).

Gal, Annie and Minker, Jack. A natural language database interface that provides cooperative answers. In *Engineering of Knowledge–Based Systems. 2nd Conference on Artificial Intelligence Applications.* Washington: IEEE Computer Society Press, 1985: 352–357.

Gallant, Stephen I. Connectionist expert systems. In *Communications of the ACM* 31(2) (Feb. 1988): 152–169.

Gallo, T. et al. ObNet: an object oriented approach for supporting large, long–lived, highly configurable systems. *11th International Conference on Software Engineering. Proceedings.* May 15–18, 1989. Pittsburgh, PA.

Gammack, John G. Different techniques and different aspects on declarative knowledge. In *Knowledge Acquisition for Expert Systems: An Introductory Framework*, edited by Kidd, Alison L. New York: Plenum, 1987: 137–163.

Gebhardt, Friederich. Connections between information retrieval systems and expert systems. *Nachrichten fur Dokumentation* 36 (6) (1985): 255–263.

Genesereth, Michael R. and Ginsberg, Matthew L. Logic programming *Communications of the ACM* 28 (9) (September 1985): 933–941.

Gentner, Dedre and Stevens, Albert L. (eds.) *Mental Models.* Hillsdale, NJ: Erlbaum, 1983.

Gevarter, William B. The nature and evaluation of commercial expert system building tools. *Computer IEEE* (May 1987): 24–41.

Gevarter, William B. An overview of expert systems. U.S. Department of Commerce. National Bureau of Standards. Washington, DC: GPO. SuDoc no: C13.58.82–2505.

Gibb, Forbes and Sharif, Carolyn (comps.) Bibliography [expert systems in libraries]. In *Expert Systems in Libraries*, edited by Gibb, Forbes. London: Taylor Graham, 1985: 83–97.

Gibb, Forbes (ed.) *Expert Systems in Libraries. Proceedings of a Conference of the Library Information Technology Group and the Library and Information Research Group* (November 1985). London: Taylor Graham, 1985.

Gilmore, John H. and Howard, Charles. Expert systems tools for practitioners. In First Australian Artificial Intelligence Conference. November 1986. Melbourne, VIC.

Gibson, William. *Neuromancer.* Ace, 1984.

Gibson, William. *Count Zero.* New York: Arbor House, 1986

Gibson, William. *Burning Chrome.* New York: Arbor House, 1986.

Gilmore, John H. and Howard, Charles. GEST — The generic expert system tool. In *SPIE Applications of Artificial Intelligence.* Orlando, FL, 1985.

Glinert, Ephraim P. and Tanimoto, Stephen L. PICT: An interactive graphical programming environment. *Computer (IEEE)* 17 (11) (November 1984): 7–25.

Goldberg, Adele and Robson, David. *Smalltalk–80: The Language and Its Implementation.* Reading, MA: Addison–Wesley, 1983.

Gordon, Martha J. A human–factors approach to system design. *OCLC Newsletter,* no. 171 (January/February 1988): 17–18.

Grateful Med. U.S. Dept. of Health and Human Services. *Grateful Med: Users' Guide.* Version 4.0 Bethesda, MD. U.S Dept. of Health and Human Services, NIH and NLM.

Greenes, Robert A. Knowledge management as an aid to medical decision making and education: The EXPLORER–1 system. In *MEDINFO 86,* edited by R. Salamon, B. Blum, M. Jorgensen. Elsevier North–Holland, 1986: 895–899.

Grimson, Eric L. and Patil, Ramesh S (eds.) *AI in the 1980's and Beyond: An MIT Survey.* Cambridge, MA: MIT Press, 1987.

Grishman, Ralph. Natural language processing. *Journal of the American Society for Information Science* 35 (5) (1984): 291–296.

Guida, Giovanni and Tasso, Carlo. An expert intermediary system for interactive document retrieval. *Automatica* 19 (6) (1983): 759–766.

Gupta, Amar and Prasad, Bandreddi E. (eds.) (1988a) *Principles of Expert Systems.* New York: IEEE Press, 1988.

Gupta, Amar and Prasad, Bandreddi E. (eds.) (1988b) *Microcomputer–Based Expert Systems.* New York: IEEE Press, 1988.

Haftner, Ruth. The performance of card catalogs: a review of the research. *Library Research* 1 (1970): 199–220.

Hahn, Udo and Reimer, Ulrich. Heuristic text parsing in 'Topic': Methodological issues in a knowledge based text condensation system. In *Representation and Exchange of Knowledge as a Basis of Information Processes,* edited by H.J. Dietschmann. Elsevier North–Holland, 1984: 143–163.

Hahn, Udo. Expert systems as intelligent information systems. *Nachriften fur Dokumentation* 36 (1985): 2–12.

Halasz, Fred Seven issues for the next generation of hypermedia systems. *Communications of the ACM* 31(7) (July 1988).

Hapgood, Fred. MIT's roach motel: Artificial intelligence. *Omni* (October 1988): 38–40

Hapgood, Fred. The Omni photovore: How to build a robot that thinks like a roach. *Omni* (October 1988): 201–212.

Harline, N. LaVar. A computerized reference retrieval system. ERIC document ED 102 974 1974.

Harmon, Paul and King, David. *Expert Systems: Artificial Intelligence in Business.* New York: Wiley, 1985.

Harmon, Paul, Maus, Rex and Morrissey, William. *Expert Systems: Tools and Applications.* New York: Wiley, 1988.

Hart, Anna. *Knowledge Acquisition for Expert Systems.* New York: McGraw–Hill, 1986.

Harter, Stephen P. Scientific inquiry: a model for online searching. *Journal of the American Society for Information Science* 35 (2) (March 1984): 110–117.

Harter, Stephen P. Online searching styles: an exploratory study. *College and Research Libraries* (July 1984): 249–258.

Harter, Stephen P. and Peters, Anne Rogers. Heuristics for online information retrieval: A typology and preliminary listing. *Online Review* 9 (5) (1985): 407–424.

Hawkins, Donald T. and Levy, Louise R. Front–end software for online database searching. Part I: definitions, system features, and evaluation. *Online* (November 1985): 30–37.

Hawkins, Donald T. Applications of artificial intelligence (AI) and expert systems for online searching. *Online* 12 (1) (Jan. 1988): 31–43.

Hayes, I (ed.) *Specification Case Studies.* Cambridge, UK: Prentice–Hall International, 1987.

Hayes–Roth, Frederick, Waterman, Donald A. and Lenat, Douglas B. (eds.) *Building Expert Systems.* Reading, MA: Addison–Wesley, 1983.

Hayes–Roth, Frederick. Knowledge–Based Expert Systems. *Computer* 17 (Oct. 1984): 263–273.

Hayes–Roth, Frederick. Rule–based systems. *Communications of the ACM* 28 (9) (September 1985): 921–932.

Haykin, David. *Subject Headings: A Practical Guide.* Washington, DC: U.S. Government Printing Office, 1951.

Henco Software Inc. *INFO–DB+: Text management as a necessity: Henco and Digital team up to deliver all the information when you need it.* Waltham, MA: Henco Software Inc., 1987.

Hendler, James A. *Expert systems: The user interface.* Norwood, NJ: Ablex, 1988.

Hendrix, G. C. Developing a natural language interface to complex data. *ACM Transactions: Database Systems* 3 (March 1978): 105–107.

Herot, Christopher F. Spatial management of data. *ACM Transactions on Database Systems* 5 (4) (December 1980): 493–514.

Hickey, T.B. and Handley, J.C. Interactive display of text and graphics on an IBM PC. In *The Impact of the New Information Technology on International Cooperation, Essen Symposium – 1986.* Essen, FRG, 1987: 137–149.

Hickey, Thomas B. Information display. In *Annual Review of OCLC Research, July 1987–June 1988.* Dublin, OH: OCLC, 1988: 18.

Hildreth, Charles R. *Online Public Access Catalogs: The User Interface.* Dublin, OH: OCLC, 1982.

Hildreth, Charles R. Intelligent interfaces and retrieval methods for subject searching in bibliographic retrieval systems. *Advances in Library Information Technology* No. 2. Washington, DC: Cataloging Distribution Service, Library of Congress, 1989.

Hiz, Henry. Questions and answers. *Journal of Philosophy* 59 (10) (May 1962): 253–265.

Hjerppe, Roland. Project HYPERCATalog: Visions and preliminary conceptions of an extended and enhanced catalog. *Intelligent Information Systems for the Information Society. IRFIS 6,* edited by B.B.C. Brookes. North–Holland, 1986: 211–225.

Hollaar, Lee. A testbed for information retrieval research: The Utah retrieval system architecture. In *Research and Development in Information Retrieval. Eighth Annual In'tl. ACM SIGIR Conference.* Baltimore: Assn. for Computing Machinery, 1985: 227–232.

Hollan, James D., Hutchins, Edwin L., and Weitzman, Louis. STEAMER: An interactive inspectable simulation–based training system. *AI Magazine* 5 (2) (Summer 1984): 15–27.

Holler, Frederick. Toward a reference theory. *RQ* 14 (4) (Summer 1975): 301–309.

Horowitz, Roberta S. and Weiner, John M. Article processing after retrieval. In *MEDINFO 86,* edited by R. Salamon, B. Blum, M. Jorgensen. Elsevier North–Holland, 1986: 550–552.

Hudson, Judith and Walker, Geraldine. The year's work in technical services research, 1986. *Library Resources and Technical Services* (December 1987): 275–286.

Huet, B. and Pourriat, J.L. Premisses for an information systems design method integrating an intelligent module. In *MEDINFO 86,* edited by R. Salamon, B. Blum, M. Jorgensen. Elsevier North–Holland, 1986: 592–596.

Humphrey, Susanne M. and Kapoor, Anil. The MedIndex system: research on interactive knowledge–based indexing of the medical literature. LHNCBC Technical Report 88–1. Bethesda, MD: U.S. Dept. of Health and Human Services/Public Health Service/National Institutes of Health. 1988.

Hunt, V. Daniel. *Artificial Intelligence and Expert Systems Sourcebook.* New York: Chapman and Hall, 1986.

Hurley, Bernard J. Information transaction processing in a tandem environment. *Library and Information Technology Association (LITA) 2nd National Conference.* Boston, MA. October 5, 1988.

Hutchins, Edwin L., Hollan, James D., and Norman, Donald A. Direct manipulation interfaces. In *User Centered System Design: New Perspectives on Human–Computer Interaction,* edited by Norman, D.A. and Draper, S.W. Hillsdale, NJ: Erlbaum, 1986: 87–124.

Immroth, John Phillip. Analysis of Vocabulary Control in Library of Congress Classification and Subject Headings. Littleton, CO: Libraries Unlimited, 1971: 90–101, 107–8.

Informatics 8. *Advances in Intelligent Retrieval: Informatics 8.* London: Aslib, 1985.

Ingwersen, Peter. Search procedures in the library – analyzed from the cognitive point of view. *Journal of Documentation* 38 (3) (Sept. 1982): 165–191.

Ingwersen, Peter. Online man–machine interaction facilities: A cognitive view. In *Representation and Exchange of Knowledge as a Basis of Information Processes,* edited by H.J. Dietschmann. Elsevier North–Holland, 1984: 325–358.

Ingwersen, Peter, Kajberg, Leif, and Pejtersen, Annelise M. (eds.) *Information Technology and Information Use.* London: Taylor Graham, 1986.

Ingwersen, Peter and Pejtersen, Annelise M. User requirements – empirical research and information systems design. In *Information Technology and Information Use,* edited by Ingwersen, Peter. London: Taylor Graham, 1986: 111–125.

Ingwersen, Peter. Cognitive analysis and the role of the intermediary in information retrieval. In *Intelligent Information Systems: Progress and Prospects.* Chichester, England: Ellis Horwood (1986): 206–237.

Jachowicz, J. L. Application of classification as a basis for the formulation of a thesaurus. *Bombay: Third International Study Conference on Classification as a Basis for the Formulation of Thesaurus* (1975): 18–24.

Jackson, M. *System Development.* Englewood–Cliffs, NJ: Prentice–Hall, 1983.

Jackson, Peter. *Introduction to Expert Systems.* Reading, MA: Addison–Wesley, 1986.

Jacobson, Carol E. and Witges, Shirley A. (comps.) *Proceedings of the Second Conference on Computer Interfaces and Intermediaries.* Alexandria, VA: Office of Information Systems and Technology, Defense Technical Information Center, 1986. NTIS AD A174–000–0.

Jahoda, Gerald and Braunagel, Judith S. *The Librarian and Reference Queries: A Systematic Approach.* New York: Academic Press, 1980.

Jahoda, Gerald and Olson, Paul E. Models of reference – analyzing the reference process. *RQ* 12 (Winter 1972): 148–160.

Jahoda, Gerald et al. The reference process: modules for instruction. ERIC document ED 136 765, 1976.

Jahoda, Gerald. The process of answering reference questions: a test of a descriptive model. ERIC document ED 136 769, 1977.

Jahoda, Gerald, Braunagel, Judith, and Nath, Herbert. The reference process: modules for instruction. *RQ* (Fall 1977): 8–12.

Janosky, Beverly, Smith, Philip J. and Hildreth, Charles. Online library catalog systems: an analysis of user errors. *International Journal of Man–Machine Studies* 25 (1986): 573–592.

Jenkins, Richard A. *Supercomputers of Today and Tomorrow: The Parallel Processing Revolution.* Blue Ridge Summit, PA: Tab Books, 1986.

Johnson, Jeff A. The desktop metaphor as an approach to user interface design. In *The Range of Computing. 1985 ACM Annual Conference.* Association for Computing Machinery, 1985: 548–549.

Jones, Kevin P. (ed.) *Informatics 7: Intelligent Information Retrieval.* London: Aslib, 1983.

Jones, Kevin P. Ten years of informatics. In *Advances in Intelligent Retrieval: Informatics 8.* London: Aslib (1985): 263–309.

Jones, Kevin P. and Bell, Colin L. M. MORPHS – an intelligent retrieval system. *Aslib Proceedings* 38 (3) (March 1986): 71–79.

Kallfass, Monika and Seeger, Thomas. From the stereotype approach of knowledge representation to a polymorphous concept of knowledge organization. In *Representation and Exchange of Knowledge as a Basis of Information Processes,* edited by H.J. Dietschmann. Elsevier North–Holland, 1984: 61–73.

Kantor, Paul B. Information retrieval issues in the design of expert systems. *Proceedings of the American Society for Information Science Annual Conference* (1986): 113–117.

Kantor, Paul B. Scholar's cross–reference system. In *Annual Review of OCLC Research, July 1987–June 1988.* Dublin, OH: OCLC, 1988: 26–27.

Karna, Kamal N. (ed.) *Expert Systems in Government Symposium.* New York: IEEE, 1985.

Kehoe, Cynthia A. Interfaces and expert systems for online retrieval. *Online Review* 9 (6) (1985): 489–505.

Kelly, George A. *The Psychology of Personal Constructs.* New York: Norton, 1955.

Kerschberg, Larry (ed.) *Expert Database Systems: Proceedings from the First International Workshop.* Menlo Park, CA: Benjamin/Cummings, 1986.

Kidd, Alison L. (ed.) *Knowledge Acquisition for Expert Systems: A Practical Handbook.* New York: Plenum Press, 1987.

Kidd, Alison and Cooper, Martin B. Man–machine interface issues in the construction and use of an expert system. *International Journal of Man–Machine Studies* 22 (1985): 91–102.

Kimura, Michio. Steps toward feasible consultation systems: The knowledge–based antibiotic medication counselling system ANTICIPATOR. In *MEDINFO 86*, edited by R. Salamon, B. Blum, M. Jorgensen. Elsevier North–Holland, 1986: 276–281.

King, Donald W. and Palmour, Vernon E. User behavior. In *Changing Patterns in Information Retrieval: 10th Annual National Information Retrieval Colloquium.* Washington: ASIS, 1974: 7–33.

Kinoshita, June and Palevsky, Nicholas G. Computing with neural networks. *High Technology* (May 1987).

Kinoshita, June. Neural networks at work. *Scientific American.* (November 1988): 134–135.

Korfhage, Robert R. Intelligent information retrieval: issues in user modelling. In *Expert Systems in Government Symposium*, edited by Karna, Kamal N. Washington: IEEE Computer Society Press, (1985): 474–482.

Kostrewski, Barbara. Structural considerations for the derivation of application linked reference languages for medical information systems. In *Informatics 5. Analysis of Meaning.* London: Aslib, 1979: 148–154.

Krawczak, Deb, Smith, Philip J., Shute, Steven J. and Chignell, Mark. EP–X: A knowledge–based system to aid in searches of the environmental pollution literature. In *Engineering of Knowledge– Based Systems. Second Conference on Artificial Intelligence Applications.* New York: IEEE (1985): 552–557.

Kroenke, David M. and Dolan, Kathleen A. *Database Processing: Fundamentals, Design and Implementation.* 3rd. ed Chicago, IL: Science Research Associates, 1988.

Kuhn, Allen D. and Cotter, Gladys A. The DoD Gateway Information System (DGIS): User interface design. In *Proceedings of the 49th Annual ASIS Meeting* 23. American Society for Information Science. (1986): 150–157.

Kuhns, J. L. Data retrieval and relational logic. *Drexel Library Quarterly* 14 (2) (April 1978): 90–105.

Kunz, W. and Rittel, H. How to know what is known: designing crutches for communication. In *Representation and Exchange of Knowledge as a Basis of Information Processes*, edited by H. J. Dietschmann. Elsevier North–Holland, 1984: 51–60.

Kurdyla, Edward M., Jr. Interview on electronic publishing and information delivery at OCLC. *OCLC Newsletter* (November/December 1988): 26.

Lamb, M.R., Auster, E.W. and Westel, E.R. A friendly front–end for bibliographic retrieval: the implementation of a flexible interface. In *Pro-*

ceedings of the 48th Annual ASIS Meeting 22. American Society for Information Science. (1985): 229–235.

Lancaster, F. Wilfrid. Trends in subject indexing from 1957 to 2000 In *New Trends in Documentation and Information*, edited by Taylor, P.J. 1980.

Lancaster, F.W. Microelectronics and the communications revolution. In *Application of Mini- and Micro- Computers to Information, Documentation, and Libraries*, edited by C. Keren and L. Perlmutter. Elsevier, 1983: 111–119.

Lesk, Michael. Automatic sense disambiguation. In *Annual Review of OCLC Research, July 1987–June 1988*. Dublin, OH: OCLC, 1988: 62–64.

Levy, Joe. Computers that learn to forget. *New Scientist* (August 11, 1988): 36–39.

Levy, Louise. Gateway software: Is it for you? *Online* (November 1984): 67–79.

Liebowitz, Jay. *Introduction to Expert Systems*. Santa Cruz, CA: Mitchell Publishing Co, 1988.

Liebowitz, Jay. Common fallacies about expert systems. *Computers and Society* 16 (4) (Winter/Spring 1987): 28–33.

Lindley, D.V. The probability approach to the treatment of uncertainty in artificial intelligence and expert systems. In *Proceedings of the Calculus of Uncertainty in Artificial Intelligence and Expert Systems Conference*. Washington, DC: George Washington University, 1984.

Lippmann, Walter. *Public Opinion*. New York: Macmillan, 1922.

Lubbock, Georgette. Meaning in IR: The problem behind the problem. In *Informatics 5. Analysis of Meaning*. London: Aslib, 1979: 293–302.

Luconi, Fred L. et al. Expert systems: the next challenge for managers. *Sloan Management Review* (Summer 1986): 3–14.

Lynch. In Hudson, Judith and Walker, Geraldine. The year's work in technical services research, 1986. *Library Resources and Technical Services* (December 1987): 275–286.

MacCafferty, Maxine and Gray, Kathleen. *Analysis of Meaning: Informatics 5*. London: Aslib, 1979.

MacKay, D.M. Informational analysis of questions and commands. In *Information Theory*, edited by Colin Cherry. London: Butterworths, 1961: 469–476.

Macleod, Ian A. Handling multiple data bases in document retrieval. In *Research and Development in Information Retrieval. Eighth Annual In'tl ACM SIGIR Conference*. Baltimore: Assn. for Computing Machinery, 1985: 26–32.

Mah, C. P. and D'Amore, R.J. *N-Gram Indexing: A New Alternative in Text Processing*. McLean, VA: PAR Government Systems Corporation, 1985.

Mandel, Carol A. and Herschmann, Judith. Online subject access – enhancing the library catalog. *Journal of Academic Librarianship* 9 (3) (1983): 148–155.

Mandel, Carol. Multiple thesauri in online library bibliographic systems: a report prepared for Library of Congress Processing Services. Washington, DC: Cataloging Distribution Service, 1987.

Mandler, George. Organization and memory. In *The Psychology of Learning and Motivation: Advances in Research and Theory.* Vol. 1, edited by K.W. and J.T. Spence. New York: Academic Press, 1967.

Mannock, K.L. and Leung, C.H.C. An expert system for efficient office object management. In *Expert Systems 85. Proceedings of the 5th Technical Conference of the British Computer Society.* Cambridge Univ. Press., 1985: 241–258.

Marchionini, Gary and Shneiderman, Ben. Finding facts vs. browsing: knowledge in hypertext systems. *Computer* 21 (1) (January 1988): 70–80.

Marcus, Richard S. An experimental comparison of the effectiveness of computers and humans as search intermediaries. *Journal of the American Society for Information Science* 34 (6) (1983): 381–404.

Marcus, Richard S. Development and testing of expert systems for retrieval assistance. In *Proceedings of the 48th Annual ASIS Meeting* 22. American Society for Information Science. (1985): 289–292.

Marcus, Richard S. Design questions in the development of expert systems for retrieval assistance. In *Proceedings of the 49th Annual ASIS Meeting* 23. American Society for Information Science. (1986): 185–189.

Marcus, Richard S. CONIT: expert retrieval assistant. In *MEDINFO 86*, edited by R. Salamon, B. Blum, M. Jorgensen. Elsevier North–Holland, 1986: 1156.

Marcus, Richard S. Issues for expert systems for retrieval assistance. In *Second Conference on Computer Interfaces and Intermediaries for Information Retrieval.* Alexandria, VA: Defense Technical Info. Ctr., 1986: 213–214.

Markey, Karen. Subject Searching in Library Catalogs: Before and After the Introduction of Online Catalogs. *OCLC Library Information and Computer Science Series.* Dublin, OH: OCLC, 1984.

Markey, Karen. Dewey decimal classification online project: evaluation of a library schedule and index integrated into the subject searching capabilities of an online catalog. OCLC Report No: OCLC/OPR/RR–86/1, 1986 Dublin, OH: OCLC.

Markey, Karen and Visine–Goetz, Diane. Increasing the accessibility of Library of Congress subject headings in online bibliographic systems. *Annual Review of OCLC Research, 1988* (1987–88) 32–34.

Maron, M.E. Theory and foundations of information retrieval. *Drexel Library Quarterly* 14 (2) (April 1978): 1–9.

Martin, James H. Knowledge acquisition through natural language dialog. In *Engineering of Knowledge–Based Systems. 2nd Conference on Artificial Intelligence Applications.* Washington: IEEE Computer Society Press, 1985: 582–586.

Martin, James and Oxman, Steven. *Building Expert Systems: A Tutorial.* Prentice Hall: Englewood Cliffs, NJ, 1988.

McCall, R., et al. A database model as the basis of a workstation for the designer. In *Representation and Exchange of Knowledge as a Basis of Information Processes,* edited by H. J. Dietschmann. Elsevier North–Holland, 1984: 301–324.

McCarthy, John. Some expert systems need common sense. In *Computer Culture: The Scientific, Intellectual, and Social Impact of the Computer,* edited by H. Pagels. New York: New York Academy of Sciences, 1984: 129–137.

McCone, Gary K. Expert systems or librarian ex machina [Artificial Intelligence/Expert Systems Interest Group program report]. *LITA Newsletter* 30 (Fall 1987): 3–4.

McCorduck, Pamela. *Machines Who Think, a Personal Inquiry into the History and Prospects of Artificial Intelligence.* San Francisco: Freeman, 1979.

McDermott, John. R1: The formative years. *AI Magazine* 2 (1981): 21–29.

McGraw, Karen L. Artificial intelligence: The competitive edge in integrated systems development. *T.I. Engineering Journal* 3 (Jan.–Feb. 1986): 1–12.

McGraw, Karen L. Guidelines for producing documentation for expert systems. *IEEE Transactions on Professional Communications* 29 (4) (Dec. 1986): 42–47.

McGregor, D.R. and Malone, J.R. An architectural approach to advances in information retrieval. In *Advances in Intelligent Retrieval: Informatics 8* (1985): 35–46.

Meadow, Charles T. and Cochrane, Pauline. *Basics of Online Searching.* New York: Wiley, 1981.

Meadow, Charles T., et al. A computer intermediary for interactive database searching. I. Design. *Journal of the American Society for Information Science* 33 (September 1982): 325–332.

Meadow, Charles T., et al. A computer intermediary for interactive database searching. II. Evaluation. *Journal of the American Society for Information Science* 33 (November 1982): 357–364.

Meadow, Charles T., et al. OAK – a new approach to user search assistance. In *Second Conference on Computer Interfaces and Intermediaries for Information Retrieval.* Alexandria, VA: Defense Technical Info. Ctr., 1986: 215–223.

Meredith, Joseph C. Machine–assisted approach to general reference materials. *Journal of the American Society for Information Science* 22 (May–June 1971): 176–186.

Meredith, Joseph C. Refsearch Search System (REFSEARCH) User's Manual. U.S. Dept. of Health, Education and Welfare. Office of Education. Bureau of Research. Final Rpt. Project 7–1085. grant no. OEG–1–7–071085–4286. Berkeley, 1971.

Metzler, Douglas P., et al. An expert system approach to natural language processing. In *Proceedings of the 48th Annual ASIS Meeting* 22. American Society for Information Science. (1985): 301–307.

Micco, H. Mary. An exploratory study of three subject access systems in medicine: LCSH, MeSH and PRECIS. Ph.D. Dissertation. University of Pittsburgh, 1980.

Micco, H. Mary and Smith, Irma. Designing an expert system for the reference function subject access to information. In *Proceedings of the 49th Annual ASIS Meeting* 23. American Society for Information Science. (1986): 204–210.

Micco, Mary and Smith, Irma. Expert systems in libraries: do they have a place? *Library Software Review* (Jan.–Feb. 1987).

Micco, Mary and Smith, Irma. Expert systems and vocabulary control: from the perspective of a reference librarian. Unpublished manuscript.

Michie, Donald. Automating the synthesis of expert knowledge. *Aslib Proceedings* 36 (9) (Sept. 1984): 337–343.

Michie, Donald. Current developments in artificial intelligence and expert systems. *Zygon* 20 (4) (December 1985): 375–389. Reprinted from Handbook of information technology and office systems. Amsterdam: Elsevier, 1986.

Michie, Donald Current developments in artificial intelligence and expert systems. In *Handbook of Information Technology and Office Systems*, edited by A. E. Cawkell. Amsterdam: Elsevier Science Publishers, 1986.

Michie, Donald. *On Machine Intelligence.* 2nd edition. Chichester, England: Ellis Horwood, 1986.

Mili, Hafedh and Rada, Roy. A statistically built knowledge base. In *Expert Systems in Government Symposium*, edited by Karna, Kamal N. Washington: IEEE Computer Society Press, 1985: 457–463.

Miller, George A. The magical number seven, plus or minus two: Some limits on our capacity for processing information. *Psychological Review* 63 (March 1956): 81–97.

Miller, Perry. *Expert Critiquing Systems: Practice–Based Medical Consultation.* New York: Springer–Verlag, 1986.

Minsky, Marvin. A framework for representing knowledge. In *The Psychology of Computer Vision*, edited by P. Winston. New York: McGraw–Hill, 1985.

Minsky, Marvin. *Society of Mind.* New York: Simon and Schuster, 1986.

Minsky, Marvin. A framework for representing knowledge. In *Mind Design*, edited by J. Haugeland. Cambridge, MA: MIT Press, 1981: 95–128. Also in Brachman & Levesque (1985): 245–262.

Mischo, William H. Expanded subject access to reference collection materials. *Journal of Library Automation* 12 (4) (December 1979): 338–354.

Mishkoff, Henry C. *Understanding Artificial Intelligence.* Indianapolis: H.W. SAMS, 1988.

Mitev, Nathalie Nadia and Walker, Steven. Information retrieval aids in an online public access catalogue: Automatic intelligent search sequencing. In *Advances in Intelligent Retrieval: Informatics 8.* London: Aslib, 1985: 215–226.

Morehead, David R. and Rouse, William B. Human–computer interaction in information seeking tasks. *Information Processing and Management* 19 (4) (1983): 243–253.

Morehead, David R. and Rouse, William B. Models of human behavior in information seeking tasks. *Information Processing and Management* 18 (4) (1982): 193–205.

Mukhopadhyay, Uttam, et al. An intelligent system for document retrieval in distributed office environments. *Journal of the American Society for Information Science* 37 (3) (1986): 123–135.

Najarian, Suzanne E. Organizational factors in human memory: implications for library organization and access systems. *Library Quarterly* 51 (3) (1981): 269–291.

Nau, D.S. Expert computer systems. *IEEE Computer* (February 1983): 87–91.

Neches, Robert, Swartout, William R. and Moore, Johanna D. Enhanced maintenance and explanation of expert systems through explicit models of their development. *IEEE Transactions on Software Engineering* SE–11 (11) (November 1985): 1337–1351.

Negroponte, Nicholas. *Soft Architecture Machines.* Cambridge, MA: MIT Press, 1975.

Neill, S.D. Problem solving and the reference process. *RQ* 14 (4) (Summer 1975): 310–315.

Nelson, Ted. Interactive systems and the design of virtuality. Part I. *Creative Computing* 6 (11) (November 1980): 56–62.

Nelson, Ted. Interactive systems and the design of virtuality. Part II. *Creative Computing* 6 (12) (1980): 95–106.

Nelson, Ted. A new home for the mind. *Datamation* 28 (3) (March 1982): 169–180.

Newell, Allen and Simon, Herbert A. *Human Problem Solving*. Englewood Cliffs, NJ: Prentice Hall, 1972.

Nguyen, Long Thanh and Greenes, Robert A. A framework for the use of computed links in the EXPLORER–1 knowledge management system. In *MEDINFO 86*, edited by R. Salamon, B. Blum, M. Jorgensen. Elsevier North–Holland, 1986: 891–894.

Niehoff, Robert. *Evaluation of the Vocabulary Switching System: Final Report*. Columbus, OH: Batelle Memorial Institute, 1984.

Nilsson, Nils. Fundamentals and current research. [Artificial Intelligence: Convergence of Mind and Machine?] Speech at American Library Association Annual Conference. San Francisco, CA. June 30, 1987.

Noerr, Peter L. Information navigation. In *Informatics 5. Analysis of Meaning*. London: Aslib, 1979: 221–226.

Noerr, Peter and Bivins Noerr, Kathleen. The electronic scroll. In *The Application of Mini- and Micro– Computers in Information, Documention, and Libraries*, edited by C. Keren and L. Perlmutter. Elsevier North–Holland: 41–54.

Norman, Donald A. Some observations on mental models. In *Mental Models*, edited by Genter, Dedre and Stevens, Albert L. Hillsdale, NJ: Erlbaum, 1983: 7–14.

Norman, Donald A. Cognitive engineering. In *User Centered System Design: New Perspectives on Human–Computer Interaction*, edited by Norman, DA and Draper, SW. Hillsdale, NJ: Erlbaum, 1986: 31–61.

Norman, Donald A. and Draper, Stephen W. (eds.) *User Centered System Design: New Perspectives on Human–Computer Interaction*. Hillsdale, NJ: Erlbaum, 1986.

Nowak, Elzbieta J. and Szablowski, Bogumil F. Expert systems in scientific information exchange. *Journal of Information Science* 8 (1984): 103–111.

Nycum, S. N. Legal liability for expert systems. In *MEDINFO 86*, edited by R. Salamon, B. Blum, M. Jorgensen. Elsevier North–Holland, 1986: 1069–1071.

OCLC Online Computer Library Center. *Annual Review of OCLC Research. July 1987–June 1988*. Dublin, Ohio: OCLC.

Obermeier, Klaus K. Expert systems – enhancement of productivity? In *Productivity in the Information Age. Proceedings of the 46th ASIS Annual Meeting* 20. American Society for Information Science, 1983: 9–13.

Obermeier, Klaus and Cooper, Linda E. Information network facility organizing system (INFOS) – an expert system for information retrieval. *1984: Challenges to an Information Society. Proceedings of the 47th ASIS Annual Meeting* 21. American Society for Information Science, 1984: 95–98.

Oblitey, William W. A formal language model for local area network configuration. Ph.D. IDIS–University of Pittsburgh, 1988.

Oddy, R.N. Information retrieval through man–machine dialogue. *Journal of Documentation* 33 (1) (March 1977): 1–14.

Oddy, Robert. Retrieving references by dialogue rather than by query formulation. *Journal of Informatics* 1 (1) (April 1977): 37–53.

Oddy, Robert N., Palmquist, Ruth A. and Crawford, Margaret A. Representation of anomalous states of knowledge in information retrieval. In *Proceedings of the 49th Annual ASIS Meeting* 23. American Society for Information Science, 1986: 248–254.

O'Malley, Claire E. Helping users help themselves. In *User Centered System Design: New Perspectives on Human–Computer Interaction*, edited by Norman, DA and Draper, SW. Hillsdale, NJ: Erlbaum, 1986: 377–398.

O'Neill, Edward T. and Aluri, Rao. Library of Congress subject heading patterns in OCLC monographic records. *Library Resources and Technical Services* 25 (Jan./Mar. 1981): 63–80.

O'Neill, Margaret and Morris, Anne. Expert systems in the United Kingdom: an evaluation of development methodologies. *Expert Systems* 6(2) (April 1989): 90–99.

Owen, David. Answers first, then questions. In *User centered system design: New perspectives on human–computer interaction*, edited by Norman, DA and Draper, SW. Hillsdale, NJ: Erlbaum, 1986: 361–375.

Paice, Chris. Expert systems for information retrieval? *Aslib Proceedings* 38 (10) (Oct. 1986): 343–353.

Pao, Miranda Lee. Semantic and pragmatic retrieval. *1984: Challenges to an Information Society. Proceedings of the 47th ASIS Annual Meeting* 21. American Society for Information Science. (1984): 134–136.

Parrott, James R. Expert systems for reference work. *Microcomputers for Information Management* 3 (3) (September 1986): 155–171.

Parrott, James R. REFSIM: a bimodal knowledge–based reference training and consultation system. *Reference Services Review* 16 (1–2) (1988): 61–68.

Partridge, Derek. *Artificial Intelligence: Applications in the Future of Software Engineering*. Chichester, England: E. Horwood, 1986.

Penniman, David W. Tomorrow's library today. In *Annual Review of OCLC Research, July 1987–June 1988*. Dublin, OH: OCLC. (1988): 59–60.

Petersen, Toni. The AAT: A model for the restructuring of LCSH. *Journal of Academic Librarianship* 9 (September 1983): 207–210.

Pfleeger, Shari Lawrence. *Software Engineering: The Production of Quality Software*. New York: Macmillan, 1987.

Phrabha, Chandra. Managing large retrievals. *Annual Review of OCLC Research, 1987–1988*.

Pierce, John R. *Languages and Machines: Computers in Translation and Linguistics.* Washington, DC: National Academy of Sciences/National Research Council. Pub. No. 1416. 1966.

Pollack, Michael A. and Greenes, Robert A. A pictorial simulation construction kit for enhancing knowledge–based learning. In *MEDINFO 86*, edited by R. Salamon, B. Blum, M. Jorgensen. Elsevier North–Holland, 1986: 887–890.

Pollitt, A.S. A rule–based system as an intermediary for searching cancer therapy literature on MEDLINE. In *Intelligent Information Systems: Progress and Prospects.* Chichester, England: Ellis Horwood, 1986: 82–126.

Pollitt, Arthur Steven. Expert systems and the information intermediary: tackling some of the problems of naive end–user search specification and formulation. In *Intelligent Information Systems for the Information Society*, edited by B.C. Brookes. Elsevier North–Holland, 1986: 100–108.

Pollitt, Steven. CANSEARCH: An expert systems approach to document retrieval. *Information Processing and Management* 23 (2) (1987): 119–138.

Pool, Ithiel de Solla. Culture of electronic print. *Daedulus* 111 (Fall 1982): 17–31.

Pool, Ithiel de Solla. *Technologies of Freedom.* Cambridge, MA: Belknap Press, 1983.

Porter, M.F. An algorithm for suffix stripping. *Program* 14 (3) (July 1980): 130–137.

Pratt, Allan D. *The Information of the Image.* Norwood, NJ: Ablex, 1982.

Preece, Scott E. Process–modeling retrieval interfaces. In *The Information Community: An Alliance for Progress. Proceedings of the 44th ASIS Annual Meeting* 18. American Society for Information Science. (1981): 274–75.

Prerau, David S. Selection of an appropriate domain for an expert system. *AI Magazine* (Summer 1985): 26–30.

Psotka, Joseph. Intelligent design environments and assistant systems. In *Expert Systems in Government Symposium*, edited by Karna, Kamal N. Washington: IEEE Computer Society Press, 1985: 225–228.

Putnam, L. A general empirical solution to the macro–software sizing and estimation project. *IEEE Transactions on Software Engineering* SE–4 (4) (1978): 345–361.

Quillian, Ross M. Semantic memory. In *Semantic Information Processing*, edited by Minsky, Marvin. Cambridge, MA: MIT Press, 1968: 227–270.

Quinlan, J. Ross. Discovering rules by induction form large collections of examples. In *Expert Systems in the Microelectronic Age*, edited by Michie, Donald. Edinburgh: Edinburgh University Press, 1979: 33–46.

Quinlan, J. Ross. Learning efficient classification procedures and their application to chess end–games. In *Machine Learning: An Artificial Intelligence Approach,* edited by Michalski, Ryszard et al. Los Altos, CA: Morgan Kaufmann, 1983.

Rada, Roy and Coccia, Craig. A knowledge base for retrieval evaluation. In *The Range of Computing* 1985 ACM annual conference. Association for Computing Machinery. (1985): 360–367.

Rada, Roy et al. A medical informatics thesaurus. In *MEDINFO 86,* edited by R. Salamon, B. Blum, M. Jorgensen. Elsevier North–Holland, 1986: 1164–1172.

Rada, Roy and Martin, Brian K. Augmenting thesauri for information systems. *ACM Transactions on Office Information Systems* 5 (4) (October 1987): 378–392.

Raeth, Peter G. Two PC–based expert system shells for the first–time developer. *Computer (IEEE)* 21(11) (Nov. 1988): 73–80.

Rajinikanth, M. and Bose, Prasanta K. A knowledge–based approach to database query processing. *Artificial Intelligence and Its Applications,* edited by Cohn, A.G. and Thomas, J.R. New York: Wiley, 1986: 107–121.

Reddy, Raj and Zue, Victor. Tomorrow's computers — the challenges: Speech understanding. *IEEE Spectrum* (November 1983): 84–87.

Reddy, Raj, et al. *The HEARSAY Speech Understanding System: An Example of the Recognition Process.* New York: IEEE Transactions on Computers. C–25: 427–431.

Reichgelt, Han and Harmelen, Frank van. Relevant criteria for choosing an inference engine in expert systems. In *Expert Systems 85. Proceedings of the Fifth Technical Conference of the British Computer Society.* Cambridge Univ. Press., 1985: 21–30.

Reichman, Rachel. *Getting Computers to Talk Like You and Me: Discourse Context, Focus, and Semantics (an ATN Model).* Cambridge, MA: MIT Press, 1985.

Rennels, Glen. Computational Model of Reasoning from the Clinical Literature. Springer Verlag Lecture Notes in Medical Informatics, no. 32. New York: Springer–Verlag, 1987.

Rennels, Glenn D., Shortliffe, Edward H., et al. Reasoning from the clinical literature: The roundsman system. *MEDINFO 86,* edited by R. Salamon, B. Blum, M. Jorgensen. Elsevier North–Holland, 198.

Rich, Elaine. User modeling via stereotypes. *Cognitive Science* 3 (1979): 329–354.

Rich, Elaine. *Artificial Intelligence.* New York: McGraw–Hill, 1983.

Richardson, John R. Toward an expert system for reference service: a research agenda for the 1990's. *College and Research Libraries* 50 (2) (March 1989): 231–248.

Richer, M. Five commercial expert systems tools: an evaluation. *The Artificial Intelligence Report* 2 (8) (August 1985).

Rigby, Malcolm. The UDC in mechanized subject information retrieval. In *Subject Retrieval in the Seventies: New Directions: An International Symposium*, edited by Hans Wellisch and Thomas D. Wilson. Westport, CT: Greenwood Press, 1972.

Ripley, G. David. DVI – a digital multimedia technology. *Communications of the ACM* 32 (7) (July 1989): 811–822. [special issue]

Roach, J. and Wilding, M. Improving human–computer interaction by learning a model of user preferences. In *Engineering of Knowledge-Based Systems. 2nd Conference on Artificial Intelligence Applications*. Washington: IEEE Computer Society Press, 1985: 364–369.

Robertson, David, et al. The ECO browser. In *Expert Systems 85. Proceedings of the Fifth Technical Conference of the British Computer Society*. Cambridge Univ. Press., 1985: 143–156.

Robertson, S.E. Progress in documentation: theories and models in information retrieval. *Journal of Documentation* 33 (2) (June 1977): 126–148.

Robertson, Stephen E. Indexing theory and retrieval effectiveness. *Drexel Library Quarterly* 14 (2) (April 1978): 40–56.

Robertson, S.E. Between aboutness and meaning. In *Informatics 5. Analysis of Meaning*. London: Aslib, 1979.

Robertson, S.E. and Sparck–Jones, Karen. Relevance weighting of search terms. *Journal of the American Society for Informations Science* 27 (3) (May–June 1986): 129–46.

Rogers, Jean B. *A Turbo PROLOG Primer*. Reading, MA: Addison–Wesley Publishing Co, 1987.

Rosenberg, Steven. Expert systems and the design of powerful user interfaces. In *The Information Community: An Alliance for Progress. Proceedings of the 44th ASIS Annual Meeting* 18 American Society for Information Science. (1981): 285–87.

Rosenberg, Victor. Application of Psychometric Techniques to Determine the Attitudes of Individuals Toward Information Seeking. Center for the Information Sciences. Lehigh University. Studies in the Man–System Interface in Libraries, Report no. 2, Bethlehem, PA, 1966.

Roualt, Jacques. Linguistic methods in information retrieval systems. In *Advances in Intelligent Retrieval: Informatics 8* (1985): 148–162.

Rubin, D.C. and Kontis, T.C. A schema for common cents. *Memory and Cognition* 11 (1983): 335–341.

Ruth, Christopher and Stephen Ruth. *Developing Expert Systems Using 1st–Class*. Santa Cruz, CA: Mitchell Publishing Inc., 1988.

Safran, Charles, et al. A computer programm for interactive searches of a medical database. In *MEDINFO 86*, edited by R. Salamon, B. Blum, M. Jorgensen. Elsevier North–Holland (1986): 545–549.

Salamon, Roger, Blum, Bruce, and Jorgensen, Mogens (eds.) *MEDINFO 86. Proceedings of the Fifth Conference on Medical Informatics.* Amsterdam: Elsevier North-Holland, 1986.

Salton, G. Some characteristics of future information systems. In *Application of Mini– and Micro– Computers to Information, Documentation, and Libraries,* edited by C. Keren and L. Perlmutter. Elsevier, 1983: 11–23.

Salton, G., et al. Automatic query formulations in information retrieval. *Journal of the American Society for Information Science* 34 (4) (1983): 262–280.

Salton, Gerard and McGill, Michael J. *Introduction to Modern Information Retrieval.* New York: McGraw–Hill, 1983.

Salton, Gerard. On the use of knowledge based processing in automatic text retrieval. In *Proceedings of the 49th Annual ASIS Meeting* 23. American Society for Information Science. (1986): 277–287.

Salton, Gerard. Another Look at Automatic Text–retrieval Systems. *Communications of the ACM* 29 (7) (July 1986): 648–656.

Salton, Gerard. Automatic phrase construction for the representation of text content. In *Annual Review of OCLC Research, July 1987–June 1988.* Dublin, OH: OCLC, 1988: 30–31.

Saracevic, Tefko and Baxter, Matthew A. On a method for studying the structure and nature of requests in information retrieval. In *Productivity in the Information Age. Proceedings of the 46th ASIS Annual Meeting* 20. American Society for Information Science. (1983): 22–25.

Saracevic, Tefko, Kantor, Paul, Chamis, Alice, and Trivison, D. A study of information and retrieving. I. Background and methodology. *Journal of the American Society for Information Science* 39 (3) (1988): 161–176.

Saracevic, Tefko and Kantor, Paul. A study of information seeking and retrieving. II. Users, questions, and effectiveness. *Journal of the American Society for Information Science* 39 (3) (1988): 177–196.

Saracevic, Tefko and Kantor, Paul. A study of information seeking and retrieving. III. Searchers, searches, and overlap. *Journal of the American Society for Information Science* 39 (3) (1988): 197–216.

Schank, Roger and Abelson, Robert P. *Scripts, Plans, Goals and Understanding: An Inquiry into Human Knowledge Structures.* Hillsdale, NJ: Erlbaum, 1977.

Schank, Roger C. and Riesback, Christopher (eds.) *Inside Computer Understanding: Five Programs Plus Miniatures.* Hillsdale, NJ: Erlbaum, 1981.

Schank, Roger C. and Childers, Peter G. *The Cognitive Computer: On Language, Learning and Artificial Intelligence.* Reading, MA: Addison–Wesley, 1984.

Schroder, J.J. Study of strategies used in online searching: 3. Query refining. *Online Review* 7 (3) (1983): 229–236.

Schwartz, Tom J. [et al.] Artificial intelligence in the personal computer environment. [and other papers] In *The Range of Computing*. 1985 ACM annual conference. Association for Computing Machinery. (1985): 484–491.

Scripps–Howard News Service. Fuzzy logic: Scientists worldwide have itch to put "fuzzy logic" to use. *Pittsburgh Press,* May 28, 1989.

Sejnowski, Terrence J., Koch, Cristof, and Churchland, Patricia S. Computational neuroscience. *Science* 241 (September 9, 1988): 1299–1306.

Settel, Barbara (ed.) Subject description of books: A manual of procedures for augmenting subject descriptions in library catalogs. Syracuse, New York: Syracuse University, School of Information Studies, 1977. Research Study No.3.

Settel, Barbara and Cochrane, Pauline. Augmenting subject descriptions for books in online catalogs. *Database* (December 1982): 15–23.

Shafer, G. *A Mathematical Theory of Evidence*. Princeton, NJ: Princeton University Press, 1976.

Shapiro, Ezra. AI, AI, oh! [VP Expert shell] *Byte* (June 1987): 321–323.

Shapiro, Stuart C. (ed.) *Encyclopedia of Artificial Intelligence* (2 vols.) New York: Wiley, 1987.

Shaw, Mildred L.G. and Gaines, Brian R. An interactive knowledge–elicitation technique using personal construct technology. In *Knowledge Acquisition for Expert Systems: An Introductory Framework*, edited by Kidd, Alison L. New York: Plenum, 1987: 109–136.

Shepherd, Michael A., Lo, A. and Phillips, W.J. A study of the relationship between user profiles and user queries. In *Research and Development in Information Retrieval. Eighth Annual In'tl. ACM SIGIR Conference*. Baltimore: Assn. for Computing Machinery, 1985: 274–281.

Shneiderman, Ben. *Designing the User Interface: Strategies for Effective Human–Computer Interaction*. Addison–Wesley: Reading, MA, 1987.

Shoval, Peretz. Knowledge representation in consultation systems for users of retrieval systems. In *Application of Mini– and Micro– Computers to Information, Documentation, and Libraries*, edited by C. Keren and L. Perlmutter. Elsevier, 1983: 631–643.

Shoval, Peretz. Principles, procedures and rules in an expert system for information retrieval. *Information Processing and Management* 21 (6) (1985): 475–487.

Simon, Herbert A. *Models of Thought*. New Haven: Yale Univ. Press, 1979.

Simonds, Michael J. Database limitations and online catalogs. *Library Journal* (February 1984): 329–330.

Sinkankas, George Martin. A study of the syndetic structure of the Library of Congress List of Subject Headings. Paper for M.L.S. University of Pittsburgh, 1975.

Skuce, D., et al. A rule–oriented methodology for constructing a knowledge base from natural language documents. In *Expert Systems in Government Symposium,* edited by Karna, Kamal N. Washington: IEEE Computer Society Press, 1985: 378–385.

Slatter, Philip E. *Building Expert Systems: Cognitive Emulation.* Chichester, England: Ellis Horwood, 1987.

Sloman, Aaron. Real time multiple–motive expert systems. In *Expert Systems 85. Proceedings of the Fifth Technical Conference of the British Computer Society.* Cambridge Univ. Press., 1985: 213–224.

Sloman, Aaron. An overview of some unsolved problems in artificial intelligence. In *Informatics 7: Intelligent Information Retrieval.* Cambridge: Aslib, 1984: 3–15.

Smith, Irma and Micco, Mary. Developing an expert system for the reference function. Unpublished paper, PRLC Annual Meeting. Pittsburgh, PA, 1987.

Smith, Karen E. Hypertext — linking to the future. *Online* 12 (2). (March 1988): 32–40.

Smith, Karen F. Robot at the reference desk? *College and Research Libraries* 47 (September 1986): 486–90.

Smith, Linda C. Artificial intelligence applications in information systems. In *Annual Review of Information Science and Technology* 15, edited by Martha E. Williams (1980): 67–105.

Smith, Linda C. and Warner, Amy J. A taxonomy of representations in information retrieval design. In *Representation and Exchange of Knowledge as a Basis of Information Processes,* edited by H.J. Dietschmann. Elsevier North–Holland, 1984: 31–49.

Smith, Linda C. Knowledge–based systems, artificial intelligence and human factors. In *Information Technology and Information Use,* edited by Ingwersen, Peter, et al. London: Taylor Graham, 1986: 98–109.

Smith, Linda. Machine intelligence vs. machine–aided intelligence as a basis for interface design. In *Second Conference on Computer Interfaces and Intermediaries for Information Retrieval.* Alexandria, VA: Defense Technical Info. Ctr., 1986: 107–112.

Smith, Linda C. Artificial intelligence and information retrieval. In *Annual Review of Information Science and Technology* 22, edited by Williams, Martha E. New York: American Society for Information Science/Elsevier, 1987: 41–77.

Smith, Philip J. and Chignell, Mark. Development of an expert system to aid in searches of the Chemical Abstracts 1984: Challenges to an information society. *Proceedings of the 47th ASIS Annual Meeting* 21. American Society for Information Science. (1984): 99–102.

Smith, P.J., Krawczak, D., Shute, S. and Chignell, M. Bibliographic information retrieval systems: increasing cognitive compatibility. *Information Services and Use* 7 (1987): 95–102.

Smith, P.J., Shute, S., Chignell, M. and Krawczak, D. The role of the human factors engineer in designing the interface to a knowledge–based system. Technical Report #OSU–CSEL–126, The Ohio State University, Columbus, OH, 1988.

Smith, P.J., Shute, S., Galdes, D., and Chignell, M. In search of knowledge–based search tactics. *Proceedings of the 12th Annual International ACMSIGIR Conference on Research and Development in Information Retrieval.* 1989: 3–10.

Smith, P.J., Shute, S., and Krawczak, D. Developing semantically–based search systems. *Advances in Man–Machine Systems Research* 5, edited by W. Rouse (1989): 93–152.

Sowizral, Henry A. Expert systems. In *Annual Review of Information Science and Technology* 20, edited by Martha E. Williams (1985): 179–199.

Sparck–Jones, Karen. A statistical interpretation of term specificity and its application in retrieval. *Journal of Documentation* 28 (March 1972): 11–20.

Sparck Jones, Karen. Problems in the representation of meaning in information retrieval. In *Informatics 5. Analysis of Meaning*. London: Aslib, 1979: 193–201.

Sparck Jones, Karen. Intelligent retrieval. In *Informatics 7: Intelligent Information Retrieval.* Cambridge: Aslib, 1984: 136–143.

Sparck Jones, Karen. Proposals for R&D in intelligent knowledge based systems (IKBS). *Journal of Information Science* 8 (1984): 139–147.

Sparck Jones, Karen. Issues in user modelling for expert systems. In *Artificial Intelligence and Its Applications*, edited by Cohn, A.G. and Thomas, J.R. New York: Wiley, 1986: 183–195.

Sparck Jones, Karen. Information retrieval. In *Encyclopedia of Artificial Intelligence*, Vol. 1. edited by S.C. Schapiro. New York: Wiley, 1987: 421.

Srihari, Sargur N. (ed.) Computer Text Recognition and Error Correction. Piscataway, NJ: IEEE Computer Society Press, 1985.

Stanfill, Craig and Kahle, Brewster. Parallel free–text search on the connection machine system. In *Communications of the ACM* 29(12) (December 1986): 1229–1239.

Stanfill, Craig and Waltz, David. Toward memory–based reasoning. In *Communications of the ACM* 29 (12) (December 1986): 1213–1228.

Stanfill, Craig. *Parallel Computing for Information Retrieval: Recent Developments.* 1988.

Stefik, Mark, et al. The organization of expert systems, a tutorial. *Artificial Intelligence* 18 (2) (1982): 135–173.

Stefik, M., Bobrow, D.G., et al. WYSIWIS revised: Early experiences with multiuser interfaces. *ACM Transactions on Office Information Systems* 5 (2) (April 1987): 147–167.

Stefik, Mark. The next knowledge medium. *AI Magazine* 7 (1986): 34–46.

Stiles, William G. Ranganathan, cognition, and expert systems. *Canadian Journal of Information Science* 10 (June 1985): 16–24.

Subrahmanyam, P.A. The "software engineering" of expert systems: is Prolog appropriate? *IEEE Transactions on Software Engineering* SE11(11) (November 1985): 1391–1400.

Subramanian, V., Biswas, G. and Bezdek, J.C. Document retrieval using a fuzzy knowledge–based system. *Optical Engineering* 25 (3) (March 1986): 445–455.

Svenonius, Elaine and Schmierer, Helen F. Current issues in the subject control of information. *Library Quarterly* 47 (3) (1977): 326–346.

Svenonius, Elaine. [Humphrey Clinker] discussed in OCLC Annual Reserch Report – 1988. Dublin, OH: OCLC, 1988.

Swigger, Keith. Questions in library and information science. *Library & Information Science Research* 7 (1985): 369–383.

Tait, J.I. Automatic request parsing and variant generation. In *Informatics 7: Intelligent Information Retrieval.* Cambridge: Aslib, 1984: 53–64.

Taylor, Robert. *Question–Negotiation and Information–Seeking in Libraries.* Center for the Information Sciences. Lehigh University. Studies in the Man–System Interface in Libraries. Report no. 3. Bethlehem, PA, 1967.

Taylor, Robert. Question–negotiation and information seeking in libraries. *College & Research Libraries* (May 1968): 178–194.

Taylor, Robert S. On the study of information use environments. In *Proceedings of the 49th Annual ASIS Meeting* 23. American Society for Information Science. (1986): 331–334.

Teitelman, W. and Masinter, L. The Interlisp programming environment. *Computer (IEEE)* (April 1981): 25–33.

Teskey, F.N. *Principles of Text Processing.* Chichester, UK: Ellis Horwood, 1982.

Teskey, Niall. Extensions to the advanced interface management project. In *Annual Review of OCLC Research, July 1987–June 1988.* Dublin, OH: OCLC, 1988: 31–32.

Thinking Machines Corp. The Connection Machine Family: Parallel Computers That Are Easy to Program (sales brochure). Cambridge, MA: Thinking Machines Corp.

Thompson, Craig W. Using a menu–based natural language interface to ask map– and graph–valued database queries. In *Association for Computing Machinery. 1985 ACM Annual Conference. Proceedings* (1985): 328–338.

Thompson, Craig W., Kolts, John and Ross, Kenneth M. A toolkit for building "menu–based natural–language" interfaces. In *Association for Computing Machinery. 1985 ACM Annual Conference. Proceedings* (1985): 318–327.

Thompson, Roger H. and Croft, W. Bruce. An expert system for document retrieval. In *Expert Systems in Government Symposium*, edited by Karna, Kamal N. Washington: IEEE Computer Society Press, 1985: 448–456.

Thunderstone Software Reference: Knowledge Management Through Text Understanding. Cleveland, OH: Expansion Programs International, 1988.

Tichy, Walter F. What Can Software Engineers Learn from Artificial Intelligence? *Computer (IEEE)* (November 1987): 43–54.

Timpka, Toomas. Decision support for general practitioners; Design and implementation by integrating paradigms: Hypertext, knowledge based systems and online library. In *MEDINFO 86*, edited by R. Salamon, B. Blum, M. Jorgensen. Elsevier North–Holland, 1986: 96–100.

Todd, Henry. Multivariate analysis of discriminate patterns in an expert system. *AI Magazine* (Summer 1984).

Toliver, David E. Whether and whither micro–based front ends? In *Second Conference on Computer Interfaces and Intermediaries for Information Retrieval.* Alexandria, VA: Defense Technical Info. Ctr., 1986: 225–234.

Tolle, John E., et al. Display formats project. *Annual Review of OCLC Research* (July 1985–June 1986): 14.

Tong, Richard M., et al. RUBRIC: An environment for full text information retrieval. In *Research and Development in Information Retrieval. Eighth Annual In'tl. ACM SIGIR Conference.* Baltimore: Assn. for Computing Machinery, 1985: 243–251.

Torrero, Edward A. (ed.) *Next Generation Computers.* New York: IEEE, 1985.

Tou, Frederich N., et al. RABBIT: An intelligent database assistant. In *Proceedings of the American Association for Artificial Intelligence.* 1982: 314–318.

Treleaven, Philip C. and Lima, Isabel Gouveia. Fifth generation computing. In *Informatics 7: Intelligent Information Retrieval.* Cambridge: Aslib, 1984: 79–91.

Tucker, Lewis W. and Robertson, George C. Architecture and applications of the the Connection Machine. *Computer (IEEE)* 21 (8) (August 1988): 26–38.

Turing, Alan. Computing machinery and intelligence. *Mind* 59 (1950) 433–460.

Turing, Alan. Computing machinery and intelligence. In *Computers and Thought*, edited by Feigenbaum, Edward A. and Feldman, J. New York: McGraw–Hill, 1963.

Turner, Judith A. Figuring out the rules for how the brain works. [Carver A. Mead and forthcoming book, *Analog VLSI and Neural Systems*] *Chronicle of Higher Education* (October 26, 1988): A3.

Turner, Judith Axler. Plan for $5–million prototype of electronic research library announced. *Chronicle of Higher Education* (June 1, 1988): A27.

Tyugu, Enn. *Knowledge–Based Programming*. Reading, MA: Addison–Wesley, 1988.

United States Dept. of Agriculture. National Agricultural Library. AquaRef: Aquaculture Information Center's Expert Advisory System.

Vavrek, Bernard. The nature of reference librarianship. *RQ* 13 (Spring 1974): 213–217.

Vavrek, Bernard F. Communications and the reference interface. Doctoral dissertation, University of Pittsburgh, Graduate School of Library and Information Sciences, 1971.

Vedder, Richard G., et al. Five PC–based expert systems for business reference: An evaluation. *Information Technology and Libraries* 8 (1) (March 1989): 42–54.

Vickery, A., Brooks, H.M. and Vickery, B.C. An expert system for referral: The PLEXUS project. In *Intelligent Information Systems: Progress and Prospects*. Chichester, England: Ellis Horwood, 1986: 154–183.

Vickery, A. and Brooks, H.M. PLEXUS – the expert system for referral. *Information Processing and Management* 23 (2) (1987): 99–117.

Vickery, Alina and Brooks, Helen. Expert systems and their applications in LIS. *Online Review* 11 (3) (1987): 149–165.

Vickery, B.C. Structure and function in retrieval languages. *Journal of Documentation* 27 (2) (June 1971): 69–82.

Vickery, B.C. Knowledge representation: a brief review. *Journal of Documentation* 42 (3) (Sept. 1986): 145–159.

Vigil, Peter J. The psychology of online searching. *Journal of the American Society for Information Science* 34 (4) (1983): 282–287.

Vigil, Peter J. The software interface. In *Annual Review of Information Science and Technology* 21, edited by Martha E. Williams (1986): 63–86.

Vinge, Vernor. Marooned in Realtime. New York: Bluejay Books, 1986.

Vinge, Vernor. *True Names and Other Dangers*. New York: Simon and Schuster, 1987.

Vries, J.K. et al. An intelligent information retrieval system for laser disc medical archives. In *MEDINFO 86*, edited by R. Salamon, B. Blum, M. Jorgensen. Elsevier North–Holland, 1986: 1148.

Waldron, Vincent R. Interviewing for knowledge. *IEEE Transactions on Professional Communications* 29 (2) (June 1986): 31–34.

Walker, Adrian (ed.) *Knowledge Systems and PROLOG: A Logical Approach to Expert Systems and Natural Language Processing.* Reading, MA: Addison–Wesley, 1987.

Walters, John R. and Nielsen, Norman R. *Crafting Knowledge–Based Systems: Expert Systems Made Realistic.* New York: John Wiley & Sons, 1988.

Waltz, David. Information Retrieval on the Connection Machine. Paper presented at the Library and Information Technology Association (LITA) 2nd National Conference. Boston, MA. October 5, 1988.

Warner, Amy J. Natural language processing. In *Annual Review of Information Science and Technology* 22, edited by Williams, Martha E. New York: American Society for Information Science/Elsevier, 1987: 79–108.

Warren, Kenneth S. (ed.) *Selectivity in Information Systems: Survival of the Fittest.* New York: Praeger, 1985.

Waterman, Donald A. *A Guide to Expert Systems.* Reading, MA: Addison–Wesley, 1986.

Waters, Samuel T. Answerman, the expert information specialist: An expert system for retrieval of information from library reference books. *Information Technology and Libraries* (September 1986): 204–212.

Watstein, Sarah and Kesselman, Martin. Artificial intelligence: A Library Hi–tech bibliography. *Library Hi–Tech Bibliography* 1 (1987): 1–9.

Watters, C.R., et al. Integration of menu retrieval and Boolean retrieval from a full–text database. *Online Review* 9 (5) (1985): 391–402.

Weibel, Stuart L. Connectionist models of computation: Their potential in information systems. In *Annual Review of OCLC Research, July 1987–June 1988.* Dublin, OH: OCLC, 1988: 11–12.

Weil, Cherie B. Automatic retrieval of biographical reference books *Journal of Library Automation* 1 (4) (December 1968): 239–249.

Weil, Cherie B. Classification and Automatic Retrieval of Biographical Reference Books. Dissertation. University of Chicago, Graduate Library School, 1967.

Weizenbaum, Joseph. ELIZA, a computer program for the study of natural language communication between man and machine. *Communications of the Association of Computing Machinery* 9 (1966): 36–45.

Weizenbaum, Joseph. *Computer Power and Human Reason.* San Francisco: Freeman, 1976.

Wenger, Etienne. *Artificial Intelligence and Tutoring Systems: Computational and Cognitive Approaches to the Communication of Knowledge.* Los Altos, CA: Morgan Kaufmann, 1987.

Wenig, Raymond P. *Expert Systems: Practical Applications of Artificial Intelligence.* Franklin, MA: International Management Services, 1988.

Wersig, G. and Hennings, R.D. The intellectual architecture of information systems: A broad research agenda. In *Representation and Exchange of Knowledge as a Basis of Information Processes*, edited by H.J. Dietschmann. Elsevier North–Holland, 1984: 7–30.

Wessels, Michael B. and Niehoff, Robert. Synonym switching and authority control. In *Authority Control: The Key to Tomorrow's Catalog.* Phoenix, AZ: Oryx, 1982: 97–118.

Weyer, Stephen A. and Borning, Alan H. A prototype electronic encyclopedia. *ACM Transactions on Office Information Systems* 3(1) (Jan 1985): 63–88.

White, Marilyn Domas. The reference encounter model. *Drexel Library Quarterly* 19 (2) (Spring 1983): 38–55.

Wiederhold, Gio. Structural versus application knowledge for improved database interfaces. In *Second Conference on Computer Interfaces and Intermediaries for Information Retrieval.* Alexandria, VA: Defense Technical Info. Ctr., 1986: 17–96.

Wiener, Norbert. *Cybernetics.* Namur, Belgium Proceedings of the 1st–5th Congress, International Association of Cybernetics, 1961.

Wilkinson, John P. and Miller, William. The step approach to reference service. *RQ* (Summer 1978): 295–301.

Williams, Martha E. Transparent information systems through gateways, front ends, intermediaries, and interfaces. *Journal of the American Society for Information Science* 37 (4) (1986): 204–214.

Williams, Martha E. Information retrieval research: Interface comparison, database selecetion and transparent systems. *OCLC Research Reports* (1986–1987): 33–34.

Williams, Martha E., et al. Comparative analysis of online retrieval interfaces. In *Proceedings of the 49th Annual ASIS Meeting* 23. American Society for Information Science. (1986): 365–370.

Williams, P.W. Recent developments in the use of microcomputers to access online systems. In *Application of Mini– and Micro– Computers in Information, Documentation, and Libraries*, edited by C. Keren and L. Perlmutter. Elsevier, 1983: 645–653.

Williamson, Robert E. ANNOD – A navigator of natural–organized (textual) data. In *Research and Development in Information Retrieval. Eighth Annual In'tl. ACM SIGIR Conference.* Baltimore: Assn. for Computing Machinery, 1985: 268–273.

Wilson, Patrick. Some fundamental concepts of information retrieval. *Drexel Library Quarterly* 14 (2) (April 1978): 10–23.

Winett, Sheila G. and Fox, Edward A. Using information retrieval techniques in an expert system. In *Engineering of Knowledge–Based Systems. 2nd Conference on Artificial Intelligence Applications.* Washington: IEEE Computer Society Press, 1985: 230–235.

Winograd, Terry. *Language as a Cognitive Process: Syntax.* Reading, MA: Addison–Wesley, 1981.

Winograd, Terry and Flores, Fernando. *Understanding Computers and Cognition: A New Foundation for Design.* Horwood, NJ: Ablex, 1986.

Winston, Patrick Henry. *Artificial Intelligence.* 2nd. ed. Reading, MA: Addison–Wesley, 1984.

Wolf–Terroine, M. *A Macrothesaurus; Why? How?* Bombay, India: Third International Study Conference on Classification Research, 1975: 56–73.

Wong, S.K.M. and Yao, Y.Y. A statistical similarity measure. In *Tenth International ACM–SIGIR Conference on Research and Development in Information Retrieval.* New Orleans, June 3–5, 1987. New York: ACM Press.

Woods, W.A. Lunar rocks in natural English: explanations in natural language question answering. In *Linguistic Structures Processing,* edited by Zampoli, A. Amsterdam: Elsevier North-Holland, 1977.

Wylensky, Robert. *Lispcraft.* New York: W.W. Norton, 1984.

Yaghmai, N. Shahla and Maxin, Jacqueline A. Expert systems: A tutorial. *Journal of the American Society for Information Science* 35 (5) (Sept. 1985): 297–305.

Yankelovich, Nicole and Meyrowitz, Norman. Reading and writing the electronic book. *Computer* 18 (10) (Oct. 1985): 15–29.

Yankelovich, Nicole, et al. Intermedia: the concept of a seamless information environment. *Computer* 21(1) (Jan. 1988): 81–96.

Yin Wei, Mulliner, K. and Zin Lin. Interactive journal title searching via a network of concept–atoms. In *The Range of Computing.* 1985 ACM annual conference. Association for Computing Machinery, 1985: 457–461.

Yin, Khin Maung with Solomon, David. *Using Turbo PROLOG.* Indianapolis, IN: Que Corporation, 1987.

Yourdon, Edward. *Managing the System Life Cycle.* New York: Yourdon Press, 1982.

Yu, Clement T. and Lee, T.C. Non–binary independence model. In *1986 ACM Conference on Research and Development in Information Retrieval.* Pisa, Italy: September, 1986: 265–268.

Yu, Clement T. and Salton, Gerard. Precision weighting: An effective automatic indexing method. *Association for Computing Machinery Journal* 23: 76–88.

Zadeh, L.A. *A Theory of Approximate Reasoning in Machine Intelligence.* New York, NY: John Wiley & Sons, 1979.

Zarri, G.P. Expert systems and information retrieval: An experiment in the domain of biographical data management. *International Journal of Man–Machine Studies* 20 (1) (1984): 87–100.

Zarri, Gian Piero. Interactive information retrieval: An artificial intelligence approach to deal with biographical data. In *Advances in Intelligent Retrieval: Informatics 8* (1985): 101–119.

Zarri, Gian Piero. Artificial intelligence and information retrieval: A look at the RESEDA project. In *Informatics 5. Analysis of Meaning*. London: Aslib, 1979: 166–179.

Zloof, M.M. Office–by–example: A business language that unifies data and word processing and electronic mail. *IBM Systems Journal* 21(3) (1982): 272–304.

Index

ABI/INFORM, 284
abduction, 154
acceptance testing, 315
access language, 267
acoustic/phonetic analysis, 6
ADA, 182
adaptive interfaces, 233, 335
adjacency operator, 241
advanced interface management, 242, 335
advisory systems, 229, 289, 329
agenda, 103
ambiguity, 4, 8-9, 32, 238
American Association for Artifical Intelligence, 328
analog computers, 324
analogy, 25
anaphora (unclear antecedent), 9, 98
Anglo-American Cataloging Rules, 329
Answerman, 256
antecedents, 86
application programs, 272
approval, 307, 314
AquaRef, 256
arity, 152
ARPA, 5
articulation techniques, 139
artifical intelligence
    characteristics of research, 1-2
    history of, 24-25
    marketplace, 316
    technology in libraries, 327-328
artifical realities, 337
assertions, 43
ATN, 7-8
attributes, 45, 47-49
audit trails, 315
automatic correction, 233
automatic indexing, 176
automated knowledge acquistion, 136

B+ tree, 166
backtracking, 36, 277
backward chaining system, 36
Bagger, 25
Bayesian analysis, 39, 147
behavioral
    knowledge, 123
    models, 80
    studies of searchers, 79
belief functions, 147
Belkin's theory, 118
bibliographic records, 244
bibliographies, 268
binary independence model, 177
Biographical Reference Assistant, 86-87
blackboard architecture, 1, 2, 52-53, 95, 100-102
black box mentality, 235
book counts, 215
Boolean algebra, 23, 94
breadth first search, 48
British National Bibliography, 147
Broad Subject Ordering, 92
browsing, 18, 96, 103, 170, 173, 179, 181, 239, 242, 334
BRS, 284
brute force, 41, 170, 175, 177
BSO, see Broad Subject Ordering
budget, 266, 284
Business Periodicals Index, 286
Business Reference Tools, 259, 260

C, 64, 151
C++, 182
CALIBAN, 244, 334
Cansearch, 232
Cardiac-2, 149
career oportunities, 339
cataloging, 329
categorization, 88
categorization schemes
    in reference work, 76, 79
CD-ROM, 268, 271, 324
certainty, 88, 154
C-framer, 162
chalkboard, 250
channel, 68, 89
chunking, 119, 298
circulation records, 166, 171
citation
    analysis, 118
    index, 140
    pearl growing approach, 82
classification, 76, 179, 211, 220
    categorical, 150
    of reference works, 79, 89
closed world systems, 41
CLOUT, 7
clustering, 157, 175-177
Coder, 335
codification, 285
cognition, 119
cognitive
    overload, 179, 228, 241, 315, 335
    process, 79, 118
    psychology, 119
COLAB, 250
communications, 262
    network, 183
    script, 284, 286
    software, 281, 287
Compact DISCLOSURE, 286
compiled knowledge, 120, 300
compiler, 63
composite documents, 335
Compustat, 286
computational
    analysis, 79
    engine, 182
Consensus system, 91
concept, 238
    analysis, 100
    definition, 96
    hierarchies, 238
    relationships, 241
    network, 241, 289
conceptual
    chaining, 13
    dependency model, 11-13
concurrent access, 183
confidence factors, 147-148
conflict
    resolution, 51-52
    resolution strategies, 155, 255
    rules, 100
CONIT, 87, 94
Connection machine, 165, 177
connectivity, 282
constraints, 164, 273, 284, 311
COCOMO
    constructive cost model, 298
consultation, 257, 276, 277, 284, 286, 288
    system, 113
context, 70, 150, 164, 231
    sensitive help, 233
control, 73, 155, 233
controlled vocabulary, 97
core resources, 258
cooperating expert systems, 330
cosine method, 177
cost estimation, 294-295
costs, 171
criteria for expert system development, 110
cross reference facility, 62
crystal storage, 325
Cybernetics, 23

D display language, 242
DARPA (Defense Advanced Research Projects Agency), 4
database management systems, 166, 281, 329-330
databases, 85, 93, 164, 183, 230, 231, 247, 253, 284, 286
  front-ends, 93
  documentation, 270
data dictionary, 298
datagloves, 337
Data Pro reports, 287
data structures, 147, 166
data vs. knowledge, 107
dBASE III Plus, 262, 286
debugger, 276
debugging, see tracing
Debuggy, 19
decision making, 162
decision trees, 45, 309
declarative languages, 278
decomposition, 151
deduction, 138, 154
deep reasoning capabilities, 312
Deep Thought, 318
deliverable systems, 277
demons, 4, 314
Dempster-Shafer method, 147
DENDRAL, 26-27
depth-first search, 48
design
  model, 227
  process, 298
desktop metaphor, 249
development
  environments, 319
  facilities, 62
  tools, 267, 272
Dialog, 98
dialogue, 225, 228, 233, 287, 288
Digital Video Interactive, 325
direct manipulation, 246
discourse, 70, 82
discourse analysis, 123, 132
discrimination, 176
display technology, 236
distributed
  expert systems, 330
  parallel processing, 333
  processing, 183, 324
document display, 239
documentary knowledge, 123
documentation, 315
domain, 109, 271, 274
  consultation, 102
  expert, 267
  knowledge, 102
  rules, 99
  selection, 258
downward migration, 322-323
DYK, 252
dynamic, 227

electronic encyclopedia, 241
electronic library, 183
Electronic Mail Indexing and Classification system, 175
electronic manuscript standard, 171
Electronic Publishing and Information Delivery project, 171
ELIZA, 7
ellipses, 98
embedded systems, 64, 322
Emperor I, 180
EP-X, 237, 238, 239, 335
equipment malfunction, 315
error detection and correction, 19-20, 237
ethical issues, 339
evaluation, 96, 109
  of search results, 301
expert, definition of, 291
expert knowledge, 118
expert systems, 3, 53, 273
  evaluation criteria, 59
  history of, 22-30

shells, 53, 61, 272, 277, 280, 320
tools, 53
expertise, 107, 258
experts, cooperating, 330
Explainer, 103
explanation, 39, 96, 109, 236, 277, 285
facilities, 262, 265, 311
Exsys, 63
eyeball tracking, 336
Eyes-as-output project, 336

facet classification scheme, 92, 96
facets, 157, 160, 179, 226, 284, 310
F & S Index, 287
feasibility study, 294
feedback, 23, 68
Fifth Generation Computer Systems, 28
fileboxes, 181
file servers, 183
filtering, 293
filters, 69, 176, 225, 226, 282, 283, 284
First Class Fusion, 154
formal logic, 154
format, 150
forward chaining systems, 40
frame-based knowledge representation, 156, 162
frame-based languages, 57
frames, 100-101, 147, 151, 157, 227, 238, 274
front-ends, 93, 329-330
full-text databases, 123, 178
functional decomposition, 298
function-oriented programming, 243
FRUMP, 13
fuzzy logic, 147-149

games and game playing, 24
gatekeeper, 268
gateways, 93, 282
General Problem Solver, 25
generate-and-test system, 113
global memory, 100
goal-oriented interview, 125
goal seeking, 35-36
Grafics, 289
graphic
images, 225
languages, 326
graphically oriented, 320-321
graphics, 62, 242
growth, 318
Grundy system, 227, 334
Guidon, 20

handles, 89
hardware, 62, 258
trends, 322
HARPY speech understanding system, 5, 325
Hearsay I, II, 4-5, 102, 325
Hepatitis knowledge base, 91, 331-332
heuristics, 155
of online searches, 82
hierarchical
browsing, 239
classification, 92, 96
relationships, 158, 238
hill climbing search, 50
holographic images, 253
hooks, 286
human
experts, 118
information processing, 66
information processing model, 119
/machine interaction, 223
hybrid representation schemes, 320
Humphrey Clinker problem, 178
HyperCard, 213
HYPERCATalog, 243
hyperlibraries, 181

hypermedia, 178-180
hyperspace, 182
hypertext, 165, 178-179, 211, 220, 241, 277, 288, 334

Icon, 178, 246
ICPSR, 286
idea tactics, 81
idealized representation, 126
ID3 induction algorithm, 138, 154
if...then rules, 273
IIDA, 94, 234
implications, 338
imprecision, 9-10
inaccuracy, 10-11
incompleteness, 10
inconsistencies, 314
indexing, 156, 164, 284
induction, 138, 154
  table, 274
  tools, 60
inference engine, 50-51, 182, 262, 276
information
  access to, 171, 268
  display, 242
  format, 267
  machine, 21
  retrieval, 164, 241, 249, 323, 325
  resources, 75, 92
  searching, 235
  seeking, 66-67, 71, 85, 122, 229
  space, 333
  system, 85, 22
Information Retrieval-Natural Language Interface, 97
infrastructure, 213
inheritance, 61, 163
input/output technologies, 325
institutional profiles, 257
integrated library systems, 328
intelligent browsing, 328
Integrated Pertial Parser (IPP), 13
Intel million-transistor chip, 322
intelligent systems, 237
intelligent tutoring system, 3, 17-19, 233
Intelligent Typewriter, 5
interaction, 225
interactive video, 326
interface, 168, 178
  adaptive, 233, 335
  design, 226, 232
  management, 102, 242, 335
intermediary, 70, 86, 238
internal cognitive states, 136
interpersonal interaction, 136
interpretation, 238
intersection, 170
interviewing strategies, 124
introspection,127
inverse document frequency method, 176
inverted index, 166, 170
IR/NLI, 97
isa links, 159-160
I3R, 101

Japanese initiative, 28
joystring, 337

keys, 165
keyword indexing, 168, 171
knowledge
  acquisition, 108, 116, 268
  artifacts, 339
  bases, 116, 262, 273, 280, 281, 330, 332
    indentification of, 310
    updating of, 117-118
  engineer, 122, 267
  engineering, 107, 298-299
  interviewer, 123
    techniques, 124
  libraries, 331-332
  network, 331

refinery, 140, 331
representation, 108, 126, 183, 264, 274
standards, 330
techniques available, 58
sources, 270
structures, 73, 248
techniques, 123
transfer, 289
knowledge-based
data systems, 168
front-ends, 330
knowledge-driven systems, 231
KRL, 180
Kurzweil Voice System 3000 speech recognition system, 5
KWIC, 164, 171, 173
KWOC, 164, 171, 173

LCSH, 270
laser discs, 268, 324, 326
LIFER natural language interface, 7

linguistic analysis, 79
linked lists, 165, 179, 287
links, 157, 179, 211, 220, 245, 253, 269, 276, 324
LISP, 1, 53, 237, 258, 272, 278, 280, 322-323
machines, 150
Sun Common, 162
Tutor, 19-20
workstations, 323
logic-based languages, 60
Logic Theorist, 25
Loops, 57
LUNAR question answering system, 6

machine
induction, 139
translation, 2, 15-16
MACSYMA, 26, 109
maintenance, 275, 315
mapping, 211
MARC, 165-166, 171, 211
market research, 271
Media Lab, 249, 336
medical expert systems, 321
Medindex system, 147, 162
MeSH (Medical Subject Heading), 162
memory, 119
mental models, 226, 228, 241, 245
mentor, 268
Mercury, 328
messages, 68
meta-knowledge, 103, 137, 155, 237, 255
Meta-level Reference Works, 270
METAMORPH, 177-178
metaphors, 247, 334
metarules, 50, 137, 151, 155, 311
microcomputer-based expert system shells, 139
Microsoft Windows, 243
minimal spanning tree algorithm, 176
mistakes, 237
MIT Media Lab, see Media Lab
modality, 109, 120
models, 65-67, 227, 334
binary independence model, 177
communication models, 67-70
frame based models, 72-75
information processing models, 71
models of reference sources, 75
non-binary interdependence, 177
online searching behavioral models, 80
modular
design, 99
structure, 262

modularity, 320
module, 102, 150
monitoring, 68
Monkeys and Bananas, 25
Moody's, 288
MONSTRAT, 132
morphological analysis, 6, 177
multimedia, 183
multimodal system, 121
multiple worlds, 314
MYCIN, 20, 27, 113, 136, 148, 156

N-grams, 164, 175
National Library of Medicine, 242, 321
natural language, 2, 77, 92, 211
- ELIZA, 14-15
- interfaces, 7
- SHRDLU, 15
- specifying facts, 32-33

navigation, 182
- systems, 321

need, 68
Nestor Writer, 21-22
networks, 225
NL menu, 231, 238
neural networks, 3, 21, 332-333
- history of, 23-24

nonmonotonic reasoning, 149, 227, 314
nonverbal communication, 70
notational system, 145
NOTECARD, 179-181
numeric data construct, 142

object-oriented
- approaches, 320-321
- languages, 58-59
- programming, 165, 182, 242, 250

Objective-C, 182
objects, 243, 249
- complex, 275

OCLC, 171, 183, 242, 252
OCR, see optical character recognition
Office-by-Example, 248
online
- database, 271
- interviews, 133
- retrieval, 65
- searching, 65, 80-83, 129, 249
  - project MONSTRAT, 133

OPAC, 52, 165, 170-171, 228, 242, 243, 247, 248, 259, 268, 270, 271, 282, 286, 287
opacity, 139
optical character recognition, 325
optical computing, 324
organizing, 108
Overdoc, 253

Paper Chase, 237
pattern matching, 1, 21-22
- developing predicate
- unification, 33

parallel
- architectures, 323
- computers, 323
- processing, 165, 177, 323

parallelism, 325
parsing
- ATN, 7-8
- bottom-up, 7-8
- semantic grammar, 7-8
- top-down, 7-8

pathfinders, 268, 270, 289-290
pattern, 147, 151
- matching, 94
- recognition, 235

PC-based consultation systems, 328-329
performance standards, 314
permuted titles, 174
personal computers, 322-323
- in cataloging, 329
- in reference, 329

personal construct psychology, 141

personnel costs, 266
physical data structures, 166
Plan-Generate-Test method, 26-27
PLEXUS knowledge based reference system, 92
plumbing metaphor, 69
Pointer, 21
poisoning, 314
pragmatics, 98
PRECIS, 164, 173, 175
precision, 82, 171
predicate calculus, 151, 153
predicates, 33
primitives, 238
printed index, 247
probability, 155
  rankings, 39
  weightings, 147
probes, 125
problem
  internal representation, 99-100
  solving, 154
  space, 111
process flow diagram, 298
procedural knowledge, 155
production rule systems, 155-156
profiles, 284
programming languages, 272
Project HYPERCAT, 334
Project Mercury, 183
Project MONSTRAT, 132
PROLOG, 1, 32, 56, 92, 151, 154, 168, 258, 272, 274, 275, 278, 280

proof of concept, 267
proofreading, 17
property lists, 147
propositions, 152
protected modes, 233
protocol
  analysis, 73, 127, 129, 298
  retrospective, 128
  search, 112
prototype, 150, 277, 284, 292
  system, 279
Prospector, 27
proximity searching, 170
Put-that-there, 336

qualifiers, 89
quantification, 145, 153
query, 66, 67, 69, 71, 73, 227, 229, 244
  builders, 93
  building, 287
  by example, 248
  formulation, 85, 90, 96
  formulation template, 244
  languages, 112, 231
  subject, 283, 294
  systems, 334
  terms, 176
question answering systems, 6-7, 113
Question & Answer natural language understanding system, 7

Rabbit, 230, 231
ranking
  of outcomes, 38
  of recommended tools, 76
ready reference, 257
recall, 81, 171, 239
recognition, 239
recognize-act-cycle, 156
redundancy, 323
Reference Advisory System, 232
Reference Assistant, 183, 328
reference, 329
  books, 310
  interview, 65-67, 72, 121, 229, 160
  process, 120
  query, 310
  sources, 257

works
biographical, 88
for cancer therapy, 96
language for describing, 90
matrix, 78
related to gardening, 92
reflective probes, 126
Refsearch, 88
relational database management systems, 164-165, 166, 171
relevance, 170, 177
feedback, 94, 101, 140, 229
remote access, 183
representation formalisms, 164
request probes, 126
requirements
analysis, 291
specification, 298
repertory grids, 141
RESEDA, 91
retrieval
descriptive, 230
retrospective protocols, 128
review articles, 116
robotics, 2, 16-17
roles, 174
Roundsman project, 162
rule-based tools, 59
rules, 36
domain, 99
matching, 100
run-time version, 277

scope notes, 220
screen design, 278
screen management facilities, 62
scripts, 73, 151, 160, 282
reference interview, 74
search
behavior, patterns of, 234
breadth first, 48
depth first, 48
fragments, 310
hill-climbing, 50
protocols, 112
strategy, 72, 265, 301, 314
conceptualist, 81
negotiation, 17-18
operationalist, 81
tactics, 80, 99
searcher
attributes, 134
behavior, 79, 134
/client interactions, 132
semantic, 234
analysis, 8
nets, 147, 160
primitives, 11-12
serendipity, 178, 242, 252
shells, 58, 272, 277, 280
development, 320
PC-based expert systems, 61
short-term memory, 119, 127
SHRDLU, 15
similarity measures, 176
singularity, 252
skeletons, 249
slots, 157, 159-160
Smalltalk, 57, 80, 182
social issues, 339
software, 258
engineering, 291
trends, user acceptance, 319
Software Architecture Machines Project, 249
sources, 90
spatial data management, 251, 336
specification languages, 307
spectral holes, 325
speech production, 6
Speech Understanding Research Project, 4
speech understanding, 4-6
staff education, 338
stampsheet, 250
standardization, 321, 339
statistical user model, 227

statistical
    clustering, 175
    weighting, 245
statistics sources, 260
stemming algorithm, 94
storage media, 183
STEAMER, 245, 334
structured objects, 151
subject
    access, 179
    classification, see classification
    headings, 171
    maps, 220
    query, 282
supermicros, 63
SUR, 4
syndetic structure, 112, 213, 217
synonyms, 177
syntactic analysis, 6-7
syntax, 234
system
    degredation, 315
    limitation, 315
    security, 315
systems analysis
    evaluation, 315
    performance, 314
    requirements, 294
    specification, 270
    testing, 294

tactics, see search tactics
target records, 242
task
    activation, 100
    analysis, 129
    categories, 109
    rule clusters, 100
taxonomy, 157
    question types, 236
TEIRESIA, 136
template forms, 249
term
    frequency, 177
    selection, 96
    weight, 177
thesaurus, 211, 225, 244, 250
thrashing, 234
Tomus, 211
tools
    answer providing, 78
    library, 75
    metalevel, 75
toy
    problems, 25
    systems, 255
tracing, 276, 311
training and support, 63
translations, 43
transphasors, 324
tree structure, 158, 244
truth maintenance, 149, 313
Turbo PROLOG, 272
Turing test, 24
turnkey expert systems, 318
tutorial modality, 267

ULSI: Ultra Large Scale Integration, 324
uncertainty, 147
universal quantifiers, 153
user
    acceptance, 267
    behavior, 226, 228, 232
    interactions with, 132
    interface, 178, 223, 224, 277, 280, 304
    modelling, 113, 226, 334
    profile, 310
    stereotypes, 227, 310

validation, 310, 311, 313
vector, 175-177
verbal
    dialog, 326
    protocol analysis, 123, 128
verbalizations, 122

verification, 39, 307, 315
VLSI: Very Large Scale Integration, 324
videodisc, 180
virtual computers, 335
virtuality, 245
VISICALC, 245
vision systems, 16-17
visual metaphors, 326
vocabulary control, 151
VP-Expert, 59, 272, 274, 275, 280

weights, 38, 244
What-if capability, 277, 313
windowing, 178, 278
windows, 246, 277, 334
word fragments, 175
working memory, 43, 155
working set, 239
workstations, 178, 180, 183, 250, 258
world knowledge, 310
WORM disks, 326
writing errors, 17
writer's workbench, 17
WYSIWIS, 250

XCON, 27-28

Z specification, 307